Date Due

Oct 15 '46			
Dec 17 '46			
Apr 1 '66			
Apr 15 '66			
Apr 24 '68			
Oct 22 68			
Apr 21 '70			

A History of Ohio

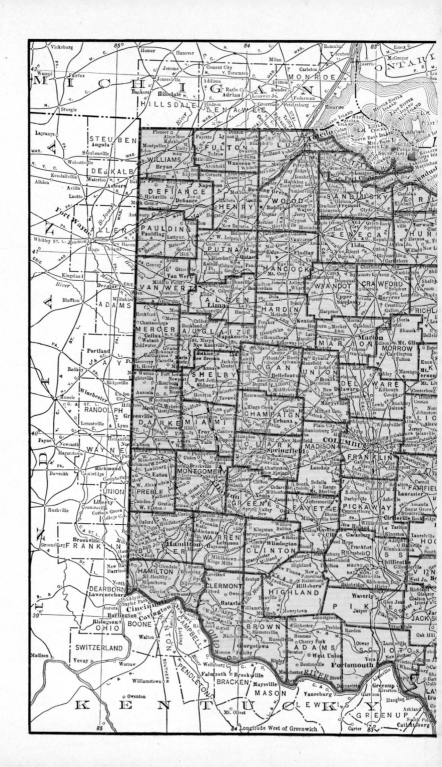

TO

T. M. R.

AND

H. C. W.

PREFACE

PROFESSOR Elbert J. Benton, of Western Reserve University, in *The American Historical Review*, October, 1926, found occasion to note the "monumental evidence of the backwardness of Ohioans in writing their own state's history" and even raised the query whether such indifference might be "an evidence of the low state of culture in the oldest community of the Old Northwest." Anyone acquainted with the literature of American history recognizes the lack of any satisfactory volume or series of volumes which present in a critical way the story of Ohio. The difficulties to be encountered in the essaying of such a work need not be minimized: there is the problem of amassing accurate data in a field relatively neglected by the scientific historian; there is the necessity of subordinating local pride to the grim dictates of impartial judgment; and there is the skepticism in some quarters as to the value of state history to any except those of strictly antiquarian interests.

The present volume is offered in the belief that the history of a state whose population is approximately equivalent to that of Switzerland and Norway combined is in itself worthy of attention. Because of the significant rôle played by Ohio in the development of the United States, the history of the state may serve, moreover, not to accentuate any undesirable provincialism, but to explain the contribution of a single state to the larger life of the nation. As natives of Ohio, the members of whose families for three generations have been born within its borders, and as teachers for practically a decade at Ohio's largest institution of higher learning, the authors trust that they may possess, in some degree, a sympathetic appreciation of the nature of their task. In the preparation of this volume, not only the better-known printed works, but many private letters and unpublished sources have been consulted. Since the book is intended primarily for undergraduate students and the general reader, footnote references to sources have been omitted. At the conclusion of each chapter, however, bibliographical notes on certain important sources for the period treated have been added.

To those who have been of assistance to the authors, especially to Professor Carl Wittke, of the Ohio State University—the editor of the series, who has rendered invaluable advice and unfailing encouragement—their heartfelt appreciation is extended. For any errors of fact or interpretation, however, the undersigned alone must be held at fault.

Eugene H. Roseboom
Francis P. Weisenburger

COLUMBUS, OHIO

TABLE OF CONTENTS

MAPS

A History of Ohio

CHAPTER I

THE LAND AND THE FIRST INHABITANTS

The Physical Basis

OHIO is a political, not a geographical, unit. Its eastern and southern boundaries were determined by Pennsylvania and Virginia, while its western and northern (west of Lake Erie) boundaries were fixed by a Congress in whose actions political considerations were an important factor. Only Lake Erie, itself a part of the Canadian boundary, constituted a natural limit for any state that might be erected immediately west of Pennsylvania. On the other hand, the Ohio River, though a logical southern line, was by no means a barrier confining population to a particular area. Rather, it was a unifying factor that tended to create a community consisting of the people along both banks. Thus Ohio furnished no peculiar local environment that separated its people from their neighbors or enabled them to develop institutions, ideas, and customs characteristic of Ohioans alone.

These facts, however, do not deny the existence in the state of a certain local color, particularly in the years preceding the Industrial Revolution and the revolution in transportation, when the New Englander, the Pennsylvanian, the southerner, the Scotch-Irishman, the Irishman, and the German were being amalgamated into the "Buck-

1

eye." True provincialism could have no existence in Ohio, swept as it was by successive waves of migration from the east, which not only constantly brought new infusions into its racial strains but carried westward thousands of Ohioans, who settled in Iowa, Kansas, and other Western states. Every improvement in transportation and communication meant the further acceleration of this process, while industrialism, developing in the cities, drew to Ohio workers from all parts of the nation and of Europe as well. That this condition contributed to Ohio's economic greatness and that it stimulated intellectual life, there can be no question; but it is equally true that it has prevented the development of any genuinely native art, literature, or culture that can be regarded as characteristically Ohioan. Provincialism could not flourish in a state that was the highway of the nation.

Thus, from the beginning, accessibility has been the keynote of Ohio's history. No mountains, deserts, swamps, or large bodies of water segregated its inhabitants from their fellow Americans. Lake Erie, on the north, and the Ohio River, on the south, invited alike the Indian, the trader, and the pioneer to enter the "Buckeye State." The Maumee, the Sandusky, and the Cuyahoga Rivers, accessible from the lake, were open to the skillful paddlers of canoes, who could proceed southward to the low portages, over which their boats could be carried a short distance to the headwaters of the Great Miami, the Scioto, and the Tuscarawas-Muskingum Rivers, respectively, and thence to the Ohio—the vast interior was thus open to the voyagers. Or, reversing the process, the lake region was equally accessible from the great river.

When the canal era came, Ohio's system of artificial waterways, following the rivers and cutting across the portages, furnished the connecting links in an all-water route from New York City to the Mississippi River. Hitherto isolated localities found easy access to markets, and Ohio's rapid development in the decades from 1830 to 1850 owed much to this factor. But Ohio was equally well situated for transportation by land. That the old National Road should be built across the "Buckeye State" was no accident but the natural consequence of Ohio's central location. With the dawn of the railway era, after 1850, the great east-and-west trunk lines were constructed across the state, thus offering the shortest and easiest routes to the great prairies. Nature interposed no serious barriers to the new method of transportation in Ohio, and the network of rails spread in the state until there was scarcely a village more than a few miles from a railroad. Motor transportation, at a much later date, has carried the process still further and brought even the isolation of rural life to an end. Finally, the hills of the south and southeast, resisting longest, have, generally, also yielded to the march of progress.

Ohio's location contributed much to its economic development. As the easternmost state of the Middle West, it was the nearest to the great Eastern markets, whether by the Erie Canal, the National Road, or the great railroad systems. Down the Ohio and Mississippi were the Southern markets, especially important before the advent of the railway. The Lakes offered water routes for the transportation of Ohio's coal to the great Northwest, and from the Lake Superior region came the rich iron ore to make the Cleveland-Youngstown District the iron and steel center of the nation.

But the state had advantages, other than accessibility and favorable location, for a varied economic life. Nature endowed it with a rich soil and valuable mineral resources. Lying in three different physiographic provinces, Ohio is a borderland possessing the characteristics of all three.[1] The eastern half of the state lies almost entirely in the Allegheny Plateau. This plateau reaches nearly to Lake Erie on the north, extends diagonally southwest from near Cleveland to Morrow County, turns almost due south along the eastern edges of Delaware, Franklin, and Pickaway Counties to Ross County, where it bends southwest again, and then resumes its southern course through Highland and Adams Counties to the Ohio River. West of this line lie the Lake Plains and the Central Plains, separated from each other by an irregular line extending from Van Wert County, in the northwest, eastward to Cuyahoga, where it joins the boundary of the Allegheny Plateau.

Dividing the Allegheny Plateau into two distinct areas is the glacial boundary running from Columbiana County in the east, westward to Holmes County, thence irregularly southwest to Brown County, on the Ohio River. The Lake and Central Plains and the northern and western parts of the Allegheny Plateau were all once within the area of the great ice sheets. Below the glacial line lie the hill counties of the southeast, an old area much cut up by streams and marked by steep valleys and narrow ridges, often containing valuable coal deposits but of little use for agriculture. Fertile sections exist along the river bottoms and on some of the more level uplands, but much of the region is unsuited to any but the more primitive types of agriculture, familiarly called "hill farming," while some portions are not cultivated at all. Although containing one fourth of the area of the state, the unglaciated region produces but one eighth of the crops.

---

[1] The area of Ohio is 44,803 square miles, including the state's share of Lake Erie. Without the latter the area is 41,263 square miles. These figures have been worked out by Professor C. E. Sherman, Department of Civil Engineering, Ohio State University, who has had charge of the state topographic survey.

Of the area north of the glacial line, the Lake Plains include only a narrow strip of lake shore east of Cleveland, but they widen to the west and embrace all or parts of

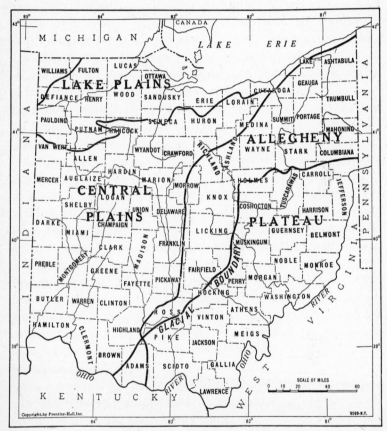

Physiographic Provinces of Ohio

fifteen northwestern counties from Erie County to the Indiana line. This section was once under the waters of Lake Erie and consequently is so level that drainage constituted a serious problem for the early settlers. The "Black Swamp" in this area was the last part of the state to be settled.   Once drained, the soil was found to be as rich as any in the state.

The Central Plains, including the western and south-western counties, lie in the glaciated area and consist of wide stretches of flat country, broken occasionally by gently rolling hills.   One of these glacial hills near Bellefontaine, Logan County, rises to a height of 1,550 feet above sea level, the highest point in the state.   Down in the extreme south-western corner, near Cincinnati, on the Ohio River bank, at the low water mark is the lowest land, 440 feet above sea level.   The land in these plains was well eroded when the glaciers came, and this condition permitted the soil carried by the great ice sheet to be spread rather evenly and to a considerable depth.   Often the drift is more than one hundred feet deep.

That part of the Allegheny Plateau which includes north-eastern and parts of central Ohio also lies in the glaciated area.   Here the hills were rounded off and the valleys partially filled to make possible a more gentle topography and to create a soil more suitable for agriculture than the unglaciated hills to the south and the east.   While not as fertile as the plains, this region contains much excellent pasture land.   However, the advance of the ice was retarded here and reached over only the northern and western edges of the Plateau.

The significance of glaciation in Ohio can hardly be over-estimated.   The great ice sheets rounded off the hills and filled the valleys, thus creating a surface easily tilled and less likely to be washed away.   The ice also carried along and ground up rocks from a variety of sources and, in melting, deposited this new soil, many feet deep, on the old surface to give it a complexity and richness lacking in the unglaciated area.   Swamps and poor drainage are often found in glacial regions; but these disadvantages can be overcome,

and, in any case, do not offset the great benefits produced
many thousand years ago by the huge masses of ice. Ohio
agriculture owes much to the work done by the great
glaciers.

Ohio's mineral resources are also proof of nature's
beneficence to the "Buckeye State." Coal, clay, stone,
sand and gravel, gas, petroleum, and salt are the more
essential ones. Of these, coal and clay are, of course, the
most important, both being found chiefly in the unglaciated
plateau of the southeast and serving to offset the lack of
tillable soils in this section. Iron ore also exists here, but
it has not been used for many years because of its inferior
quality as compared with that of the Lake Superior ores,
so easily imported by way of the Lakes. The other
mineral resources are not so localized as clay and coal—
oil, for example, having been found in many parts of the
east and southeast and in an important area in the northwest.

One natural resource was both a hindrance and a necessity to the pioneer. Heavy forests of oak, maple, hickory,
walnut, elm, and other deciduous trees covered most of the
state and constituted a serious obstacle to agriculture.
In the early days of settlement, wood was primarily used for
the making of houses, furniture, and fences, and for fuel, but
with these needs supplied, much timber had to be burned
to clear the land. As a consequence, Ohio today is forced
to import much of the wood required for building and
industrial purposes.

The climate of Ohio is popularly regarded as disagreeable,
because of the extremes of heat in summer, the low temperatures of winter, and the great variability of the weather
from day to day. Yet it is well suited for the growth of
the great crops of the temperate zone. The mean annual
temperature is about fifty-one degrees, with the extreme
south (Lawrence County) averaging fifty-five degrees,

and the northeast (Lake, Geauga, and Ashtabula Counties), forty-eight degrees. The length of the growing season (between killing frosts) is sufficient for most crops, extending from 150 days in several parts of the north to 178 days in the Ohio Valley and in much of the lake shore region, with two small areas—one in the southwest, the other in the north—reaching 192 days. The phenomenon of the extreme north's rivaling the Ohio River counties in length of growing season is due to the modifying influence of Lake Erie upon temperatures. The earliest frosts are as likely to occur in the valleys of the south, which fill with cold air, as anywhere in the state, whereas portions of the lake shore are affected last of all.

Rainfall varies from thirty-one to forty-two inches annually, and one half of this amount falls during the growing season—a vital factor in the production of crops. The Ohio River counties have the heaviest precipitation and the lake region has the lightest, though the latter has its rainfall distributed more evenly throughout the year. The drainage basin of the Ohio River is subject to rather frequent floods, some of them, such as those in 1884 and 1913, constituting major disasters in the state's history. At the other extreme is the terrible drought of 1930, which, however, was not local in extent.

The winds of Ohio are southwesterly, though the spiral movement of the cyclonic storms results in a great variation in climate from day to day and from place to place. The lake in winter, with its warmer temperature, has a tendency to attract these storms, thus making it rougher in winter than in the other seasons.

In general, Ohio's climate shows no marked differences from one part of the state to another. There are no mountain barriers, and all sections are nearly equally accessible to the winds, rains, and temperature changes of the Middle

West. Disagreeable as the extremes of heat and cold may be and ranging sometimes from ten degrees below zero to one hundred degrees above in a single year, the climate is favorable to agriculture; there is also something to be said for the stimulating effect of such variations of temperature upon human beings who seek a livelihood in this part of the United States.

The Mound Builders

If man, as is generally supposed, came to North America across Bering Strait perhaps ten thousand years ago, his migration to the upper Mississippi Valley was much more recent. Centuries must have passed before the Rocky Mountain barrier was crossed and eastern North America entered. Some time after the great glaciers receded from what is now Ohio, the first human beings came to this region. What manner of men these were, whence they came, how long they remained, what types succeeded them—all these things are veiled in the mists of the dim past. Only with the advent of the Mound Builders, so called, do we have definite evidence of the character of Ohio's prehistoric inhabitants.

Perhaps two or three thousand years ago, when the Mediterranean world was revolving around the civilization of the Greeks or was being dazzled by the glory of Rome, the Scioto Valley and the Miami Valleys were inhabited by men who preserved knowledge of their culture for the archæologists of another race by building mounds of earth. With no system of writing by which to record their deeds, they have left no chronicles of their wars and conquests, of their rise and decline, of their rulers and their follies. Yet singularly enough, we know many of the intimate details of the daily lives of these aborigines—their tools and weapons, their carvings and ornaments, their burial customs, their agriculture and commerce, and their food products. We are able to distinguish cultural differences and to divide the peoples accordingly, but the great questions of their origin and their disappearance remain unanswered. We have a fragment of a story—a bit of description, vivid enough but without plot and without beginning or ending.

Mound building, particularly for burial purposes, is a common trait among barbarian peoples, a feature which, with the advance toward civilization and the use of better building materials, leads to the construction of temples, pyramids, or other imposing structures. Most of the eastern half of the United States lies in the general mound-building area, with the Allegheny Mountains from Virginia northward serving as a sort of eastern boundary. Geography largely determined the mound builder's location, as primitive man was controlled entirely by his environment. Hills and swamps were avoided, while well-watered valleys provided an easy means of subsistence for peoples dependent on hunting, fishing, and primitive agriculture for an existence. The Ohio Valley, including two thirds of Ohio and parts of several neighboring states, is thickly dotted with mounds and earthworks of various kinds. More than five thousand such evidences exist in the state of Ohio alone, with the county of Ross, in the Scioto Valley, the greatest center of these remains.

Burial mounds are by far the most numerous remains. They range in size from almost imperceptible elevations to the great mound at Miamisburg, which reaches a height of sixty-eight feet. A second type, known as effigy mounds, of which Ohio has only three or four identified as such, was designed to represent some animal and possessed a religious significance or a ceremonial purpose. The most famous of all such works is the Great Serpent Mound in Adams County, 1,330 feet in length along its coils and averaging about three feet in height. It is in the form of a serpent with what appears to be an egg held in its distended jaws. The "Alligator," or "Opossum," Mound, in Licking County, cannot be so clearly identified, but its ceremonial aspect is evident enough. Also in Licking County, at Newark, is a bird-shaped figure, while parts of what seems to be a second serpent mound exist in Warren County. Effigy mounds, exceptional in Ohio, are quite numerous in Wisconsin and some adjacent areas, the product of a different culture from that of the Ohio Valley.

The enclosures fall into two general groups: those built on hilltops, which seem to have served a defensive purpose, and those more or less geometric in character, which from their location could hardly have been fortifications but which must have had some ceremonial or social significance. Of the first group Fort Ancient in Warren County is the best-known example. Located on a kind of promontory overlooking the Little Miami River and consisting of three and one half miles of walls, this fortification was admirably situated to provide a defense for a large number of people against their enemies. Among other examples of defensive works are Fort Hill in Highland County and Spruce Hill Fort in Ross County.

The numerous geometric enclosures vary greatly in height, extent, and shape. They are usually found in conjunction with burial mounds and are one of the chief characteristics of the Hopewell type of culture, soon to be described. Although not geometrically perfect, the circles, squares, and other figures are surprisingly accurate, since the methods of measurement these primitive peoples used must have been very crude.

Other remains in the form of village sites, flint quarries, pictured rocks, graves, and numerous relics of individual handiwork reveal much information of great interest about the prehistoric inhabitants of Ohio. These mound-building peoples have been divided by the archæologists into certain cultures based upon their customs. Thus, in Ohio are found the Hopewell, the Fort Ancient, and the Adena types.

The Hopewell peoples derived their name from a group of earthworks in Ross County on the land of M. C. Hopewell. Over twenty important centers of this culture exist in Ohio, being particularly noteworthy in Ross, Licking, Scioto, Washington, and Hamilton Counties. The presence of Hopewell Builders is marked by geometric embankments, in close association with groups of mounds. The mounds cover what were once sacred buildings where religious rites were observed and where burials took place. Cremation was used in the great majority of burials, though enough exceptions exist to show that for some special reason, perhaps in the case of an important personage, at times the body was buried uncremated. When the sacred building was to be abandoned, it was destroyed by fire and covered with earth to make the mound. From the Hopewell practices of offering gifts as sacrifices to the gods and of burying valuables with the individual, a great deal of information as to cultural development has resulted. Particularly in their manufacture of pipes, ornaments, pottery, and implements is the work of these people outstanding. Their use of copper, obtained evidently from the Lake Superior region, and of mica, probably obtained from the southeastern seaboard, indicates some form of exchange or commerce with distant peoples.

The Fort Ancient culture was first recovered by an exploration of the mounds and village sites in the neighborhood of the old fortification. It extends over a wide area of the Ohio Valley, overlapping the Hopewell region and indicating the presence of a larger population. The Fort

Ancient peoples were less advanced culturally than the other Mound Builders in Ohio, and their mounds are less imposing. Wood, stone, clay, and bone were the chief materials with which they worked, and their carvings and ornaments are inferior to the Hopewell products. They did not use copper or mica. Though usually burying bodies in mounds, they did not practice cremation.

A third culture found in Ohio has been called the Adena, from a mound located near Adena, the home of Thomas Worthington, in Ross County. Mounds have furnished the chief evidences of this culture, as village sites and forts or enclosures have not been discovered. The great Miamisburg Mound in Ohio and the still larger Grave Creek Mound in Marshall County, West Virginia, are examples of this type. The Adena peoples built carefully shaped, conical mounds, placed the bodies of their dead in them in log sepulchers, and did not practice cremation. Copper and mica were known and used, but not so extensively as in the Hopewell culture. The sculptured pipes of the Adena peoples show real artistic development. They are tubular in form, unlike the Hopewell pipes, which are of the platform type. In general the Adena peoples seem to rank somewhere between the Fort Ancient and Hopewell types in cultural advancement.

These three cultures, and perhaps others not as yet identified, occupied two thirds of the state of Ohio and parts of Pennsylvania, West Virginia, Kentucky, and Indiana, with some Hopewell evidences being found even in Illinois, Iowa, Michigan, and Wisconsin. On the other hand, northern Ohio belonged to the Great Lakes area of prehistoric Indian culture. This region has not been so carefully explored as the southern valleys, but the smaller, more scattered mounds, enclosures, and village sites point to an early Algonquian occupancy succeeded in turn by an

Iroquoian people and by the Eries, who were still in the region in the early seventeenth century. The fact that the earthworks in this section are less striking than to the south and the fact that they are associated with known branches of the Indian race have caused them to be regarded with less interest and speculation than the earthworks of the Ohio Valley peoples.

Despite the notion, held for a long time, that the Mound Builder remains were of great age, the facts seem to indicate that these peoples flourished as late as the centuries just preceding the discovery of America, contemporary in part with the Middle Ages of European history. Furthermore, the glamour of mystery is considerably lessened when we learn that the old belief that they were a separate and superior race of people has no acceptance with the archæologists. The Mound Builders were Indians, inferior to some of the historic tribes, superior to others, in cultural attainments, but with no distinctive traits that cannot be found, in some degree, among the Indians of later times. They hunted and fished and practiced primitive agriculture, raising corn, beans, and tobacco with crude implements for cultivating the soil. They quarried flint and made from it tools and weapons; but their chief metal, copper, was not smelted, but was hammered into the desired shape. While mound building was exceptional with the Indians as the white man found them, it existed in certain tribes and may have been far more general at an earlier period. In other words, the Mound Builders may have been the ancestors of some of the red men of today.

What became of these peoples who once occupied the Ohio Valley may only be conjectured. Certainly they seem to have had no connection with the Indians that the whites found living in Ohio, for these, as will be seen, were recent immigrants into an unoccupied region. Conquest and extinction by, or merger with, stronger neighbors was the probable fate, though it may have been preceded by a period of decadence that invited eventual destruction. Migration to some distant region is another possibility, which would have involved change of habits and, perhaps, absorption by other peoples. Whatever their fate, it seems strange that the Hopewell people, the most advanced of Ohio's prehistoric types, should have been so completely absorbed or obliterated as to leave upon no later Indian tribe an impress that could prove a relationship. Yet such is the case. Their disappearance was complete. The records of their existence, however, were implanted in their mounds and earthworks, and the archæologists of today are thus enabled to reconstruct with surprising accuracy the civilization of these lost peoples.

Ohio takes high rank among the states of the Union in archæological research. For many years the Ohio Archæological and Historical Society has been exploring mounds and village sites, until today it has in its museum at Columbus a magnificent display of the remains of early cultures not surpassed anywhere in the world. From the middle years of the nineteenth century, when E. G. Squier and E. H. Davis published their pioneer work, *Ancient Monuments of the Mississippi Valley*, down to the present day, Ohio has been fortunate in having earnest and scholarly archæologists constantly adding to the fund of information about its prehistoric peoples. Outstanding figures among them in recent years have been Warren K. Moorhead, Gerard Fowke, William C. Mills, and Henry C. Shetrone. *The Mound-Builders*, by Dr. Shetrone, director of the Archæological Society, published in 1930, gives Ohioans an admirable account of the state's prehistoric inhabitants based upon the latest researches in the field.

The Archæological Society has also done an excellent work in securing the conversion into state parks of the more outstanding remains of the Mound Builders, thus insuring their preservation for future generations.

The Indians of Ohio

When French and English began their struggles for the Ohio Valley in the middle of the eighteenth century, they found the present state of Ohio occupied by a number of Indian tribes who were themselves recent immigrants into the region. The earliest of these had come in scarcely more than a half-century before. The absence of any native tribes is accounted for by the defeat and apparent extermination of the Eries by the Iroquois in the 1650's. The Eries, or the Cat Nation, had occupied the southern shores of Lake Erie from western New York westward into northern Ohio. How much of the present state they possessed, it is impossible to know, as the only information we have concerning them comes from French Jesuit missionaries who knew of them through the Iroquois, bitter enemies of the Eries. One of the Jesuit *Relations* describes them as follows:

"The Cat Nation is very populous, having been reënforced by some Hurons, who scattered in all directions when their country was laid waste, and who now have stirred up this war which is filling the Iroquois with alarm. Two thousand men are reckoned upon, well skilled in war, although they have no firearms. Notwithstanding this, they fight like Frenchmen, bravely sustaining the first discharge of the Iroquois, who are armed with our muskets, and then falling upon them with a hailstorm of poisoned arrows, which they discharge eight or ten times before a musket can be reloaded."

But this bravery and skill availed them nothing in the end. The Jesuit *Relation* for 1656 records their destruction the previous year. The warriors of the Iroquois confederacy besieged the chief fighting force of the Eries in one of their strongholds, apparently near the site of Erie, Pennsylvania. Using their canoes as scaling ladders, the assailants climbed the palisade, and, after a desperate struggle, exterminated most of the defenders. After this crushing defeat, the identity of the Eries is lost, the remnants being absorbed by other Indian nations. Thus the earliest Ohio Indians disappeared from history. Apparently for many years the present state was uninhabited, except, perhaps, for scattered groups of no importance, though it was crossed and recrossed by war parties of Iroquois whose conquests extended to the Mississippi River.

By the beginning of the eighteenth century, the Miamis had spread into western Ohio. Forced from the Wisconsin region by the pressure of hostile tribes, they came southeastward into Indiana and Ohio, their chief town, Pickawillany, being located near the present city of Piqua, Miami County. The Miamis have been characterized as possessing a milder and more courteous disposition than their neighbors, practicing agriculture with much success, and preferring travel by land to the use of canoes. They are often referred to by writers as Piankashaws and Weas, the names of two of the six bands into which they were divided.

The Shawnees, or Shawanoes, seem to have come from the Cumberland and Tennessee Valleys northward into Pennsylvania and Ohio, though it is not at all clear just when or by what route this migration took place. The chief movement came in the second quarter of the eighteenth century, but there is some evidence that bands of Shawnees were living in or crossing Ohio long before that

time.   They seem to have been rather nomadic in character,
for groups of them appear in several different parts of the
country in the early years of European colonization.   In
Ohio, by 1750 the Shawnees were established in the Scioto
Valley with their sphere of influence extending well up into
the northern part of the state.   A fierce, aggressive, proud
people, they offered the most desperate and prolonged
resistance to the white advance of all the Ohio tribes, the
names of Cornstalk, Blue Jacket, and Tecumseh being
outstanding in their history.

A third group of red men occupied the northern and
northwestern area of the present state.   These were called
Wyandots by the English, originally *Wendat* in their own
language.   They consisted of a part of the Hurons who
were driven out of eastern Canada and across Lake Huron
by the Iroquois conquests and who, after a temporary
sojourn in the vicinity of Mackinac Island, in northern
Michigan, drifted southward, part of them coming into
the Maumee and Sandusky Valleys of northwestern Ohio
and even spreading down into the central part of the state—
an area overlapping the area of the southern Indians.
Though few in numbers, the Wyandots, themselves of
Iroquois stock, recovered their morale and established
themselves as brave fighters who ordinarily were less cruel
in their treatment of prisoners than were the other tribes.

The Delawares were the fourth of the important Ohio
tribes.   Late comers into the state from the east, they
occupied the Muskingum Valley and other parts of eastern
Ohio, constituting, together with the Shawnees, the chief
barrier to white advance into the Ohio Valley.   The
Delawares had suffered defeat and ignominious treatment
at the hands of the Iroquois in their original Delaware
Valley home and in addition had been forced westward by
English occupation of their lands.   But relieved for a time

of both dangers, they speedily recovered their fighting prowess and were far from deserving the term "women," applied to them by the Iroquois in their days of humiliation.

Besides these important tribes, several detached bands from other nations were scattered through the state in friendly contact with their more powerful neighbors. In northwestern Ohio groups of Ottawas, from the upper Great Lakes region but originally from Ontario, settled in close proximity to the Wyandots. Pontiac, one of the greatest of Indian leaders, was an Ohio-born Ottawa. From the powerful Iroquois confederacy in New York came scattered bands to establish villages in Ohio. The Tuscarawas, the Sixth Nation of the league, gave their name to a river in the eastern part of the state, where some of them resided. From the Iroquois also came some groups of Senecas to set up a few towns on the upper Scioto and on the Sandusky. They were later called the "Senecas of the Sandusky," but are better known as "Mingoes," a name said to imply a stealthy or treacherous disposition. They were few in numbers and came to Ohio not long before the American Revolution, but they achieved a unique fame chiefly through the eloquence of a warrior named Logan at the time of Dunmore's War. A few Cherokees, representatives of a great southern people, lived for a time in Ross County, while occasionally wanderers or outlaws from other tribes appeared in the state but had no significance in its history.

The Ohio Indians represented the two great linguistic stocks of the eastern United States and Canada. Of the four major nations, the Miamis, Delawares, and Shawnees were of Algonquian stock, while the Wyandots were of Iroquoian stock, though not members of the confederacy of that name. The pressure of white settlement on the seaboard and wars among themselves had produced a general displacement of Indians from their traditional homes, and now resulted in a mingling of peoples in Ohio that was to be further complicated as the whites pressed into the Ohio Valley. Numerically the total Indian population in the present state probably did not exceed fifteen thousand in the period preceding the American Revolution. There were no territorial boundaries, as there was room for all, and there was little occasion for rivalry. Nearly all the Ohio Indians had in times past felt the heavy hand of the conquering Iroquois nations of New York and even in the eighteenth century were subject to a nominal overlordship by them, for the Iroquois still had a vague claim to the Ohio Valley. But more important than this relation was the need for common action in resisting the white advance. Though without any central organization, the various Ohio tribes nevertheless acted together in emergencies to offer a serious barrier to white settlement.

Selected Bibliography

PHYSIOGRAPHY: For an account of Ohio's physical features and their relationship to its economic development, see Roderick Peattie, *Geography of Ohio, Ohio Geological Survey, Fourth Series, Bulletin 27* (Columbus, 1923). More elementary is William M. Gregory and William B. Guitteau, *History and Geography of Ohio* (Boston, 1922), pp. 94–218. Convenient accounts are found in Rufus King, *Ohio, First Fruits of the Ordinance of 1787* (Boston, 1903), pp. 1–6; Henry Howe, *Historical Collections of Ohio* (Cincinnati, 1888), Vol. I, pp. 51–89; C. B. Galbreath, *History of Ohio* (5 vols., Chicago and New York, 1925), Vol. I, pp. 3–13 (geology of Ohio).

Much material on the physical history of Ohio may be found in the publications of the United States Geological Survey and the volumes of the Geological Survey of Ohio. For a broad view of the significance of the Ohio Valley in American history, see Frederick Jackson Turner, "The Place of the Ohio Valley in American History," *Ohio Archæological and Historical Quarterly*, Vol. XX (1911), pp. 32–47.

PREHISTORIC RACES: The best account in this field is Henry C. Shetrone, *The Mound-Builders* (New York, 1930). Pages 165–279 deal especially with Ohio, but the earlier pages should be read to understand the broader significance of the subject. The same author has an excellent article entitled "The Indian in Ohio," in *Ohio Archæological and Historical Quarterly*, Vol. XXVII (July, 1918), pp. 274–508. Pages 458–507 deal with the prehistoric Indians. (In the separately printed edition, the pages are 196–245.) Other references are E. O. Randall and Daniel J. Ryan, *History of Ohio* (5 vols., New York, 1912), Vol. I, pp. 3–80; C. B. Galbreath, *History of Ohio*, Vol. I, pp. 25–55; Gerard Fowke, *Archæological History of Ohio* (Columbus, 1902).

Accounts of explorations of mounds and village sites are scattered through the volumes of the *Ohio Archæological and Historical Quarterly*. The locations of Ohio mounds, villages, and other remains may be found in W. C. Mills, *Archæological Atlas of Ohio* (Columbus, 1914).

OHIO INDIANS: See the article by Shetrone, cited above, especially pp. 305–321 (in the separately printed edition, pp. 43–59); C. B. Galbreath, *History of Ohio*, Vol. I, pp. 89–101; Randall and Ryan, cited above, Vol. I, pp. 155–179; Theodore Roosevelt, *The Winning of the West* (4 vols., New York, 1894–96), Vol. I, pp. 70–87 (the paging is different in other editions); Rufus King, *Ohio*, pp. 20–24 and 53–55; James W. Taylor, *History of the State of Ohio* (Cincinnati, 1854), pp. 29–40. Much material on the early migrations of the Ohio Indians appears in C. A. Hanna, *The Wilderness Trail* (2 vols., New York, 1911), *passim*.

The above accounts are descriptions of the various Ohio tribes. The narrative histories of the relations of the Indians and the whites will be cited in the succeeding chapters.

CHAPTER II

THE FRENCH AND THE ENGLISH IN THE NORTHWEST

The First Europeans

WHILE French traders and Jesuit priests were penetrating as far westward as Lake Superior in the first half-century of their colonization on the St. Lawrence, Lake Erie and the region south of it were still unknown to Europeans as late as the 1660's. The Five Nations of the Iroquois, warring almost incessantly with their Huron and Algonquin neighbors and usually hostile to the French, offered an effective barrier to the progress of the latter into New York, Pennsylvania, and Ohio. Not until 1669 do we have definite evidence of Frenchmen paddling along the shores of Lake Erie, the last of the Great Lakes to be discovered. It is quite possible that some wandering French fur trader, or *coureur-de-bois*, had entered the Ohio country earlier, as the monopolistic system of handling this trade and the lure of the woods converted many a good French subject into a kind of freedom-loving barbarian, roaming the forests and living the life of the Indian. These *coureurs-de-bois* penetrated far into the interior, and it is not impossible that the first white man south of Lake Erie belonged to this class of French adventurers.

With the coming of Réné-Robert Cavelier, Sieur de la Salle, to New France, the mists begin to lift a little and the Ohio Valley comes into written history. La Salle, young, ambitious, and possessed of an indomitable will and a passion for exploration, secured an estate on the St. Lawrence a few miles from Montreal in 1666 and became a feudal proprietor. Hearing from some Senecas of a distant river called the Ohio,[1] he determined to find it in order to satisfy his love of exploration and to develop a profitable trade or find the much-sought route to China. Joining forces with two Sulpitian priests bent on a missionary enterprise, he set out with guides and attendants, a party of twenty-four, for the Seneca villages near Lake Ontario. Unable to secure guides here for the Ohio, the party proceeded to the western end of the lake, where they met Louis Joliet, explorer and fur trader, returning from the upper lakes. He had come by way of Lake Erie, making the first recorded instance of a white man on its waters (1669). Joliet persuaded the missionaries that the Indians of the lake region needed their aid, and consequently La Salle was forced to rely for his Ohio exploration on his own resources.

The next two years are veiled in mystery. The records of La Salle's life during these years are lost, and only through secondhand information can his activities even be conjectured. It seems that he secured a guide, proceeded from Lake Erie to a stream flowing into the Ohio, reached the latter river, and explored it to the falls, or rapids, at the site of the present Louisville. Deserted by his men, he had to return, apparently without reaching the Mississippi,

---

[1] The origin of the name "Ohio" is a matter of controversy. The Ohio River was called by the French "La Belle Rivière" (*the beautiful river*), a translation of the Iroquois term "Oyo," supposed to mean "beautiful" and given its present form by the English. Another version, while accepting the Iroquois origin, derives the name from a word applied to any principal stream and meaning "great" or "fine." As the Iroquois regarded the Allegheny-Ohio as the principal river of their country, the use of the term seemed fitting. On the other hand, it has been claimed that the Miamis had a word meaning "very white river" which began with Ohui or Ohi (*very*), which they applied to the whitecaps on the Ohio, as stirred up by the wind. The traders shortened it to "Ohio." The reader will find the different views summarized in A. B. Hulbert, *Historic Highways*, Vol. IX, pp. 17-20, and in C. A. Hanna, *The Wilderness Trail*, Vol. I, pp 293-294.

though this fact is not entirely clear. This exploration he made in the winter of 1669–1670 or the spring of the latter year. The chief basis for this account of La Salle's work is a book printed some years later by an anonymous friend to whom the explorer related the narrative while on a trip to Paris. The book is full of inaccuracies and geographical errors, but this defect might be attributed to the author's lack of knowledge of America and his dependence on his memory for the facts told him. The historian Parkman accepted this account of La Salle as substantially correct, and most writers on Ohio history are inclined to agree with him. The French later proclaimed La Salle the discoverer of the Ohio, and maps as early as 1673 and 1674 were so marked. On the other hand, it has been argued that the evidence is insufficient and unreliable and that the claims of the French to the region explain their desire to make La Salle the discoverer. The matter constitutes an interesting historical problem lacking definite proof but with the probabilities favoring La Salle.

The intrepid French explorer next devoted his efforts to an exploration of the Mississippi, which he attempted to reach by way of Lake Michigan and the Illinois country. In the course of his journey of 1679 he constructed the first ship to sail on Lake Erie, the "Griffin," but it was lost on the return voyage from Lake Michigan. After this date, La Salle's name is no longer associated with Ohio history, though it looms large in the story of the French in the Mississippi Valley.

The first English to appear on Lake Erie were sent by the redoubtable Thomas Dongan, Royal Governor of the Province of New York. Unwilling that the French should control the fur trade of the upper lakes and with it the destinies of the Indians, Dongan in 1685 licensed certain traders to engage in trade with the Western tribes. Led by a young Dutchman of Albany, Johannes Rooseboom, an expedition of eleven canoes went along Lake Erie and up Lake Huron to the Mackinac region, returning successfully with rich stores of furs. Rooseboom led a second expedition the following year, but the French and their Indian allies intercepted and captured the English traders, and no further efforts were made by Dongan in the West, though he secured from the powerful Iroquois in New York an acknowledgment of their allegiance to the English Crown. Apparently the route taken by Rooseboom followed the north shore of Lake Erie. The first recorded exploration of the Ohio shore came in 1688, when the picturesque young Frenchman, La Hontan, coursed along the southern border with a body of Indians in canoes. His well-known lack of veracity and some blunders of geography have cast doubts upon his exploit, though the fact that he had his headquarters at the lower end of Lake Huron and made frequent trips up and down the Lakes makes his story probable enough.

But the Ohio region attracted neither French nor English as yet. The outbreak of the great European struggle between Louis XIV and William of Orange in 1689 involved their colonists in America (where it was called by the English colonists "King William's War"), and the New York-New England frontier became the scene of a bloody warfare. The region west of the mountains was of little importance, as the English were filling in the seaboard and the few scattered French in the remote interior constituted as yet no menace to their advance. After the Peace of Ryswick, in 1697, the French hold on the Mississippi Valley was strengthened by the beginnings of settlement on the Gulf coast in 1699, and by the establishment of Detroit in 1701 by La Mothe Cadillac to guard the important water connection between Lakes Huron and Erie. For a time, as early as the 1680's, a post existed near the mouth of the Maumee, but it was not maintained.

The second intercolonial war (1701–1713), known in America as Queen Anne's War, started from European causes, and the fighting in America was not of great importance. New England and South Carolina, exposed to French and Spanish attacks, bore the brunt of the war, while New York, protected by Iroquois neutrality, and Pennsylvania, governed by Quaker legislators, were largely indifferent to the struggle. The Ohio Valley was too remote to be involved, though the victors in Europe might have forced the vanquished to cede title to all their American possessions and claims. By the Treaty of Utrecht (in 1713) England was satisfied with Newfoundland, Acadia, the Hudson Bay region, and a protectorate over the Iroquois, while to France were left her St. Lawrence possessions and whatever she might make out of her vague claims to the Mississippi Valley and the Great Lakes region.

The Advance of the Trader

The first half of the eighteenth century constitutes a little-known period of Ohio's history. In these years the Indian nations, already referred to, were moving into the present state, most of which they were to hold until Anthony Wayne's famous legion dispossessed them near the end of the century. Penetrating the Ohio Valley and reaching even the Lakes, in defiance of French priority, came the packhorses of the English traders. From as far south as Carolina they came, bringing rum and gunpowder, cloth and blankets, hatchets and beads—to apprise the redskin of the advantages of the white man's civilization, usually cheating and debauching him in the process. To the merchants of Philadelphia and Charleston and other centers went the skins and furs and a goodly share of the profits.

Exported to England, these products of the Indian's skill and effort added to the income of that commercial element that was tending more and more to shape the destinies of the tight little isle. Long before the heroic figure of Daniel Boone reached the Ohio Valley, these agents of British business were quietly at work rounding up consignments of furs and hides to be transported to the seaboard. By the 1740's they were causing alarm to French officials, tapping the lake area and diverting from Montreal part of the Northwestern Indian trade.

Although less active at first, by the middle of the century Pennsylvania traders were dominant in Ohio. Virginians operated farther south, while the New Yorkers used the Iroquois as middlemen in drawing the business of the Western Indians to Albany. The king of the Pennsylvania traders was George Croghan. He was born in Ireland and in 1741 came to America, where he soon made a name for himself by the extent of his operations. His agents and associates were active from Lake Erie to Kentucky and from western Pennsylvania to the Wabash, while at several strategic points in this region he had located important storehouses. Croghan was distinctly superior to his rivals in enterprise, tact, and fairness in dealing with the Indians, and soon became a valuable, if unofficial, representative of the interests of Pennsylvania and of the British Government in the contest with the French. This earliest exponent of big business in the Ohio Valley was keenly aware of the mutual advantages present in the close relationship of government and business.

New York, Pennsylvania, and Virginia each played a part in shaping the destinies of Ohio in the first half of the eighteenth century. Rival land claims, Indian relations, and the activities of traders furnished the fuel for controversies between colonial officials, gave the home govern-

ment much concern, and were the occasion for numerous
conferences between Indian chiefs and agents of the various
governors. Virginia claimed the entire Ohio country
under her charter of 1609, which gave her the land "from
sea to sea, west and northwest." Pennsylvania's charter
of 1681, though not a sea-to-sea grant, extended westward
beyond the forks of the Ohio, thus taking in a part of
Virginia's claim. New York, lacking a charter, was
sedulous over the interests of the Iroquois, who claimed the
Ohio country as far as the Mississippi by right of conquest.
It was not the policy of the British Government or of any
of the Colonies to ignore the Iroquois claims, as the Six
Nations served as a buffer against the French, and their
alliance was eagerly sought. However, by various agreements they were induced through the medium of rum and
other gifts to surrender parts of their claims to lands beyond
the mountains. Just what was conceded was vague
enough, and the right of the Iroquois to make such grants
very dubious. The Delawares and the Shawnees, after
moving into the Ohio Valley, felt no longer so subservient
to the Six Nations and resented the inferior position in
which they were placed. But the absence of settlers down
to the middle of the century prevented serious trouble
over lands while the Pennsylvania traders were winning the
Ohio Indians with cheap goods.

The third of the struggles between France and Great
Britain involving colonial possessions lasted from 1744 to
1748. Like the first two wars, it had no great significance
in America and was merely a forerunner to the decisive
struggle that was to settle the fate of vast colonial possessions. The Iroquois were again pawns in the Anglo-
French rivalry on the Canadian border but were shrewd
enough to be able to preserve their neutrality and reap
considerable advantages from it. In the West a part of the

Shawnees yielded to French pressure, but soon repented and, with other Western Indians, allowed the Pennsylvania traders to draw them into close relations with the English. These traders, reaching the vicinity of Detroit and the French line of communications from the Maumee to the Wabash, instigated a plot that for the moment threatened to wipe out French power in this region.

Nicolas, a Huron (Wyandot) chief, dissatisfied with his treatment by the French at Detroit, established his head-quarters on Sandusky Bay and permitted Pennsylvania traders to establish a post there. The nature of this relationship is evident from a letter to the Pennsylvania authorities signed by three Indian chiefs in the spring of 1747, in which they stated that five Frenchmen had been killed near Detroit, a fort that they soon hoped to have in their possession. A French scalp was sent along as a proof of their liking for the English. The letter was in the handwriting of George Croghan, who himself soon wrote that he had returned from the woods "and has brought a Letter a french scalp and some Wompom for the Governor from a part of the Six Nations Ingans That has thire Dweling on the borders of Lake Arey."

But Nicolas was unable to carry out his plans against the French. His grandiose scheme of a concerted attack upon them by an alliance of Northwestern Indians collapsed when the French, warned by various acts of violence, strengthened their posts and prepared to punish the conspirators. Nicolas reluctantly submitted and was forgiven, but presently fled from the Sandusky region when the fact that he was still trading with the English was found out by the French.

Nevertheless, English influence was increasing in the Ohio country. A visit to Philadelphia by ten Ohio Indians in November, 1747, resulted in the dispatch of presents and the promise of larger gifts to all the Ohio Indians the following year. Croghan, acting for Pennsylvania, distributed goods in the spring of 1748 and paved the way for a conference at Lancaster, Pennsylvania, a few weeks later, when representatives of the Six Nations and of the principal Ohio tribes met Pennsylvania and Virginia officials. The Miamis were newcomers at the conference, having come from the distant Wabash Valley to share in the presents and trade of the English. A treaty of friendship was expected to cement the Western Indians to the English cause.

Soon afterward, Conrad Weiser, a German, long the agent of Pennsylvania to the Iroquois but new to the Ohio Indians, proceeded to the upper Ohio, accompanied by the invaluable Croghan and Andrew Montour, a Canadian half-breed interpreter. Traders and Indians assembled to meet Weiser at Logstown, some eighteen miles below the forks of the Ohio. Croghan had an important trading house here, and the location was convenient for meeting the Ohio tribes. Presents valued at £700 were distributed, of which Virginia had contributed £200 and Pennsylvania the rest. With many expressions of satisfaction, the Indians accepted the gifts and announced their desire to regard the English as true brothers. English influence now seemed paramount among the Indians in the Ohio country.

In the same year, the Treaty of Aix-la-Chapelle closed the war between France and England. But colonial officials on both sides continued their efforts to control the Indians, for it was evident that the peace was only a truce that might be broken at any time. Even had the feeling of the colonial officials been otherwise, the clashing interests of traders would soon have compelled the respective governments to lend their assistance.

The Struggle for the Ohio Valley, 1749–1763

French officials viewed the rise of English influence among the Western Indians with considerable apprehension, for it was becoming evident that control of the Ohio Valley was the key to the interior. While earlier the portages across Wisconsin and Illinois had been the usual routes from the St. Lawrence region to the Mississippi, the French were now finding it more convenient to proceed up the streams flowing into the lower lakes and over to the branches of the Ohio. The important Maumee-Wabash route had to be protected against the English, but such protection was hardly possible unless the upper Ohio were under French control. There could be no security for traders or for the settlers in the Illinois country unless the English were stopped at the forks of the Ohio, the junction of the Allegheny and Monongahela Rivers.

The first step for the French to take was to restore their influence among the Indians, and to accomplish this Celoron de Blainville (sometimes called Bienville) led an expedition into the Ohio country in 1749. He was sent out by the able and energetic Marquis de Galissonière, a naval commander of distinction who was temporarily serving as governor-general of New France. Celoron's task was to warn the English traders that they should leave the country, to take formal possession of the Ohio Valley for France by burying lead plates inscribed with the claims of Louis XV, and to win the Indians from their English alliance. Accompanied by two hundred and fifty men, mostly Canadians, with a few French officers and soldiers and some Indians, he proceeded from the St. Lawrence up the Lakes to a point on Lake Erie (the mouth of Chautauqua Creek) where an eight-mile portage would take them to Lake Chautauqua. The outlet of this lake

led to the Allegheny, and the Allegheny to the Ohio proper.
Stopping at intervals to bury his plates—a formality
bordering on the ridiculous—and to confer with the
Indians, Celoron finally reached the mouth of the Great
Miami on August 28. Leaving the Ohio, he went up the
Miami to Pickawillany, then the capital of the Miamis and
a center for English traders. After a few days here the
expedition proceeded overland to the Maumee, down to
Lake Erie, and eastward to the St. Lawrence. Two of the
six plates were later found, one in 1798 at the mouth of the
Muskingum, the other in 1846 on the Kanawha.

This display of French power was injurious rather than
helpful. Celoron's force was not strong enough to overawe
the Indians, while the English traders ignored his orders to
depart. At Logstown, according to the Jesuit chronicler
of the expedition, the leader of the English traders, "who
saw us ready to depart, acquiesced in all that was exacted
from him, firmly resolved, no doubt, to do nothing of the
kind as soon as our backs were turned." Indeed, Croghan
himself, at the request of the Governor of Pennsylvania,
followed Celoron to counteract the latter's activities and to
preserve English influence.

In the following year rumors of another French expedition led Governor Hamilton to send Croghan and Montour
west with presents to hold the Indians loyal. They had
reached the Wyandot town on the present site of Coshocton,
where Croghan had a storehouse, when they were surprised
by the arrival of an Englishman on a mission quite different
from that of the trader. This was Christopher Gist, agent
of the Ohio Land Company.

The Ohio Land Company was organized in 1748 at the
suggestion of Thomas Lee, a member of the Governor's
Council of Virginia. A number of prominent Virginians
and Marylanders, including Lawrence and Augustine

Washington, were associated with him, while a London merchant was influential in interesting the British Government. Their petitions to the King asked for five hundred thousand acres of land between the Monongahela and Kanawha Rivers on either or both banks of the Ohio. Two hundred thousand acres were to be selected at once and were to be free from quitrents or any royal tax if the company should colonize one hundred families on the land in seven years and build a fort for their protection. The British Government approved the plan in 1749, the desire to block the French advance into the Ohio Valley being not the least important reason for its favorable action. The company began at once to import goods from England, for the Indian trade was expected to bring in large profits. A store was established at Will's Creek, Maryland, and a road to the forks of the Ohio was planned. To secure an accurate report on the nature of the country and the disposition of the Indians, the company employed Christopher Gist to go to the upper Ohio Valley. A surveyor, trader, and experienced woodsman, he was well fitted for a task that required days of travel through virgin forests, physical endurance in a high degree, and keenness of observation, as well as tact in dealing with the red man.

Crossing the mountains to the Ohio River, he followed that stream to a point near the present western boundary of Pennsylvania. Then he proceeded into the eastern part of Ohio, to arrive on December 14, 1750, at the Wyandot town, where he met Croghan and Montour. After a month's stay here, he accompanied the representatives of Pennsylvania across eastern Ohio to a great swamp (now Buckeye Lake), thence to the site of present Lancaster, and then southwest to the "Pickaway Plains" (near the site of present Circleville), stopping at a number of Indian villages on the way. They followed the Scioto to its mouth, where an important Shawnee town (now Ports-mouth) was located. After conferences with the Indians, the party proceeded in a northwesterly direction to the Miami town of Pickawillany (Piqua). Here "Old Britain," chief of the Miamis, received them with much favor, show-ing his English leanings by refusing presents from Detroit and sending away a delegation of Ottawas who brought them. Gist left the Pennsylvania agents here and returned to the Ohio River, proceeding homeward across Kentucky and the mountains of Virginia. His diary, with its terse descriptions of the beauty and richness of the Ohio country, is one of the most valuable documents of the early history of the state.

Gist had been duly cautious in concealing the purposes of the Ohio Company, but it soon became evident to the Pennsylvania traders that he represented a dangerous rival that not only would injure their trade, but would arouse Indian hostility by its plan to occupy with its settlers a large tract of land. Furthermore, the uncertainty of the western limits of the Quaker colony afforded an opportu-nity for Virginia to claim the upper Ohio Valley, thus adding to the difficulty of the Pennsylvanians' dealing with the Indians, who were being sedulously courted by French agents in spite of England's apparent dominance. Indian fears of French attacks were heightened by the failure of the Quaker Assembly of Pennsylvania to provide for a fort at the forks of the Ohio, though the Governor favored the measure. It was thus left to Virginia to assume the aggressive.

Unhampered by such difficulties as assemblies or inter-colonial rivalries, French officials at Quebec urged upon Celoron, now in command at Detroit, the dispatch of a large expedition into the Ohio Valley to punish the Indians and to drive out the English traders. Celoron was unwilling to risk the consequences of such an aggressive measure and held back. The matter was solved by Charles Langlade, a Canadian half-breed, who in June, 1752, without formal official sanction, led a band of two hundred and fifty Ottawa and Chippewa Indians and a few French in an attack upon Pickawillany. The place was surprised while many of the warriors were absent, some thirty Indians were killed, five traders were captured and one killed, and their goods, worth £3,000, were confiscated. The body of "Old Britain," the Miami chief, was boiled and eaten by the victors. The affair was not, as it is sometimes stated, the first battle of the "French and Indian War," for neither France nor England was officially involved, nor was it followed by any hostile measures. However, it marked the beginning of the decline of English influence among the Western Indians, which only a bold policy could offset.

In the spring of 1753 Governor Duquesne of New France sent an expedition to occupy the upper Ohio Valley. A chain of forts to extend from Presque Isle (now Erie, Pennsylvania) was begun, but disease and the problem of supplies prevented their completion at this time. Governor Dinwiddie, of Virginia, concerned over the interests of the Ohio Land Company, sent young George Washington to warn off the French, but this attempt was of no avail. Far more to the point was the sending of Captain William Trent in February of 1754 to erect a fort at the forks of the Ohio. The work was not finished, however, for the French appeared in force, took possession, and completed the fort, which they named Duquesne for the governor of New France. Washington, now in command of a body of Virginia troops, surprised and captured a detachment of French advancing toward his fortified camp at Great Meadows and began the "French and Indian War." But he himself was soon compelled to surrender to superior numbers of the enemy on July 3, 1754, and control of the Ohio Valley definitely passed to the French.

The Ohio Indians, overawed by the French, were no longer ready to risk themselves for Virginia and Pennsylvania, and the efforts of Croghan held but a small number faithful. However, a British army was sent over in 1755 under General Edward Braddock to drive the French from the Ohio Valley. Success would have meant the speedy desertion of the French cause by the fickle Indians, who felt no great loyalty to either side. But Braddock's disastrous defeat a few miles from Fort Duquesne destroyed what little English influence was left among the Indians, and they now openly went on the warpath for the victorious French. Of the Iroquois, only the Mohawks took an active part on the English side.

The formal declarations of war in 1756 began the fourth great struggle between France and Great Britain for world empire. The former had the aid of Austria and Russia, in Europe, while the rising German state of Prussia was allied with Britain. This Seven Years' War (the "French and Indian War" in American history) did not end until 1763, though by 1760 the triumph of the British was assured in America. After initial blundering and failures, the British Government, directed by the great imperialist statesman, William Pitt, overcame the Bourbon power on the seas and sent armies to America in the years 1758 and 1759 to capture the French strongholds from Louisburg on the Gulf of St. Lawrence to Fort Duquesne at the western extremity of the French line of defense. The English colonists loyally aided Pitt with men and money and shared in the final triumphs.

For Ohio history, the most significant event of the war was the capture of Fort Duquesne by General John Forbes in the fall of 1758. But this victory was a triumph of peace rather than of armed force, for the way had been prepared by the pacifist emissary of the Province of Pennsylvania, Christian Frederick Post, a missionary of the Moravian Brethren, who at the risk of his life went to the Ohio Indians and persuaded them to adopt a neutral policy. Deserted by their Indian allies and short of supplies because of the British control of the seas, the French abandoned Fort Duquesne without a battle, and Forbes occupied it in November, 1758, renaming it Fort Pitt. The war in the West was over. By the Treaty of 1763, Canada and the eastern half of the Mississippi Valley became English territory.

SELECTED BIBLIOGRAPHY

La Salle's achievements are recorded in one of Francis Parkman's classic volumes, *La Salle and the Discovery of the Great West* (Boston, 1907). Chapter II deals with the supposed discovery of the Ohio River. On this point, see also Justin Winsor, *A Narrative and Critical History of America* (8 vols., Boston and New York, 1889), Vol. IV, pp. 201–246 (containing maps and critical comments); C. A. Hanna, *The Wilderness Trail*, Vol. I, p. 143, and Vol. II, pp. 87–92 (a critical treatment of La Salle's work); *Western Reserve Historical Society Tracts*, No. 38 (an article by Col. Charles Whittlesey); Randall and Ryan, *op. cit.*, Vol. I, p. 103, and Vol. III, pp. 117–129; Rufus King, *History of Ohio*, pp. 29–45. Much material on the penetration of the French into the interior may be gleaned from Frank H. Severance, *An Old Frontier of France* (2 vols., New York, 1917). The familiar story of French and English rivalries is told in many accounts, of which the following are for convenient reference: Charles Moore, *The Northwest under Three Flags* (New York, 1900), pp. 63–105; Randall and Ryan, Vol. I, pp. 172–375; J. W. Taylor, *History of Ohio*, pp. 55–80 and 115–126; King, *op. cit.*, pp. 46–79; C. B. Galbreath, *History of Ohio*, Vol. I, pp. 57–86 and 101–106.

Dealing more especially with Indian relations and the problems of the trader are Hanna, *op. cit.;* Joseph S. Walton, *Conrad Weiser and the Indian Policy of Colonial Pennsylvania* (Philadelphia, 1900), and A. T. Volwiler, *George Croghan and the Westward Movement* (Cleveland, 1926). The broader significance of Celoron's work is portrayed in George Wood, "Celoron de Blainville and French Expansion in the Ohio Valley," *Mississippi Valley Historical Review*, Vol. IX, pp. 302–319. The journals of the expedition may be read in *Expedition of Celoron to the Ohio Country in 1749* (C. B. Galbreath, ed., Columbus, 1921). *Christopher Gist's Journals* (W. M. Darlington, ed., Pittsburgh, 1893) constitute another valuable source of early Ohio history. *Early Western Travels* (R. G. Thwaites, ed., Cleveland, 1904), Vol. I, contains the journals of Conrad Weiser, George Croghan, Christian Frederick Post, and Thomas Morris.

CHAPTER III

THE STRUGGLE WITH THE INDIAN, 1763–1783

Pontiac's Conspiracy and Bouquet's Expedition

*T*HE elimination of the French was by no means the end of England's problems in America. In fact, the difficulties with the Indians and with her own colonists following the Seven Years' War made the burdens of empire seem greater than its benefits. The relations of mother country and colonists belong to the story of American independence, but the Indian problem is peculiarly a part of Ohio's history.

Indian policy was concerned primarily with two fundamental factors: trade and lands. The white trader was eager to profit from the former; the pioneer and the land speculator were concerned with the latter. Upon the British Government rested the responsibility of protecting the Indians from white rapacity and of maintaining peaceful relations, no small task when the elimination of the French danger permitted the trader and the land-hungry to swarm into the Ohio Valley regardless of the rights of the Indian. The agents of the government were well chosen for their work. Sir William Johnson, at the head of the Northern Department (including the Northwestern Indians), had the confidence of the Iroquois and for years had skilfully managed Indian affairs in New York. His deputy, more directly concerned with the Ohio Valley, was the erstwhile trader, George Croghan, who more than any other man knew how to deal with the Western Indians and to retain their friendship. But the efforts of these agents proved unavailing in quieting the Indians. Despite conferences and presents, the red men were growing more and more restless and suspicious, and in 1763 Pontiac's great uprising resulted.

A number of factors explain this outbreak. A throng of unscrupulous traders, disregarding licenses and attempts at restriction, cheated the Indians and aroused their hatred. The British commander-in-chief, General Jeffery Amherst, unappreciative of the difficulties involved, restricted sales of ammunition and enforced upon the Indian agents a policy of economy that greatly reduced the amounts of presents and contributed to Indian unrest. The contrast between this attitude and the attitude of the English when the war was going on was not lost upon the Indian. French traders added to the unrest by spreading false rumors and engaging in intrigues, while in the background there was growing among the Ohio Valley Indians the feeling that their lands would be seized next. Only a leader was needed, and the Ottawa chieftain, Pontiac, supplied this need.

Simultaneous surprise attacks upon the scattered British posts in the West proved so successful that nine forts were captured, while only three held out through the summer of 1763. The post on Sandusky Bay, the only British fort on Ohio soil, was the first to fall. The garrison of fifteen men was wiped out and the officer in command taken prisoner. But the key to the Ohio Valley, Fort Pitt, resisted until relieved by Colonel Henry Bouquet in August. Detroit likewise resisted a long siege, and the failure of the Indians to take these two strongholds led to the collapse of the conspiracy.

British authority had now to be restored in the Northwest and the abandoned posts reoccupied. To over-awe the still rebellious tribes, two expeditions were sent west in 1764: one under Colonel John Bradstreet to Detroit, following the southern shore of Lake Erie, the other under Colonel Henry Bouquet, marching into Ohio from Fort Pitt. Conferences were to be held with the Indians, English prisoners surrendered, and peace treaties signed. Bradstreet accepted the assurances of the Wyandots, Ottawas, and other northern Ohio Indians and inflicted no punishment upon them. Disregarding orders from General Thomas Gage, now British Commander-in-chief in North America, Bradstreet did not march to attack the Scioto Valley Indians, but returned to Niagara. Regardless of the peaceful attitude of the Indians around Detroit, the Ohio tribes remained unpacified.

Their pacification was accomplished, however, by Bouquet's expedition in the fall of 1764. Bouquet was a Swiss soldier of fortune who had spent many years in the British service and who had learned by experience how to deal with the Indians. Refusing to negotiate at Fort Pitt, he marched with fifteen hundred men into eastern Ohio to the Tuscarawas-Muskingum Valley, where he established headquarters on the site of the present city of Coshocton. Overawed by his presence in the heart of the Indian country, the Ohio tribes came to his camp to offer their submission. More than two hundred white prisoners were released—some after years of captivity—and promises were made that others would be brought to Fort Pitt the following spring, when a formal treaty would be signed. Bouquet, assured that the Ohio Indians were really desirous of peace, returned to Fort Pitt after an absence of only two months.

The more difficult task of pacifying the tribes of the Illinois country was left to George Croghan. Diplomacy instead of force was necessary here, for it was impossible to send a large British army so far into the interior. Under circumstances of great hazard to himself and his companions,

Croghan won over the tribesmen, including the redoubtable Pontiac himself, to an acceptance of English rule. By the close of the summer of 1765, the Western Indians had given their submission, and an English garrison was established in the Illinois country. Once more the boats of the traders were passing unmolested down the Ohio River.

British Policy and Western Land Projects, 1763–1774

Closely related to the Indian problem was the question of the disposal of the great interior region west of the Alleghenies. To permit the Colonies with sea-to-sea claims to exercise jurisdiction here would invite confusion and trouble not only among the Colonies themselves, because of overlapping claims, but also in their relations with the Indians, for the eager frontiersmen had little regard for the rights of the red men. An imperial control of some sort seemed necessary. But the imperial authorities were faced with the same problem—whether or not to permit settlement in the interior, and, if they permitted it, how to regulate it in order to avoid Indian troubles. The British Government, controlled for the most part by selfish politicians, was hardly in a position to adopt a consistent, statesmanlike policy; but to its credit, in the years following Pontiac's Conspiracy, it succeeded in avoiding Indian wars and in preventing a rush of settlers into the Ohio Valley to seize Indian lands.

The Royal Proclamation Line of 1763 was established to confine settlement east of the Alleghenies. The government recognized the need of an Indian boundary beyond which white settlers could not proceed without government authorization, and designated the mountains because there was no time to fix a definite line in agreement with the Indians and have it surveyed. Already pioneers and land speculators were pushing into the interior, and Pontiac's Conspiracy had broken out. The establishment of such a line would not prevent future cessions of land by the Indians to the British Government and the properly regulated colonizing of such lands, but it did attempt to restrain settlement until the government could control it. The fur trade also needed to be protected, and presently two Indian districts were created west of the mountains to safeguard the red men from unscrupulous whites. The leading land speculators regarded the policy of the Proclamation as only temporary and made plans to secure the most desirable lands as soon as the region should be opened. The frontiersmen paid little attention to the line, squatting on Indian lands as before.

Believing that the West would soon be opened to settlement, some of the speculators organized companies to secure large tracts from the Crown. Several of these projects were launched in the 1760's, but only one came near to success. This was the Walpole Company, better known as the Vandalia Project, from the name it proposed to give its new colony. Thomas Walpole, a London banker, and a number of prominent Englishmen were stockholders, as well as George Croghan, Governor William Franklin, of New Jersey, Sir William Johnson, and other colonial capitalists. Benjamin Franklin acted as lobbyist for the company with the British Government. It petitioned for a grant south of the Ohio, west of Pennsylvania and Virginia, and as far west as the Kentucky River, an area including approximately the present state of West Virginia and the eastern part of Kentucky. The project was pressed especially after the Iroquois, by the Treaty of Fort Stanwix, in 1768, surrendered their claims to a vast tract south of the Ohio and as far west as the Tennessee.

But the British Government had to give its consent— and this was less easy to obtain. Rival speculators and companies wanted grants, and protested to the British ministers, though some were bought off with shares in the reorganized company. The old Ohio Land Company still had hopes of being revived, and the Virginia soldiers, who had been promised land bounties, had expected them to be located in this area. Virginia naturally objected to this disregard of her charter claims. But skilful lobbying overcame all objections, and it seemed in 1773 as if the new colony would soon be an actuality. Apparently the charter was about to be granted. If Vandalia had been colonized, Ohio would soon have had settlers, for the Ohio River boundary would not have bothered the frontiersmen; but delays and obstructions prevented any action until the Revolution broke out and ended British control.

One of the leading speculators of the Virginia group was George Washington, who had long been interested in Western lands. Through his agent, Captain William Crawford, he selected a number of tracts in the Ohio Valley and had them surveyed, although final title could only be obtained when Virginia's right to the Ohio Valley was recognized by the Crown. In 1770 Washington made a trip to Fort Pitt and then down the Ohio to the mouth of the Great Kanawha, looking for desirable land. On this journey he encountered a rival speculator, George Croghan, who attempted to sell the Virginian a part of his own holdings. Only his demand for cash prevented the sale. Croghan's titles depended on the success of the Vandalia scheme and of royal confirmation of some Indian purchases.

Washington never lost interest in the West, and in the trying years following the Revolution advocated a scheme for connecting the headwaters of the Potomac and the Ohio to furnish an Eastern outlet for Western goods. In his will he listed tracts of land in sections that now constitute Kentucky, Ohio, and West Virginia totalling more than forty-one thousand acres.

The last significant measure of the British Government applying to the West was the Quebec Act of 1774. It was designed primarily to give to Canada a permanent government without a representative assembly, and a satisfactory legal system—a measure quite suited to the French population; but it extended the boundaries of the province of Quebec to the Ohio River on the south and to the Mississippi on the west. Since the French villages in the Illinois region contained the only permanent residents in this area, excepting the Indians, and since the preservation of the fur trade was an object of the act, the measure did not seem unreasonable. Yet it disregarded the Western land claims of several seaboard Colonies, already irritated by British commercial restrictions, and seemed to the frontiersmen to guarantee Indian possession of the lands north of the Ohio. It also created resentment because of the privileged position it gave to the Roman Catholic Church, though this was suited to the religious desires of the French. The measure would have aroused less opposition had it not been enacted at the time when Parliament was passing laws to punish Boston and Massachusetts for the "Boston Tea Party." Though the Quebec Act had no connection with these coercive acts, it was associated with them in the popular mind and was later mentioned in the Declaration of Independence as an act of British tyranny. Its significance in Ohio history is slight. Acts of Parliament meant little to Americans in 1775.

Lord Dunmore's War

Despite the evident desire of the British Government to proceed cautiously in securing land cessions and permitting settlement, the Ohio Indians were becoming increasingly concerned over the appearance of hunters, surveyors, and occasional squatters west of the Indian boundary. They were further incensed at the action of the Iroquois nations in 1768 at Fort Stanwix when the region south of the Ohio River was ceded to the Crown with no regard for the claims of the Ohio tribes, particularly the Shawnees. This ill feeling was fanned into a flame by a number of irritating incidents on both sides and came to a climax in the spring of 1774. Alarmed at rumors of Indian depredations, Dr. John Connolly, agent at Fort Pitt for Virginia's Governor, Lord Dunmore, issued a proclamation calling on the frontiersmen to arm in their own defense, as war was at hand. Settlers on the exposed frontier began to flee to the settlements for safety, and killings by both frontiersmen and Indians occurred frequently.

One of the overt acts was furnished by a group of surveyors and frontiersmen who gathered at the mouth of Wheeling Creek and determined to begin hostilities. Captain Michael Cresap was chosen as leader, though he was not responsible for the acts of violence that followed, popularly called "Cresap's War." The first bloodshed came when two Indians in a canoe on the Ohio were fired upon and killed. Other killings speedily followed, making war inevitable. The most atrocious act was the cold-blooded murder of a number of unarmed Mingo Indians at "Baker's Cabin," some fifteen miles above the present site of Steubenville on the Virginia side of the river. A villainous character by the name of Greathouse was the leader of the whites. The Indians were made drunk and then killed. Among them was a sister of the Mingo chief, Logan, and perhaps other relatives. Logan, holding Cresap responsible, went on the warpath, and the frontier was soon aflame.

The Indians of the Ohio country did not present a united front. The Shawnees furnished the backbone of their resistance, being aided by Mingoes, Wyandots, and scattered groups from other tribes. Owing to the influence of the Moravian missionaries, the majority of the Delawares held aloof. The more distant Northwestern tribes and the Iroquois were not involved in the war.

On the other hand, Virginia alone of the English Colonies was responsible for the war. Claiming the region around Fort Pitt, and controlling that frontier village despite Pennsylvania's claims,[1] the Old Dominion, under its aggressive Royal Governor, Lord Dunmore, set about to crush the Ohio tribes and establish its title to the great Northwest. Pennsylvania adopted a policy of neutrality, while the hostile tribes on their part attempted to distinguish between Virginians and residents of the Quaker colony. The trading interests of the latter made them less objectionable than the Virginia speculators and home-seekers.

On June 10, 1774, Lord Dunmore called out the militia of the western counties, and the war was on. The Governor sent out Colonel Angus McDonald to raid the Shawnee towns, but the expedition did little but stir up the Indians to a greater fighting pitch. The more important work was left to Dunmore himself, who assembled a force of militia at Fort Pitt, and Colonel Andrew Lewis, who called out the frontiersmen of the southwestern counties. The original plan was for a junction of the two forces at the mouth of the Big Kanawha, but Dunmore, coming down the Ohio from Fort Pitt, proceeded only as far as the Hocking, and then marched up that valley toward the Shawnee villages on the Pickaway Plains, where he expected Lewis to join him.

---

[1] Fort Pitt was no longer a British post, since the troops had been removed in 1772.

The latter, with some eleven hundred backwoodsmen, followed the Kanawha to the Ohio, and on October 6 encamped at Point Pleasant at the junction of the two rivers. Here, in the early morning of October 10, he was attacked by more than a thousand warriors, mostly Shawnees, under the leadership of the crafty and skilful Cornstalk. They had crossed the Ohio the night before, unobserved by Lewis's scouts, and were within two miles of the sleeping Virginian troops when they were discovered by hunters. A desperate battle ensued between Indians and Lewis's frontiersmen with the result in doubt until late in the day, when the braves began to retire: that night they retreated across the Ohio and returned to the Shawnee towns. One fifth of Lewis's forces were killed or wounded, while the number of Indian casualties was smaller; but the failure of the attack of the Indians and their withdrawal gave the Virginians a hard-earned victory.

The battle of Point Pleasant has sometimes been called the first engagement of the American Revolution, but this is hardly the case. Great Britain was in no way involved, as the Indians were fighting on their own initiative to defend their lands against the aggressions of the frontiersmen. Nor were the latter conscious of upholding the American cause against the mother country, particularly since a royal governor had called them to arms. It was rather the beginning of another chapter in the long struggle of the red men to save their lands from the unceasing pressure of the whites. Not until Wayne's victory in 1794 was the contest for the Northwest terminated.

However, Point Pleasant was long celebrated in frontier annals for the heroic deeds of the participants. Stories and ballads recited around the fireplaces of log cabins made the battle take on an epic character to the generation that listened to the fireside chronicles, the spirit of which is exemplified by the following verse:

> Like thunder from heaven our rifles did roar,
> Till twelve of the clock, or perhaps something more,
> And during this time the Shawnees did fly,
> Whilst many a brave man on the ground there did lie.

The news of Point Pleasant reached Dunmore as he was marching toward the Shawnee towns, and was soon followed by overtures for peace from Cornstalk. Eight miles from the chief Indian village, the Governor established Camp Charlotte, in what is at present Pickaway County, and here terms were agreed upon. The Indians were to restore prisoners and property and to regard the Ohio River as their boundary line. More definite terms were to be arranged at Fort Pitt the following spring. While the negotiations were under way, Colonel Lewis approached Camp Charlotte with his victorious army. Doubting his ability to control the frontiersmen in the presence of their hated enemy, Dunmore ordered them to march back to Point Pleasant, as the war was over. Only with considerable reluctance did they finally agree to do this: destroying the Shawnee villages would have been far more to their taste.

A group of Mingoes refusing to join in the negotiations were punished by an expedition sent against their villages (on the present site of Columbus), which were destroyed. Logan, the Mingo chief, had not opposed peace, though he did not take part in the discussions. He had not fought at Point Pleasant, for he was at the time leading a raid on the Virginia frontier. Now, his vengeance satisfied, he recounted his mistreatment at the hands of the whites in a famous speech to Dunmore's envoy that, if not written down and translated exactly as he gave it, at least expresses admirably in its English version the sense of injustice and the burden of sorrow that weighed upon him. His pathetic eloquence has immortalized him as his deeds as a warrior could never have done.

Before their withdrawal from Ohio soil, the officers of Dunmore's army passed a resolution expressing their sympathy for the American cause, then represented by the First Continental Congress at Philadelphia. This resolution was accompanied by an expression of confidence in their commander, Lord Dunmore—a fact that seems to prove clearly without foundation the stories later circulated to the effect that Dunmore provoked the war in the interests of Great Britain to keep the frontiersmen occupied. It was even charged that he had tried to accomplish the destruction of Lewis's force by giving him no aid at Point Pleasant, but there are no indications in any of Dunmore's private letters that he was guilty of such duplicity, nor were such charges made at that time. On the contrary, all the evidence points to his sincerity and zeal in upholding the rights of the Province of Virginia. The aspersions cast upon him later by frontiersmen and frontier writers were doubtless inspired by their dislike of the Governor resulting from his actions in support of the British Government in the first year of the Revolution. His course then made them suspect him of motives that could not have been present earlier.

The results of Dunmore's War were important. It kept the Ohio tribes quiet during the first two years of the Revolution and gave the little Kentucky settlements an opportunity to become established without molestation. It furnished military experience for many officers and soldiers who later took part in the Revolution: for example, Andrew Lewis, Daniel Morgan, George Rogers Clark, Isaac Shelby, and William Crawford. It strengthened Virginia's claim to the trans-Allegheny region, for she alone had been responsible for the war and its successful

outcome.   Her paper claims could now be reënforced by
an argument based upon conquest.   The Quebec Act was
seemingly made a dead letter to the frontiersmen.

Ohio during the Revolution

The struggle for the Ohio country during the American
Revolution was essentially a renewal of the conflict between

Ohio in the Revolutionary Period

Indian and frontiersman that had begun with the French
and Indian War, had been reopened for a time by Pontiac

in 1763, and after some years of quiet, had entered upon a
new phase in Dunmore's War, when the Ohio Indians
seemed in imminent danger from the westward advance
of the whites.   Whether the Revolution had come or not,
further wars were inevitable if the Indians were to be
dispossessed of their lands.   The outbreak of hostilities
between mother country and Colonies merely hastened the
renewal of the old struggle.   This time, British encouragement and assistance made the area of conflict more widespread and the result more doubtful than they had been in
1763 and in 1774.

At first, the Ohio Indians, still smarting from their
defeat at Point Pleasant, were reluctant to go on the warpath at the behest of British authorities.   Indeed, the
Indians seemed bewildered at the rapid turn of events in
1775.   The very tribes that had been punished by Dunmore
the year before were now being urged by his agent, Connolly,
to attack the frontier settlers.   Connolly's efforts were
nullified, however, by the formation of a committee of
public safety at Pittsburgh that took control of the region
and asked Congress for action to quiet the Indians.   Both
Virginia and Congress appointed commissioners to complete the preliminary treaty, made by Dunmore the year
before, and a great gathering of tribes was held at Pittsburgh in September, 1775.   The outcome was a treaty to
insure the friendship of the Indians and to secure their
neutrality in the war.   Thus, the immediate danger of
Indian attack was removed, the settlement of Kentucky
was allowed to proceed peacefully, and the West could send
its riflemen to join the army of Washington, then encircling
the British forces in Boston.

The fall of 1775 also saw the capture of Dunmore's agent,
Connolly, who was planning to arouse the Indians, and,
with the aid of British troops in the Northwest and in

Canada, seize Pittsburgh and invade Virginia from the west. He was arrested in Maryland on his way west, and his plan came to nothing. A more spectacular undertaking on the American side in 1776 was the exploit of Captain George Gibson, a young Virginian, who, with Lieutenant William Linn and fifteen men, went down the Mississippi to New Orleans to secure powder. After some difficulties with the Spanish authorities that were ironed out by Oliver Pollock, an American merchant, Gibson succeeded in his mission and sent ninety-eight barrels, with forty-three men to convey them, up the Mississippi and the Ohio. The expedition arrived at Wheeling on May 2, 1777, narrowly escaping capture at the falls of the Ohio at the hands of a band of Indians sent by the unfriendly Spanish officials at St. Louis. The value of this precious cargo to the American cause can hardly be overestimated.

It was becoming increasingly evident in 1776 that the Indians would soon be involved in the war, and Washington himself suggested that they be enlisted in the American cause. Congress authorized the Commander-in-chief to engage two thousand Indians and to offer rewards for prisoners, but this decree was counteracted by two factors that gave the British authorities an advantage in bidding for their support. One was the work of Canadian officials, particularly Sir Henry Hamilton, in command at Detroit, in offering every inducement to win the Western tribes. Congress, with its limited means, could not outbid the British. A second factor weighing heavily against the Americans was the natural hostility between frontiersman and red man that produced the inevitable crop of irritating incidents leading directly to war. The depredations of a band of hostile Mingoes, known as "Pluggy's Band," created consternation along the frontier in the fall of 1776 and made open war seem imminent, though Colonel George

Morgan, Indian agent at Pittsburgh, was making every effort to preserve peace between the various tribes and the frontiersmen.

The principal overt act, as in Dunmore's War, was furnished by lawless frontiersmen. Cornstalk, coming to Fort Randolph (Point Pleasant) in the spring of 1777 to warn the commander that the Shawnees were about to go on the warpath, was murdered in cold blood with his son and two companions in the confines of the fort by militia-men. The soldiers had been infuriated at the killing of a young Virginia volunteer by some marauding braves across the Kanawha and had vented their rage on the high-minded Shawnee chief. This act of despicable treachery was followed by a general rising of the Ohio tribes, excepting the Delawares, against the frontier. Both Congress and Governor Patrick Henry, of Virginia, attempted to make amends to the Shawnees, but the damage could not be repaired.

The story of the next six years is one of bloodshed and horror, of war in its cruelest form, with whites vying with Indians in acts of atrocity. Ohio was as yet unsettled but was crossed by bands of hostile braves, on their way to attack the Kentucky settlements or the Pennsylvania and Virginia frontiers, and by retaliatory expeditions of Americans intent on punishing the tribesmen by scattering their bands and destroying their Ohio villages. No important battles were fought on Ohio soil, but a number of bloody minor engagements and acts of individual prowess, peculiar to frontier warfare, made these years take on an almost legendary character to the succeeding generations. The names of Daniel Boone, the Poe brothers, George Rogers Clark, Simon Kenton, and William Crawford, among the American heroes, and of "Hair-Buyer" Hamilton and the three Tories, Alexander McKee,

Matthew Elliott, and Simon Girty, on the British side, speak for themselves.

The year 1777, besides being the period of raids on frontier settlements in Kentucky and on the upper Ohio, was marked by an unsuccessful attack on Fort Henry (now Wheeling) by a band of two or three hundred Indians and some Detroit rangers in September. The little band of defenders offered such desperate resistance that the besiegers soon withdrew in discouragement. The siege was immortalized in frontier annals by Major Samuel McCullough's reputed descent on horseback down a precipitous slope some three hundred feet high to escape the Indians who had intercepted him as he was about to enter the fort.

The year 1778 is famous in the history of the Revolution for the exploits of George Rogers Clark in the Northwest. His capture of Kaskaskia, Cahokia, and Vincennes in the Illinois country with one hundred and fifty men constitutes the most important accomplishment in the West during the war. The frontier rejoiced especially at the capture of Sir Henry Hamilton, the hated "Hair Buyer," at Vincennes in February, 1779. In Kentucky, Boonesborough underwent a ten-day siege late in the summer of 1778, but the resistance of Boone, Kenton, and their followers was too much for the four hundred and fifty assailants, mostly Indians with a few French Canadians.

In the same year, two attempts were made to invade the Ohio Indian country. General Edward Hand in February led five hundred men from Fort Pitt into eastern Ohio against the Indians on the Mahoning with the ultimate intention of moving against Sandusky. But only a few women and children and one man had been captured when heavy rains and melting snows put an end to the campaign. Soon afterward Alexander McKee, Matthew Elliott, and

Simon Girty fled from Fort Pitt to Detroit, where, as partisan leaders, they rendered valuable aid to the British cause.

In the fall General Lachlan McIntosh, General Hand's successor at Pittsburgh, prepared to attack Detroit, and established Fort Laurens on the Tuscarawas River in what is at present Tuscarawas County. Lacking supplies enough to proceed further, he retired, leaving at the fort a garrison of one hundred and fifty men under Colonel John Gibson. Here, in February, 1779, Simon Girty and Captain Henry Bird began a siege with a force of Indians and a few British soldiers that ended when both sides became nearly exhausted from lack of food. But the post was in too exposed a position to make it worth while to risk its garrison, and in August, 1779, it was evacuated, after being in almost constant danger of Indian attack from the time of its establishment. It was the first American fort on Ohio soil.

On the Kentucky front, in the early summer of 1779, occurred an offensive thrust of nearly three hundred frontier volunteers under Colonel John Bowman against the Shawnee center on the Little Miami near the present site of Xenia. Though outnumbering the Indians three to one, the expedition accomplished little beyond the destruction of huts and crops and the acquisition of plunder. It did, however, prevent an intended invasion of Kentucky, and caused some alarm in Detroit lest the Indians, in discouragement, should abandon the British cause. In the same summer, George Rogers Clark's plan to attack Detroit, though not carried out for lack of men and supplies, produced a near-panic in that place.

The year 1780 was marked by a raid upon Kentucky by British and Indians and a retaliatory expedition against the Ohio Indians by Clark. The first, planned by Major Arent S. De Peyster, in command at Detroit, as part of a general offensive in the West, was aimed at the newly established but important town of Louisville. However, fearing that the post might prove too difficult to take, the motley array of Indians, Canadians, and British soldiers turned to attack the weaker Kentucky settlements. Two of these were easily captured, but the problem of supplies, the heavy rains, and the unruly actions of his Indian allies led the commander, Captain Henry Bird, to order a retreat. The immediate effect was a retaliatory expedition led by George Rogers Clark. With nearly a thousand backwoodsmen from all parts of Kentucky, the hero of Vincennes pushed up the Little Miami in August, arriving at the Indian center of Old Chillicothe (near Xenia) in time to see burning the huts of the Shawnees, who had abandoned their towns and fled some twelve miles to their capital near the present site of Springfield. Clark pursued them and fought a successful engagement (the Battle of Piqua) with a remnant of the tribesmen, though most of the Indians, alarmed at the size of this frontier army, had fled into the forest. The town was soon in flames and the crops around it destroyed by the avenging frontiersmen. Clark's force then returned to the Ohio and dispersed. The blow was a severe one to the Shawnees, and for the rest of the year the Kentuckians enjoyed a temporary respite from the horrors of Indian warfare.

Again in 1781 the Americans took the offensive and planned two expeditions into the Indian country. The first of these expeditions, in April, was directed against the Delaware center of Goschochgung (Coshocton). Led by Colonel Andrew Brodhead, commander of the forces at Pittsburgh, three hundred regulars and volunteers proceeded into eastern Ohio and surprised the Indian towns. Brodhead had been warned by the Moravian missionaries that the Delawares were about to abandon their neutrality, and

decided to strike first.[2]   The expedition was quite successful, seizing the Indian towns without a shot's being fired.
Fifteen warriors were killed in cold blood for their supposedly wicked deeds and a number of others murdered on
the march back by the undisciplined militiamen.   The
power of the Delawares was broken in eastern Ohio, and
they withdrew to the Scioto-Sandusky region.

Far more important was the plan of George Rogers Clark
to capture Detroit.   Only through possession of this key
point could Americans hope to end the Indian danger in
the Northwest.   But misfortune dogged Clark's steps from
the outset.   Though both Washington and Governor
Jefferson, of Virginia, approved, they could render little aid,
military or financial.   Colonel Brodhead at Fort Pitt
would not coöperate, and finally Clark was forced to start
down the Ohio with less than one fifth of the two thousand
men deemed necessary for the success of the enterprise.
He had expected reënforcements to overtake him before he
reached Louisville, but only 107 militia under Colonel
Archibald Lochry set out to join him.   These, short of
ammunition and supplies, were unable to catch up with
the main expedition and were cut off by a superior force of
Indians on August 24 a few miles below the mouth of the
Great Miami.   Forty-two were killed and the rest captured.
In the face of this disaster, Clark could not hope to attack
Detroit, and the plan was abandoned.

While the war was drawing to a close on the seaboard with
the capture of Cornwallis at Yorktown in the fall of 1781, it
continued its bloody course for another year in the Northwest.   The chief events center around the misfortunes of
the Moravian missionaries and their Indian converts.

---

[2] A band of the Delawares, led by their chief, Captain Pipe, had aided
the British from the first, but the majority, influenced by the Moravians,
had held aloof.

From the days of the French and Indian War, the Moravian Brethren, a German Protestant sect of simple, Quaker-like tenets, had been interested in the problem of Christianizing the Indians. As early as 1761, Reverend Christian Frederick Post had tried to establish a mission among the Delawares on the Muskingum, but the times were too unsettled to permit its success. Work with the Delawares in Pennsylvania was encouraging but encountered the suspicions of the frontiersmen, who thoroughly distrusted the Indian as a neighbor. The best opportunities seemed to be offered by the Delawares on the Tuscarawas, in eastern Ohio, and here in 1772 was begun the mission of Schoenbrunn (*Beautiful Spring*) by David Zeisberger and John Heckewelder. Soon other little villages were established,[3] and in them were congregated several missionaries and their families and the converted Indians, many of them from Pennsylvania, who were taught the virtues of the Christian way of life and the duty of nonresistance to the use of force.

The Revolution brought the dangers of war to the Moravians, whose villages lay on one of the principal war-paths between the hostile centers of Detroit and Pittsburgh. War parties from both sides stopped for refreshment at the missions and received the same friendly treatment. The influence of Zeisberger and Heckewelder was important in keeping most of the Delawares neutral until 1781, and it was due to the latter's warnings that Colonel Brodhead was able to attack and destroy the towns of the hostile tribesmen before they could carry out their plans against the Americans. But in return the Moravians

---

[3] Schoenbrunn and Gnadenhutten (1772) were abandoned, and Lichtenau (near Coshocton) became the mission center in 1776. The latter was abandoned in 1779–1780, and New Schoenbrunn (1779) and Salem (1780) were established and Gnadenhutten reoccupied (1779).

gained only the ill will of the frontier militia, who were with difficulty restrained by Colonel Brodhead from plundering the mission towns. The borderers could not understand neutrality and pacifism and only remembered that bands of marauding savages had rested and received food from the Moravians. The American commander urged the missionaries and their Indians to withdraw behind the American lines, but they would not abandon their beloved villages.

On their part, the British Indians were irritated at the refusal of the Moravian converts to take part in the war, and tried to embroil them. The first blow came in the fall of 1781. A band of Indians from Sandusky and Detroit with a few British rangers came to the towns on the Tuscarawas, and, after much plundering, forced the Christian Indians and their Moravian teachers to go with them to the Sandusky region. Here the hapless converts erected a few huts—"Captives' Town"—and faced a winter of starvation, as their savage hosts had abandoned them to their fate. However, the missionaries themselves were summoned to Detroit, where they had to undergo an examination before the commandant, De Peyster. The latter declared himself satisfied that the Moravians were innocent of wrongdoing and permitted them to return to Captives' Town.

A more serious blow now befell the Christian Delawares. Facing starvation in their new quarters, they were permitted by their Wyandot masters in February to send one hundred and fifty of their number back to the Tuscarawas to gather the corn left in the fields at the time of their forced departure. Here, with a few others who had remained at their old homes, they were found by a company of ninety volunteer militia from the Pittsburgh area, mostly frontier ruffians, led by a certain Captain David Williamson. Aroused at recent Indian raids and atrocities, and refusing to believe that the Moravian converts were not party to them, the borderers took matters into their own hands and decided to wipe out the villages. No resistance was offered, and the Indians were disarmed and imprisoned in two cabins at Gnadenhutten while their captors debated their fate. Only eighteen of the ninety voted for mercy, the rest favoring immediate execution. The captives, informed of their decision, were allowed to spend the night in singing and praying, and next morning were led out by twos and murdered in cold blood. Sixty-two adults and thirty-four children perished, two boys miraculously escaping.

Having disposed of the Indians at Gnadenhutten and Salem in this fashion, the bloodthirsty frontiersmen proceeded to Schoenbrunn to complete their work, but the inhabitants had been warned in time and had fled. The killers then gathered together the plunder and returned to the neighborhood of Pittsburgh, where public opinion seems to have been divided as to the justice of the deed. Posterity has had but one opinion on this question, namely, that their action stands out as one of the most atrocious massacres in the annals of warfare. Prisoners have been killed in cold blood on numerous occasions in Indian wars, but the murder of a group of noncombatant neutrals who had been taught to regard nonresistance as a Christian virtue by a band of whites, supposedly Christians, is almost without parallel.

This massacre, in March, 1782, began a year of such horrors that it has been called the "bloody year." Regardless of what had happened in the East, the war was not yet over in the West. The most important offensive operation was an expedition of four hundred and eighty mounted volunteers, mostly Pennsylvania borderers, including many of Moravian infamy, against the Wyandot center of Sandusky (near the site of Upper Sandusky) in May and June, 1782. A company of Detroit rangers under Captain William Caldwell and some Lake Indians came to the aid of the Ohio tribesmen, and a battle was fought near the Wyandot town. The first day (June 4), there was no decisive result, and the struggle continued in desultory fashion another day; but reënforcements of Shawnees and Canadians alarmed the Americans, who decided to retreat that night. The retreat speedily became a disorderly flight that was not checked until the deserted Wyandot town was reached next morning. A successful stand against their pursuers that afternoon (the battle of the Olentangy) saved the little army and enabled it to retire without further interference. But among the fifty missing was the unfortunate commander of the expedition, Colonel William Crawford. Elected to the position by popular vote, he had attempted the impossible in trying to conduct a successful campaign with undisciplined frontier volunteers in the heart of the Indian country. Separated from his command and captured by the Delawares, he was burned to death with horrible tortures. The Moravians were being avenged.

Success in defeating Crawford's expedition encouraged the Indians, and a raid against Bryan's Station in Kentucky followed in August. Defeated in trying to take the place, and fearful of the arrival of relief from other settlements, the Indians and rangers under Captain Caldwell withdrew. A body of Kentuckians, overtaking the enemy, was led into an ambush at the Blue Licks on the Licking River on August 19 and the worst disaster of the Revolution in the West followed. Sixty-six Americans were killed and four were captured. The last British offensive came in September, when Fort Henry was besieged by Captain Andrew Bradt with nearly three hundred Indians and rangers.

The garrison of eighteen men, besides women and boys, resisted so bravely that the siege was abandoned in three days. The attack was made memorable by the exploit of Betty Zane, sister of the commanding officer, who at the risk of her life ran from the fort to a fortified cabin near by and returned with a badly needed supply of powder for the garrison.

Even before the siege of Fort Henry, orders from his superiors came to De Peyster at Detroit to act only on the defensive, and no more raids were organized against the frontier. But the Kentuckians, aroused by the defeat at Blue Licks, struck one more retaliatory blow at the Indians. George Rogers Clark, taking the field for the last time, in November led 1,050 mounted riflemen up the Miami Valley against the Shawnee towns. One detachment went as far as Loramie's (or Lorimier's) Store, a British trading post at the head of the Miami. No resistance was offered by the fleeing tribesmen, whose towns were burned and whose supplies were destroyed by the avenging Kentuckians. This raid, made in November, 1782, marked the close of the Revolution in the West. General Irvine had planned to assist Clark by leading an expedition from Fort Pitt against the Sandusky towns, but as his troops were assembling, orders came for him not to proceed, as Sir Guy Carleton, the British commander at New York, had put an end to the Indian war.

The story of the peace negotiations lies outside the field of Ohio history, but it is of interest to know that the obtaining of American title to the vast region west of the Alleghenies was largely due to the insistence of the commissioners, John Jay and John Adams, upon this point, in opposition to the French proposal that the Northwest remain in British hands. By disregarding French advice and breaking their own instructions, they made terms with the British commissioners that made the Mississippi and the Great Lakes the western and northern boundaries. Diplomacy rather than conquest won the Northwest, for most of Ohio and the important Detroit area were under British-Indian control despite Clark's conquest of the Illinois country. But the British Government, headed by the liberal-minded Lord Shelburne, was desirous of winning the United States away from the French and anxious to retain the commerce of the states as before the war, and made concessions that were not pleasing to France and her ally, Spain, whose hopes of confining the new nation to the area east of the mountains were thereby shattered. Thus Ohio became part of the United States of America, though whether title to the Ohio country was vested in Congress or in certain claimant states remained to be settled, while the sullen tribesmen for years to come were to dispute actual possession with the land-hungry frontiersmen.

Selected Bibliography

The period from 1763 to 1783 is covered in a number of general works. An excellent brief account is Frederick A. Ogg, *The Old Northwest* (New Haven, 1919, *Chronicles of America Series*, Vol. XIX). Burke Aaron Hinsdale, *The Old Northwest* (New York, 1888), is an older work of much value. Written in entertaining style but concerned chiefly with frontier wars is Theodore Roosevelt, *The Winning of the West* (4 vols., 1894–1896, but published in other editions): the first two volumes cover this period. Justin Winsor, *The Westward Movement* (Boston, 1897), gives much space to the Northwest. Charles Moore, *The Northwest under Three Flags* (New York, 1900), pp. 205–278, continues through this period. The histories of Ohio cited in the previous chapter may be consulted, Randall and Ryan being especially detailed on the Revolution, though not always accurate.

Pontiac's Conspiracy is brilliantly presented in Francis Parkman, *Conspiracy of Pontiac* (2 vols., Boston, 1883). Volwiler's *Croghan and the Westward Movement* is excellent on westward expansion prior to the Revolution.   There are several biographies of George Rogers Clark, but James A. James, *The Life of George Rogers Clark* (Chicago, 1928), is particularly valuable for its broad treatment of the Revolution in the West.   C. W. Butterfield, *History of the Girtys* (Cincinnati, 1890), and *Washington-Irvine Correspondence* (Madison, 1882), contain much material on the subject.   Thomas Boyd, *Simon Girty, the White Savage* (New York, 1928), is an entertaining biography.   For a sympathetic account of the Moravians, the reader should consult Edmund De Schweinitz, *The Life and Times of David Zeisberger* (Philadelphia, 1870).

Two volumes of documents on the Revolutionary period have been edited by Reuben G. Thwaites and Louise Phelps Kellogg: *Documentary History of Dunmore's War* (Madison, 1905) and *The Revolution on the Upper Ohio, 1775–77* (Madison, 1908). Miss Kellogg has also edited *Frontier Advance on the Upper Ohio, 1778–79* (Madison, 1916, *Wisconsin Historical Collections*, Vol. XXIII), and *Frontier Retreat on the Upper Ohio, 1779–81* (Madison, 1917, *Wisconsin Historical Collections*, Vol. XXIV).   The introductions to these collections of sources are excellent summaries of the years covered.   The closing phases of the Revolution are admirably covered by Milo M. Quaife in an article, "The Ohio Campaign of 1782," *Mississippi Valley Historical Review*, Vol. XVII, pp. 515–529.   The diary of the Moravian missionary, David Zeisberger, is in *Ohio Archæological and Historical Quarterly*, Vol. XXI, pp. 1–115, and in *Diary of David Zeisberger* (Eugene F. Bliss, ed., 2 vols., Cincinnati, 1885).   Heckewelder's account may be read in John Heckewelder, *A Narrative of the Mission of the United Brethren among the Delaware and Mohegan Indians* (Philadelphia, 1820).   Washington's journal of his tour of the Ohio in 1770 may be found in *Old South Leaflets*, Vol. II, General Series No. 41, and, in more complete form, with an introduction by A. B. Hulbert, in *Ohio Archæological and Historical Quarterly*, Vol. XVII, pp. 431–488.

Information as to points of historic interest may be found in *First Biennium Report of the Ohio Revolutionary Memorial Commission* (Columbus, 1931).   The commission has also issued a cartographic map, "Ohio Revolutionary Memorial Trails, 1776–1813," with explanatory notes.   Only western Ohio has been covered by the commission, however. Dealing with Schoenbrunn and its restoration, Rev. Joseph E. Weinland, *The Romantic Story of Schoenbrunn* (Dover, Ohio, 1928), presents interesting information. Charles Edwin Hopkins, *Ohio, the Beautiful and Historic* (Boston, 1931), is a book of travel containing much early history, written in an uncritical fashion.

CHAPTER IV

Ohio in the Confederation Period

Indian Relations in the Post-war Years

*T*HE Indian problem in the Northwest, like a host of other questions, domestic and foreign, inherited from the struggle for independence, remained to thwart the feeble attempts of Congress to arrive at its solution in the trying years of post-bellum reconstruction. Two factors rendered exceedingly difficult a peaceful arrangement between Indians and whites north of the Ohio. One was the continued presence of British troops and officials at Detroit, Michilimackinac, and other border posts on American soil. The other was the unceasing movement of frontiersmen and land speculators into the region claimed by the Northwestern tribes. On its part, Congress could neither get rid of the first nor control the second. Even a stronger government would have found the problem a serious one, but to the Government of the Confederation a solution was impossible.

The presence of the British in the Northwest was due ostensibly to the failure of the United States to live up to the terms of the Treaty of 1783. The confiscation by various states of private debts owed to British merchants before the war was apparently the crux of the difficulty, since the treaty had provided that the collection of these debts should not be interfered with. John Jay, American Secretary for Foreign Affairs, wrote in 1786 that "there had not been a single day since it took effect, on which it (the treaty) had not been violated in America by one or other of the

States." Such an admission would seem to justify the British attitude; yet far more important than the charge of treaty violation was the desire of British officials in Canada to retain the valuable fur trade of the Northwest for their merchants. The surrender of the border posts would carry with it control over the Indians and consequent loss of this trade. The Northwest Company, organized in 1783, was a powerful factor in persuading Canadian officials, and through them the British Government, that a business of half a million dollars or more might be thrown away through evacuation of the Western posts.

Fed and clothed largely from British sources, and influenced by British agents not to surrender their lands, the Ohio tribes looked with growing uneasiness at the throngs of prospective settlers encroaching on their claims. The overflow from Kentucky and Pennsylvania seemed about to spread into the Ohio country in such volume that, unless speedily checked, resistance would be hopeless. Despite the impossibility of obtaining valid titles from state or central government, and in the face of a proclamation of Congress against their entry, the land-hungry continued their efforts. In the words of Washington,[1]

> Such is the rage for speculating in, and forestalling of lands on the No. West of the Ohio, that scarce a valuable spot, within any tolerable distance of it, is left without a claimant. . . . In defiance of the proclamation of Congress, they roam over the Indian side of the Ohio, mark out Lands, survey and even settle on them. This gives great discontent to the Indians, and will unless measures are taken in time to prevent it, produce a war inevitably with the western tribes.

His solution was to have Congress declare all measures to secure land north of the Ohio illegal and make the vio-

---

[1] In a letter to Jacob Read, Nov. 3, 1784. See *The Writings of George Washington* (W. C. Ford, ed., New York, 1891), Vol. X, pp. 416 to 419.

lators thereafter outlaws and "fit subjects for Indian vengeance."

Rather tardily, in 1784, Congress took up the problem of satisfying the Indians and appointed commissioners to treat with the various tribes for the purpose of drawing boundary lines. At Fort Stanwix, in the fall of 1784, negotiations were conducted with the Iroquois, and their claims to the region north of the Ohio were surrendered. The Ohio tribes, however, resented this action, and further negotiations were necessary to placate them. Accordingly, at Fort McIntosh, in western Pennsylvania, the commissioners of Congress arranged a treaty with the Wyandots, Delawares, Chippewas, and Ottawas in January, 1785. The Indians were granted an area bounded on the east by the Cuyahoga and the Tuscarawas as far as the crossing above Fort Laurens, on the south by a line from this point to the portage between the Great Miami and the Maumee, and on the west by the Maumee to Lake Erie. Thus, a tract including perhaps a third or a fourth of the present state of Ohio was to become a great Indian reservation.

There remained the task of dealing with the Shawnees and the more western tribes, and Fort Finney was established at the mouth of the Great Miami as a convenient point for the negotiations. Wyandots and Delawares came for the rum and presents, but the Shawnees had to be threatened with war before they finally appeared in January, 1786, one hundred and fifty warriors with their women and children. They accepted with some reluctance a treaty assigning them lands between the Great Miami and the Wabash. Probably the boldness and force with which George Rogers Clark, who was one of the commissioners, insisted upon their submission explains their willingness to sign. They also urged the Western tribes to come to the conference, but British influence kept the latter away and presently the Shawnees themselves were repudiating the treaty and denying that they were bound by it.

Partly as a consequence of their successful coöperation with one another during the Revolution and partly because of British advice and influence, the tribes were now tending to act as a unit and to insist that no treaties were binding unless agreed to by all. The American policy of treating with individual tribes seemed to have gained little, and a new Indian war was apparently at hand. The usual depredations occurred, and the Kentucky settlements began to suffer from raiding parties from the Wabash region.

Clark, believing that force was the only remedy, appealed to Congress, but that body, short of funds and incapable of vigorous action, delayed so long that the Kentuckians, urged on by the Virginia authorities, took matters into their own hands. Clark organized and led an expedition of twelve hundred men against the Wabash tribes in September, while Colonel Benjamin Logan in October moved against the Shawnees with eight hundred men. But the hero of Vincennes, too much addicted to liquor for his own good, but more hampered by the wretched character of his backwoods militia, accomplished little in a military way, though he secured a cessation of hostilities and a promise of a treaty in the future. Colonel Logan, helped by the absence of many warriors, who were aiding their western allies against Clark, succeeded in destroying ten Shawnee villages and their large quantities of provisions, while ten Indians were killed and thirty-four were captured. This success was marred by the murder in cold blood of Chief Molunthe, an old Shawnee who had been at the Fort Finney negotiations and who favored peace. The murderer, a ruffian officer named McGary, went unpunished.

No further hostilities occurred, but the tribes were still sullen and resentful. Murders and stealings did not cease, and boatloads of immigrants on the Ohio River were in constant danger. In conferences at Detroit, held under British supervision, the Western tribes and the Six Nations held to the idea of common ownership of the Northwest and the necessity for the consent of all to cessions. But they were not agreed as to making open war, and the peace that was but a step removed from war continued through the Confederation years.

Land Cessions and Congressional Ordinances

Four states, New York, Virginia, Massachusetts, and Connecticut, had claims on the Northwest that, however unimportant they might have seemed to the British Government in the pre-Revolution years, were not to be lightly disregarded by a Congress controlled by representatives of land-claiming states. In the Articles of Confederation the matter was not dealt with, though it was hoped that the states would voluntarily relinquish their claims. Maryland, however, demanded a more specific pledge and, alone of the thirteen states, refused to ratify the Articles until assured that the claimant states would surrender their claims. Congress in 1780 gave its word that such cessions would be disposed of for the common benefit of the United States, and that new states would be formed from the territory, to be admitted to the Union on equal terms with the old.

New York, early in 1780, led the way to union by offering to give up a claim that rested solely on her former guardianship over the Iroquois with their vague pretensions to control over the West they had once conquered. Virginia and Connecticut next promised to act, and although terms had not yet been arranged with Congress, Maryland was satisfied as to their good intentions and accepted the Articles of Confederation.

It took several years to complete the cessions north of the Ohio, as special conditions had to be met in each case. Virginia's claim rested upon the vague expression in her charter of 1609 giving her the land "from sea to sea, west and northwest," but it had been strengthened by Dunmore's War and by Clark's conquest of the Illinois country. In surrendering her claim north of the Ohio in 1784, she reserved the region between the Scioto and the Little Miami to satisfy the bounties promised to her Revolutionary veterans, provided insufficient lands remained in Kentucky for this purpose.

Massachusetts and Connecticut, with sea-to-sea charters, were involved in controversies with New York and Pennsylvania, but Massachusetts ceded her Western claims in 1785 after reaching an agreement with New York over lands in that state. Connecticut, unable to secure lands in the Quaker state, reserved ownership and jurisdiction over a region extending one hundred and twenty miles west of Pennsylvania and lying between 41° and 42° 2', though she ceded the rest of her claim to the United States in 1786. Thus, north of the Ohio Congress could provide a government and sell lands, assuming, of course, that the demands of the Indians could be satisfied.

The evolution of the territorial system that found expression in the Ordinances of 1784 and 1787 is too long a story to be recounted in connection with the history of Ohio. Suffice it to say that the idea of new self-governing commonwealths beyond the Alleghenies, in contrast with the British system of colonial dependencies, had become a well-established principle in the minds of leading Americans by the close of the Revolution. Among others, Silas Deane,

Tom Paine, Pelatiah Webster, Timothy Pickering, Theodoric Bland, Rufus Putnam, George Washington, and David Howell all affirmed this principle and in one way or another contributed to give it a practical application. A committee of Congress, composed of Howell of Rhode Island, Chase of Maryland, and Thomas Jefferson, presented to that body the Ordinance of 1784 for the government of the region beyond the mountains. Jefferson actually wrote the document, and it was quite worthy of his illustrious name.

This ordinance divided the entire West (most of it not then ceded to Congress) into some sixteen or eighteen prospective states, ten of them north of the Ohio, with the boundaries drawn in checkerboard fashion with slight regard for geographical considerations. A temporary government was to exist until a division had twenty thousand people, at which time a permanent constitution and a permanent government were to be set up. In this second stage a congressional delegate who could debate but not vote would be permitted. When a state had a free population equal to that of the smallest of the thirteen original states, it was to be admitted into the Confederation on an equal footing with the old states. Although indefinite as to details, the Ordinance seemed to give complete self-government at all stages. The original draft prohibited slavery after 1800, but this prohibition was stricken out by Congress by a close vote, as were the names (such as Assenisipia, Metropotamia, Sylvania, and Michigania) that Jefferson applied to the prospective states. The Ordinance of 1784 was never in operation, as it was superseded by the Ordinance of 1787 before actual settlement had begun.

With the cessions completed for the Northwest by 1786 and a land ordinance providing for survey and sale of lands in effect, Congress considered a plan of government for the region in its usual dilatory fashion until July, 1787, when Reverend Manasseh Cutler, representing the newly organized Ohio Company, appeared on the scene. With the prospect of the sale of a large tract of land, and with Cutler assisting the committee, Congress speedily enacted the Ordinance of 1787.

Dealing only with the Northwest and far more definite in its provisions than its predecessor, this measure established the foundation for the American territorial system. It created three stages of government for the Northwest. In the first stage—before the territory had five thousand free adult males—a governor, a secretary, and three judges, appointed by Congress, constituted the administration. The governor and the judges could not formally legislate but might select such laws of the original states as were best adapted to conditions in the territory. In the second stage—beginning when the free men numbered five thousand—there was to be added an assembly consisting of an elected house of representatives and a legislative council of five selected by Congress from a group of ten named by the house. The two houses were to choose a congressional delegate, who would have debating but not voting powers. The governor was to possess an absolute veto over measures of the assembly. The territory was to be divided into not less than three, or more than five, states. Each might be admitted on equal terms with the old states when it had a free population of sixty thousand. This was the third and final stage.

A series of "articles of compact" between the original states and the people and states of the Northwest contained the usual guarantees of individual liberty found in a bill of rights, such as religious liberty, trial by jury, and the sanctity of contracts. One of these articles forbade slavery, though fugitives could be lawfully reclaimed.[2] Education was praised, though not endowed, in the statement, "Religion, morality, and knowledge, being necessary to good government and the happiness of mankind, schools and the means of education shall forever be encouraged." Good faith was to be observed towards the Indians, and their lands and property were to be respected.

The Ordinance of 1787 was a more conservative document than the Ordinance of 1784. The latter in indefinite terms granted self-government to the prospective states from the very beginning, but the former gave to the people no share whatever in government in the first stage, and in the second stage limited such participation by granting the governor an absolute veto. In addition, a property qualification of fifty acres of land was required for voters, one of two hundred for representatives, and one of five hundred for members in the council. Such requirements were common enough then and were met without difficulty at a time when land was cheap and plentiful, yet they show that the Ordinance of 1787 was not the product of frontier democracy. In the territorial period of Ohio's history, the fact that the position of the governor was a powerful one caused much dissatisfaction.

The ordinance in its features dealing with the government of territories prior to statehood bears strong resemblance to the system of government of a British royal province, particularly one like Massachusetts under its charter of 1691. But in its provision for statehood it differs fundamentally from the old colonial system. The West, although many seaboard Americans would have so preferred it, was not to be subject to the East as the Colonies had been to Great Britain.

---

[2] The anti-slavery clause of the ordinance did not apply to the French residents of the Illinois country, who held slaves for some years after it went into effect.

Quantities of ink and of oratory have been wasted in trying to determine the authorship of this important act. Nathan Dane, of Massachusetts, who drew up the ordinance for the committee, certainly had more to do with the actual wording than anyone else and was responsible for many significant details. Manasseh Cutler undoubtedly contributed some features, for he was very anxious to have the measure passed. If his Ohio Company were to attract settlers, such legislation was necessary. His lobbying certainly hurried it through. Rufus King is often credited with originating the anti-slavery article in the Congress of 1785, though Jefferson had this principle in the first draft of his Ordinance of 1784. But the claims of authorship for all of these men are of slight importance. No one man was really responsible for the measure. It was the application from familiar precedents of principles that had been developing ever since the separation from Great Britain. Congress needed only to borrow workable features from existing or earlier systems of government and fit them to the Northwest, to carry out the accepted ideal of new states admitted after a territorial apprenticeship. As for slavery, there was little desire, even in the South, to extend it north of the Ohio. Indeed, it is hard to see how any representative group of public men in 1787 could have devised a document for the Northwest differing in any fundamental way from the act that was passed. The broad principles were too well established to be credited to any one man.

Two years prior to the adoption of the Northwest Ordinance, Congress had enacted a law for the survey and sale of lands fully as significant for the West as the Ordinance of 1787. This was the Land Ordinance of 1785. It was passed to carry out the principle of disposing of the public domain for the common benefit of all the states. It made use of the experiences of the old states in the survey and sale of their lands, and, like the Ordinance of 1787, it was not the creation of any one man.

The land, ceded by the states and purchased from the Indians, was to be surveyed into townships six miles square, beginning at the intersection of the boundary of Pennsylvania and the Ohio River. The townships were to be numbered from the Ohio River northward, and each strip of townships, called a "range," was to receive a number, the numbers beginning at the Pennsylvania line and running westward. The townships were subdivided into thirty-six sections of one square mile each. The land was to be sold at auction at not less than one dollar per acre, with a section of six hundred forty acres the minimum amount to be sold. Section Number 16 of every township was reserved for schools and four other sections were set aside for future sale by the government. Special reservations were made for Canadian refugees who had supported the Revolution and for the Moravian Indians, the latter receiving a tract including the sites of their former homes. Virginia's military district between the Scioto and the Little Miami was also recognized. The "Geographer of the United States," assisted by a surveyor from each state, was to direct the survey.

The rectangular system of surveys provided in this ordinance spared Ohio (except in the Virginia Military District) the confusion and difficulties caused in the past by an indiscriminate method of locating lands. By the older system, the individual secured a land warrant from the colony or state and then had the tract that suited him surveyed; thus new tracts often overlapped earlier purchases, and less attractive lands were left unclaimed. New England, unlike the other Colonies, had used the system of granting townships to groups of settlers with survey preceding settlement, but the townships were not uniform in shape. In Ohio there was used for the first time a rectangular system, by which the townships were subdivided into smaller squares. Sale was to follow survey; thus, questions as to what the individual was buying were avoided and the overlapping of claims was prevented. As early as 1765 Colonel Henry Bouquet had pointed out the merits of such a system, and the idea had appealed to others, including Thomas Jefferson; but to Congress was left the opportunity of putting it into effect when the Northwest was ceded to it.

The actual work of surveying the Seven Ranges (the first rows of townships adjacent to Pennsylvania and Virginia) began in the fall of 1785 under Geographer Thomas Hutchins and proceeded under great difficulties. The "Geographer's Line," drawn west from the intersection of the Ohio River and Pennsylvania's western boundary, was the northern limit of the survey and the Ohio River, the southern. Here, in the heavily forested hills of southeastern Ohio, the surveyors struggled to run their lines correctly, with the constant danger of hostile Indians, in addition to all the usual hazards of frontier life, such as disease, insects, bad weather, and an uncertain food supply. The township lines of four of the Seven Ranges were completed by February, 1787, and Congress ordered that sales be begun. The results were not very encouraging. Between September 21 and October 9, 1787, the Treasury Board sold 108,431 acres; but no townships were purchased entire, and the total received, $117,108, was mostly in depreciated Government securities. At this rate it would take many years for land sales to individuals to have any appreciable effect in reducing the national debt. Realizing this even before the auctions had begun, Congress turned its attention to making some large sales to land companies or groups of speculators, and thus arranged a contract in the same year with the Ohio Company and the holders of the "Scioto Right." As a consequence, settlement began in 1788 under the auspices of the Ohio Company before the individual purchasers of tracts in the Seven Ranges had had a chance to move in. But squatters were already farming portions of this region, and their priority as settlers will be considered in the following section.

The Beginnings of Organized Settlement

The first settlers in Ohio—disregarding the traders with their Indian wives and the Moravian missionaries and their families—were squatters who settled on the Ohio River and its branches in the southeastern counties while the Revolution was still going on. Showing as little regard for the authority of Congress or the claimant states as for the rights of the Indian, these rough, bold backwoodsmen squatted on lands that suited them and defied all efforts to dislodge them. They were a constant menace to good relations with the Indians, and by the Treaty of Fort McIntosh (1785) those squatters who settled beyond the boundary agreed upon in the treaty were outlawed and made subject to Indian vengeance by its terms.

The commissioners who arranged the treaty also authorized the dispossession of these intruders on the American side of the line. Ensign John Armstrong, under orders from Colonel Josiah Harmar, undertook the task and, with considerable difficulty, cleared the squatters from the north bank of the Ohio between Pittsburgh and Wheeling. He reported that six hundred families were settled on the Hocking and Muskingum Rivers, and that fifteen hundred persons were living on the Scioto and the Miami. He referred to them as "banditti whose actions are a disgrace to human nature." Yet, shortly before his arrival, one of their leaders, John Amberson (or Emerson), was calling an election for members of a constitutional convention, which was to meet at the mouth of the Scioto on April 20. The public notice of the election spoke of people having "an undoubted right to pass into every vacant country, and there to form their constitution," and asserted that Congress could not forbid them or sell the uninhabited lands. This was the homely political philosophy of frontiersmen, and belies their designation as "banditti."

Some of the dispossessed petitioned Congress, in their distress at being evicted, for permission to retain their lands and to receive the preference later when the region should be opened to settlement. But Congress, in a proclamation issued June 15, warned all intruders to depart, while Colonel Harmar erected Fort Harmar at the mouth of the Muskingum primarily to guard against "squatting."

Yet such measures could no more succeed in the long run than could the British Proclamation Line of 1763. By no means all of the intruders were evicted, but of those who were, many were soon back on their old locations. There was no place for them in Kentucky, where overlapping claims and a confusion over titles were driving immigrants elsewhere. North of the Ohio there was a chance at least that preëmption or squatters' rights might be made good. Had not organized settlement begun when it did, Ohio would soon have been flooded with land-hungry frontiersmen, regardless of the efforts of Congress toward a systematic survey and sale of land. As it was, many of these early intruders became permanent settlers, later securing titles from land companies or individual owners, or making other arrangements to secure lands. Others, the driftwood of the frontier, were swept on westward by the flood of population to repeat the pioneering process again and again. Land titles meant little to them.

While the history of these first settlers is veiled in obscurity, the Ohio Company appeared in 1787 to begin the work of organized colonization. Its history goes back to the efforts of a group of Revolutionary War officers, headed by Brigadier General Rufus Putnam, of Massachusetts, to secure bounty lands from Congress in the section comprising the present state of Ohio in order to establish a new state. Their petition, presented to Congress in 1783, also contained the idea of a purchase of land for public securities by "such of the Army as wish to become adventurers in the new Government." Congress took no action, as too many other matters had to be dealt with first. Putnam did not lose interest in the matter, however, and in 1785 he was appointed one of the surveyors of the Seven Ranges under Geographer Hutchins. Presently he resigned to accept a similar position in Massachusetts to survey her Maine lands, and his close friend, Brigadier General Benjamin Tupper, took his place. As a result of information acquired by Tupper in the West, plans were formulated to organize a company, and "a Piece styled Information" appeared in several Massachusetts newspapers in January, 1786. This newspaper notice called upon all persons interested to meet at a number of different towns to elect delegates to a meeting at the Bunch of Grapes Tavern in Boston on March 1.

Eleven men met on that date—five of them signers of the petition of 1783—and the organization of the Ohio Company was begun. The total capital was not to exceed one million dollars in Continental certificates, to be subscribed in shares of one thousand dollars each, and to be used to purchase land in the Northwest. A year passed before any further action was taken, and then, on March

8, 1787, a meeting was held and two hundred and fifty
shares were found to have been subscribed. General
Samuel H. Parsons was sent to New York to present a
memorial to Congress. That body lacked a quorum and
did not act on the matter, but meanwhile the leaders in
the company became dissatisfied with Parsons's work, as he
seemed to favor a location west of the Scioto, instead of
next to the Seven Ranges, as was preferred by the company.
Consequently, Reverend Manasseh Cutler was sent in his
place to oresent the matter to Congress.

Dr. Cutler was "the more-or-less dissatisfied pastor" of
the Congregational Church at Ipswich, Massachusetts,
who, with a small salary and a large family, saw in the
Ohio Company an opportunity to improve his fortunes.
A graduate of Yale, he had taught school, studied law,
entered the ministry, served as army chaplain, and delved
in the natural sciences and medicine and was a member of
the leading honorary societies of his day. His versatility,
wide acquaintance, and skill at meeting all manner of men
made him a veritable Franklin, to use Professor Hulbert's
comparison.

The wheels began to turn rapidly soon after Dr. Cutler's
arrival in New York. The Ordinance of 1787 was taken
up by Congress and within eight days passed in a form
satisfactory to him. With regard to the purchase of lands,
he found certain difficulties in the way and allied with a
group of New York speculators, headed by William Duer,
Secretary of the Treasury Board (the financial department
of the Government), to make a joint purchase far larger
than that which the Ohio Company could make alone.
By the most skilful kind of wirepulling, including the
company's support of General Arthur St. Clair, president
of Congress, for the governorship of the Northwest Territory, the deal was finally arranged with Congress.

The contract called for two purchases, one for the Ohio Company and the other for Duer and his associates, the "Scioto Company"; but both purchases were made in the names of Cutler and Winthrop Sargent, the latter being the secretary of the Ohio Company. The first purchase included a tract of land bounded by the Seventh Range on the east, the Ohio River on the south, and the western limit of the Seventeenth Range on the west and extending as far north as was necessary to give the company one and one-half million acres, in addition to reservations of one section in each township for schools, another section for religion, three sections for later disposal by Congress, and two whole townships for a university. The company was to pay five hundred thousand dollars down and the same amount when the survey was completed, but since payment could be made in depreciated Government securities worth perhaps twelve cents on the dollar, the price was actually much lower than indicated. As finally surveyed, the tract with its reservations included 1,781,760 acres.

The Scioto purchase lay to the north and west of the Ohio Company's purchase and contained 4,901,480 acres, an enormous tract of great value, which was to be paid for in four semiannual installments at the price of $66\frac{2}{3}$ cents an acre. The first installment was to be due six months after the boundary of the tract was surveyed by the Government surveyors. The contract for this purchase was really an option to buy, instead of an outright purchase, and proved to be purely a scheme of some shrewd speculators to make large profits with little investment. Nevertheless, their influence helped the Ohio Company to secure its contract, and Duer even advanced funds to Cutler to help it meet its first payment. Congress was desirous of selling a far larger amount than the New England associates could finance, in order to reduce the public debt and to strengthen the Government, and it was well that the Ipswich minister fell in with these wolves of the "Wall Street" of his day. Otherwise Congress might have listened to one of the several other schemes then being urged upon it.

The Ohio Company later encountered financial difficulties due to the Indian war and could not pay its second installment. It had already paid for and received 750,000 acres; so Congress in 1792 added 214,285 acres, to be paid for with Army warrants, and 100,000 acres, to be granted free to actual settlers within five years in one-hundred-acre tracts.

In the winter of 1787–1788, two advance parties set out from Massachusetts and Connecticut for the Ohio Company's purchase, joining forces at Sumrill's Ferry, Pennsylvania, where they built boats to carry them down the rivers that led to the Ohio. On April 1 they began their journey, and on April 7 they arrived at Fort Harmar, at the mouth of the Muskingum. Here, on the east bank, under the supervision of the father of the Ohio Company, Rufus Putnam, was founded the town they called at first Adelphia but soon changed to Marietta. The final name was chosen in honor of Queen Marie Antoinette of France, whose kind treatment of Benjamin Franklin in the Revolutionary years endeared her to the war veterans who were establishing this settlement.

The early settlers of Marietta and its vicinity were of a different sort from the rough backwoodsmen who had done so much to push the frontier westward. Some of them had attended Harvard or Yale; the leaders had been officers in the Revolution, and, consequently, members of the fraternal order of the Cincinnati; and a number belonged to the American Union Lodge of Free Masons, which was trans-

ferred to Marietta and which remains, after many vicissitudes, the oldest in the state. Respect for law and order
and the religious and educational ideals of New England
predominated in the new community. When the dignified
and polished Scotch soldier, Arthur St. Clair, arrived on
July 9 with his credentials as Governor of the Northwest
Territory, he found himself in a congenial atmosphere.
The formal welcome he received fitly typified the character
of the new colony. Under such happy auspices was
organized settlement in the future Buckeye State begun.

Selected Bibliography

Most of the general works cited in the preceding chapter on
the Revolution extend through the Confederation period.
Hinsdale's *The Old Northwest* is especially useful for this period,
as it emphasizes the questions of land claims, state cessions, and
the ordinances of Congress. The Ordinances of 1784 and 1787
are discussed in Jay A. Barrett, *Evolution of the Ordinance of
1787* (New York, 1891). A pamphlet by W. F. Poole, *The
Ordinance of 1787, A Reply* (Ann Arbor, 1892), briefly covers
the controversy over the authorship of that document. C. B.
Galbreath, "The Ordinance of 1787, Its Origin and Authorship,"
Ohio Archæological and Historical Quarterly, Vol. XXXIII, pp.
111–175, reviews the problem and reaches conclusions favorable
to Nathan Dane. The Ordinance itself may be consulted in
Barrett, *op. cit.*, pp. 81–89, *Ohio Archæological and Historical
Quarterly*, Vol. V, pp. 50–57, and *Old South Leaflets*, General
Series, No. 13.

The Records of the Ohio Company (A. B. Hulbert, ed., *Marietta
College Historical Collections*, Vols. I and II, Marietta, 1917),
not only contain the proceedings of the company, but include an
excellent introduction by the editor (pp. xv–cxxxvii), which is
the best history of the company. Volume III of this series,
Ohio in the Time of the Confederation (Marietta, 1918), is a
valuable collection of documents relating to government, land
surveys, and colonizing projects in this period. *The Life,
Journals and Correspondence of Rev. Manasseh Cutler* (W. P.

and J. P. Cutler, eds., 2 vols., Cincinnati, 1888), reveals Cutler's part.in the history of the Ohio Company. A brief sketch of Putnam is found in Mary Cone, *Life of Rufus Putnam* (Cleveland, 1886). More useful are the letters of General Parsons in Charles S. Hall, *Life and Letters of General Samuel Holden Parsons* (Binghamton, N. Y., 1905). An excellent account of the original surveys in Ohio, with maps, is found in C. E. Sherman, *Original Land Subdivisions (Ohio Coöperative Topographic Survey, Final Report*, Vol. III, 1925). (The treaties of Fort McIntosh and Greenville and the laws affecting land surveys are included in the volume. Particularly valuable is the large map by C. E. Sherman and W. D. Turnbull accompanying the volume.)

CHAPTER V

The Territorial Period

Early Settlements

*M*ARIETTA, settled in 1788, did not long remain the sole authorized American community in the old Northwest. In 1786 Benjamin Stites, a native of New Jersey, then residing in Pennsylvania, while engaged in a trading expedition down the Ohio, had explored the valleys of the Big and Little Miami Rivers. Thrilled with a realization of the fertility of the area, he had rushed eastward at once in the hope of negotiating for its exploitation. Success crowned his efforts to the extent that he stimulated the interest of John Cleves Symmes, a native of Long Island who had settled in New Jersey in 1770, who had fought in the Revolutionary War and had served for six years as a judge of the state supreme court, and who was then a Member of the Congress of the United States. As a result, Symmes in the spring of 1787 went down the Ohio as far as the falls of that river (Louisville) and possibly into the Wabash Valley. He considered plans for a colony on his own account in that area and even issued a circular addressed to the people of Kentucky inviting them to share in his intentions.

The remoteness of the Wabash Valley, however, caused him to change the site of his venture to the valleys of the Miamis. He enlisted the support of such men as Jonathan Dayton (who was to be a member of the United States Constitutional Convention and subsequently speaker of the House of Representatives), Elias Boudinot (for many years a Member of Congress), and John Witherspoon (a signer of the Declaration of Independence and president of the College of New Jersey, now Princeton), and appealed to Congress for a grant of two million acres. A tentative contract was arranged, but Symmes soon saw that the strip would be too large and endeavored to have it reduced to one-half the original size.

The Board of the Treasury replied that it could not make a single grant of all the land between the Little and Big Miamis, but that it was willing to sell him a million acres with a frontage of twenty miles extending eastward from the mouth of the Big Miami. This restriction was embodied in a contract signed by the agents of Symmes on October 15, 1788. Already, however, the latter, impelled by an excessive zeal, had initiated the granting of land along the Little Miami, whose mouth is fourteen miles east of the boundary mentioned in the contract of 1788. Hence, efforts were made by friends of Symmes to induce Congress to readjust this boundary. Such a law was passed in 1792, and as a result, the President issued in 1794 a patent for the amount of land that had been paid for, 248,500 acres (exclusive of reservations for certain purposes) extending from one Miami to the other.

Subsequently, however, Symmes again demanded the full one million acres for which he had contracted, and he proceeded to sell warrants for land that lay beyond the limits of his patent of 1794. Complications in regard to titles arose as a result, and although Congress allayed the difficulty by granting special concessions to settlers who had found themselves innocent victims of the controversy, Symmes failed to establish his own claims and died in extreme poverty some years later (in 1814).

The first actual settlement in this area, established on a grant received from Symmes (but to which at that time

Symmes had no legal title), was begun by Stites in November, 1788, a short distance below the mouth of the Little Miami. It was called Columbia.[1] Its importance, however, was soon overshadowed by another community, which had already been laid out and which was settled but a few weeks later.

The site of the latter town, opposite the mouth of the Licking River, had been purchased from Symmes in January, 1788, by Matthias Denman, a New Jersey land speculator, who interested in the project Robert Patterson, the founder of Lexington, Kentucky, and John Filson, a Kentucky teacher, pioneer, and chronicler. Filson is said to have suggested the name for the place—Losantiville (*L* for *Licking; os* for *mouth; anti* for *opposite; ville* for *city*). He participated in the laying out of the streets for the new community, although he did not live to see the town established, for he disappeared during an exploring trip in the Miami Valley in the fall of 1788 and was never heard of thereafter. His share of the proprietorship was assumed by Israel Ludlow, the only one of these entrepreneurs who is known to have located personally in the Miami Valley. As the old year blended into the new, the first houses were being erected, and during the following fall a protective stockade, Fort Washington, was occupied by troops from Fort Harmar. Governor St. Clair then moved to the village, designated it as the capital of the Northwest Territory, and rechristened it Cincinnati after the noted post-Revolutionary society.

Meanwhile (in January, 1789), Symmes himself had laid out the village of North Bend farther to the west where the Ohio River bends more to the north than at any point west of the mouth of the Great Kanawha. This place

---

[1] This village was annexed to Cincinnati in 1872.

was to be undistinguished except as the home of William Henry Harrison, whose wife was a daughter of Symmes.

A few years later Symmes sold the land for the founding of Dayton (1795) to Governor St. Clair; James Wilkinson, the wily military leader of the West; Jonathan Dayton; and Israel Ludlow. The recent Treaty of Greenville[2] gave hope that Indian troubles, which had brought failure to an earlier project (Venice) on the same site, would be avoided. Symmes, as it turned out, did not receive land in this vicinity from the Government; hence the founders of Dayton, like others in the Western country, had later to secure actual title from the Federal authorities.

A plan of settlement that was associated with much intrigue and disappointment was that of the Scioto Company, which had linked its fortunes with those of the Ohio Company in order to enlist sufficient support in Congress for the proposed grant to the latter group. Chief among the promoters of the Scioto organization was William Duer, a New York capitalist, the Secretary of the Board of the Treasury of the United States. An option had been secured on the land west of the Ohio Company's grant as far as the Scioto River, and it was planned to sell a part of this area to Europeans in exchange for United States securities, which were then deemed by persons abroad to be practically worthless. Joel Barlow, the poet of the Revolutionary period and author of the rather bombastic *Columbiad*, was chosen as the European representative, but achieved no success in his promotional ventures until he encountered William Playfair, an unscrupulous, worldly-wise Englishman. Their coöperation produced, as a scheme for facilitating sales, the *Compagnie du Scioto*, to which were transferred three million acres, to be

---

[2] See page 99.

paid for by 1794. A land office was opened, and plats and maps were exhibited, with a town Gallipolis, "city of the French," shown nearly opposite the mouth of the Great Kanawha. An alluring prospectus was issued, setting forth the attractions of the region—tobacco superior to that of Virginia, catfish up to eighty pounds in weight, and nature that provided the necessities of life. For good measure, it was added that the United States capital would probably be established there, and all was attested by the official United States Geographer.

The speculative fever spread rapidly in France, which was then on the eve of its great Revolution, for the people believed that America offered the realization of their ideal of "liberty, equality, and fraternity." The company actually could sell only preëmption rights, as Congress had not received compensation for the land and still held title to it. Nevertheless, purchasers received documents purporting to be deeds, and about one hundred and fifty thousand acres had been disposed of by 1790. Suspicions, however, soon became aroused, sales stopped, the scheme was denounced as a swindle, and the speculative bubble had burst.

The five or six hundred persons who had already embarked for America faced serious difficulties. Not only did Barlow have no funds with which Duer could pay Congress for the lands, but, by accurate survey, Gallipolis was found to be outside the Scioto Company's grant. The settlers (who had come to America *via* Alexandria, Virginia, and were assisted by agents of the company to reach the western side of the mountains) soon found that, being for the most part members of the professional and artisan classes, they were scarcely fitted for the rigors of pioneer life. Eighty cabins had been built for them by the Scioto Company at Gallipolis (within, as it proved, the Ohio Company's grant), and, although Congress ceded to them (in 1795) "the French Grant" of twenty-four thousand acres, extending eight miles along the Ohio River in what is now Scioto County, practically all of them preferred to remain at their first settlement, paying a second time for the land that they had occupied.

After the establishment of Marietta, Cincinnati, and Gallipolis, the fourth permanent center of settlement was made (in 1791) at Massie's Station, later called Manchester (after the home city of the Massie family in England), twelve miles above the present Maysville, Kentucky, in what is now Adams County. The restriction upon settlement in the Virginia Military District[3] having just been removed, this was the first town to be established in that region. The founder was Nathaniel Massie, a native of Virginia, who as a young man of twenty had settled in Kentucky and who had later become a surveyor of the Military District. After planting the colony at Manchester, he gradually became familiar with the Scioto Valley to the northeast and decided that the junction of Paint Creek with that river constituted an advantageous site for a city. Lots were offered gratis to the first one hundred settlers, but the group that set forth in 1795, which included many Kentuckians, was forced back by the Indians. In 1796, however, the first cabins were erected at Chillicothe, a community that developed with considerable rapidity and became a center of Virginia and Kentucky influence in the developing commonwealth.

Shortly afterwards another Virginia surveyor, Lucas Sullivant, saw the natural advantages of the area at the junction of the Scioto and Whetstone (Olentangy) Rivers, the site of a former village of the Mingo Indians. Accord-

---

[3] See page 72.

ingly, Franklinton, named for the great Revolutionary statesman, was established in August, 1797, and though it was of only slight importance for some years, the high

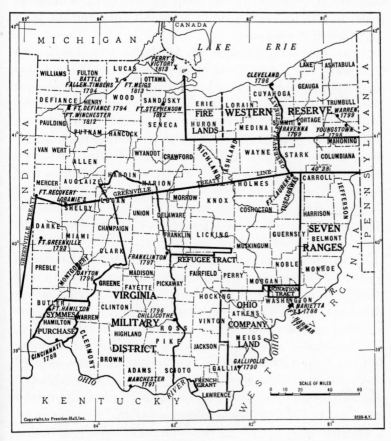

Land Divisions, Early Settlements, and Military Posts

bank of the Scioto to the eastward was made the state capital (in 1816), and developed into the present city of Columbus.

While southern and central Ohio were thus receiving their first accessions of settlers, northern Ohio was not without its attractions. Connecticut, as has been shown, in making her cession of Western lands to the Federal Government in 1786, had reserved a strip south of Lake Erie, north of the forty-first parallel, and extending one hundred and twenty miles westward from the Pennsylvania line. In 1792 Connecticut granted half a million acres at the westward end of this "Connecticut Reserve" or "Western Reserve" to those inhabitants of certain Connecticut towns whose property had been destroyed by Tory raids during the Revolution. Eighteen hundred and seventy persons thus received lands in what is now Huron and Erie Counties, an area appropriately called "The Firelands," where the present-day names of such communities as Norwalk and New London indicate the former Connecticut homes of many of the early inhabitants. In May, 1795, practically all of the rest of the Reserve was offered for sale, the proceeds to serve as a perpetual fund for the Connecticut common schools, and a few months later the land was sold without survey to thirty-five buyers for prices totalling one million two hundred thousand dollars.

The Connecticut Land Company, headed by Oliver Phelps, a prominent land speculator, was formed to assist the venture, and Moses Cleaveland, a Yale graduate and an attorney and director for the company, became general agent. With a party that included surveyors, the latter proceeded to the new territory in the spring and summer of 1796, after arrangements had been made with the Iroquois as to their title to all land east of the Cuyahoga River. Immediately Cleaveland (the name later shortened to Cleveland) was established at the mouth of the river (in 1796). This region rapidly increased in population from only fifteen families in 1798 to over thirteen hundred inhabitants in 1800, and remained for many decades a center of distinct New England influence. Settlers, however, came from other sections. Youngstown was founded in 1798; in the spring of 1799 Ephraim Quinby, of Washington County, Pennsylvania, began improvements that marked the beginnings of the city of Warren; and in the latter year, Ravenna was founded by Benjamin Tappan.

Indian Troubles

The beginnings of this westward movement of the white man had alarmed the Indian, and such treaties as had been made did not deter him from murder and plunder in a desperate effort to turn back the tide of settlement. At first there were only six hundred United States troops along the Ohio River to protect the whole Northwest.

In 1789 St. Clair attempted to improve conditions by a treaty at Fort Harmar (opposite Marietta on the Muskingum) that restated and confirmed the earlier agreements. The Shawnees, Miamis, and some others were not present, and St. Clair aimed to reënforce tribal jealousies by treating each group as an individual nation. Difficulties continued, however, the British utilizing the posts that they still held in the Northwest as centers of influence hostile to the Americans. Two raids by United States troops into the Indian country did not improve the situation, and in 1790 Congress authorized the President to call the militia of Virginia, Kentucky, and western Pennsylvania to assemble at Fort Washington (Cincinnati) to prepare for a more ambitious movement against the natives.

The army of between fourteen and fifteen hundred men in all, less than a fourth of whom were regulars, was intrusted to General Josiah Harmar, a native of Philadelphia and a veteran of the Revolution, who for a number of years had been engaged in Indian warfare and for whom the fort across the Muskingum from Marietta had been named. The militia was untrained, disorderly, and jealous of the regulars, and the commissary was poorly organized, but Harmar pushed northward for a distance of one hundred and seventy miles through the Miami Valleys and into the valley of the Maumee as far as the Miami villages at the site of what is now Fort Wayne, Indiana.

A number of Indian villages were burned and supplies of corn were destroyed, but one detachment of the army under Colonel John Hardin was routed by the savages, and later, when on the return march another group of four hundred men was sent back to retrieve the situation, they too were repulsed. The army returned to Cincinnati, and a court of inquiry in 1791 found that the commander had acted in honorable fashion. Harmar subsequently returned to Pennsylvania, where he died in 1813.

The Indians, now bristling with self-confidence, renewed their depredations to such an extent that, in response to the petitions of the frontiersmen, Washington ordered mounted columns to raid the Indian villages in the Wabash Valley to the westward. To establish more decisively American prestige in these areas, Arthur St. Clair was placed in charge of a new army of three thousand men, recruited in large part from the indigent and profligate of the eastern cities. St. Clair, who was a native of Scotland, had served in the British Army during the French and Indian War, subsequently settling in Pennsylvania and holding the rank of colonel in the American Army during the Revolution. Now, as first governor of the Northwest Territory and commander of the armed forces, he planned to build a chain of forts in the western part of what is now Ohio, at intervals of twenty-five miles, from the

Ohio River to Lake Erie. Though a soldier of ability, St. Clair found the odds against him. He was inexperienced in Indian warfare, almost too ill to mount his horse, and many of the troops were unruly and untrustworthy. Starting northward in September, 1791, he erected the first of the line of fortifications, which included Fort Hamilton and Fort Jefferson. On November 3, the army encamped on the banks of the east fork of the Wabash. By that time many had deserted, regulars had been detached from the main columns to prevent unruly militia from raiding the supplies, and the numbers had dwindled to fourteen hundred men. At dawn of the next day a surprise attack under the leadership of Little Turtle threw the army into disorder and then into panic. St. Clair's personal bravery—three mounts were shot from under him, and eight bullets pierced his clothing and one grazed his gray hair—could not avert disaster, and though a remnant of. the army cut through and escaped, almost half of it was annihilated, and huge baggage stores were lost. Washington was overcome with chagrin at the news of this overwhelming defeat, but a commission exonerated St. Clair from blame.

St. Clair's military position now (in April, 1792) fell to Anthony Wayne, who had won a major-generalship for his gallant services in the Revolution, and who had later campaigned against the Creek Indians in Georgia. Delayed for a time by the possibility of negotiations with the Indians, Wayne at length collected twenty-five hundred men near Pittsburgh and proceeded in the spring of 1793 to Cincinnati. After months of careful drilling in frontier methods and in the organization of scouts and spies, the advance northward was begun in October. Eighty miles from Cincinnati the winter was spent in further drill at the newly erected Fort Greenville, while on the site of

St. Clair's defeat a stockade was constructed, significantly designated as Fort Recovery (in December, 1793).

The British assumed a threatening attitude. Fort Miami had been rebuilt below the rapids of the Maumee (in April, 1794), near the outskirts of the present Toledo, and late in June an unsuccessful attack was made by the Indians upon Fort Recovery. A month later, however, Wayne's forces, joined by an army of Kentucky volunteers under Major-General Scott, began their march northward into the valley of the Auglaize. At the junction of this river with the Maumee near the reputed birthplace of the great Pontiac, Wayne erected his strongest fort, which was named Defiance.

Overtures of peace having been proposed by Wayne but not accepted by the enemy, he advanced down the Maumee Valley, and the two armies met on August 20, 1794, at Fallen Timbers (above the present Toledo), so-called because here were found rows of dead trees felled by a hurricane some two years before. The enemy army consisted of somewhat under two thousand warriors, probably commanded by Blue Jacket, as Little Turtle—the ranking chief—had disagreed with the proposed arrangements. The battle had been carefully planned, and the Americans charged in open order in two lines with horsemen on the flanks. In less than an hour the Indian army was in flight, and, as Roosevelt says, the Americans had won the greatest battle of forty years of warfare with the redskins.

For three days the Americans continued the work of devastation, after which they retired up the Maumee and eventually reached the juncture of the St. Joseph and St. Mary's Rivers (the scene of Harmar's defeat), where a fort was erected by Colonel Hamtramck and named in honor of the victor of the recent campaign.

Wayne himself was back at Greenville in November. The following June a council of over eleven hundred prominent tribesmen was held, and in August the Treaty of Greenville was signed by over ninety representatives of the Indians. This agreement, ratified by the United States Senate in December, provided for the cessation of hostilities and for a mutual restoration of prisoners with a gift of $20,000 in goods to the Indians to be followed by an annual appropriation of goods worth $9,500. A boundary was also established, running from Lake Erie *via* the Cuyahoga and the Tuscarawas Rivers to a point above Fort Laurens, thence westward *via* a point near Loramie's Station to Fort Recovery, and southwestward to the Ohio opposite the mouth of the Kentucky. All the region to the east and south of this line was surrendered to the whites, who were also allowed some posts and reserves in the Indian country. Partly because of Wayne's frank and fair method of treatment, the Indians remained true to their agreement. Indian warfare was now forever at a close in Ohio, and in the Northwest peace reigned until Tecumseh took the warpath again sixteen years later.

The terms of Jay's Treaty, with England (in 1794), also contributed to the solution of the problems of the Northwest, as the posts in that region, supposedly American since the Treaty of Paris (1783), were surrendered, and the area between the Ohio and the Lakes westward to the Mississippi for the first time was solely under the jurisdiction of the United States.

Early Government in the Northwest

The Ordinance of 1787, as has been noted, provided for a first stage of government in which the authority would rest in a governor, a secretary, and three judges appointed by the governor. The governor was intrusted with the executive power, the three judges with the judicial power, and the governor and the judges, acting as a legislative council, with power in matters of a legislative nature. The ordinance also provided for the creation of tribunals inferior to that constituted by the three judges, and for the appointment of subordinate officers. Before this formal institution of control could be achieved, temporary civil governments were established at Marietta, Columbia, and Cincinnati.

With the inauguration of the more permanent arrangements of government, Arthur St. Clair became the governor, Winthrop Sargent, the secretary, and James M. Varnum, Samuel H. Parsons, and John C. Symmes[4] the judges of the Territory. St. Clair was absent for a considerable time during the early part of the territorial period; hence his prerogatives fell, when the occasion arose, to Sargent, a native of New England who had been an able officer in the American Revolution. The latter was, however, almost stupidly tactless as an executive and met considerable opposition from two of the three judges who shared authority with him, and also from the general populace, who resented his autocratic attempts to suppress what he considered "licentiousness," such as the sale of liquor to soldiers and the firing of guns at night.

The expenses of the Territorial government were met largely by special fees and by appropriations of the Federal Government, but local expenses were met by taxes assessed upon individuals according to their wealth and ability to pay. In 1795 the Governor and judges proceeded to revise the Territorial laws and to establish a complete legal system by the adoption of statutes of the original states, principally Pennsylvania. A comprehensive statute

---

[4] John Armstrong had been appointed a judge but declined to serve.

providing for county taxes was passed, and three years later (in 1798) a Territorial tax on land was levied for the first time, land being divided into three classes, according to quality, for purposes of assessment.

Settlements had been made very cautiously previous to the Treaty of Greenville; but with the passing of the earlier, practically imperative necessity of blockhouse protection, the new communities developed with amazing rapidity.

In 1795 a concerted opinion developed around Cincinnati advocating an advance to the second stage of government, but St. Clair and Sargent lent no aid to the movement. In November, 1797, agitation again arose and meetings were held with a view to achieving statehood; and although this goal was not at once attained, St. Clair undertook to determine by a census whether the five thousand adult males necessary to a progression to the second, or representative, stage of organization were within the Northwest Territory. The number proved to be in excess of the required minimum, and in December, 1798, St. Clair issued a proclamation for the election of the lower house of twenty-two members (from the whole Northwest Territory), fifteen to come from the five counties of the later state of Ohio and seven from the four counties comprising the old French settlements of the present Michigan, Indiana, and Illinois.

The judges henceforth were to be limited to purely judicial functions, while the governor was to retain his appointive power and his general executive authority and to possess an absolute veto upon all legislative acts. The lower house of the legislature met in preliminary session at Cincinnati in February, 1799, to nominate ten persons, from whom President Adams chose five for the Council, and reassembled in September to turn its attention to the business of law-making. Acts were passed dealing with the organization of the militia and with judicial procedure, with the sale of liquor to Indians, and with the establishment of a system of taxation.

Territorial expenses were to be met by assessments on land, divided into three classes; local revenues were to be secured from taxes on houses, lots, horses, cattle, bond servants, bachelors, ferries, and retailers. In practice, the revenue for Territorial purposes was raised with difficulty, and often a considerable problem arose in relation to the balancing of accounts; but this was achieved, and when Ohio entered the Union, Territorial finances were in a fairly satisfactory condition.

The first Territorial legislature received a petition from Virginians to permit them to bring their slaves into the Virginia Military District, but such a plea was unanimously rejected. The Territory was entitled to a delegate in Congress, and for this position William Henry Harrison, Secretary of the Territory, was chosen over the Governor's son, Arthur St. Clair, Jr.

A year later (in 1800) Harrison, in conjunction with Albert Gallatin, sponsored a new Federal land law that reduced the minimum acreage that could be purchased from six hundred and forty to three hundred and twenty acres, extended four years' credit, and established land offices at Cincinnati, Marietta, Chillicothe, and Steubenville. With these more liberal opportunities, a further incentive was given to many to move to the new territory, and soon a movement was in full sway for the formation of the state of Ohio.

The Movement for Statehood

Governor St. Clair, as has been indicated, had been a strenuous opponent of any statehood movement. Well realizing that the Ordinance of 1787 required sixty thousand people in a given area before it could be organized into a state, he employed the strategy of seeking divisions of the Northwest Territory in such a manner as to prevent any one of them from soon attaining the requisite number. As early as January, 1790, he had written to James Ross, of Pittsburgh, proposing one future territory centering in the Muskingum Valley, another comprising the Miami Valley area, and a third extending eastward and westward from the Wabash River. Other possible divisions were proposed from time to time, but the opponents of statehood always sought to arrange these in such a way as to accomplish the purpose of their own group.

St. Clair was interested in securing the division of the Territory also because the large area from the western boundary of Pennsylvania to the Mississippi made it extremely difficult to hold court with proper frequency in the more remote counties. St. Clair himself had the gout and hence was personally averse to extended journeys. The difficulty was partially remedied in 1795 by the repeal of the statute of limitations (which had outlawed cases not presented within a certain period), thus removing a reason for the anxiety as to the frequency of the court sessions, and by the modification of the ordinance so as to give a single judge the power to hold court.

After the advance of the Territory to the second stage, as a result of the census of 1798, the inhabitants of the western counties felt keenly the burden of sending delegates to the new Territorial legislature. Indeed, the distance to Cincinnati was so considerable as to cause the inhabitants of Vincennes to petition Congress to return the Territory to the first stage. Not being able to obtain this action, these persons became interested in suggested divisions of the Territory.

Accordingly, St. Clair returned to his previous suggestion of 1790, a plan that by dividing the Republican Scioto Valley would strengthen the conservative forces and postpone statehood. Marietta would probably be the seat of government of one district, Cincinnati that of another, and Vincennes that of the third. The importance of Chillicothe would be materially reduced by the realization of this proposal, hence certain leaders of that place urged a rival plan upon William Henry Harrison, Territorial Delegate to Congress. The result was a Federal act (of May 7, 1800) embracing the proposals presented by Harrison and providing for two separate governments divided by a line drawn from the mouth of the Kentucky to Fort Recovery, thence directly northward to the international boundary. The territory to the west of this line was designated as Indiana Territory, with its seat of government at Vincennes, and that to the east retained its existing name and the established political machinery. Vincennes and Chillicothe were to remain the seats of government until other provision might be made by the respective legislatures.

In the meantime, antagonism had been rapidly developing between St. Clair and the legislature of the Territory— particularly because, when the first session of the latter adjourned in December, 1799, St. Clair had vetoed eleven bills, six of them providing for the creation of new counties. The Governor claimed for himself the power to create such new subdivisions and to establish local seats of justice; but this opinion directly conflicted with the desires of certain influential persons to make their own communities the seats of county government. Another basis for antagonism was St. Clair's deep-seated opposition to statehood, based upon the conviction that Ohio was too far distant from the central government, that it would constitute another Republican state dangerous to Federalist supremacy in national affairs, and that the people were too ignorant and too ill-qualified for more active participation in governmental policies. Such a viewpoint intensified the hostility of a people imbued with the unequivocal democracy of the frontier.

The rapid increase in the population of the Territory and the general success of the Jeffersonians in the elections of 1800 were factors favorable to the Republicans, who now commenced a correspondence with their party friends at the National Capital. Thomas Worthington, a native of Virginia, who as a young man of twenty-five years had come to the Scioto Valley in 1798 and who was a prominent member of the Territorial legislature, was instrumental in pressing the plans of the Ohio Republicans for statehood, and attempted to secure newspaper support for their proposals.

Thus, the issues were clearly drawn. The St. Clair faction, with its stronghold at Cincinnati and forming a coalition with the political leaders of Marietta, urged the continuance of St. Clair as governor, the restoration of the seat of government to Cincinnati, and the alteration of the Division Act of 1800 along the lines suggested by St. Clair. In this way Cincinnati and Marietta would become permanent centers of government. A secondary feature of the strategy of this group was to placate the disfranchised inhabitants of the back-country districts of Hamilton County by securing for them congressional relief as to land titles. Another aspect of the St. Clair proposals was a demand to be made upon John Cleves Symmes that he should cede, in accordance with his contract with the United States, one of the most desirable townships in his purchase for a university. This last proposition gives a reason for William Henry Harrison's opposition to the

Cincinnati plan, since he, although a resident of the Cincinnati neighborhood, as the son-in-law of Symmes considered the interests of his wife's father.

A considerable degree of success for a time attended the efforts of the Cincinnati group. As Territorial Delegate to succeed William H. Harrison, who had been appointed Governor of Indiana Territory, William McMillan, of Cincinnati, was elected by the legislature for the unexpired term, and Paul Fearing, of Marietta, was elected for a new term. President Adams, who had decided to appoint Senator Tracy, of Connecticut, governor, was persuaded to give the office again to St. Clair (for three years, beginning February, 1801). The Territorial legislature was induced to pass a bill providing, with the consent of Congress, for the change of the boundaries of the proposed states so as to locate one east of a line drawn northward from the Scioto River, and another bill for the return of the capital to Cincinnati.

The Scioto Valley Republicans had, on the other hand, definite plans of their own—the removal of St. Clair, the prevention of congressional assent to the re-division bill, and, if possible, the granting of immediate statehood. Against the re-division, an emphatic protest was registered in the legislature, and Thomas Worthington and Michael Baldwin, the latter a native of Connecticut and a promising lawyer of Chillicothe, who later fell a prey to dissipation, were sent to Washington to represent the interests of the Scioto group. Many persons who had resented the autocratic attitude of St. Clair, because of his opposition to an extension of the franchise, signed petitions that were systematically forwarded to Washington in opposition to the acceptance of the re-division. William B. Giles, a noted Virginia Congressman, took up the cause in the House of Representatives, and Congress rejected the proposal of the Territorial legislature by a vote of eighty-one to five. Charges were drawn up against St. Clair accusing him of a usurpation of legislative powers, a misuse of the veto, an exaction of arbitrary fees, an attempt to dismember the Territory, a neglect of the militia, and other abuses of his authority, but President Jefferson refused to sanction his removal.

The President, however, agreed with Congress as to the advisability of the creation of the new state, and an Enabling Act received the executive approval on April 30, 1802. This act provided that a constitutional convention should be elected in October, to meet on the first Monday in November to decide whether it would be expedient to frame a constitution. If the members of the convention decided in the affirmative, they were to proceed to that task or were to call another convention for the purpose. The western boundary of the state was to be the meridian from the mouth of the Great Miami to a line drawn eastward through the southern bend of Lake Michigan.

Some persons, including Paul Fearing, the Territorial Delegate, found objections to the Enabling Act; but the bonfires that burned before many a cabin in the Territory upon receipt of the news of the passage of the act gave evidence of the essential popularity of the measure. Even St. Clair came to recognize the futility of further opposition to statehood, and his friends at Cincinnati allowed it to be known that, if the re-division of the Territory were accomplished, they would urge Congress to admit each division to the Union separately as soon as it had a population of thirty-three thousand, which was then the basis of representation in the Federal House of Representatives.

The Democratic Republicans, however, under the astute leadership of Worthington, were aggressive and resourceful in the field of political organization. The desire of the

Republicans at the National Capital for additional representation in Congress and the ambitions of local personages for mail contracts or for positions under the Federal Government or the state government were carefully stimulated in the interests of the plans of the Chillicothe leaders. Local politicians, thus incited to action, were instrumental in the propagation of Republican organizations, one that served as the model for others in southwestern Ohio being established even at the enemy's citadel, Cincinnati.

The backwoodsmen could vote, since one year's residence and the payment of taxes were the only requisites to the franchise, and their importance at the polls was multiplied by the law of 1800, which provided for voting by districts within the county rather than by the casting of ballots at the county seats, as was required by the old law of 1799. These circumstances helped to insure a victory for the Jeffersonians. In Chillicothe, in particular, keen interest developed in relation to the choice of delegates, and Duncan McArthur, later to be governor of the state, wrote that the place was "glutted with handbills and long tavern harangues."

Thirty-five delegates were chosen to this first Ohio constitutional convention: two from the Western Reserve, twenty-six from the Ohio River counties, and seven from the interior area. Thomas Worthington in his diary analyzed the political division of the members by classifying twenty-six as Republicans, seven as Federalists, and two as of doubtful status. The convention met and organized on the first day of November, 1802, the presiding officer being Edward Tiffin, a native of England and a graduate in medicine of the University of Pennsylvania who had come to Chillicothe from Virginia in 1798 and had served as speaker of the Territorial house of representatives. Such delegates as were unfavorable to immediate statehood saw the uselessness of opposition. Ephraim Cutler (a son of Manasseh Cutler, the able representative of the Ohio Company) was the exception, as he steadfastly voted his dissent as a matter of principle.

During the sessions of the convention, Arthur St. Clair expressed a desire to address the members. Permission was granted by a narrow vote of the delegates, with the provision that he should speak in an unofficial capacity. The remarks made by St. Clair before the convention naturally were differently received by Republican and Federalist partisans. By Jefferson his speech was considered intemperate and indecorous; by Jacob Burnet, a graduate of Princeton who had come to Cincinnati in 1796 and had been a member of the Territorial council, as "sensible and conciliatory." In his discourse St. Clair declared that the Enabling Act was "in truth a nullity," since "for all internal affairs" the Territory was "no more bound by an act of Congress than . . . by an edict of the first consul of France," and that opposition ought to be registered against legislation by which over five thousand persons were "divested of the rights they were in possession of without a hearing—bartered away like sheep in a market—transferred to another government." The speech was reported to Jefferson, and as a result Secretary of State Madison sent a letter to St. Clair notifying him of his removal from the governorship. The letter was delivered to the Governor by Charles Willing Byrd, the Secretary of the Territory, who had received with this communication the news of his own promotion to be acting governor. Thus, there passed from official life the former president of Congress, who had been for fourteen years the Governor of the Northwest Territory. St. Clair, a broken and impoverished old man, retired to Pennsylvania, where he died in the summer of 1818.

The convention completed its task before the end of November, after only twenty-five days of work, and the constitution was signed by every one of the members. Thomas Worthington was designated to carry the document with the convention's message to Congress in Washington.

The Governor, popularly chosen for a two-year term, was seriously restricted in his powers, owing in part to the recent difficulties with St. Clair, in part to the general distrust of executives during the post-colonial period, and in part to the democratic tendencies of the Jeffersonians. He was to be head of the militia; he could grant pardons and reprieves, fill vacancies during the recess of the legislature, and call the legislature into special session; but he was denied the veto power. In short, the governorship became a position of honor rather than of power.

At the head of the judicial system was a supreme court of three judges—the number later increased to four[5]—who were chosen by the legislature and were required to hold court annually in each county. Common pleas courts were also provided for in each county, where two (or three) associate judges were to hold court with a president judge, who was assigned to a circuit, there being three circuits in the state. In addition, justice courts and other inferior jurisdictions were to be created at the discretion of the legislature.

True to Jeffersonian standards, the legislature became the dominant branch of Ohio's government. Judges, who held seven-year terms, and all state officials except the governor were chosen by it. The legislature itself was bicameral, the lower house always to be composed of not less than twenty-four members nor more than seventy-two, and the upper house never to consist of less than one-

---

[5] From 1808 until the second Ohio constitution went into effect in 1852, there were four judges, except from 1810 to 1816.

third or more than one-half the number in the lower body.

Local officials such as justices of the peace, sheriffs, and coroners were chosen by popular election, which permitted the participation of virtually all whites of male sex over twenty-one years of age, for, although the suffrage was limited to those who paid a state or county tax, work upon the roads was considered a fulfilment of that requirement. The proposal for enfranchising the Negro within the state received, in the convention, a tie vote (17:17), which was broken in favor of the negative by the chairman, Edward Tiffin, who stated the close proximity of Kentucky and Virginia as the reason for his disapproval.

The constitution included the customary bill of rights with provisions for freedom of speech, of religion, and of assembly; humane treatment of prisoners; speedy and impartial trials; and prohibitions upon disproportionate punishments, upon poll taxes, and upon hereditary privileges. A convention for amending the constitution might be called by a two-thirds vote of both houses of the legislature, after such a call had received the approval of a majority of the voters.

As was often the custom at that period, the constitution was not referred to the people for ratification, but a call was issued for electing members to the legislature, to convene on the first Tuesday in March, 1803, the writs to be issued by the president of the convention rather than by the governor of the Territory. Such procedure called forth little criticism at the time, and we may well infer that political inertia and ignorance are not an exclusive possession of recent decades from the attitude of one Ohioan of that day, whose only comment was that the people of his neighborhood did not like the constitution "at all because it had no pictures in it."

SELECTED BIBLIOGRAPHY

This period is covered in Randall and Ryan, Vol. II, pp. 505–600 and Vol. III, pp. 35–141; in Galbreath, Vol. I, pp. 193–261; in King, pp. 229–269; in Chaddock, "Ohio before 1850, a Study of the Early Influence of Pennsylvania and Southern Populations in Ohio," *Columbia University Studies in History, Economics, and Public Law*, Vol. XXXI, pp. 47–62; and in Hinsdale, pp. 285–315 (rev. ed.).

For accounts of the beginnings of Cincinnati and the Miami Valley, see Charles T. Greve, *Centennial History of Cincinnati and Representative Citizens* (2 vols., Chicago, 1904); and Charles F. Goss, *Cincinnati, the Queen City* (4 vols., Chicago, 1912). Jacob Burnet, *Notes on the Early Settlement of the Northwest Territory* (Cincinnati, 1847), is a valuable contribution by a Cincinnati pioneer who became a United States Senator. Important also is Beverley W. Bond, Jr., *The Correspondence of John Cleves Symmes, Founder of the Miami Purchase* (New York, 1926). The planting of Gallipolis is discussed by John L. Vance in "The French Settlement and Settlers of Gallipolis," *Ohio Archæological and Historical Quarterly*, Vol. III, pp. 45–81, and by Theodore T. Belote in *The Scioto Speculation and the French Settlement at Gallipolis* (Cincinnati, 1907). The life story of the founder of Chillicothe is told by his grandson, David M. Massie, in *Nathaniel Massie, a Pioneer of Ohio* (Cincinnati, 1896). The early history of the Western Reserve is narrated in Alfred Mathews, *Ohio and her Western Reserve* (New York, 1902). Clarence D. Laylin, "The Firelands Grant," is in the *Ohio Archæological and Historical Quarterly*, Vol. X, pp. 435–450. Of importance for the land surveys is W. E. Peters, *Ohio Lands and Their Subdivision* (Athens, Ohio, 1918).

The best work on St. Clair is *The St. Clair Papers: the Life and Public Services of Arthur St. Clair, with his Correspondence and other Papers*, arranged and annotated by W. H. Smith (2 vols., Cincinnati, 1882). *St. Clair's own Narrative of the Campaign against the Indians, 1791* was published in Philadelphia in 1812 and has since been reprinted. "Winthrop Sargent's Diary while with General Arthur St. Clair's expedition against the Indians" is in the *Ohio Archæological and Historical Quarterly*, Vol. XXXIII, pp. 237–282. Events related to the Treaty of

Greenville are treated in Frazer E. Wilson, *The Peace of Mad Anthony* (Greenville, 1909). A popular but reliable biography of Wayne is Thomas Boyd, *Mad Anthony Wayne* (New York, 1929). Biographical sketches of Winthrop Sargent, Secretary of the Northwest Territory, are in the *Ohio Archæological and Historical Quarterly*, Vol. XXXV, pp. 583–601 (by B. H. Pershing), and Vol. XXXIII, pp. 229–236 (by C. S. Sargent).

Two articles of merit by Randolph C. Downes are "Trade in Frontier Ohio," *Mississippi Valley Historical Review*, Vol. XVI, pp. 467–494, and "The Statehood Contest in Ohio," *Ibid.*, Vol. XVIII, pp. 155–171. By the same author is "Thomas Jefferson and the Removal of Governor St. Clair in 1802," *Ohio Archæological and Historical Quarterly*, Vol. XXXVI, pp. 62–77. "The Struggle for Statehood" by Ruhl J. Bartlett is in *Ibid.*, Vol. XXXII, pp. 472–503.

The first constitution of Ohio is in *The Constitutions of Ohio* (Isaac F. Patterson, ed., Cleveland, 1912), pp. 73–97; Daniel J. Ryan, "From Charter to Constitution," *Ohio Archæological and Historical Quarterly*, Vol. V. The development of the judicial system of Ohio, both before and after statehood, is carefully analyzed by Francis R. Aumann in "The Development of the Judicial System of Ohio," *Ohio Archæological and Historical Quarterly*, Vol. XLI, pp. 195–236.

CHAPTER VI

State and National Politics under the Republicans

The Early Years of Statehood

AMONG the utterances of Thomas Jefferson in his inaugural address of March 4, 1801, were the now familiar words of conciliation: "We are all Republicans; we are all Federalists." When Ohio entered the Union in 1803 as the "first fruits of the ordinance of 1787," the initial clause of this quotation rather literally served to explain the then existing political situation in the new commonwealth. The triumph of the movement for statehood had meant a very general eclipse politically of the Federalists in the state, who showed themselves to be surprisingly weak even in readily recognizable centers of New England migration such as the Western Reserve. In fact, an impotence characterized their forces in the state to the extent that in the initial contest for the governorship they generally refrained from voting or cast blank ballots in opposition to the Democratic-Republican candidate, Edward Tiffin; and the latter, who just previous to his first election had served as president of the constitutional convention, was easily returned two years later for a second administration (in 1805). Moreover, in the first Presidential election in which Ohio participated (the election of 1804), in the entire state only three hundred and sixty-four votes were cast for C. C. Pinckney, the Federalist candidate.

Yet, the supremacy of Jeffersonianism in the state can be exaggerated, for, in the contest for the single seat in the National House of Representatives to be filled by an Ohioan in 1803, the leading Federalist candidate, William McMillan of Hamilton County, polled about half as many votes as the successful Republican nominee, Jeremiah Morrow.

The early years of statehood in Ohio were not characterized by events of unusual significance. As Salmon P. Chase later expressed it, aside from the Burr Conspiracy the period "was marked by few striking or important incidents. The attention of the general assembly was chiefly bestowed on local legislation. The erection of new counties, and the incorporation of towns, banks, manufacturing companies, academies, and religious societies, indicated the rapid progress of the state in population, wealth and character."

The first session of the legislature that met in the new statehouse, in Chillicothe, probably the first stone public building within the boundaries of the Northwest Territory, was opened by an address by the Governor. Naturally the first legislature faced the task of carrying into effect many provisions of the new state constitution and of providing fundamental acts for the insuring of orderly life in the new body politic. The tax laws of the Territory were slightly modified and continued in force, and in the session of 1803–1804 somewhat improved, the main reliance still resting upon revenues from lands, two thirds of the receipts to be paid into the state treasury and one third into the various county treasuries.

During the first sessions of the legislature, laws were enacted regulating marriages, providing for the punishment of crime, establishing the beginnings of an educational system, and dealing with the supervision of elections. The passage of a general statute continuing in effect all Territorial laws not conflicting with the new constitution or new enactments removed the necessity for the immediate consideration of detailed legislation of every important category.

The first Ohio Legislature, composed of fourteen senators and thirty members of the house, included twelve persons who had served in the preceding constitutional convention. Chillicothe Republicans were well represented among the new state officials, with Tiffin as governor, Nathaniel Massie as speaker of the senate, Michael Baldwin as speaker of the house, and William Creighton, Jr., as secretary of state. Another Chillicothe Republican was chosen Senator in April, when Thomas Worthington, of that place, and John Smith, of Cincinnati, became Ohio's first Representatives in the upper House of the national Congress. Since the Democratic Republicans held the political control of the state practically unchallenged, such credit and such criticism as are directed to the successes and failures of the legislature during the early years of statehood must to a large degree fall upon them.

Their strength and weakness lay largely in a confidence in a powerful legislature, dominating the other branches of the government and responsible to the voters at frequent elections. Naturally this attitude weakened the authority of the governor, except as he could exert influence through the force of his personality, and placed the judiciary in a relationship of actual or potential subserviency. At this time, however, in some state and Federal courts elsewhere in the nation the doctrine that judges might declare legislative enactments void if they found the acts contrary to provisions of the state constitution or the Federal Constitution was being promulgated. If this principle were adopted by members of the bench in Ohio, a heated contest would be extremely probable. Such a situation had developed by 1807. Two years before, the legislature had given local justices jurisdiction without a jury trial in cases involving amounts not exceeding fifty dollars. A suit involving thirty-two dollars and brought by a certain Daniel M'Faddon against Benjamin Rutherford was decided in favor of the plaintiff in justice's court in Steubenville and was ultimately appealed to the supreme court of the state. Since the Ohio constitution guaranteed trial by jury and the Federal Constitution insured the right of jury trial save in contracts involving less than twenty dollars, the court held the law under which the justice's decision had been made to be unconstitutional. Thus, in the history of the Ohio judiciary, a decision was rendered comparable to the *Marbury* vs. *Madison* pronouncement (in 1803) in the history of the nation. By this time, Governor Tiffin had resigned to become a United States Senator, and Acting Governor Thomas Kirker (1807–1808), a native of Ireland, called attention to the problem of legally collecting obligations of amounts between twenty and fifty dollars, and urged that an adjustment be made by the legislature.

That body, however, was more immediately concerned about the results of the election of 1807. In this contest Return Jonathan Meigs, Jr., of Marietta, had received a clear majority over Nathaniel Massie, of Chillicothe, but a question of ineligibility to office on the basis of residence was raised against Meigs, who had been absent for a time as a Federal judge of the Territory of Louisiana. Massie pushed the contest, apparently in the interests of his friend, Kirker. The legislature declared against the eligibility of Meigs, though it proceeded to elect him to the state supreme court; and Kirker continued to act as governor until a new election could be held in the fall of 1808.[1]

In this new appeal to the electorate, strong competition developed between Thomas Worthington and Samuel Huntington, with Kirker as a minor candidate. All three contestants were nominally Democratic Republicans, but Worthington was an especial advocate of legislative supremacy, while Huntington had been one of the judges who had upheld the prerogatives of the judiciary. Like Kirker, Worthington represented the liberal faction of the party, and probably would not have announced his intention of running had he known that the former was to enter the lists. The Federalists of the state had no candidate, but seem to have concentrated upon Huntington, a native of Connecticut, who, in view of the division of the opposition, was enabled to secure the governorship, which he held from 1808 to 1810. The legislature elected at the same time, however, was unfriendly to the powers of the judiciary, and soon a committee of the house brought charges of impeachment against George Tod, who had participated with Huntington in the *Rutherford* vs. *M'Faddon* case, and against Calvin Pease, a circuit judge, who had taken a similar stand in a different case. The charges were argued before the state senate, which in each case on the crucial charge rejected conviction by a vote of fifteen to nine, a two-thirds majority being necessary for removal.

Another means of placing the judiciary in a position of subordination, however, was derived from a provision of the Ohio constitution that specified seven years as the term for justices of the supreme and the inferior courts. It was now resolved by the legislature (in 1810) that this meant that the term of office for such judges as had been appointed

---

[1] Thereafter, until the constitution of 1851 became effective, Ohio's governors were elected in the even-numbered years.

since 1803, as well as for those whose terms began in that year, should end in 1810. Obviously, those who wished to see the judgeships filled with men deferential to the will of the legislature sponsored this move, and the judges who were subsequently appointed were persons who were considered to be favorable to such principles. Thus frontier democracy made unstinting efforts to make the judiciary as well as the legislative and executive branches of the state government responsive to the popular will. The frontiersmen held an unwavering faith in a government by the people, and the idea of judges interposing legal objections to the work of their representatives was not one to be endorsed widely at the log cabin fireside.

Doubtless some votes for the so-called "Sweeping Resolution" were gained from members from the vicinity of Zanesville by a supposed agreement that the capital of the state would be moved for a time from Chillicothe to Zanesville. At any rate, the capital was located at the latter place from 1810 to 1812, when the legislature, after much lobbying on the part of representatives of various localities, accepted the proposition of certain landowners[2] to lay out a town "on the east bank of the Scioto River, opposite Franklinton" and to provide the necessary land and public buildings for a statehouse, state offices, and a penitentiary. Temporarily, Chillicothe was designated as the seat of government, but in 1816 the newly-platted Columbus became the permanent capital.[3]

---

[2] Alexander McLaughlin, John Kerr, Lyne Starling, and James Johnston.

[3] The new town (east of the Scioto) was located on a strip known as the Refugee Tract, granted in 1801 to sympathizers with the patriot cause in the American Revolution who as such had been refugees from Canada and Nova Scotia. The tract extended as far north as Fifth Avenue and as far south as Steelton, at the present site of Columbus, and eastward about forty-eight miles from the Scioto River. Only a small portion of the lands set aside were ever claimed by refugees.

The Burr Conspiracy

While the struggle between the legislature and the judiciary was in progress, one of the two original Senators from Ohio, John Smith, was experiencing embarrassing difficulties due directly to the activities of Aaron Burr, recently Vice President of the United States. The latter, ostracized from Eastern society by the circumstances of his duel with Hamilton in the spring and summer of 1805, had taken a trip down the Ohio and Mississippi Rivers to New Orleans. In the course of this journey he had stopped at Blennerhassett's Island, fourteen miles below Marietta in the Ohio River, the Arcadian establishment of an Irishman of means and culture from whom the island took its name. Having interested Blennerhassett in his plans, Burr had spent a day at Cincinnati with Senator Smith, was later entertained by Andrew Jackson in Tennessee and by Governor Claiborne at New Orleans, and on the return journey stopped to see Jackson again, and also Henry Clay at his home near Lexington, Kentucky. In Ohio once more, he saw Senator Smith a second time, at Cincinnati, and Governor Tiffin, at Chillicothe.

In the summer of 1806, Burr started on a second trip down the Ohio, accompanied by his daughter, the beautiful and gifted Theodosia Alston. Making further arrangements for boats and men, he proceeded to Chillicothe, Cincinnati, and then to the Southwest.

The actual intent of Burr is still confused by conflicting evidence and may have been the clouded intention of an irrational mind. At times he spoke of an attack upon Spanish territory in the Southwest, where an independent state could be erected; at times of the assumption of disputed land claims in the West; and on other occasions of an assault upon territory included in the Louisiana Purchase.

To have carried out the last of these ideas would have been, of course, a treasonable enterprise. Hence, suspicious rumors were abroad in 1806 in regard to his purposes, and President Jefferson accordingly delegated John Graham as a secret agent to the West. Governor Tiffin, being persuaded that Burr had designs against the territorial integrity of the country, sent a special message to the legislature of the state on December 2, imparting information as to these supposedly treasonable purposes.

The legislature at once sanctioned repressive measures against the expedition, boats and supplies were seized, and the militia was called out at Marietta and Cincinnati. Much frenzied excitement manifested itself, Blennerhassett's home was wrecked by the Virginia Militia, and the affair in relation to Ohio came to an end. Burr being brought to trial, the Ohio Legislature in turn called upon Senator Smith to resign. A United States Senate committee, headed by J. Q. Adams, conducted a lengthy investigation, ultimately recommending expulsion under a "strong presumption of guilt." The Senate failed to comply, but by a narrow vote (19:10), and with the other Ohio member, former Governor Tiffin, voting in the affirmative. Smith saw fit to resign, removing to Louisiana, where he resumed his former activities as a preacher. It is now generally believed that Smith was wholly innocent of any unpatriotic purpose but placed himself in a vulnerable position by his steadfast refusal to repudiate a friend whom he believed to be likewise guiltless of any intended injury to his country.

The Tammany Organization

Personal jealousies doubtless entered into this attack upon Smith, for, although the Republican Party was generally united on questions of national concern, sectional animosities and individual ambitions were prominent factors in state politics. At times this situation led to more or less informal arrangements between certain Republicans and the Federalist minority, the former on such occasions being designated as "Quids" by the majority faction in their own party. The "Sweeping Resolution" of 1810, with its attack upon the integrity of the courts, alarmed some of the conservative Republicans—a situation which caused those party men who had sponsored the resolution to take counsel lest the Quids and Federalists should combine for the repeal of the measure. Accordingly, the regular Republicans were instrumental in the formation of Tammany societies that followed the model of such organizations in New York and other seaboard states. These societies brought forth one of their number, Thomas Worthington, for the governorship in 1810. He was opposed by Return Jonathan Meigs, Jr., of Marietta, then a United States Senator, a Republican of the same type as Huntington, and a Yankee by heredity and association, whose close affiliation with some of the Federalists made him more acceptable to that group than Worthington. The New England settlers gave such considerable support to Meigs that he was elected, though the sting of defeat was mitigated for his opponent by the latter's election to the United States Senate for the remainder of Meigs' term.

In this session of the legislature, the Tammany men were able to resist any action against the "Sweeping Resolution," even though a concerted effort was made in that direction. A year later (in January, 1812), however, the legislation that embodied the principle of the "Sweeping Resolution" was repealed, and the power of the society had clearly passed its zenith in the state.

In the Presidential election of 1812, nevertheless, the Tammany feeling was still so strong that a Tammany group of electors and an anti-Tammany list, both pledged to Madison and Gerry, the Republican candidates, were submitted to the voters in opposition to the ticket favoring De Witt Clinton and Gerry. Clinton had been nominated by the Republicans of New York and was then indorsed by the Federalists as a peace candidate. His position on this question and his advocacy of internal improvements and a protective tariff attracted considerable support. The strength of the various elements in the contest may be judged to some degree from the 7,420 votes cast for the Tammany ticket in contrast to 3,301 cast for the Clintonian, and 1,051 for the anti-Tammany men. The Tammany society, however, faded rapidly as the dominating political group. The War of 1812 overshadowed lesser considerations; and the passing of the Tammany power, signalizing the reunification of the Republicans, was indicated in February, 1813, by the overwhelming majority given in the legislature to Jeremiah Morrow to fill the vacancy in the United States Senate caused by the resignation of Alexander Campbell.

The War of 1812

Some recent historians have come to the conclusion that the entrance of the United States into the War of 1812 was "unnecessary, impolitic, untimely and rash,"[4] for American grievances against France were at that time exceptionally serious, while not only were those against Great Britain less acute than in 1807, but the British Parliament was approaching them in a mood of conciliation. Ostensibly, the declaration of war was due chiefly to Great Britain's maritime practices, yet the seat of America's seagoing interests, New England, was almost fanatically opposed to hostilities. The real clue to the spirit and the

---

[4] Muzzey, *The United States of America*, Vol. I, p. 252.

votes that compelled the conflict was to be found among the pioneers of the West, who, with the frontier love of action, welcomed an encounter that promised to remove forever the menace of Indian aggression and to gain possibly a part or all of British North America beyond the Great Lakes. The fear of the red man rather than a conscious covetousness of British soil was doubtless the dominant reason in Ohio for that Western bellicosity that caused the eccentric John Randolph, of Virginia, to exclaim: "Agrarian cupidity, not maritime right, wages this war. . . . Ever since the report of the Committee on Foreign Relations came into the House, we have heard but one word—like the whippoorwill, but one eternal, monotonous tone— Canada, Canada, Canada."

Yet it is highly probable that a majority of Ohioans did not actively concern themselves with the possibilities of a conflict, and of those who did, many were worried about the woeful state of unpreparedness in the Northwest. Governor Meigs in April, 1812, wrote of his fear that should the British get possession of Detroit, "the Indians on both sides of the Lakes might join them and the frontiers of Ohio be harrassed by the murderous Incursions of numerous savages." In Congress, Senator Worthington interested himself in legislation for the organization of six companies of rangers to defend the frontier (January, 1812) and for the authorization of one hundred thousand militiamen to be held in readiness for instant service (April, 1812). At the same time, he sought to convince President Madison of the exposed, unprotected condition of the borders in the Northwest. The Ohio Legislature was rather indifferent to the problem of protection, and the attitude of the people of the state is indicated in the statement of Governor Meigs in April, 1812, that, in case of a failure of volunteers, a draft would be necessary.

Neither of Ohio's Senators voted for the declaration of war, and one of them, Thomas Worthington, voted in the negative.[5] The latter, returning from Congress in July, 1812, noted that sentiment in the area between Wheeling and Lancaster (Ohio) seemed to be divided as to the war, "those advocating it making much noise, those opposed to it being more quiet."

Governor Meigs had suggested in January that a general treaty committing the Indians to a policy of peace ought to be arranged before the British secured their allegiance. Late in the summer, negotiations were carried on with the red men at Piqua, and although the British had been partially successful in keeping the tribes from attending, those who assembled gave "the most positive assurance of their determination to keep peace."

Some Ohioans were opposed to an unnecessary conflict, but the population as a whole felt the necessity of supporting the war. The militia, however, was ignorant of discipline, poorly officered, lacking in equipment, and inadequate in its commissary department. One prominent Ohioan estimated that seven tenths of the militia officers were "entirely ignorant of the military discipline." The wretched state of the equipment, moreover, caused much disgruntlement, and one officer complained that the "militia cannot march without a new blanket, a new gun and bayonet, shoes, etc., and every company . . . must have a team of 4 horses to haul their baggage or they cannot march."

---

[5] Senator Campbell did not attend the War Congress of 1812. Illness in his family and the expectation of an adjournment kept him at home. Later he resigned. Worthington wrote to his wife in explanation of his own negative vote: "I have done my duty and satisfied my conscience. Thousands of the innocent will suffer, but I have borne my testimony against it, and thank God, my mind is tranquil . . . now that the step is taken, I am bound to submit to the will of the majority, and use my best exertions to save my country from ruin."

Some felt that Governor Meigs was inept at meeting the demands of the situation. Former Governor Tiffin and a future governor, Duncan McArthur, were of this opinion, and advocated a change in the chief executive following the next elections. Nevertheless, when the Federalists brought forth Thomas Scott, of the state supreme court, Meigs was accepted by the Republicans as the lesser of two evils and was easily reëlected (in 1812).

Even before the declaration of war, the Ohio Militia had been turned over to General William Hull at Dayton (on May 25, 1812). Hull had served creditably in the Revolutionary War, but had grown old and corpulent, and his selection for the command was most unfortunate. Proceeding northward *via* Urbana, Fort Findlay, and the lower Maumee Valley through a wilderness of miry trails, the army reached Detroit in July, but only after a schooner carrying stores and baggage and even military papers had been captured by the British on Lake Erie. Hull was overcautious and indecisive, and finally, without resistance, surrendered the post at Detroit. Most of Hull's army, including Colonels Duncan McArthur and Lewis Cass, were from Ohio; hence, indignation as a result of Hull's ignominious action was keenly felt throughout the state.

Governor Meigs, in his annual message of December, 1812, with bombastic rhetoric appealed for a vigorous prosecution of the war. He declared in part,

> On the ocean your impressed brethren are compelled by the torturing lash to raise their unwilling arms against the country of their birth, and in maritime exile drag out an unhappy existence. On the west the hordes of barbarians, stimulated by British influences, tear alike the scalp from the mother and the infant in her arms and with relentless fury stain the land of freedom with the blood of her sons.

In the meantime, William Henry Harrison, who had gained something of a military reputation in the Northwest as a result of his meeting the Indians in an encounter at Tippecanoe Creek (Indiana) in 1811, had been appointed Brigadier General to coöperate with Hull. Kentucky placed in his charge two or three thousand men to go to the relief of Detroit, but while en route to Cincinnati they learned of Hull's surrender. Joined by volunteers, the army pushed northward *via* Piqua, St. Mary's, and Defiance. Troops from Pennsylvania and Virginia crossed the state *via* Wooster and Upper Sandusky, and militiamen from Ohio journeyed from Urbana *via* Fort McArthur (in the present Hardin County) toward the appointed rendezvous at the rapids of the Maumee.

Because James Winchester, a Tennessee planter whose commission as brigadier general antedated that of Harrison, demanded recognition, the latter turned over to him a part of the forces—an action that militated against any early advance. President Madison finally placed Harrison in supreme command, but without securing thereby the whole-hearted support of Winchester.

Although Harrison's army exceeded that of the enemy in numbers, it was undisciplined, and transportation problems, always difficult at that time in the region of the "Black Swamp" (south of the present site of Toledo), increased with the approach of winter. The commissary department, thoroughly disorganized in the Northwest since the surrender of Hull, suffered from the impaired credit of the Government; on December 21, General Winchester at Defiance (where a newly erected fort had been named in his honor) had issued his last barrel of flour, and his troops were subsisting on poor beef and hickory roots.

The administration desired an immediate attack upon Detroit, so Harrison ordered Winchester to occupy a base at the rapids of the Maumee. This was done, but Winchester, without extensive investigation and without authority from Harrison, decided to send a detachment to Frenchtown (now Monroe, Michigan). An engagement there resulted in the American occupation of the place, with luxuries of various kinds, but a false sense of security prevailed, to be rudely terminated by an attack by Indians and British. Harrison, at Upper Sandusky, was advised too late of the expedition to be able to send troops to assist Winchester's men, who were disastrously defeated at the Battle of the River Raisin.

Harrison then moved his depot to Fort Meigs below the rapids of the Maumee, where he successfully resisted a siege by the British. Late in July, the fort was again attacked by Colonel Proctor, the British commander, who finally decided to move over to the Sandusky River and ascend it to Fort Stephenson, the present site of Fremont, which a council of officers had decided to abandon. This order eventually was not insisted upon, and Major George Croghan, a Kentucky-born youth of twenty-one years, whose father's uncle was the famous Indian trader of the same name, with a single cannon and only one hundred and fifty men successfully beat off a force of probably twelve hundred British and Indians.

The methods employed by the Government in the raising of troops were ineffective; therefore, Harrison appealed for aid to Governor Shelby, of Kentucky, who soon arrived at Upper Sandusky with thirty-five hundred men. Thus reënforced, Harrison hastened to Fort Meigs, where news came to him of the victory of Oliver H. Perry over the British at the Battle of Put-in-Bay. With the lake, as a result, under American control, the army under Harrison began the invasion of Canada, and at the Battle of the River Thames won a victory possibly momentous in its effects upon the terms of peace. In this encounter the great Indian chieftain, Tecumseh, whose birthplace was supposedly the Shawnee village near the present site of Springfield, Ohio, met his death, and circumstances decreed that the war in the Northwest should come to an end.

Financially, Ohio had contributed her portion of the expenses of the war. Four thousand dollars had been appropriated for the purchase of blankets for the Ohio militia in the national service, and forty thousand dollars had been expended for the payment of bounties at twelve dollars a month to Ohio militiamen who continued to serve under Harrison. Three successive direct tax levies were made upon the state between 1813 and 1816, and in each case Ohio met her quota promptly, saving a considerable discount that was offered for speedy compliance with the act. Part of the funds for these requisitions was borrowed from banks for a time, but in 1815 the tax upon land was increased seventy-five per cent, while taxes were established upon bank stock and upon processes and proceedings in law and equity. On the military side, not only 24,521 enlisted men but 1,759 officers, including leaders such as Harrison, McArthur, and Cass, were citizens of the state.

Political Matters at the Close of the War

Toward the end of the struggle (in 1814), Ohio's Governor, Return J. Meigs, Jr., resigned his position to receive from Madison an appointment as the first postmaster-general of the United States to be selected from Ohio. Othniel Looker, a Revolutionary soldier, who was then speaker of the state senate, served as acting governor until the end of the term (1814).

The close of the war found in the chief executive's chair at Columbus the able and urbane Republican, Thomas

Worthington, who professed an indifference to political preferment yet long played an active rôle in Ohio official affairs. In the election of 1814, he had proved much too formidable an opponent for Looker, who carried only four counties in a contest that created little interest because of the focusing of attention at that time upon the war. Worthington's inaugural address was in reality a war message calling for renewed energy in the prosecution of the conflict. He undertook to organize the militia more effectively and pressed plans for military changes upon the legislature, but the confirmation of rumors of peace in February, 1815, put an end to the immediate need for such action. In 1816 Worthington was easily reëlected over Colonel James Dunlap, of Chillicothe, and Judge Ethan Allen Brown, of the state supreme court.

Worthington's administrations were years of rapid increase in population, of growth in trade and industry, of wildcat banking and feverish speculation. During this time, the completion of the penitentiary at Columbus enabled the legislature to accomplish a thorough revision of the criminal code whereby long terms at hard labor were substituted for stripes on the bare back at the whipping post. In the same session of the legislature, provision was made for the first time for the care of the insane, who, if dangerous, were to be incarcerated in the county jail unless relatives or friends furnished bond for the safe-keeping of the person elsewhere. The need for caring for the poor also was recognized in the passage of a law authorizing the erection of county infirmaries for the destitute. Hitherto, only such relief had been available as the township overseers had found it possible to dispense, and even under the revised system this continued to be the common practice, as the poor were cared for under a contract awarded to the lowest bidder.

The session of the legislature that met in the winter of 1817–1818 largely gave up its time to a "windy warfare" over the taxation of the United States Bank. Ethan Allen Brown, the leading candidate for the governorship in 1818, actively favored the carrying out of such a program and was elected by a vote of 30,194 to 8,075 over James Dunlap of Chillicothe. The question of the taxation of the bank was a paramount one at the time. It reflects a typical frontier attitude and demands more detailed attention.

The Struggle with the Bank of the United States

With the closing months of the War of 1812, difficult financial conditions had produced rather generally in the country, with the exception of New England, a suspension of specie payments, an expedient that had become necessary in Ohio about the first of January, 1815. Economic conditions in the East at the same time were sending westward an unprecedented number of settlers, creating an increase in population, a demand for credit, and an inflation of prices. All of these circumstances helped produce an appearance of unusual prosperity and gave opportunity for the establishment of banks and the issuance of notes unsupported by adequate financial resources. These financial organizations were created by special acts of the legislature, as a result of much pressure exerted by interested parties, and considerable trading of votes by legislators active in aiding the plans of influential constituents. For a time considerable profits were realized by the banks, and the state, wishing to secure a share of the dividends, passed a law in February, 1816, the Bonus Act, requiring every bank receiving a charter under certain conditions to grant to the state a twenty-fifth interest in its business, the dividends from which were to be applied to the securing of more stock until one sixth of the total was owned by the state.

With the establishment of a branch of the United States Bank at Cincinnati in 1817, feeling was engendered against the institution because of the tendency of its adequately secured note issues to displace those of state banks and because of its favored position by virtue of its exemption from the taxes paid by the local banks. Politicians and local bankers were active in arousing hostile sentiment; an appeal was made in the state legislature to the Jeffersonian principle of State rights; and in December, 1817, a committee was created by the lower House of the Ohio Legislature to determine the expediency of taxing the Ohio branches of the United States Bank. Although the committee advised against such procedure, the house of representatives voted in favor of a tax, but ultimately postponed action until the next session.

The heyday of speculation and extravagance following the war had reached a crisis in the summer of 1818, when the United States Bank,[6] with a branch at Cincinnati and a new one at Chillicothe, established in the spring of 1818, became frightened at the excesses to which the extension of credit had gone, and faced the problem of the conservation of its assets. As a result, a sudden restriction of credits by the Bank took the form of an order requiring the Cincinnati branch to collect the balances due from the state banks, at the rate of twenty per cent every thirty days. The local banks immediately faced a crisis, specie was drained in wholesale fashion to the East, and the notes of many Ohio banks were refused at the state treasury in the payment of taxes. The foreclosure of mortgages at a

---

[6] Upon the passage of the bill creating the Second Bank of the United States in 1816, three Ohio Congressmen voted in the affirmative, as did Senator Morrow; two Congressmen voted in the negative, as did Senator Ruggles.

time when no reasonable sale could be obtained and a precipitate decline in the prices on all produce were features of this financial crisis, from which Ohio did not fully recover for a number of years.

By an act of February 8, 1819, an annual tax of fifty thousand dollars was levied on each branch of the United States Bank within the state, to be collected with unlimited right of search under the direction of the state auditor. According to this legislation, popularly termed the "crowbar law," such authority was granted in collecting the tax that, if the state auditor could not find the money in the banking room, he was impowered "to go into each and any other room or vault of such banking house, and every closet, chest, box, or drawer in such banking house to open and search."

In March the position of the bank was fortified by the famous decision of Chief Justice John Marshall in the case of *McCulloch* vs. *Maryland*, a judicial pronouncement which affirmed the constitutionality of the bank and denied the right of a state to tax the note-issues of the institution. In September, notice was given to Ralph Osborn, the Ohio Auditor, that the bank had petitioned the United States circuit court asking for an injunction against the collection of the tax. At the same time, a subpœna was served upon him to appear before the court to answer the petition. Osborn, advised by legal talent that these processes did not in themselves serve as an injunction, issued a warrant to John L. Harper to collect the tax. The latter thereupon forcibly took from the Chillicothe branch a sum in excess of one hundred thousand dollars, two thousand of which he kept as payment for his services.

The bank appealed once more to the circuit court and secured an injunction against Osborn and Harper, restraining them from paying over the money or making a report of its collection to the legislature. The money was, never-theless, paid over to the state treasurer. Harper and his assistant, Thomas Orr, were thereupon arrested and con-fined to prison until the following January, when they were freed by the circuit court because of irregularities as to their arrest.

In the meantime, the legislature designated a committee to consider the problem. The latter group on December 12, 1820, advised that the case of *McCulloch* vs. *Maryland* be ignored as a "maneuver of consummate policy," which could be treated as Georgia had done the decision of *Fletcher* vs. *Peck;* it asserted that the state was sovereign and, as such, the judge of its own powers; it recommended that the bank be outlawed from the state, no jailor to imprison nor any judge, jury, or recorder to take action to safeguard the interests of the bank; and it reaffirmed the state's right to tax the institution.

The report received the approval of the legislature in an act of January 29, 1821, withdrawing the protection of the state laws from the United States Bank. In Septem-ber, the United States circuit court ordered Osborn to return one hundred thousand dollars to the bank and to pay interest upon the part of that sum that was in specie. Thereupon an appeal was made to the Supreme Court of the United States, where the case, *Osborn* vs. *Bank of the United States*, enlisted some of the best legal talent avail-able, Henry Clay, Daniel Webster, John Sergeant, and William Wirt, the last-mentioned the Attorney General of the United States, as counsel for the bank, and John C. Wright and Charles Hammond, appearing for the state.

Hammond, who was both an able lawyer and an experi-enced journalist, argued that the circuit court could not assume jurisdiction in a case against a state, and that only the Supreme Court could act in an injunction suit. He also maintained that the bank was not exempt from the taxing power of the state, since it was essentially a private corporation and not a branch of the Government.

John Marshall, in his decision of March 19, 1824, following the precedent of *McCulloch* vs. *Maryland,* sustained the contentions of the circuit court in every particular except the matter of interest,[7] and declared the Ohio law "repugnant to the law of the United States, made in pursuance of the constitution, and therefore void."

Thus, Ohio, like other states, such as Kentucky and Maryland, had engaged in a contest with the bank and had had her fling in the field of nullification of unpopular Federal measures. The excitement of the Missouri slavery controversy detracted from the attention that the incident might otherwise have secured; and the revival of prosperity, the reduction in the price of lands by the law of 1820, the increasing importance of sectional issues, and the development of a more nationalistic viewpoint in Ohio gradually led to a marked change in public opinion. In January, 1826, the Ohio Legislature repealed its enactment outlawing the bank from its borders (a law that had been essentially a dead letter) and in the next decade when South Carolina appealed to the doctrine of nullification in her opposition to the protective tariff, Ohio frowned upon such a theory as "revolutionary" and "pernicious."

The Movement for Internal Improvements

Another matter that created widespread attention during this period was the agitation for a state canal system. A leader in this movement was Governor Brown, who was

---

[7] Marshall held that since the parties had been restrained by the circuit court from using the money, they ought not to be charged with interest.

easily reëlected in 1820 over his principal opponent, Jeremiah Morrow. Brown did not serve out his second term, however, for upon the death of United States Senator William A. Trimble in 1821, he was elected to the latter's place. Allen Trimble, Speaker of the Ohio Senate and a brother of the deceased Senator, then assumed the duties of acting governor, an office that he occupied from January to December, 1822.

The securing of adequate roads and a canal system seemed to be a factor upon which the future prosperity of Ohio, still in its frontier stage of development, was dependent. As early as 1800 arks or "New Orleans boats" (that were usually broken up following the completion of the voyage) had descended the Ohio and Mississippi Rivers, laden with fruit, fowl, cider, pork, lard, flour, and similar products. Keel boats and the more capacious barges were also used, the latter usually making two trips to New Orleans and back in a year. Transportation by barge was less expensive than the use of the overland route over the mountains from Philadelphia, hence groceries and heavy articles were usually brought up the river. Especially in the inland areas of the state, transportation rates were so high that settlers found themselves deprived of the articles they desired and unable to market the products of their farms.

In the hope of improving conditions, at the session of the first Ohio Legislature, an act was passed authorizing a lottery to raise money for the improvement of the navigation of the Muskingum and Cuyahoga Rivers, but this measure did not accomplish its purpose. Even with the introduction of the steamboat in 1811 upon the Ohio River, reducing the time and cost of sending freight downstream to New Orleans to a mere fraction of the former amount, the interior counties could find access to markets only in case roads were also available.

The value of good roads had not been lost sight of. The Enabling Act, under the terms of which Ohio was admitted to the Union, provided that, with Ohio's exemption of the United States lands within her boundaries from taxation, five per cent of the proceeds of such lands should be employed for the building of roads within the state.[8] By 1805 about twelve thousand dollars had been provided, and the necessary surveys were begun. More comprehensive plans were subsequently authorized by Congress, and the Cumberland Road was started in 1811, to be completed as far west as Wheeling seven years later.

The results from the expenditure of the "three per cent fund" were not so fortunate. Road commissioners in the counties were intrusted with the money, which was largely used for local projects. These projects necessarily lacked the value that they would have possessed if they had been units in a carefully integrated state system. By 1816, although about $173,000 from this fund had been expended in the state, local roads were still exceedingly inadequate.

Canals, however, were to constitute the chief means in Ohio for improving access to markets. As early as 1807, Senator Worthington had proposed a resolution asking Secretary of the Treasury Gallatin to report a plan for the employment of the power of Congress for the opening of roads and canals, with a list of such undertakings as might deserve Government aid. Nothing was done immediately, but the Cumberland Road developed from a report of Gallatin made a year later.

Later, New York sought the coöperation of other states in securing aid from the National Government for the construction of the Erie Canal. Congress refused such help; but after the War of 1812, which had clearly demon-

---

[8] It was later arranged that three per cent should be used for common highways within the state and two per cent for the national highway.

strated the need for better facilities of transportation and communication, New York decided to go ahead with the project on her own account. Assistance from Ohio was sought, and although a committee of the Ohio House of Representatives favored such a course, the senate refused to pledge financial aid.

Toward the end of Worthington's second administration (in 1818) the Governor called the attention of the legislature to the need for internal improvements. Shortly afterwards, Governor Ethan Allen Brown, later known as the "Father of the Ohio Canals," in his inaugural address emphasized the need for "a cheaper way to market for the surplus produce of a large portion of our fertile country." Less than a month thereafter, in his first message to the legislature, he stressed the popular ignorance that surrounded the canal question and urged the need of employing engineering talent in ascertaining the feasibility and cost of a canal connecting the Ohio River and Lake Erie. Much discussion developed in the legislature over the matter, but over a year passed before an act was secured (in February, 1820) providing for three canal commissioners who were to engage a capable engineer. This action, however, was to be dependent upon the acquiescence of Congress in a proposition for a donation and sale to Ohio of public lands lying upon and near the proposed route. Congress failed to grant the desired concessions, hence nothing was accomplished for two more years.

In the meantime, Governor Brown refused to allow the legislature to lose sight of the matter, and as a result of his insistence, a committee of the house reported early in 1822 as to "the probable expense, the profits, the means" of building the canal. The committee concluded that the project could be built at less expense than that of New York in building the famous Erie Canal, that the benefits would be not only in the form of cheaper transportation but also in the tolls received, and that construction could be carried on by either private or state capital. A law was passed (in February, 1822) providing for a competent engineer to examine the country between the Ohio River and Lake Erie and for the appointment of seven commissioners to determine the practicability and relative expense of various proposed routes. Thus, the first positive step was taken toward the construction of the Ohio canal system.

Three principal lines of construction were considered: a western one *via* the Miami and Maumee Valleys, a central one *via* the Scioto and Sandusky Rivers, and an eastern one through the Muskingum and Cuyahoga Valleys. One of the best of the engineers of the Erie Canal, James Geddes, having been employed in 1823, the commissioners made a preliminary report of their investigation but urged an extension of time for the determining of the advantages of the various routes. This extension was granted by legislative authority, and a year later (in 1824), the commissioners made a recommendation for a canal from the lake *via* the valley of the Cuyahoga and through the upper part of that of the Muskingum, *via* the Licking Valley and down the lower part of the valley of the Scioto. A second canal was also urged *via* the Maumee and Miami River Valleys.[9] The plan was distinctly a compromise of the various plans aiming to obtain the support of the legislators from various sections of the state.

The legislature, however, delayed final action and authorized a further examination of the Sandusky-Scioto

---

[9] The canal commissioners originally intended to carry the one canal across the Scioto Valley to the Miami River, the waterway thus traversing the state from northeast to southwest, but this plan was found to be impracticable because of topographical hindrances.

route and of the possible terminal points upon Lake Erie. During the summer of 1824, surveyors were busy on the proposed routes, and following the election of legislators

Ohio Canals, the National Road, and Zane's Trace

favorable to the program (October, 1824), an act was passed in February, 1825, definitely providing for the beginning of the construction of the canals.

This measure provided for a board of canal commissioners of seven members, who were empowered to fix the route and begin the construction of a canal from the mouth of the Scioto to the lake by way of Licking Summit and the Muskingum, and of one from Cincinnati to Dayton. A "canal fund" was established, to be managed by a board of three commissioners, who were given the right to borrow money and to make arrangements as to its management. The board was soon organized; surveyors were engaged; and by April the first loan for four hundred thousand dollars had been secured from Eastern capitalists.

The work was formally begun on July 4, 1825, when at Licking Summit, near Newark, Governor Morrow and other persons of prominence took part in the ceremonies, a part of which included the turning of the first spadeful of earth by the guest of honor, De Witt Clinton, of New York, the father of the Erie Canal. Less than three weeks later, on July 21, at Middletown, a similar occasion, also graced by the attendance of Governor Clinton, marked the beginning of the Miami Canal. Ohio's dreams were at last on the road to realization!

SELECTED BIBLIOGRAPHY

The chief events of this period are considered in Randall and Ryan, Vol. III, pp. 146–308, and in King, pp. 296–367. Two scholarly articles on the politics of this period are those by William T. Utter: "Judicial Review in Early Ohio," *Mississippi Valley Historical Review*, Vol. XIV, pp. 3–25, and "Saint Tammany in Early Ohio," *Ibid.*, Vol. XV, pp. 321–341. A suggestive interpretation of political forces is Homer C. Hockett, *Western Influences on Political Parties to 1825* (Columbus, 1917). Details of Burr's activities may be found in S. H. Wandell and Meade Minnegerode, *Aaron Burr* (2 vols., New York, 1925), Vol. II.

Life and Times of Ephraim Cutler, a member of the first constitutional convention, by his daughter, Julia Perkins Cutler (Cincinnati, 1890), is highly informative, but its objectivity is subordinated at times to the claims of family pride. Other biographies of significance are William E. Gilmore, *Life of Edward*

Tiffin (Chillicothe, Ohio, 1897); A. C. McLaughlin, *Lewis Cass* (Boston, 1891), pp. 1–53; and Josiah Morrow, "Jeremiah Morrow," in *Old Northwest Genealogical Quarterly*, Vol. IX, pp. 1–27, 99–133, and 227–254.

For an interpretation of Western influences making for war, see Julius W. Pratt, *Expansionists of 1812* (New York, 1925); Louis M. Hacker, "Western Land Hunger and the War of 1812: a Conjecture," in *Mississippi Valley Historical Review*, Vol. X, pp. 365–396; and Julius W. Pratt, "Western Aims in the War of 1812," *Ibid.*, Vol. XII, pp. 36–51.

A detailed account of the war in the West is Robert B. McAfee, *History of the Late War in the Western Country* (Lexington, Ky., 1816), later reprinted (Bowling Green, Ohio, 1919). The activities of the chief commander from Ohio are summarized by Beverley W. Bond, Jr., in "William Henry Harrison in the War of 1812," *Mississippi Valley Historical Review*, Vol. XIII, pp. 499–516. Also useful is "Northern Ohio during the War of 1812," with an introduction by E. J. Benton, *Western Reserve Historical Society Tracts*, No. 92 (Cleveland, 1912).

Banking in the state is carefully analyzed in C. C. Huntington, "History of Banking and Currency in Ohio before the Civil War," *Ohio Archæological and Historical Quarterly*, Vol. XXIV.

For the struggle with the Bank of the United States, see Huntington, *op. cit.*, pp. 313–329; Randall and Ryan, Vol. III, pp. 311–331; Jean D. Cheetham, "State Sovereignty in Ohio," *Ohio Archæological and Historical Quarterly*, Vol. IX, pp. 290–302; and J. B. McMaster, *History of the People of the United States* (8 vols., 1884–1928), Vol. IV, pp. 495–504.

The story of Ohio's canals is told in Randall and Ryan, Vol. III, pp. 335–363. Painstaking studies are E. L. Bogart, *Internal Improvements and the State Debt in Ohio* (New York, 1924); C. C. Huntington and C. P. McClelland, *History of Ohio Canals, their Construction, Cost, Use and Partial Abandonment* (Columbus, 1905); and W. F. Gephart, "Transportation and Industrial Development in the Middle West," *Columbia University Studies in History, Economics, and Public Law*, Vol. XXXIV. A life of one who was a notable figure in the development of Ohio's canals is J. L. Bates, *Alfred Kelley, his Life and Work* (Columbus, 1888).

CHAPTER VII

THE RISE OF JACKSONIAN DEMOCRACY

The Transition to New Party Loyalties

*I*N 1825, not only the undertaking of considerable plans for canals constructed by state funds, but the beginnings of an extensive system of education at public expense[1] and the inauguration of a new method of taxation served to indicate that in Ohio the simple frontier economy was passing.

The revision of the revenue laws at this time accomplished the abandonment of the primitive practice of depending for revenue almost wholly upon taxes secured from the land, classified in three groups according to its quality. The principle of the general property tax was now introduced, and town lots and buildings, dwelling houses, horses and cattle, pleasure vehicles, and the capital of merchants and brokers were subjected to taxation.[2] So successful was this change that the auditor of the state in 1831 reported, "The receipts from taxation annually exceed our calculations."

In national politics conspicuous changes were also to be noted, for throughout the nation the Federalist Party ceased to function after 1816, save in local elections. In that year, Ohio's electoral vote was, of course, given to the Republican candidate, James Monroe, who during the

---

[1] See Chapter VIII.

[2] In 1831 the list of things taxable was greatly enlarged. Fifteen years later (in 1846) a thoroughgoing application of the general property tax was made.

first year of his administration (1817), on a tour of the northern states, passed through Ohio, journeying *via* Delaware, Columbus, Circleville, Chillicothe, Lancaster, and Zanesville. Again in 1820, Monroe received Ohio's electoral vote in the practically unanimous vote of that year. The lull in partisan activities during the so-called "Era of Good Feeling" (Monroe's administrations until 1824) was broken, however, by a feverish contest that developed in relation to the question of his successor. Calhoun, De Witt Clinton, and William H. Crawford[3] had political friends throughout the nation, but during the early days of the campaign, for various reasons each was definitely eliminated from the Presidential contest in Ohio. Clay was nominated by a legislative caucus at Columbus in January, 1823, and for a while it appeared that he and Adams would be the principal candidates in Ohio. The latter, it was thought, would receive the support of those of New England and Federalist antecedents, who admired his character and superior training, and of those who believed that opposition to slavery should be a primary consideration in the contest. Clay, on the other hand, was the arch-supporter of internal improvements and a protective tariff and both personally and politically a representative of the West and its fundamental economic interests.

Early in 1824, however, a rising tide of enthusiasm that began to show itself in favor of Jackson, the hero of New Orleans, caused one Ohioan to exclaim, "Strange! Wild! Infatuated! All for Jackson! His victory at New Orleans

---

[3] The congressional caucus was used for the last time in this election. Attended by only a fraction of the Members of Congress and declaring for Crawford, a Georgian, it was presided over by Senator Benjamin Ruggles, who was the only Ohioan to attend and who did not enhance his political influence by so doing.

was not more unaccountable than his political success is
becoming." Jackson appealed to the Western farmer
not only as a war hero but as the embodiment of the
common man's interest. Regional factors also contributed
to his large vote, as his candidacy was favored by the
large Scotch-Irish and German population of eastern
Ohio, immigrants to whom the gospel of Jacksonian
Democracy proved especially alluring.

Clay's strength was diminished by a feeling that he was
serving as "a second fiddle" to Crawford, to whom his
influence would be swung if no one received a majority
in the electoral college. It was further affected by his
former connection as an attorney for the United States
Bank, an affiliation that made him especially unpopular in
the vicinity of Cincinnati.

Adams' expected support failed to materialize, for the
slavery issue receded into the background and prejudices
could easily be aroused on the frontier because of his
family and social connections. Hence, when the votes
were counted in Ohio, he was found to have secured only
12,280 votes in contrast to 18,489 for Jackson and 19,255
for Clay.

Thereafter, with the election referred to the House of
Representatives for decision, in view of the failure of any
candidate to secure a majority of the nation's electoral
vote, Clay was eliminated from consideration because of
the provision in the Constitution limiting a choice to one
of the three highest. Ten Ohio Congressmen preferred
Adams; two preferred Jackson; and two, Crawford. A
major question that confronted these men was whether
they considered Western or Northern interests the more
important. The decision of the Ohio delegation, which
helped to bring Adams to the Presidency, was due partly to
a belief that a northerner like Adams better represented

the economic interests of the state, and partly to a belief that he was the more capable man.

With Clay elevated to the position of secretary of state at the beginning of Adams's administration, the Clay and Adams groups in Ohio, as elsewhere, joined to form the administration party, though considerable friction developed within the organization between the former followers of Clay and Adams. For some time, no effective strength was mustered by the opposition, Presidential preferences being little stressed when Allen Trimble, of Hillsboro, who had been speaker of the state senate since 1819 and Acting Governor in 1822, was elected to the governorship in 1826. In the same year, of the ten Congressmen who had favored Adams in the House election of 1825, the eight who were seeking reëlection were all successful.

In other words, the older Ohio politicians of the type who had dominated political life in Ohio since its admission to the Union, were still in active control. The same forces that had elected Jeremiah Morrow, of Warren County, governor in 1822 and 1824 were still running strong. Morrow had been a member of the legislature of the Northwest Territory and of the constitutional convention of 1802, had been Ohio's sole Congressman for ten years (1803–1813), and had served as state senator, United States Senator, and state canal commissioner.[4]

Gradually, however, newspaper editors and ambitious politicians, who for personal or other reasons were discontented with the existing political situation, were joining the Jackson ranks. By means of an extensive organization extending even to townships and sometimes to school

---

[4] A further illustration of the continued power of the established leaders is found in the fact that, of the four candidates in the senatorial election in the Ohio Legislature in 1825, all had been in Ohio in the days of the Territorial régime, and the successful candidate, William H. Harrison, had been a Territorial Delegate to Congress at that early period.

districts, an aggressive campaign was carried on to send Jackson to the White House in 1829.

The contest throughout the nation was one of intense personal antagonisms, but nowhere was this truer than in the rough environment of the West. A region characterized by an unquestioning belief in democracy was a particularly favorable place for the inculcation of the idea that "the will of the people" had been thwarted by a "corrupt bargain" (that was never proved), according to which, it was claimed, Clay had thrown his influence in the House for the election of Adams in return for his appointment to the office of secretary of state. Hundreds of votes, moreover, were probably lost in Ohio to the administration by the constant reiteration of the assertion that the common man's hard-earned taxes were being squandered to provide frivolities such as a billiard table for the President's son in the White House.

On the other hand, publicists favorable to Adams were not hesitant in replying in like vein, and Charles Hammond, the noted Cincinnati editor-lawyer, published documentary evidence to prove that Jackson had married Mrs. Jackson before a divorce from her first husband had been legally effective. The campaign soon degenerated into mudslinging, which was bound to leave effects for years to come.

In the elections in October, 1828, Governor Allen Trimble, an anti-Jacksonian, was reëlected over John W. Campbell, the Jacksonian candidate, who previously had been a Congressman for ten years and was later to be United States district judge. At the same time, the administration men secured a majority of the seats in the State Legislature. Yet the three Jacksonian Congressmen from Ohio were reëlected, and in five other districts administration Members were supplanted by followers of the "Hero of New Orleans." No wonder that one of the defeated

Congressmen exclaimed: "It seems as if some maddening influence were abroad in the land whose cause and mode of operation is too occult to admit of full comprehension."

The Jacksonian forces made renewed efforts to carry the state for their national leader in November, when over twice as many votes were cast as in any previous year. Success crowned their endeavors, as Jackson polled 67,597 votes in contrast to 63,396 for Adams.

Immediately, followers of Adams and Clay were deeply concerned as to the possibility of removals from office, and in many cases their fears were soon realized when, upon Jackson's accession to power, editors and local politicians who had helped to secure his election were given their positions. John McLean, of Ohio, who had succeeded Return J. Meigs, Jr., as Postmaster General in 1823, and who had used his office to help Jackson's election, was unwilling to make a large number of removals and so was given a position as Associate Justice of the United States Supreme Court. He was the first citizen of Ohio to become a member of that tribunal—a position that he occupied until his death in 1861. William Henry Harrison, Ohio's only representative in a foreign country, then serving as minister to Colombia, was recalled. Joel Buttles, postmaster at Columbus practically since the establishment of the office at that place, was removed, and soon postmasters at many other towns had felt the results of the election and the operation of the "spoils system," which Jacksonian Democracy had definitely established in Federal affairs.

Jacksonians benefitting by the changes included former Governor E. A. Brown and John Hamm, a political leader of Zanesville, who were made *chargés des affaires* to Brazil and Chile, respectively. The United States Senate, however, refused to confirm some of Jackson's Ohio appointments, and on the whole, removals in the state were made neither so rapidly nor so extensively as has sometimes been supposed. In the fall elections of 1829 the Jacksonian organization was functioning well, and both houses of the State Legislature became Democratic, enabling that party to make judicial and other state appointments for the first time.

In national politics a matter causing considerable anxiety to Jacksonian politicians was the President's veto (in May, 1830) of a bill providing for a subscription by the National Government to stock in a road from Maysville, Kentucky, on the Ohio River, to Lexington, in the same state. By this act the President seemed to announce his opposition to Federal improvements. The President asserted that the project was essentially a local one, not properly an object for national assistance, but others maintained that the mail of six states would have been carried over the road. The road was of particular interest to Ohioans because it would connect at a point opposite Maysville with Zane's Trace, the first continuous road through Ohio, running from Wheeling in a southwesterly direction *via* Lancaster and Chillicothe.[5]

Ohioans, moreover, for many years had been staunch upholders of the idea of "the American System" (a protective tariff the receipts from which were used to finance internal improvements). This had been well illustrated in 1827, when each party had attempted through its Representatives in Congress to secure a liberal grant to Ohio in the form of public lands to aid the state in its canal project. Apparently, at that time, the Jacksonian Members presented their bill first, but John Woods, an administration Member from Ohio who was on the committee on

---

[5] In 1796, Congress had authorized the improvement of this road, and two years later teams began to use it.

roads and canals, was in a position to report first the administration measure that granted half a million acres of land to the state. The passage of the bill, of course, would have made a similar bill sponsored by the Jacksonians wholly out of the question. In the Senate, however, the Jackson men had their bill incorporated as an amendment to the original one, and in that form it became law, Ohio receiving a double grant of public lands and each party claiming the responsibility for this benefit to the state.

On the Maysville Road Bill each Senator and each Representative from Ohio had voted in the affirmative, hence grave concern attended the President's veto of that project. In the fall of 1830, indeed, the Jacksonians suffered a distinct setback in the state, due probably in part to this veto but also to unfortunate appointments and the usual reaction that confronts a new President in mid-administration elections. One of the Ohio Jacksonians felt moved to write: "It has turned out worse than we feared, and we are completely foiled at every point of the compass." Their opponents had secured the election as governor of Duncan McArthur, a former Congressman, soldier, and land speculator of Ross County, by a very narrow margin over Robert Lucas, of Pike County, had carried the legislature,[6] and had elected eight out of fourteen Congressmen.

This reaction created consternation among politicians in other parts. "O recreant Ohio," exclaimed a leader in northern New York, while Thomas Ritchie, the renowned Virginia editor, wrote to Van Buren, "The apparent backsliding of Ohio ought to be explained if it admit of any. It does not look well."

That the Maysville veto did not do more permanent harm to Jacksonian interests in the state may have been

---

[6] This result secured the election of a new anti-Jackson senator, Thomas Ewing, in the seat of Jacob Burnet, who did not seek reëlection.

attributable not only to the essential strength of the party organization, but also to the fact that the public demand for internal improvements was passing its crest. Ohio, as we have seen, on her own account, and at heavy expense, was constructing a system of canals between the Great Lakes and the Ohio River, hence she was not so keenly interested as formerly in appropriations by the Federal Government.

The enthusiasm aroused by the building of canals from Cincinnati to Dayton and from Portsmouth to Cleveland led to legislation for the extension of the former to the junction of the Auglaize and Maumee Rivers (Defiance) in 1831. This project (completed in 1845) was supplemented by the building of the Wabash and Erie Canal, authorized in 1834 in coöperation with the state of Indiana for the linking of Lake Erie with the Wabash River, and finished in 1842. Branch canals were also built to a considerable extent, and by 1847 the state waterway system was virtually complete. Seldom does one find a more compelling example of the transitory value of the fulfilment of many of man's most cherished dreams. Almost at once the advent of the devastating competition of the railroads became evident. By 1835 work had reached completion on the first thirty-five miles of the Mad River and Lake Erie Railroad; within a few years this line (from Springfield to Sandusky) and the Pennsylvania and Ohio (from Pittsburgh to Massillon) had been opened for service; and by 1851 the Cleveland, Columbus and Cincinnati Railroad was ready for operation.[7] The canals, of course, contributed much to the development of the state,

---

[7] In 1852, the Cleveland and Pittsburgh line was opened. In the same year, the Michigan Central and Michigan Southern lines were put in operation; and in 1853, the connecting link between Cleveland and Toledo being completed, through railroad service between Chicago and the Eastern seacoast was available.

and the tonnage carried increased annually until just preceding the outbreak of the Civil War. In 1856, however, the revenues fell below the cost of operation, and the subsequent history of Ohio's canals is one of an increasingly futile struggle against superior competition.

Anti-Masonic Complications

One of the strange products of the interplay of political forces in the United States in the years around 1830 was the Anti-Masonic Party. The intense democracy of the frontier areas reacted strongly against the secrecy of fraternal orders, and in 1826 a certain William Morgan, of Batavia, New York, indicated an intention of revealing the esoteric secrets of Freemasonry. Members of this lodge became concerned, and as early as September, 1826, a newspaper on the Western Reserve (at Ravenna) cautioned the Masonic fraternity of the state against the man "calling himself Captain Morgan." After the unexplained disappearance of this individual, supposedly done away with by Masons, heated opposition to Masonry and secret orders arose in New York State and spread into Ohio. One editor early in 1827 protested against the censuring of a whole organization for the alleged outrageous acts of a few of its members, while another complained that between the prejudices of the Masons and the Anti-Masons he could scarcely pursue a policy that would satisfy his subscribers.

The Western Reserve area, peopled largely by New Englanders, and geographically connected with the Anti-Masonic areas of Pennsylvania and New York, was at all times the stronghold of the movement in the state. Although several years passed before the movement reached its height in Ohio, newspapers championing the cause were founded, and county organizations were begun.

By the summer of 1830, a state convention of thirty delegates met at Canton, and the movement seriously concerned
the National Republican[8] leaders, as it drew votes principally from their party. In the fall of that year, in
Ashtabula, Geauga, and Portage Counties, the Anti-
Masons entrenched themselves in the county offices.
They also carried fifteen seats in the legislature, but the
nature of their principles was such as to make them on state
issues practically indistinguishable from the National
Republican members.

For some time, John McLean, of Ohio, had been developing Presidential ambitions, which had probably affected
his attitude as Postmaster General under Adams. Subsequently, he hoped that if Jackson were not a candidate for
reëlection in 1832, he might be nominated for the Presidency.
In 1830 he was asked concerning his opinions by the
Pennsylvania and Ohio Anti-Masons and replied that, since
he was not acquainted with the principles of Masonry, he
could "neither approve nor condemn them." Delegates
from Ohio attended the national convention of the party
in Baltimore in September, 1831 (the first of its kind in the
United States), and one of their number maintained that
McLean would have been nominated if his letter of declina-
tion had not been received during the sessions. But
McLean had no enthusiasm for a hopeless cause and
fully understood that he could not successfully oppose
Clay and Jackson.

The National Republicans wished to combine their
forces with the Anti-Masonic element in the state elections
of 1832. Governor McArthur, who was a Mason, promised
that he would renounce any claim to reëlection if a candidate who was neither a Mason nor an Anti-Mason could be

---

[8] This party was then taking form and was composed largely of those who
had supported J. Q. Adams's administration.

mutually agreed upon. The enthusiastic Anti-Masons
refused to acquiesce, however, in such a proposal. Their

(*County lines are shown as in 1832.*)

Presidential Election of 1832

Democratic............................ Jackson 81,246
National Republican.................... Clay...... 76,538
Anti-Masonic........................ Wirt......... 509

state convention at Columbus in June, 1832, offered the
nomination to two men who refused to split the opposition
to Jackson, but Darius Lyman, of Portage County, a

member of the state senate, accepted it.   The spirit of the
party was indicated by a report to the convention, which
said in part:

> We oppose Freemasonry, because it is immoral, in
> that it imposes upon its members horrid oaths, the
> taking of which is a violation of the laws of God and
> man and the obeying of which leads to the commission
> of perjury and murder. . . . We oppose it politically.
> It has seated itself in our political institutions, and not
> only claims the right, but exercises a power directly at
> variance with the laws of the land, sapping the very life's
> blood of our republican institutions.

Persons on the electoral ticket were to agree to vote for
William Wirt, the national nominee of the party, or to
resign their places.

The National Republicans in Ohio continued to be
conciliatory, and as late as June had made no nomination
for the governorship.   McArthur, however, was endorsed
by a meeting held during the sessions of the Federal court
in July, though he later indicated his willingness to retire
from the contest in favor of Lyman, if the Anti-Masons
would join in supporting an unpledged electoral ticket—
to vote for either Clay, the National Republican nominee
for President, or Wirt, as circumstances might direct.
McArthur was willing to sacrifice the possibility of success
in the contest for the governorship in order to help the
national prospects of the party.

Some headway was made in regard to an arrangement by
which both McArthur and Lyman would withdraw and a
candidate acceptable to all anti-Jacksonians would be
presented.   McArthur actually withdrew from the race in
September, against the wishes of many of his friends, but
by that time it was too late to offer a new nomination.
The National Republicans then had no choice but to

support Lyman, who was defeated by the Democratic candidate, Robert Lucas, by a vote of 71,251 to 63,185. It was under these conditions that the first Jacksonian Democrat entered upon the office of governor of Ohio.[9]

Dissension now developed among the Anti-Masons as to the advisability of supporting the unpledged ticket, or of supporting the strictly Anti-Masonic one, in the approaching Presidential election. As matters turned out, Jackson carried in Ohio practically the same counties that he carried in 1828, polling 81,246 votes in contrast to 76,538 polled for the unpledged ticket. Only 509 ballots were cast for the Anti-Masons, who continued their state conventions for a number of years although with scant enthusiasm.

The Tariff, Nullification, and Banking

During the following winter (1832–1833), the paramount question that concerned the country was the attempted nullification of the Tariff of 1832 by South Carolina. For this movement practically no sympathy existed in Ohio. When the Tariff of 1832 had been enacted, every Senator and every Representative from Ohio had favored its passage. Hence, an attempted repudiation of the law aroused not only a virile nationalistic sentiment, but also a concern for what was considered a fundamental economic interest of the state. Ohio Democrats and National Republicans accordingly rushed forward in a united front against South Carolina's position, the Ohio senate condemning her attitude in resolutions that were passed without debate and approved by the house of representatives without a dissenting vote.

---

[9] The Jacksonians also secured control of the legislature, which chose Thomas Morris, of Brown County, Senator.

As to the proper solution for Southern grievances, no such concerted opinion was found in the state. When Clay in 1833 proposed his well-known compromise tariff, which provided for gradual reductions in the import duties until 1842, party lines were disregarded by the Ohio delegation in Congress, as Senator Ewing and seven Members of the House voted in favor of the bill while six Congressmen and Senator Ruggles voted in the negative.[10] When the Force Bill was passed, giving the president enlarged powers in compelling obedience to national law, only one Ohio Congressman voted against the proposition. Yet the people of the state were undoubtedly pleased that compromise had been the solution of the immediate difficulty.

In the Presidential campaign of 1832, the result of which in Ohio has already been discussed, the question of the rechartering of the Bank of the United States was a primary one. In the summer, when the bill for a renewal of the life of the institution was before Congress, both Ohio Senators and ten of the fourteen Ohio Representatives voted in its favor, yet the prevailing sentiment in the state seemed to be that the President would surely veto the proposition. Subsequently, upon such action being taken by Jackson, the Democratic press in the state hailed his message as "a second declaration of independence" and as a triumph over "monopolies created for the benefit of foreigners and wielded by their influence."

The defeat of the bill, however, brought the banking question to the front in state political circles in 1833. During the previous eight years, the legislature had paid little attention to such considerations. In 1825 an act had been passed requiring all banks in Ohio to pay to the state four per cent on the future dividends earned by them,

---

[10] One Congressman, Joseph Vance, was absent.

but no further change was made in the state banking laws
until 1831, when this tax was raised to five per cent.
Between 1826 and 1832, the Ohio banks whose notes
circulated throughout the state had increased in number
from ten to sixteen, yet many felt that the banking facilities
of the state were still inadequate.   During the legislative
session of 1832–1833, much discussion developed in regard
to a State Bank as a substitute for the multiplication of
local banks.   Three different plans for such an institution
were presented, but a multitude of criticisms was forthcoming as those interested in the creation of additional
local banks registered their opposition.   In the end, none
of the plans was accepted by the legislature.   The capital-
ization of one of the Cincinnati banks, however, was
doubled and a new bank was chartered, supposedly to
meet the needs of business there in view of the gradual
curtailment of facilities offered by the Bank of the United
States.

The policy of the United States Bank in liquidating its
assets, looking forward to the probable close of its career in
1836, together with the removal of Government deposits
from the bank by Jackson's order, seriously affected the
financial situation in the vicinity of Cincinnati.   Numerous
local meetings were held in the state to consider the problem.
One at Cincinnati in February, 1834, adopted resolutions
signed by over forty-three hundred persons and recommending the continuance of the United States Bank with such
modifications "as experience has proved necessary."

Meanwhile Ohioans were writing to Washington com-
plaining of economic conditions.   One resident of Steubenville bewailed the fact that wheat had dropped from
seventy-five cents to thirty-seven and a half cents a bushel
in a few months, and that the financial attitude of the administration was apparently responsible.   A traveller wrote to

Vice President Van Buren that he had visited the leading cities from Baltimore westward and had found that the commercial despondency was greatest at Cincinnati. Even ardent friends of Jackson admitted that some of their number were falling away and that many steadfast followers of Jackson in Cincinnati felt that the bank was necessary to commercial prosperity.   Outside of Cincinnati the President's policies were more popular: in January, 1834, both houses of the Ohio Legislature adopted resolutions instructing the Congressmen and requesting the Senators of the state to use their influence against the rechartering of the bank and in sustaining the removal of public deposits.

Governor Lucas in his annual message of 1833 suggested that the completion of a large part of the state's canal system had meant the withdrawal from circulation of funds expended for that purpose and urged the creation of a State Bank as a corrective measure.   In the legislature, however, the friends of local banks and those hoping for . charters for new institutions once again used their influence against the proposition, as did supporters of the United States Bank.   The result was the creation of ten new local banks, the revival of two banks that had ceased to do business, and the failure of the proposal for a State Bank.

The largest of these new institutions was the Ohio Life Insurance and Trust Company of Cincinnati, capitalized at two million dollars, one half of which was for banking purposes.   This company became one of the most powerful organizations of its kind in the country and tended to arouse tremendous opposition among those Democrats who were unfavorable to vested privileges of any kind. Efforts were made, accordingly, early in 1836, to induce the legislature to repeal the charter of the corporation, but four prominent Democrats were members of its board of directors, and the friends of the institution were able to secure the postponement of action in the matter.

The Locofoco, or anti-bank, faction of the Democratic Party, however, in general exhibited a controlling strength in the state, and during the legislative sessions of 1834–1835 and 1835–1836 only one new bank was incorporated, the Bank of Manhattan—in the newly established village of Toledo. The same group expressed serious objection to the large amount of paper notes of lower denominations than five dollars issued by the banks and which, circulating in excessive quantities, tended to drive specie from the channels of trade. The result was the passage by the legislature in March, 1836, of an act taxing the banks of the state twenty per cent (instead of five per cent as provided by the act of 1831) unless they should surrender their rights to issue or circulate bills of less than five dollars after July 4, 1837.

A somewhat different financial problem presented itself to the next session of the legislature. The payment of the national debt of the country and the accumulation of a surplus in the Federal Treasury largely from tariff proceeds and from the sale of public lands had led to the passage by Congress of the Deposit Act of 1836, by which all of the Federal surplus above five million dollars was to be distributed among the states in proportion to their representation in the electoral college. Naturally various proposals were made in regard to Ohio's share, which was estimated at approximately $2,676,000. Turnpikes, canals, and common schools were mentioned as proper outlets for the fund, while plans for its application to the payment of the state debt, for its division among the various counties, and for the establishment of a State Bank also had their champions.

"Individual cupidity" was at work in the urging of
schemes favorable to individual and other special interests,
and the resulting legislation was somewhat of a compromise. Ohio's share of the Federal surplus was to be
distributed to the counties in proportion to their adult population, with the various county commissioners acting as
boards of fund commissioners for the control of the county
quotas. The money might be loaned by them to companies incorporated for internal improvement purposes,
to the state, or to individuals. Interest was to be paid
upon the loans and was to be used chiefly for the encouragement of common schools within the county. It was
planned that the principal of the loans should be returned
to the state by 1850, for a means of paying the canal debt,
and although some counties were slow in their repayments,
the last obligation on this account was paid in 1875.

The Boundary Dispute with Michigan

A matter of considerable interest to the people of the
Old Northwest during Jackson's second administration
was the disputed Ohio-Michigan boundary. Deeply rooted
in the misunderstandings of previous decades, the controversy may be studied in its beginnings by a reference to
the Ordinance of 1787 and the actions of the Ohio constitutional convention of 1802. The ordinance described
the boundary between the upper and lower tiers of the
prospective states of the Northwest as "an east and west
line drawn through the southerly bend or extreme of
Lake Michigan"—a specification that was recognized both
in the Ohio Enabling Act of 1802 and the act for the organization of Michigan Territory in 1805. A Frenchman,
Guillaume De l'Isle, and later two British map makers,
Lewis Evans and John Mitchell, however, had produced

maps that contributed to the general belief of this period that a parallel drawn eastward from the southern extremity of Lake Michigan would strike Lake Erie at a point somewhat north of Maumee Bay; and doubtless the Congresses that approved of the above-mentioned acts were of the belief that the boundary of Ohio would strike the lake as these map makers had indicated.

When the Ohio constitutional convention of 1802 was in session, an old beaver trapper appeared and informed the delegates that the southern tip of Lake Michigan lay much farther south than they supposed or the maps indicated. Hence the constitution of Ohio embodied the boundaries mentioned in the Enabling Act but with the following proviso: "If the southerly bend or extreme of Lake Michigan should extend so far south that a line drawn due east from it should not intersect Lake Erie or if it should intersect the said Lake Erie east of the mouth of the Miami river of the Lakes [the Maumee] then . . . . with the assent of Congress of the United States, the northern boundary of the state shall be established by, and extended to, a direct line from the southern extremity of Lake Michigan to the most northerly cape of the Miami bay." Congress neither accepted nor rejected this proviso; but the discussion of the matter continued. Later, in 1817, the boundary was surveyed, such procedure having been directed by an act of Congress in 1812, but the Surveyor-General of Ohio directed Mr. Harris, who was to run the line, to do so according to the proviso of the Ohio constitution—an order that aroused so much protest from Michigan that the boundary was marked by another surveyor named Fulton.

In 1831, Michigan Territory in vain sought a compromise settlement, and by 1833 the contest had begun in earnest. Michigan, through her legislative council, gave notice that she would meet any efforts "to rob her of her soil." Nevertheless she proposed negotiations as a means of settlement, but Governor Robert Lucas, who had been reëlected in 1834, in a special message to the Ohio Legislature during February, 1835, disdainfully rejected the proposal. He suggested that all counties bordering on the northern boundary of Ohio should extend to a line drawn from the southern end of Lake Michigan "to the most northern cape of Maumee Bay," and that township organization be extended accordingly. The legislature complied by calling for the re-marking of the northern line to which jurisdiction was to be extended. Michigan authorities took steps to prevent this, whereupon President Jackson wrote to both Acting Governor Mason of Michigan and Governor Lucas of Ohio, stating that he had asked the opinion of the United States Attorney General and expressing a hope that the contestants would restrain themselves until Federal authorities could render a decision. Richard Rush and Benjamin C. Howard were then dispatched by Jackson as peacemakers.

The boundary commission began its work, but while proceeding eastward from the northwest corner of Ohio along the Harris line, nine of the party were seized by Michigan men and taken to Tecumseh, in Michigan Territory. All but one were admitted to bail or discharged, but accounts of the incident were exaggerated in Ohio, and Governor Lucas issued a proclamation to convene the legislature in special session on June 8. Rush and Howard proposed that Ohio should be allowed peacefully to run the line and that the people should submit to the legal processes of either government until the whole matter could be settled by the Federal judiciary. Lucas expressed a willingness to accept these proposals, but Mason, opposed to the idea of joint occupation, refused.

The Ohio Legislature appropriated three hundred thousand dollars to extend Ohio's jurisdiction and to re-mark the boundary line. To prevent the "abduction" of Ohio citizens, imprisonment from three to seven years was prescribed as the penalty for such an offense. As a tribute to the Governor, the county of Lucas was erected, largely in the disputed territory.

The act providing for the organization of Lucas County had specified that common pleas court should be held in Toledo on September 7. Both Ohio and Michigan troops by the preceding day had been quartered on opposite sides of the Maumee to aid respectively in carrying out and in frustrating this plan. The Ohio judges and officers of the court, in the quiet of the night, stole into the sleeping village of Toledo, and by three o'clock the court had been organized and adjourned and an official record made in hurried fashion by the glare of a tallow dip. The officials then repaired to a neighboring tavern, duly registered, and were preparing to drink a toast to the occasion, when someone startled them by stating that Michigan troops were near at hand. Very precipitously the group rode away, though actually the Michigan men did not know of the occurrence for four days. Ohioans considered that they had won a moral victory, for Ohio's jurisdiction had been asserted in the disputed area.

Jackson informed Lucas that if a crisis arose, he would maintain the laws at all hazards, and that he relied on Attorney General Butler's opinion that the law of the United States provided for the boundary as claimed by Michigan, until the other had been declared to be such by Congress.

Ohio's good will, however, was not to be cast carelessly aside, especially in the year previous to a doubtful Presidential election. In the summer, Lucas had determined to send three mutual friends of himself and Jackson to Washington to confer with the President. One of these, William Allen, of Chillicothe, wrote to Van Buren about the party's prospects in the state: "I need not, therefore, suggest to you the necessity of your counsels and influence at Washington. The truth is the President must agree to the proposed terms or all is lost with his friends in this state, beside the more important consequences to the general welfare of the State and the Union." The electoral votes of Indiana and Illinois were also involved, as the northern boundaries of those states were likewise concerned.'

Although the President had to enforce the laws of a territory, still he could replace an officer who insisted on doing so, and Jackson proceeded to do that by removing Acting Governor Mason. John S. Horner, of Virginia, was appointed in Mason's stead, and the "Toledo War" was over. Ohio ceased to attempt to exercise authority beyond her old boundaries and proceeded unmolested to re-mark the line that she desired. Civil processes were dropped, and Michigan remained in unquestioned possession of the tract.

The question was then transferred to the halls of Congress, and in June, 1836, a law was passed to provide for the admission of the state of Michigan with the boundaries desired by Ohio but with a grant of nine thousand square miles to Michigan (the western part of the Upper Peninsula). J. Q. Adams felt that this was "one of the most remarkable examples of the usurpation of power and perpetration of wrong by Congress that has occurred since the Government of the United States has existed," all due to the fact that "there were twenty-nine members of the House from the states of Ohio, Indiana, and Illinois, all interested against the rights of Michigan; and . . . thirty-five Electoral votes from those states to be lost to any candidate for the Presidency or Vice Presidency at the then approaching Presidential election."

Ohio secured an area eleven miles wide at the eastern terminus and seven miles wide at the western end, amounting to four hundred square miles or about one third of the area of Rhode Island. The commercial interests of Toledo were particularly happy at the outcome. Plans were developing for the Wabash and Erie Canal, and persons interested in the future of Toledo hoped that it would be the terminus of the waterway. Of the approximate five hundred inhabitants of the town, only four were said to be opposed to adherence to Ohio.

The Presidential Contest of 1836

Even before Jackson's second inauguration, the followers of Supreme Court Justice John McLean were looking forward to a possibility of his nomination in 1836. Sentiment in his favor began to manifest itself, and by December, 1833, meetings were being held to advocate his candidacy. The first test of McLean's strength, however, came in the fall of 1834. General James Findlay, of Cincinnati, who had been a member of the legislative council of the Northwest Territory, had served in the War of 1812, and was an Ohio Congressman from 1825 to 1833, was urged to assume the leadership of the movement by running for the governorship. Findlay had formerly been a Jacksonian, and it was felt that he might well secure the support of the disgruntled Jackson men and of the old National Republicans, who were the leading elements in the new Whig Party. Some of the old National Republicans felt no enthusiasm for Findlay in view of his former affiliations, and suggested the name of Joseph Vance, of Champaign County, a prominent Congressman; but in August the latter withdrew from the race, which then rested between Findlay and Governor Lucas, the Democratic nominee. Enthusiastic Whig support for Findlay failed to materialize, and in the fall election, unable even to carry his home county of Hamilton, he ran behind the rest of the Whig ticket. Lucas's majority of approximately eight thousand votes in 1832, however, was cut down to about four thousand, and the Jacksonian majority of twenty-four members in the legislature gave way to a Whig advantage of fourteen members.

The defeat of Findlay was a severe blow to the McLean movement. One prominent Ohioan had previously written him: "Everything is going right for you and if Findlay is elected we will of course claim the state for McLean."

In spite of this distinct setback to the hopes of the Justice's friends, the control of the legislature and of the Ohio delegation in Congress by those opposed to Jackson served to stimulate the McLean leaders to further activity. Their attention was thereupon directed to the legislature, where it was expected that a nomination of McLean might be made.

In December, 1834, the Justice himself came to Columbus to use his influence, and for a time he seemed to contemplate the advisability of resigning from the Supreme Court to further his plans. It was expected also that action by members of the Ohio Legislature would result in similar nominations in other states. At length, fifty signatures from among the one hundred and eight members of the two houses were obtained to a paper endorsing McLean's candidacy. The approval of a majority of the legislators, however, could not be secured; the editor of the Columbus *Ohio State Journal*, a friend of Clay, used his potent influence against McLean's pretensions; and by

August, 1835, the prospective candidate penned a letter definitely withdrawing from the contest.

Besides McLean and Clay, who for a time had nursed their hopes for a Whig Presidential nomination in 1836, Daniel Webster, who made a visit to Ohio in 1833, was favored by some for the high office, and faint manifestations in the state were noticed in favor of Hugh L. White, of Tennessee.[11] Early in 1835, however, the name of William Henry Harrison was presented by a local meeting in his home county of Hamilton; by the end of the year considerable sentiment had developed in his favor; and in February, 1836, a huge Whig state convention at Columbus placed him in nomination.

In the meantime, Democrats from Ohio had assisted in the success of Van Buren at the national convention of the party at Baltimore in May, 1835. One well-known Democrat asserted that the "Ohio candidate" of the Whigs would "have his run of six months and then run down like an old wooden clock." Van Buren, however, did not muster the enthusiasm that had been extended to Jackson, and Harrison carried the state by a majority of almost eighty-five hundred votes, though Van Buren was the victor in the nation at large.

The Whigs in the state contest had presented for the governorship Joseph Vance, of Champaign County, who had previously been a member of the legislature and for seven terms (from 1821 to 1835) a Congressman, and he was elected by a majority of about six thousand votes over Eli Baldwin, of Trumbull County.[12] Later, Vance was to

---

[11] Both Webster and White, of course, became Whig candidates for the Presidency in their own sections of the country.

[12] At the same time, the Democrats continued in control of the legislature. The Whigs claimed with some justification that this result had been secured by a reapportionment act of the previous legislature. At any rate, the youthful William Allen, a Democrat, was now chosen to succeed Thomas Ewing in the United States Senate.

serve in the state senate, again in Congress (from 1843 to 1847), and in the constitutional convention of 1850.

SELECTED BIBLIOGRAPHY

Randall and Ryan, Galbreath, and King devote attention to the happenings of this period. Special articles are Eugene H. Roseboom, "Ohio in the Presidential Election of 1824," *Ohio Archæological and Historical Quarterly*, Vol. XXVI, pp. 157–223; Francis P. Weisenburger, "John McLean, Postmaster-General," *Mississippi Valley Historical Review*, Vol. XVIII, pp. 23–33; H. J. Webster, "History of the Democratic Party Organization," *Ohio Archæological and Historical Quarterly*, Vol. XXIV, pp. 1–39 and 43–54. Some light upon political conditions in Ohio is given in E. M. Carroll, *Origins of the Whig Party* (Durham, N. C., 1925).

Among the useful biographies are John C. Parish, *Robert Lucas* (Iowa City, 1907); R. C. McGrane, *William Allen, a Study in Western Democracy* (Columbus, 1925), pp. 1–56; Mrs. Dorothy B. Goebel, *William Henry Harrison, a Political Biography* (Indianapolis, 1926); Allen Trimble, *Autobiography and Correspondence* (Columbus, 1909), also in *Old Northwest Genealogical Quarterly*, Vols. IX, X, and XI; and Mrs. Elizabeth W. Perry, "Micajah T. Williams," *Ibid.*, Vol. I, pp. 1–15.

A scholarly monograph on the Anti-Masonic controversy is Charles McCarthy, "The Anti-Masonic Party, a Study of Political Anti-Masonry in the United States," *Annual Report of the American Historical Association, 1902*, Vol. I. Also suggestive is W. M. Cunningham, *History of Freemasonry in Ohio from 1791* (Cincinnati, 1909).

The contributions of Annah M. Soule and A. M. Schlesinger in *The Ohio-Michigan Boundary* (Mansfield, Ohio, 1916) are helpful in an understanding of the boundary controversy with Michigan. In this connection, Lawton T. Hemans, *Life and Times of Stevens Thomson Mason, the Boy Governor of Michigan* (Lansing, 1920), is significant.

C. C. Huntington, *History of Banking and Currency in Ohio before the Civil War*, and the references for the Ohio canals, which were cited in the previous chapter, are also of value. The early history of railroads in Ohio is summarized in *History of*

Transportation in the United States before 1860 (B. H. Meyer, ed., Washington, 1917), pp. 488–502.

A large part of the material for this chapter has been secured from an unpublished doctoral dissertation by F. P. Weisenburger, *Ohio Politics during the Jacksonian Period* (University of Michigan, 1929).

CHAPTER VIII

THE PASSING OF PIONEER LIFE IN OHIO

The State and its People

*B*Y 1820, immigrants had located in considerable numbers in every portion of Ohio except the northwestern
part. In that area, east of the Maumee River, was the
"Black Swamp," covering territory about one hundred and
twenty miles long and twenty miles wide, through which
"there was no road, except a mere trail through the woods."
Level, wet, and unhealthy, this district experienced no
general transformation during the following decade, when
thousands of immigrants moved into Indiana, Illinois, and
southern Michigan. The agues and fevers prevalent in
this section repelled the prospective settler, and in 1830
a pioneer judge journeyed westward from Findlay "through
an unsettled wilderness of some sixty miles" whose loneli-
ness was broken only by the intervening Indian settlement
at "Ottawa Village." The whole extreme northwestern
corner of the state (Hancock County and the region to the
north and west) had, by the census of 1830, a population
of only three thousand persons, with several of the counties
as yet unorganized.

The first few settlers in this area had come from New
York and New England, but those arriving immediately
after 1830 were in large part from Pennsylvania and southern Ohio. Foreign-born settlers had already begun to
come to the northwestern region, Germans from Frederick,
Maryland, having settled in the twenties at Tiffin and on
the Sandusky River in Seneca County. By 1832, the possi-

bilities of a town at the mouth of the Maumee (the present site of Toledo), where an unsuccessful effort had been made at a similar project in 1816, were being exploited, and within three or four years the whole valley was "alive with city-builders." Their hopes, however, were soon to be smashed by the effects of Jackson's Specie Circular, which helped to precipitate the Panic of 1837, resulting in the suspension of speculative activities for many years. Such a tardy development, however, was characteristic of no other large section of the state, and the rapid settling of the other parts was indicated by an increase of the population of Ohio to 581,434 in 1820 and to 937,903 in 1830, Ohio at the latter date having more people than Connecticut and Massachusetts combined.

East of the northwestern section and actually extending more than halfway across the state (120 miles) from the western border of Pennsylvania was the Western Reserve, with a population predominantly of New England origin but also embracing settlers from Pennsylvania and New York. Cleveland, destined to be the metropolis of the area and of the state, was in 1830 a struggling village of barely a thousand inhabitants, much less than half as large as either Columbus or Dayton. The opening of the Ohio Canal, connecting the lake with the interior and with the Ohio River, was a distinct boon to the city. The primitive log courthouse there had been displaced by a new one in 1828, and business on the lake developed in rapid fashion. Soon the increasing prosperity was evidenced by a new gray sandstone church upon the Public Square, and travelers noted that the place was "full of life, trade, and business." By 1840, the city, with six thousand inhabitants, was slightly larger than Columbus or Dayton.

Immediately south of the Reserve and northeast from the central portion of the state were the inland counties known as the "Backbone Region," so-called because these counties help to form the watershed of the state. Peopled largely by Pennsylvania Germans, who had begun to enter the area at the outset of the nineteenth century, towns such as Massillon, Alliance, and Canton, the last-mentioned in 1830 a thriving place of fifteen hundred people, had come to be important centers of trade. East of this district, on the Ohio River, the traveler reached Steubenville, founded by Germans about the beginning of the century and named in honor of the Revolutionary general. Situated on an elevation, in 1830 the town still contained many forest trees, although it was the third city of the state in population and the seat of several promising industries. Mount Pleasant, not many miles away, was also a leading manufacturing center of the West. In this vicinity the population was similar to that of western Pennsylvania and the Virginia Panhandle. Here were numbers of Scotch-Irish— light-hearted, democratic, whiskey-loving people, many of whom were of the second or third generation in America, their fathers having originally settled in Virginia, western Maryland, or western Pennsylvania.

About fifty miles to the west one came to the Muskingum River, then considered navigable for about one hundred miles from its mouth (to the present site of Coshocton). In this valley, Zanesville—then the second largest city in the state—was a most important manufacturing center, specializing particularly in window glass and bottles.

At the mouth of the Muskingum was Marietta, settled largely by New Englanders and in 1830 slightly larger than Cleveland. Yet, to travelers it had presented "a deserted aspect" and seemed to be "rapidly declining" in importance, its population possessing "little energy and less property, to add beauty and grandeur to the place."

Farther down the Ohio River from Marietta was Portsmouth, then a town of "low houses and broad, unpaved streets," the outlet of the fertile Scioto Valley to the north, where Chillicothe, Circleville, and Columbus were centers of local trade. As late as 1840, the roads in this vicinity were extremely poor, even the stage road between Columbus and Portsmouth being "actually impassable" in very rainy weather. In such cases, the Canal became the trusted means of transportation, though passengers were not always certain of a reliable time schedule. Travelers through this part of Ohio found taverns, with varying degrees of accommodation, available at intervals of only a few miles. Perhaps only a couple of beds would comprise the furnishings of a room set aside for travelers on the second floor, where the use of water was prohibited lest damage might result to the furniture below. In such cases a tub by the pump in the yard was available for the morning shave.

West of the Scioto and extending to the Little Miami River was the Virginia Military Tract. Nearly level in many places and covered with high grass or spacious forests in pioneer days, much of the region fell into the hands of speculators in land. At the eastern edge of this region, Chillicothe, peopled largely by Virginians and Kentuckians, boasted of almost three thousand inhabitants (in 1830), though for more than a decade the westward pull of population had caused some of its homes to be deserted for attractions in more remote regions. Here a market was held on each Wednesday and Saturday, and several cotton-spinning factories and a large steam flour mill added to the economic life. The leading hotels, Watson's and Madeira's, were frequent stopping places for pioneer travelers, and while the former sometimes left much to be desired in the way of cleanliness and courtesy, the accommodations of the latter were reported to be pleasant and the hospitality of the proprietor to be more acceptable because of his broad culture and extensive information.

Farther to the north and east, Lancaster, named from the Pennsylvania city, had already attained the dignity of three weekly newspapers. Settled originally by Pennsylvania Dutch, joined by Wurtembergers and some Swiss, one of its newspapers was printed in German, and, as at some other places in the state, German translations were affixed in large gold letters to all signs over the stores.

At the junction of the Olentangy (or Whetstone), the town of Columbus had experienced scant success in its early efforts at manufacturing, but a lively trade featured the economic life of the place. A traveler noted that its streets were "kept in a state of constant and lively animation by an endless train of wagons, horses and horsemen,— long-springed, four-horse stages rattling through at intervals—and a great variety of travelling and pleasure taking vehicles." Here, at the state capital, were several state institutions, including the state penitentiary, with 142 inmates in 1826; but the public buildings were "nothing remarkable," and the statehouse, the state office building, and the Federal courthouse (on the present Capitol Square) occupied only about one tenth of the ten acres set aside for that purpose, so that the remaining area served as a pasture for cattle.

Westward from Columbus, one might travel along the route that was later to mark the path of the National Road, but in the late twenties the thoroughfare was extremely poor, "generally of log causeways" which were badly assorted and had large holes in them.

In the rural districts of southern Ohio, farmhouses were often log structures, "miserable holes, having one room only," and some of the towns were built largely of wood, though in places like Springfield, brick was decidedly predominant. Here, as elsewhere, in the winter season especially, agues, chills, and fevers were common and the death rate correspondingly high.

In the southwestern part of the state one reached the Miami Valleys, where there were numerous orchards and where one traveler of a century ago found cultivation more highly developed than in any other part of the country he had visited. In the northern part of this district was Dayton, in 1830 a town of twenty-nine hundred inhabitants with several saw mills, grist mills, and cotton factories and the northern terminus of the Miami Canal. Cincinnati, of course, was "the largest and the handsomest town" of the entire state, "the Queen City of the West." By 1826 it had attained a population of sixteen thousand, and, with twenty-five thousand in 1830, it was the largest city in the West with the exception of New Orleans, and the seventh largest in the entire country. It boasted of four market houses, ten newspapers (two of them dailies), a college and a medical school, ten foundries, three boat yards, and several plants for the manufacture of flour, liquors, and cotton and woolen goods. Meat packing was so important as to give the city at that time the sobriquet, Porkopolis. Here also had been established a branch of the Second Bank of the United States, which had suspended operations after the financial stringency subsequent to 1818–1819, but which had been reopened in 1825. The houses were generally three stories in height and of brick, though the more pretentious places were of hewn stone. Some of the churches were show places of the town, and the leading hotel had the appearance of a royal residence.

Yet even Cincinnati was not far removed from pioneer days. Of several thousand persons listed in the city directory of 1825, over twenty per cent were natives of Pennsylvania, with New Jersey, New York, England, Massachusetts, Ireland, Maryland, Connecticut, and Virginia ranking in the order named as places of nativity of the inhabitants. Ohio as yet was relatively unimportant as a birthplace of the city's adult population, and the German element, later to be extremely important in the development of the place, in 1830 was just beginning to establish itself in appreciable numbers.

In 1830, only about five per cent of the population of Cincinnati was of German origin, but a rapid increase was soon to be noted. A traveler of this nationality noted the presence of about ten thousand of his countrymen in the city in 1834. His native language he found spoken everywhere, and peasants from the homeland were continually arriving. By 1840, the Germans comprised twenty-three per cent of the population of the city. With the increase in the number of persons of foreign birth, among whom some soon squandered such savings as they had brought with them, the older elements in the state began to manifest concern. Talk arose of the necessity for limiting "the swarms of indigent foreigners whom the selfish policy of sundry European governments is vomiting upon our shores, and who, from their ignorance, vicious habits, and former associations, are better calculated to swell the numbers, or increase the violence of a mob, or to assist an ambitious and unprincipled demagogue in overturning the liberties of the country, than to discharge with soberness and discretion the duties of American citizens." Yet, the "Forty-Eighters," who had left the Fatherland disappointed by the failure to attain German national unity on a democratic basis, came to Cincinnati in considerable numbers, and through their critical intelligence and artistic sensibilities, contributed immeasurably to the intellectual and cultural life of the city.

The coming of the foreigners occurred at a time when the native American Indian was rapidly disappearing from Ohio's borders. By treaties made at Greenville (in 1795), Fort Industry (in 1805), Detroit (in 1807), and at the rapids of the Maumee (in 1817), the tribes were practically stripped of land except for small reservations. In 1831, it was estimated that there were still two thousand red men in the state, and travelers occasionally noted, in the northwestern section, Indians wrapped in pieces of blankets and with leather moccasins, or a squaw "dressed in loose blue cloth coat, scarlet pantaloons, black beaver hat and feathers, and face painted bright red." Even the reservations, however, soon felt the impact of the advancing white. The Delawares ceded the remainder of their lands in 1829, and the Senecas on the Sandusky River parted with the last of their territory in 1831. Eleven years later, the relinquishing of the Wyandot reservation at Upper Sandusky marked the end of organized tribal life in Ohio.

This did not mean, however, the passing of the race problem in the state, for the Negro was seeking a residence there in increasing numbers. In 1829, over twenty-two hundred and fifty blacks were living in the city of Cincinnati alone, and numerous others were found throughout the southern part of the state. As the years went by, the color line was probably more closely drawn, and mob attacks in Cincinnati caused many Negroes to leave the city.

Only a generation had elapsed since the first efforts had been expended toward the conquering of the wilderness, as Ohioans were reminded when it was pointed out in December, 1827, that only two members of the legislature were natives of the state, and that, in all, only six such persons had served in that body. By 1830, however, the primitive pioneer life had largely passed, as people, mostly from the

Middle States, but also from the South and, in smaller numbers, from New England had entered the various sections of the state. This approach to maturity was signalized in 1838, when, for the first time, a native son, Wilson Shannon, was elevated to the position of chief executive of Ohio.

The Workaday World

The economic basis of the state in 1830 was still primarily agricultural. This was so much the case that when a young physician asked for the hand of a daughter of Duncan McArthur in marriage, the pioneer expressed concern as to whether a respectable livelihood could be made in that profession.

A newcomer, arriving upon the scene of his future labors, would grub out the small trees by the roots, cut down those less than a foot in diameter and burn them on the spot, and girdle the largest ones by chopping them round with an axe, cutting through the bark and sapwood and leaving them to stand until they fell over at the end of fifteen or twenty years. A house was generally built of logs and timbers secured from trees felled with the assistance of accommodating neighbors. The best of the houses had windows and doors, a shingled roof, a brick chimney, and a well-laid floor above and below the living quarters.

Sometimes birds and squirrels consumed large portions of the crops; the threshing of what remained was done with a flail, and, in the case of hired help, the tenth bushel was the common price for that service. This process was carried on until the farm was so large that horses became necessary to tread the grain. In the late twenties, however, primitive threshing machines began to come into use, one type being offered for sale in Cincinnati in 1828 by a company that had already placed ten in Hamilton County.

Pigs were an important source of food and commerce, and always boarded themselves by foraging in the woods, except in winter, when they were fed upon corn. Wheat also served as an important product of commerce, though the cost of transportation was apt to demand a large portion of the price received at market. At the Ohio River, fifty cents was a high price for a bushel of grain. In good weather it often took a man and two horses four days to take forty bushels of wheat thirty-five miles, and in bad weather much longer, so that the net price was only twenty-five cents cash. Money was scarce, however, and cash was seldom paid.

In the country, trade was on a grain basis, a day's work being paid for with a bushel of wheat, a bushel and a half of corn, or three bushels of oats. Shoemakers, tailors, and others took their pay in grain, the customers always procuring the leather, cloth, or iron, and the mechanic doing the work. Some articles at the stores, such as tea, coffee, powder, leather, and iron, could only be secured for cash, or for linen cloth, feathers, beeswax, and furs, which were not too heavy to transport and which were accepted by wholesale dealers in payment for goods. Grain was ground into meal at one of the many water mills erected on the banks of streams of various sizes. The smaller of the rivers sometimes went dry, making horsepower necessary, each man furnishing what was required to grind his own grain, though sometimes assisted by others with horses coming to the mill at the same time.

The women were accustomed to hard work, and in the event of the absence of the husband and father from home, would see to the managing of the home tasks, sometimes even directing the building of fences and the clearing of woodlands. Dress was very simple, the wool of a few sheep being spun, although not usually carded, at home.

Flax was also raised to serve in the manufacture of other necessary cloth.

Such an agricultural society was well-nigh self-sufficient, but money was imperative for certain purposes—chiefly, the payment of taxes. Hence, Ohio contractors secured lucrative agreements with the Army and Navy Departments, as well as with private concerns, and horses, cattle, swine, pork, whiskey, and flour were taken to distant markets—eastward to Philadelphia or Baltimore, *via* Lake Erie to Montreal or New York, *via* the Ohio River to St. Louis or New Orleans, or northward to Detroit. Of twenty-six million dollars' worth of produce reaching New Orleans annually by 1830, ten million dollars' worth of it came from Ohio, and five years later the products of Cincinnati alone amounted to six million dollars in value annually. Indeed, Cincinnati was a great *entrepôt* of the Ohio Valley, and one whose relative importance remained undiminished as long as river and canal traffic were of primary significance.

Manufacturing, however, was gaining rapidly in importance. Even an agriculturist like General McArthur, of Chillicothe, was interested in an iron furnace in southern Ohio which produced pig iron that was cast into stoves and other manufactures at a nearby forge. By 1826 the products of Cincinnati factories alone were valued at $1,850,000. A considerable amount of cotton yarn, cloth, and woolen goods was being manufactured, in some cases female help being employed. In 1828, an unusually large cotton mill, accommodating three thousand spindles, was erected in Cincinnati, and Steubenville was becoming known as a woolen manufacturing center, thirty-eight thousand pounds of wool, valued at thirty-five thousand dollars, being utilized by a single factory. Under these circumstances, Henry Clay, the sponsor of "the American System"—

with its twofold emphasis upon a protective tariff and
internal improvements—upon a visit to the state in 1827
found it expedient to observe the operations at the various
cotton and woolen mills of Steubenville and was at the
time attired in a coat produced in one of them.

Sociability and Recreation

"Oh, hell!—that fellow can take care of himself. Let's
go liquor." No mere barroom loafer or village ne'er-do-
well was speaking—on the contrary, it was a justice of the
Supreme Court of Ohio. The judges had been examining
for five minutes a prospective candidate for the bar, one
who was later to be the governor of the commonwealth.
But the quizzing was thus abruptly ended, and we may
readily visualize the judges quickly availing themselves of
that conviviality that was common to the time and the
district.

When the legislature met in Columbus, the long winter
evenings were often spent in stag wine parties, where song
and story, probably such as never reached the ears of their
ladies in the inland counties, were provocative of merriment. A scrupulous regard for the laws that they had
helped to enact was not always observed, and games of
faro and the use of roulette tables supplemented the other
forms of diversion.

The copious consumption of intoxicants was not confined
to any group or class. Even in New England settlements
where strong anti-alcoholic societies were later to be
found, distilleries were numerous. Thus, at Granville, in
Licking County, there were six, and the seventeen hundred
people in the township consumed ten thousand gallons of
whiskey annually. Farmers usually took a load of corn
to the distillery and received a barrel of liquor in exchange.
Similarly, practically all men of every condition of life

used tobacco in one form or another, and the smoking of pipes and cigars, the chewing of tobacco, and the use of snuff were far from unknown among women.

The evils resulting from an overindulgence in intoxicants soon created a considerable sentiment in favor of a more temperate manner of life, and temperance societies were formed in large numbers. Josiah Barber (a great-grandfather of James Ford Rhodes, the noted American historian), owner of one of the important distilleries in the West, at length came to feel that it was an evil business, rejected an offer to sell the property, and wrecked the establishment.

Pleasure resorts like the "Apollonian Garden," in Cincinnati, where an admission charge of twelve and one-half cents was required (redeemable in refreshments), offered such delicacies as turtle, oysters, and fruit, while a musical program was presented. A menagerie, exhibiting animals unknown to America, such as what was claimed to be the only adult lioness in the country, was opened for a period in Cincinnati in 1828 at the same time that a circus was offering entertainment in the form of horsemanship, dancing, and tumbling.

Opportunities for vice were far from unknown, though the general acceptance of the marriage relationship at an early age, often before a young man had become twenty-one years old and before a girl had become seventeen, tended to reduce the number of aberrations from conventionally accepted standards of sex morality.

The family was, indeed, a most important unit of social organization. Parties, courtships, marriages, and deaths, each formed a reason for social intercourse with outsiders in the home, while on more ordinary occasions a father and mother with a considerable number of sons and daughters found themselves a fairly self-sufficient social group.

In the rural districts, when new land was to be cleared, logrolling became something of a fraternal sport in which the whole neighborhood would engage. As the community became more settled, huskings, threshings, and house raisings became the occasion for informal parties, the men engaging in the principal work at hand, while the women utilized the time in quilting, sewing, or spinning. To give zest to the work, captains would be chosen among the men, teams being then selected to compete in finishing the task in rapid time. The job completed, supper would be served, following by dancing, unless the people were especially pious—in which case games, with forfeits paid in kisses, might serve as a substitute.

Hunting, fishing, swimming, and other forms of recreation, readily available in rural Ohio, we may rest assured, were not neglected. Even near the Ohio River, bears and wolves were numerous in the uncleared hills at a relatively late date (around 1818). Elsewhere—for instance, near Sandusky—the wolves were numerous and bold. Deer, wild turkeys, black and grey squirrel, partridge, and quail were found in varying degrees of abundance. Sometimes hunting parties numbering from two to six hundred persons would surround one or more townships and march to the center, enclosing all the game that did not succeed in forcing through the lines unhurt. As a consequence, by 1840 the largest of the wild animals had almost wholly disappeared.

The churches offered numerous opportunities for social contact, in both rural and urban districts. Camp meetings lasted several days, with thousands of persons sometimes in attendance. In the larger towns, some attended church services three times on Sunday, and the preacher might give sermons in private homes on other evenings. Doubtless an interest in sociability contributed quite as much to the success of such occasions as any concern with the doctrines of theology. Men were apt to be much engrossed in business, hence evangelists such as a Mr. Maffitt, described as "a beau in his dress," who appeared in Cincinnati in 1840, tended to draw large crowds of women, and the presence of the younger ones, in turn, acted as an attraction for the community. In the German communities, independent congregations, usually without creedal tests, and making an effort to reconcile theology with rationalism, arose as little spiritual republics, strangely like the community churches of more recent times.

In the rural districts, social classes were absent or not closely marked. The poor might complain of a want of money and others of a scarcity of it, but in a frontier economy none were wanting in bread, meat, or whiskey. Ex-Governor Worthington at Chillicothe might enjoy the revenue of twenty-five thousand acres, as he lived in a home constructed "like an Italian villa, of free stone, with stone steps on the exterior," but such agrarian capitalists were relatively few, and even these came closely enough in contact with the rank and file of their neighbors to feel a certain social unity with them. Religious denominations in a given community probably expressed some actual or potential social, as well as theological, cleavage, but such distinction could not without difficulty be carried into the affairs of the everyday world. Many women, sensitive to the refinements of genteel living, had brought to their log cabins muslins imported from Great Britain, and silks and crêpes suitable for gala-day occasions, and a Congressman, frequenting the shops of Washington, might bring home to his wife a couple of shawls and some Canton crêpe robes; but these did not make for an insuperable barrier between them and their homespun-clothed neighbors.

The democratic point of view, so characteristic of rural Ohio in its early decades, was not a deliberate choice: it was bound up with the necessity for coöperation and sociability with one's neighbors regardless of any inherent differences between individuals, and was confirmed by the general lack of economic distinctions between such persons. But, with the development of the larger towns and the attendant increase in material and cultural advantages, social differentiation was perhaps to be expected. In such a city as Cincinnati a laudable craving for the excellent and beautiful things of life combined itself, as in other generations, with a vulgar snobbery that sought to create a "select society." Thus, Harriet Martineau, the noted Englishwoman, recorded her attendance at parties in handsomely furnished homes in Cincinnati where the effort to manifest an appearance of cultivation showed a noticeable degree of self-consciousness and pedantry. Similarly, while watching a procession of school children "gay with flowers and ribands" in celebration of the anniversary of the opening of the common schools, she noted the air of superiority with which a woman informed her, "This is our populace!" People of this class frequented the stores of John Martin and T. Winter in Cincinnati where "Ladies' Curls, Ladies' Braides, Ladies' and Gentleman's Wigs, 'Otto' of Roses, Milk of Roses, Kalydor for the complexion" might be obtained. Playing cards in general were banned from "genteeler circles" and relegated to the grogshops, but dancing was not infrequent. A young suitor might take his friend for a ride in a gig on Sunday afternoons, perhaps venturing a considerable distance into the country. Each year, for a time, the pupils of Mrs. Caroline Hentz's private school on the outskirts of Cincinnati would have a May Day exhibition, with one of the number crowned queen—an occasion that offered an opportunity for young professional men and their ladies to ride out to witness the ceremonies. On summer evenings horseback riding, and in snowy weather a sleigh drawn by four horses, with tinkling bells, afforded many an hour of merriment. Excursions to Big Bone and Yellow Springs added to the possibilities in the summer season, when southerners in numbers were in the city to enjoy a milder climate than was offered them at home.

Clubs with an intellectual purpose, such as the "Society for Investigation" (founded in 1822) and the "Buckeye Club" (founded in 1833) in Cincinnati, are indications of some of the interests of professional groups. Among a few individuals, an interest in archæology was found, and in an attempt to popularize such knowledge, a Mr. Dorfeuille established "The Western Museum" in Cincinnati, where a collection of fossils and Mexican curiosities was displayed, but the task of filling up the room and the popular desire for sensationalism caused much "trumpery" to be included, such as a weird representation of the lower regions with skeletons that were caused to move by an ingenious device. Soon after the 1830's, the singing society and the *Turnvereine* of the German group made their influence felt in the intellectual and cultural life of Cincinnati.

Bookstores were few in number and confined to cities like Columbus and Cincinnati, where volumes pertaining to military and naval characters, *belles lettres*, and "the Pittsburg Navigator," and the usual almanacs were the most popular. Lectures were an occasional means of diversion. Sometimes, these were offered as a part of the midweek religious services; for instance, when a Columbus minister addressed his congregation during successive weeks on "Signs of the Times," attempting to show, among other things, that the science of geology did not conflict with divine revelation, or when a traveler from abroad gave a series of lectures at Chillicothe on Palestine and on the temperance question. Not so orthodox were the opinions of Miss Frances Wright, the Scotchwoman who lectured to crowded houses in Cincinnati on unconventional social viewpoints, and finally located in that city, or those of Robert Owen, the father of English socialism and the founder of the New Harmony Community on the banks of the Wabash, who engaged in a series of debates with Alexander Campbell (a founder of the Christian or "Campbellite" Church) during the spring of 1829.

Sculpture and painting were very meagerly developed, though some efforts along these lines were made in Cincinnati, and local poets of some talent were found, though the best-known Ohioans with abilities of that type, Alice and Phœbe Cary, were still girls of immature years, not to become prominent until the middle of the century.

To stimulate the cultivation of vocal and instrumental music, an Apollonian Society was organized in Cincinnati in 1824, but it was almost a decade later that the first important public musical performance in the city was held. Then thirty-five "instrumental performers, and six or seven vocalists, besides a long row for the closing chorus" gave a concert that indicated "a most promising" beginning for the musical development of the city. In 1839, the first German *Gesangverein* was founded in Cincinnati, and in 1846, three German singing societies combined to give the first annual *Sängerfest*. Many churches, however, were still dubious concerning the propriety of any but the simplest forms of religious music, although the new Catholic cathedral in Cincinnati in 1826 contained an organ secured from Pittsburgh. Around 1815, only a tuning fork had been used in the Presbyterian Church in the town that has become the present-day Columbus, and almost a quarter of a century later, the same congregation became agitated over the question of instrumental accompaniment. A bass viol was secretly constructed and conveyed to the choir loft—the congregation for a time failed to realize that it was not a human voice—and shortly afterwards an organ was secured through the demands of women of the congregation.

The same conservatism on the part of the religiously minded caused opposition to the drama. Nevertheless, citizens in Cincinnati secured the erection of a fine building seating eight hundred persons (in 1820). To maintain a high standard of talent, however, was difficult. When such an actor as Booth the Elder played there in *Richard III* or *King Lear*, as many as a hundred persons might be turned away, but support for the venture was indifferent, and within a few years this theater became a center of cheap amusement. Audiences became ill-mannered, and in 1830 a poster requested patrons not to crack nuts while the curtain was up and asked occupants of the upper boxes to avoid throwing shells and apple-cores into the pit. Within a few years, fire had destroyed this structure, as well as another built in 1832; but by the year of Van Buren's accession to the Presidency, a new one "richly decorated with chandaliers and paintings and curtains" was in operation. Mrs. Shaw, a star of the day, appeared here in *Robber's Wife* and in *Soldier's Daughter*, in the late summer of 1837, and was to be followed by a family of French dancers—egihteen in number—an attraction that promised to "draw full houses."

Religion

Many of the early settlers of Ohio had come West partly as a result of dissatisfaction with a conventional social order. Some from New England had desired to escape church taxes and puritanical restraints. To such, the New England Sabbath had been a "weariness," and a reaction against organized religion in the new environment was a logical result. Hence, in the early days of the present-day Cleveland, an effigy of Jesus was carried in a ribald procession, and a mock celebration of a communion service was performed. The struggle with the harsh elements in nature made many doubt the Christian doctrine of a loving Heavenly Father, and it was generally asserted that religious infidelity was more prevalent than in the East. Some complained of the hypocrisy that characterized the Presbyterian elder who on a Sunday distributed the communion elements with a piety equalling the facility with which he dealt the cards at a gambling-room on week-day evenings. Many may have agreed with the Alabaman who, convinced that he had been wronged in a business deal by a Methodist clergyman, wrote to his brother-in-law, an Ohio Congressman, that he "always detested the Methodist preachers generally" but was "now done with them altogether."

Yet, the stabilizing influence of religious organizations in new communities was early recognized, and at the time of the establishment of the first church in Cleveland, practically all adult males in the village signed the subscription list. Almost everywhere, communities were early provided with church organizations. Probably many rugged pioneers felt the passive good will for these societies that characterized the attitude of Duncan McArthur, who declared that he was pleased to hear of the progress of religion in his neighborhood and hoped that it was "founded upon reality," though after much serious thought he was not sure that he could join it.

Others were much more sure of their convictions and of the reality and efficacy of religious ministrations. A traveler in 1826 noted religious books on the table of Governor Morrow's home, and that both Morrow and ex-Governor Worthington said grace at meals. Postmaster General McLean, of Ohio, and Postmaster Burke, of Cincinnati, were high in the counsels of the Methodist denomination, and Governor Trimble affiliated with that body while chief executive of the state. The wife of one of the most prominent citizens of the state, who was at one time Governor, could write that she would spend Christmas at church, as she thought it "the most proper place to spend the day." The Speaker of the Ohio Senate, subsequently Governor, Robert Lucas, on the day that he affiliated with the Methodist Church (in 1819), could compose a hymn concluding with the stanza:

> And when the vale of death is past
> May I with saints, unite above,
> Where songs of praise ever last
> In sounding, Christ's redeeming love.

Among the denominations that were active in the West, at least two factors contributed greatly to enhance the early influence of the Presbyterians. The first of these was the large proportion of Scotch-Irish and others friendly to that denomination among the early inhabitants. This was especially true of parts of southern and eastern Ohio, where the influx from western Virginia and Pennsylvania was very great. James B. Finley, appointed Presiding Elder of the Ohio Conference (Methodist), complained in 1816 that the Calvinistic influence was "so great that Methodism could scarcely live." Even in the town of Delaware, later to be a point of radiation for Methodist influence, a Presbyterian society preceded the Wesleyan organization by almost a decade.

Another factor of assistance to the Ohio Presbyterians was an agreement known as "The Plan of Union." This arrangement, adopted in 1801 by the General Assembly of the Presbyterian Church and the Congregational Association of Connecticut, provided that a congregation could select a minister of the other kind of training, the minister retaining his former relationship and the church remaining as before. Since the Congregational churches tended to have no organization of other than a local sort, as a matter of practice the early Congregational ministers of the West were apt to unite with the presbyteries of the Presbyterian Church—a procedure that eventually tended to increase the number of Presbyterians at the expense of the Congregationalists.

At first, as has been observed, the Methodists encountered serious difficulties. In numerous places, services were held in private homes for as long as from one to three decades before it was found possible or expedient to build a meetinghouse. On the Western Reserve, especially, zealous Calvinistic preachers, well-trained according to the standards of the time, made progress in that area for the Methodists difficult.

Where the followers of Wesley were few, the Calvinists were quite indifferent to their presence, but the doctrines and demeanor of the apostles of predestination often isolated the good will of the rank and file of the population. Children of Presbyterian parents might be required to spend most of Sunday in learning and repeating the Shorter Westminister Catechism, but a warmer brand of religious expression was required in order to kindle the enthusiasm of the pioneer farmer or town "mechanic." No doubt heat enough was found by the latter in both the manner and doctrine of the minister who after 1822 dispensed a fervent Gospel from the Methodist Chapel, popularly known as "Brimstone Corner," in Cincinnati. At any rate, within a few years the building proved inadequate and was replaced with a larger structure. The Reverend Mr. Finley, who had led his Presbyterian congregation from Kentucky to Chillicothe in 1796, early saw the trend of the times and entered the Methodist fold, where his two sons became preachers of influence. The use of the circuit system, by which two riders could fulfil the needs of thirty stations, minimized the financial problem, while it offered an opportunity for social intercourse, which was dearly coveted, especially in the farming districts. The number of meetings tended to increase as the demand for human contact increased and the lack of public entertainment became evident.

A type of religious leadership even less expensive than that of the Methodist circuit-riding system was that of the Quakers, who dispensed entirely with the services of an official clergy. Although their system was less conducive to numerical growth, they were relatively numerous in parts of eastern and southern Ohio.

The emotional outlet that the Methodists offered was also supplied to some degree by the Baptists, a fact that tended to increase the numbers of the latter. The coming of the doctrines of Alexander Campbell, of the Campbellite or Christian Church, about 1826, however, served to make inroads into the actual and potential membership of the Baptist group. Campbell himself preached on the Western Reserve in 1827, and a few years later held a long series of debates on Catholicism with the Roman Catholic Bishop Purcell at Cincinnati.

In view of the observations already made on the type of religious activity popular in the early history of the state, the slow increase of the somewhat formal Protestant Episcopal Church is not surprising. Although services of this denomination had been held soon after 1792 at Steubenville, with monthly meetings there for many years, and although skeletons of congregations had been organized at various places, as late as 1816 there were only two Episcopal clergymen in the Northwest, and one of these was primarily secular in his interests.

Roman Catholics were relatively few in pioneer days, the first edifice of that denomination in the state being dedicated in Perry County in December, 1818. Cincinnati, however, soon became a center of this religious influence. Although as late as 1819 there had been in that community only a hundred Catholics, with no resident priest, seven years later the frame edifice erected in 1823 had become inadequate, and four priests and a bishop were in residence.

Other less extensive organizations were not without representatives. Thus, the First Congregational (Unitarian) Church of Cincinnati was organized in 1824; Jewish congregations soon came into being; and even communistic settlements, such as the Zoar community (near Dover) of Wurtemberg Separatists started in 1817, were established with varying degrees of success and prominence.

Among the rest, the Mormons must not be omitted. Their leader, Joseph Smith, and his wife arrived in Ohio by sleigh in January, 1831, with only a handful of followers. Establishing themselves at Kirtland, not far from Lake Erie, they at once inaugurated a feverish missionary activity, eight conferences being held on the Western Reserve in the fall of the first year. In 1833 a revelation was supposed to have been received commanding the building of a temple, which was soon undertaken. Dissension presently showed itself, however, as newspapers published articles purporting to reveal the evils of Mormon practice. Nevertheless, thousands of dollars in paper were issued, although the application for a bank charter had been refused by the state. In spite of elaborate plans for a city and the success of missionaries in far-away lands, financial trouble constituted a reason for their leaving for Missouri in 1838, the Mormon band having increased in the meantime to twenty-five thousand—the increase largely secured within the borders of Ohio.

It should be noted that many churches were quick to enter the field of moral regulation for their members— especially on the Western Reserve—and that trials of discipline were fairly common. Communicants were arraigned for such breaches of Christian practice as scandal, Sunday traveling, theft, and excessive use of intoxicants. Records are available showing members of the Vine Street Congregational Church in Cincinnati, in a little later period, brought to account for sending and accepting a challenge to fight a duel, profanity, neglect of the ordinances and of family prayers, card playing, attending cotillions and dancing parties, and running a Sunday boat. In the Congregational Church at Wellington, there was a standing committee for church trials, and although few cases of gross immorality were found, such cases as one in 1835 where a member was excommunicated for intoxication, profanity, and neglect of Christian duty were recorded. Near by at Oberlin, at about the same time, a communicant was brought to trial for the use of tea.

Schools

The early settlers, by necessity primarily interested in material matters, had at first little time or substance to devote to considerations of intellectual interest. Such meager education as was available was furnished during the first couple of decades of the statehood period by private schools supported and built, like churches, by private subscription. These facilities were inadequate;

hence, many adults were unable to read or write their names, travelers noting that some persons required aid in ascertaining the names and addresses on letters and packages. To be able to read the Bible or an almanac, to write, and to compute ordinary sums was deemed quite a sufficient academic equipment in that day.

Families of considerable means might employ a tutor for their children, as did the McArthurs near Chillicothe; but in most cases a group of parents would combine for the purpose. Generally, a teacher would agree to give his services for thirteen weeks—six days a week, eight hours a day—at the rate of a dollar or two for each pupil, perhaps one half payable in wheat at fifty cents per bushel and the balance payable in money. A minimum of twenty students was usually required. Murray's English Reader, the Columbian Orator, Dillworth's Speller, Webster's Easy Standard of Pronunciation, Pike's Arithmetic, and other textbooks brought from the old settlements were in general use.

The early schools were of primitive construction, built from round logs, with a puncheon floor hewn from saplings and a door made of clapboards. A fireplace with a stick and mud chimney, and benches made from split logs were other essential features. Light was admitted through a protection of oiled papers, though window glass was used in the better buildings.

The schools in Cincinnati, dating practically from the earliest settlement (for those who could afford the tuition charges), had gained a reputation that attracted students from neighboring states and even from the more distant South. Numerous "academies" of varying merit had been established in other towns and villages. The academy was an important link in the transition from the somewhat aristocratic New England Latin-Grammar school to the

public high school of the present day. In Ohio, the
preparatory departments of a few early colleges furnished
the nearest approximation to the Latin-Grammar schools
of the East. Many sons of Ohio, however, felt the need
of an education more practical in its scope than this
severely classical course, and in the days before the development of the high school, the private academies attempted to
meet that demand. In some cases, as at Dayton, a novel
system of instruction, "the Lancasterian Method," named
for an Englishman, Joseph Lancaster, was employed.
The plan was based on the assumption that by promoting
students in each class on a basis of merit to the position
of monitor, one teacher, who would be essentially a super-
visor, might guide the instruction of five hundred students,
thus eliminating much expense. This particular method
was a failure, but the academy continued for many years
as a vital element in the educational opportunities of the
state.

The great stimulus to popular education came, however,
with the organization of a genuine public school system.
The Ordinance of 1785 had provided that one section in
each township should be devoted to public school purposes,
but general educational legislation was not passed until
over a third of a century later. About 1820, certain men
in Cincinnati, Cleveland, and other towns began to cor-
respond in regard to the necessity for proper public instruction. To help the cause, "Solomon Thrifty's Almanac"
was published by Nathan Guilford in Cincinnati. A law
accordingly was passed in 1821 authorizing the division
of each township into school districts and the raising of
funds for the building of a schoolhouse and for the disposal
of any deficit accruing from the schooling of children whose
parents were unable to pay their share of the school
expenses. In practice, this measure meant that poor

children did not attend school, as many parents were too proud to permit them to accept free tutelage. A law of 1825, memorable in its significance, required the county commissioners to assess a tax upon property of one-half mill upon the dollar, the proceeds to be used for the school fund. Thus, a state system of public education was inaugurated, though even then funds sometimes permitted the schools to be open only for about a quarter of each year, and, in some places, such as Dayton and Portsmouth, a public school system was not established for over a decade. The private academies, inaugurated long before in the more important centers of population, were slow in yielding to the newer institutions.

No discussion of the development of education in Ohio would be complete without a reference to the work of Samuel Lewis, a native of Falmouth, Massachusetts, who secured all of his formal schooling during the first ten years of his life. After noteworthy endeavors in the cause of education in Cincinnati, in 1837 he was selected as the first "State Superintendent of Common Schools" in Ohio. A man of almost fanatical zeal, he travelled more than fifteen hundred miles during the first year of his work, usually by horseback, and visited three hundred schools and forty county seats. Discussing at every opportunity the needs and problems of education, he did notable service in popularizing the idea of free public education and in demanding that its standards should be of the best, for, as he said, "a school not good enough for the rich will never excite much interest with the poor."

The daughters of the economically favored, nevertheless, were apt to attend a "female seminary" such as that founded by a Dr. John Locke in 1823 at Cincinnati where French, music, penmanship, and needlework were taught by special teachers, and apparatus was provided for instruction in such studies as chemistry and astronomy. In such a boarding school as that opened by the Reverend and Mrs. C. C. Beatty at Steubenville in 1829, such subjects as Intellectual and Moral Philosophy, Evidences of Christianity, and the Analogy of Natural and Revealed Religion were offered. A little later (in 1833), Lyman Beecher's daughters, Catherine and Harriet, were the mistresses of a school in Cincinnati, and not a great distance away, at Oxford, the young daughter of a clergyman of Massachusetts, Miss Bethania Crocker, had made the beginnings of a school later to become the Oxford College for Women.

The earliest efforts at the establishment of schools later to be developed into institutions for higher education were stimulated by the appropriation by Congress of a township west of the Miami River (in March, 1803), and the turning over of two townships in the Ohio Company's purchase for similar purposes. The Ohio University, at Athens, was an outgrowth of the latter gift, though the first instruction, given in June, 1809, was of the type of an academy, and collegiate standards were not adopted until about 1822, when a full faculty was organized. Miami University, at Oxford, developing out of the other grant mentioned, although organized in 1809, did not begin its active career until 1824.

During this period, Philander Chase, an uncle of the later United States Chief Justice, came from Connecticut to Worthington, ten miles north of Columbus (in June, 1817). Chosen a bishop of the Episcopal Church, he also served as president of a Cincinnati college. Interested in promoting the educational work of his diocese, late in 1823 he sailed for England to secure aid, which was forthcoming in the form of twenty thousand dollars, besides books and religious articles. Soon afterwards, eight thousand acres of land were purchased in Knox County, and, with the erection of a large building in 1828, Kenyon College at Gambier became an actuality. In the same decade, Hudson had been chosen as the site for a college, and a charter was obtained for the institution that was to develop into Western Reserve University (later located in Cleveland). During the next ten-year period (1830–1840), further collegiate progress was made in the laying of the foundations of the institutions that were to become Denison University, at Granville, Oberlin College, at Oberlin, and Marietta College, at Marietta. The St. Xavier College, at Cincinnati, grew out of a parish school connected with the first Catholic church in the city, an institution that, after passing through several stages, was taken over by the Jesuits in 1840.

Newspapers

The newspaper, in early Ohio, was a potent influence among the educative forces of the time, although in the heat of party fray there was often an excessive indulgence in abusive phraseology. As early as 1793, the *Centinel of the North Western Territory* had been founded at Cincinnati by William Maxwell, though it was merely the first among a host of pioneer publications, many of which had a precarious and short-lived career. Later, after a change of its location to Chillicothe and a change of its name, it was merged in 1801 into the *Scioto Gazette*. This paper until 1807 was edited by Nathaniel Willis, the grandfather of the nineteenth-century poet, and, with some alterations in title, it has continued publication up to the present day.[1]

By 1810 ,newspapers were being published not only at Cincinnati and Chillicothe, but also at Steubenville,

[1] Since 1900, the old name, *Scioto Gazette*, has been employed.

Marietta, New Lisbon (now Lisbon), Zanesville, St. Clairsville, Lebanon, and Dayton. By 1821, the number of
these publications had increased to forty-one. During the
next five years, eighteen of these passed out of existence,
but the appealing though financially hazardous venture of
journalism produced thirty-seven new ones, making a
total of sixty in 1826. By that time, the leading papers
at Cincinnati were the Cincinnati *Advertiser*, edited by
Moses Dawson, an Irish politician of Jacksonian affiliations—a paper that in 1841 was purchased by John Brough
(later Governor of Ohio) and his brother, with the name
changed to *The Enquirer;* the *National Republican and
Ohio Political Register*, which was a descendant of the
Western Spy and Hamilton Gazette (founded in 1799),
the second newspaper published in what is now Ohio; and
the *Liberty Hall and Cincinnati Gazette*, edited by the
gifted but often inebriate Charles Hammond, who gained
great distinction both as a lawyer (for example, in the
case of *Osborn* vs. *Bank of the United States*) and as a
journalist. Earlier in his career, Hammond had attracted
widespread attention as the editor of the *Ohio Federalist*
at St. Clairsville by his hostility to the War of 1812, and
in Cincinnati he was rendering such service to the Adams-
Clay political forces as to be considered the leading administration editor of the West.

The Cleveland *Herald*, established in 1819, was, in the
twenties, the leading means of printed communication in
the present metropolis of the state. In the capital of the
state, the *Ohio State Journal and Columbus Gazette*, owned
by George Nashee and John Bailhache, was the most
influential paper. The latter paper was the continuation
of the Columbus *Gazette*, which had followed the *Western
Intelligencer and Columbus Gazette*, a newspaper established
in Columbus in 1814, and, as the *Ohio State Journal*, is

now the only morning newspaper in that city. The principal journalistic competition for this paper was offered by the *Ohio Monitor*, which had been established in 1816 by David Smith and Ezra Griswold. Smith soon secured complete control, which he exercised until 1835, when he sold it to Jacob Medary, who consolidated this publication with a paper known as the *Hemisphere*. Under this name it was published until 1837, when the title was changed to the *Ohio Statesman*, with "Samuel Medary and Brothers" designated as the proprietors.

Among the well-known editors of the state was James Wilson, who was brought from Philadelphia to Steubenville in 1815 to edit the *Herald* at that place. Formerly a *protégé* of Duane, the noted editor of the Philadelphia *Aurora*, Wilson exerted a wide influence as a journalist, and under his leadership the paper became known as the *Western Herald and Steubenville Gazette*. Though he was active as a politician and prominent in the counsels of those opposed to the ambitions and policies of Jackson, his contemporaries could hardly foresee that his grandson would become the World War President of the United States.

The papers of that day in Ohio were generally of weekly issue, though in the larger cities semiweekly publication was soon adopted, especially, in the case of Columbus newspapers, while the legislature was in session. Numerous columns were given to political news, to foreign news many days old, to patent medicine advertisements, and to the announcements of miscellaneous merchants, while the general indifference of the papers to the details of weddings and other social functions must have made them rather uninviting to many feminine eyes of that period.

Many newspapers arose to devote themselves to special causes, *e.g.*, the *Ohio Register and Anti-Masons Review*, at

Columbus, and the several abolitionist publications that are discussed elsewhere in this volume.

The foreign-language press was not without its representatives at an early period, the Cincinnati *Volksblatt* being established in 1836 and published continuously until after the Great War, while the *Westbote*, of influence in the entire Mississippi Valley, appeared in Columbus in 1843 and lasted until the year of the Armistice (1918).

Selected Bibliography

Contemporary impressions of life in Ohio during this period may be found in *Early Western Travels, 1748–1846* (Reuben Gold Thwaites, ed., 32 vols., Cleveland, 1904–1907). Other travelers have left accounts in James S. Buckingham, *The Eastern and Western States of America* (3 vols., London, 1842), Vol. II; E. S. Abdy, *Journal of a Residence and Tour in the United States* (3 vols., London, 1835), Vol. III; and Michel Chevalier, *Society, Manners, and Politics in the United States* (Boston, 1839). Of considerable interest are various memoirs: W. C. Howells, *Recollections of Life in Ohio from 1813 to 1840* (Cincinnati, 1895); W. D. Howells, *Years of my Youth* (New York, 1916); W. H. Venable, *A Buckeye Boyhood* (Cincinnati, 1911); and Harriet C. Brown, *Grandmother Brown's Hundred Years, 1827–1927* (Boston, 1930), pp. 3–108. The last three deal partly with a somewhat later period.

In the preparation of this chapter, many contemporary newspaper files have been consulted. In addition to the local histories previously cited, C. M. Walker, *History of Athens County, Ohio* (Cincinnati, 1869); James H. Kennedy, *A History of the City of Cleveland* (Cleveland, 1896); S. P. Orth, *A History of Cleveland, Ohio* (3 vols., Chicago, 1910); Alfred E. Lee, *History of the City of Columbus* (2 vols., New York, 1892); Henry Bushnell, *The History of Granville, Licking County, Ohio* (Columbus, 1889); Horace S. Knapp, *History of the Maumee Valley* (Toledo, 1872); and Nevin O. Winter, *A History of Northwest Ohio* (3 vols., Chicago, 1917), are useful. B. Drake and E. D. Mansfield, *Cincinnati in 1826* (Cincinnati, 1827); J. Kilbourne, *The Ohio Gazetteer* (Columbus, 1831); and F. J. Turner, "The Colonization of the West, 1820–1830," *American Historical Review*, Vol. XI, pp. 303–327, supply pertinent details. Randall and Ryan have a chapter on the social life of the pioneer, Vol. III, pp. 3–32.

For Indian cessions in Ohio, see H. C. Shetrone, "The Indian in Ohio," *Ohio Archæological and Historical Quarterly*, Vol. XXVII, pp. 274–510, and S. S. Knabenshue, "Indian Land Cessions in Ohio," *Ibid.*, Vol. XI, pp. 249–255. Frank U. Quillin, *The Color Line in Ohio* (Ann Arbor, Mich., 1913), is a history of race prejudice in the state. The authoritative work on German immigration is A. B. Faust, *The German Element in the United States* (2 vols. in one, New York, 1927).

For the study of religious life in early Ohio, the following are helpful: J. M. Barker, *History of Ohio Methodism* (Cincinnati, 1898); *Circuit-Rider Days along the Ohio* (W. W. Sweet, ed., New York, 1923); W. S. Kennedy, *The Plan of Union* (Hudson, Ohio, 1856); Joseph Doyle, *The Church in Eastern Ohio* (refers to the Episcopal Church) (Steubenville, 1914); *Ohio Church History Society Papers* (D. L. Leonard *et al.*, eds., 11 vols., Oberlin, 1889–1900); Harold E. Davis, "Religion in the Western Reserve, 1800–1825," *Ohio Archæological and Historical Quarterly*, Vol. XXXVIII, pp. 475–501; Margaret J. Mitchell, "Religion as a Factor in the Early Development of Ohio," *Mississippi Valley Historical Association Proceedings*, Vol. IX, pp. 75–89; and Chaddock, *op. cit.*, pp. 111–129. Historical accounts of local churches are also suggestive, for example, Arthur C. Ludlow, *The Old Stone Church* (Cleveland, 1920), and Francis E. Marsten, *After Eighty Years* (Columbus, 1886). The activities of the Mormons in Ohio are summarized in Randall and Ryan, Vol. III, pp. 399–424.

The early history of education in Ohio is given extensive consideration in Randall and Ryan, Vol. III, pp. 367–396; in Chaddock, pp. 138–151; in *Education in the Ohio Valley prior to 1840* (J. E. Bradford, ed., Columbus, 1916); and in E. A. Miller, "History of Educational Legislation in Ohio from 1803 to 1850," *Ohio Archæological and Historical Quarterly*, Vol. XXVII, pp. 7–142. William McAlpine, "The Origin of Public Education in Ohio," *Ohio Archæological and Historical Quarterly*, Vol. XXXVIII, pp. 409–447, attempts to demonstrate that New England influence upon education in Ohio has been less important than earlier historians have indicated. W. G. W. Lewis, *Biography of Samuel Lewis* (Cincinnati, 1857), and Laura C. Smith, *The*

Life of Philander Chase (New York, 1903), are biographical accounts of leaders in different phases of education in Ohio.

The early literary development of Cincinnati is treated in J. E. Kirkpatrick, *Timothy Flint* (Cleveland, 1911), pp. 185–201. Bertha-Monica Stearns, "Early Western Magazines for Ladies," *Mississippi Valley Historical Review*, Vol. XVIII, pp. 319–330, demonstrates the type of reading published in Ohio for a feminine clientele. Very brief summaries of early newspaper work in Ohio are found in Randall and Ryan, *History of Ohio*, Vol. III, pp. 175–179, and Galbreath, *History of Ohio*, Vol. I, pp. 519–532.

CHAPTER IX

POLITICAL VICISSITUDES OF A DECADE AND A HALF

Finance and Politics, 1836–1840

*E*VEN before the electorate of the nation made its choice of a new President in 1836, experienced political observers detected the beginnings of a severe economic crisis. In the summer of that year, the issuance of the so-called Specie Circular by President Jackson, requiring the payment of all purchases of Government lands in gold or silver, had resulted in a drastic curtailment of such transactions, a fact that reacted at once upon the Western banks and, in turn, upon the Eastern ones. The resultant general suspension of specie payment by financial institutions included such action by the Ohio banks, and some merchants were thrown into bankruptcy, while a few manufacturing plants were forced to close their doors. Strikes were threatened by workingmen, as their wages were reduced, and protest was registered against employers who would attend "a concert for the benefit of the indigent poor, and then proceed home and reduce the wages of their workmen." Most Ohioans, nevertheless, lived under such a simple agrarian economy that the obtaining of the necessities of life was not seriously affected by the problems of financial centers, and one writer pointed to the total ignorance of the people of central Ohio of the suffering experienced in New York and other cities.

The Panic of 1837, however, worked temporarily to the disadvantage of the Democrats of the state, who lost control of the legislature in the election of 1837. Subse-

quently, the Whig majority, at the suggestion of Governor
Vance, repealed an act which the Democrats (controlled
by the hard-money faction) had passed in 1836 and which
had prohibited the circulation of notes of less than five
dollars within the state. The bankers of the state were
usually Whigs, and they found considerable profit in the
issuing of the small notes; but the hard-money Democrats
strenuously opposed this currency, for, in the case
of the failure of a bank, the losses in this form of
money constituted a distinct hardship upon the poorer
classes.[1]

Business confidence returned by the summer of 1838,
and the banks resumed specie payment in August of that
year. In the fall, the improved economic situation distinctly favored the Democrats, and Wilson Shannon, of
Belmont County, captured the post of chief executive
from Governor Vance and the Democratic Party regained
control of the legislature. Shannon, the first Ohio-born
Governor of the state, had been elected partly by Whig
overconfidence and Democratic attacks upon the moral
character of Vance, and partly because of an episode
known as "the Mahan affair," but chiefly because
of promises of "bank reform." This reform included
proposals for making the liability of stockholders of a
bank proportionate to the amount of stock they owned,
and for altering bank charters when the public good
might require. Other parts of the program resulted in a
law again prohibiting the issuing of small notes by Ohio
financial corporations, and in a Bank Commissioner Act.
The latter statute provided for a commission of three
members, whose duty would be to see that banks maintained a specie reserve equal to a third of their bank note

---

[1] It is interesting to note that imprisonment for debt was abolished in Ohio
by a law of March, 1838.

issue and that these notes were redeemed in specie under penalty of suspension.

Business uncertainty again appeared in 1839 but produced no reaction against the Democrats, who again swept the polls in the fall elections of that year. Shannon, in his annual message, declared himself in favor of a system of independent banks, properly restricted and under the supervision of commissioners. This suggestion at once brought down upon him the wrath of the Locofoco section of the party, which was represented in Cincinnati in December, 1839, at a meeting that denied the constitutionality of any coins except gold and silver, declared the charter of any banks in Ohio uncalled-for and inexpedient, and insisted that Shannon could not be again supported for the governorship. Party discipline, however, prevailed at the Democratic state convention of the next year, and Shannon was renominated by acclamation.

The ensuing campaign, in which Shannon was opposed by Thomas Corwin, of Lebanon, whose eloquent oratory was a feature of the contest, was the spectacular one of "log cabin and hard-cider" notoriety. For years, the Whigs of the state had been energetically pushing the claims of William Henry Harrison with such prudence as was calculated to prevent a reaction against him, and their efforts had been rewarded by his nomination for President at the national Whig convention at Harrisburg, Pennsylvania, in December, 1839. Cabins were thereupon erected as local centers of activity; Harrison himself spoke at a large number of meetings in various sections of the state, evading all commitments on controversial issues but capitalizing to the fullest the part that he had played (during the War of 1812) in making, as he said "the indignant Eagle frown upon the British Lion." Every neighborhood resounded with tunes such as "General

Harrison's Quick Step" and "The Whig Waltz," while argument was lost in the boisterous singing of such stanzas as:

> What public good has Martin done?
>   None, that ever saw the sun!
> His schemes are all for "number one,"
>   Power and wealth to draw.
> Our friend is quite another man.
>   To help the People all he can
> His steady aim, his only plan,
>   For Harrison Huzza!

The same unbridled forces of Western frontier democracy that had swept Jackson into power in 1828 now displaced Van Buren with the "humble farmer of North Bend."

In the state contest Corwin was triumphant over Shannon, while in the national election Harrison carried not only the state but the nation as a whole, and for the first time a citizen of Ohio made ready to occupy the Executive Mansion in Washington. A relatively inconspicuous opponent of Harrison in the election had been James G. Birney, the candidate of the Liberty Party. Yet the appearance in politics of this organization is indicative of a trend in affairs relating to slavery that demands a consideration of the attitude of Ohio toward that important subject.

Beginnings of the Anti-slavery Movement in Ohio

In the first two decades of Ohio's history as a state, the number of Negroes was small, and although the legal position of the blacks was rigidly limited, in the primitive conditions of that time whites and blacks might even be found eating at the same table. The agitation in connection with the Missouri question had aroused considerable consternation in the state, and in the early discussions pertaining to the Presidential nominees of 1824 the possibility developed that the slavery issue might be an important one. This, however, was subordinated to other issues, and for some years the question of slavery ceased to be an important political factor in the state.

The evils of the institution, nevertheless, were quite generally recognized in Ohio. In 1826, the Presbyterian Synod of Ohio declared slavery to be "manstealing." The Presbytery of Chillicothe in the next year voted funds for the distribution of an anti-slavery pamphlet, and shortly thereafter unanimously adopted a resolution declaring slavery to be "a heinous sin and scandal." John Rankin, a minister of Ripley, had already written anti-slavery letters for the *Castigator*, a newspaper in his home town, in 1824, and these letters were printed in book form in 1826. As early as September, 1817, moreover, what was doubtless the first newspaper in the United States to advocate the immediate and unconditional emancipation of the slaves, the *Philanthropist*, was published by a Quaker, Charles Osborn, at Mt. Pleasant, Ohio. The first abolitionist society in the state had been organized previously at St. Clairsville in 1815 by Benjamin Lundy, who six years later started the publication at Mt. Pleasant of the noted anti-slavery paper, *The Genius of Universal Emancipation*.

At times, the danger to Northern interests of the domination of the Federal Government by the South became vocal. The most practical problem relating to "the peculiar institution" from the standpoint of Ohioans in the decade of the twenties, however, was that relating to the influx of freedmen, who were not welcome to remain in the South. There were expressions of opposition to the sending of "those persons to infest the towns of Ohio or

Indiana," since they were, in the words of a Columbus newspaper, "worse than drones to society," and were already swarming in the land "like locusts."

This situation accounts in large part for the keen interest expressed by many Ohioans in the American Colonization Society, which seemed to offer an outlet other than the Northern States for the blacks of free status by proposing to send the freed Negroes back to Africa. Branches of the society were formed on the Western Reserve in the fall of 1826, newspapers endorsed the movement, and even college students banded themselves into an auxiliary. Governor Trimble, in his annual message of 1827, suggested that, in case of the failure of the Colonization Society, the question of toleration of the further immigration of free blacks into the state would be seriously raised. As late as November, 1834, at the annual meeting of the Cincinnati branch, confidence in this method was expressed; Joseph Jones, a colored man from Liberia, was examined as to the prospects of the colony; and coffee and palm-fruit, as well as primitive manufactures of the Africans, were exhibited.

Nevertheless, the rapid increase in the number of Negroes in the state and the lack of any corresponding enthusiasm for the Colonization project caused realistically minded persons to express rather early their serious doubts as to its practicability. In 1829, there were 2,258 blacks in Cincinnati alone, out of a population of 24,000, while the annual receipts of the state colonization society amounted to less than five hundred dollars. As a means of dealing with the situation, in 1829 the township trustees at Cincinnati contemplated calling into force the almost obsolete state legislation of 1807, which provided that no free Negro could remain in the state without giving bond of five hundred dollars against his becoming a public charge. The matter was discussed with considerable animus in the newspapers, and a citizens' meeting was called to consider the propriety of voting township funds to remove from Cincinnati to Canada such blacks as were willing to go but lacked the necessary funds. The meeting refused to acquiesce in the proposal, but a large portion of the Negroes found it advisable to leave the city, many going to Canada.

By the end of 1834, the abolition question was being seriously agitated, so much so that the Columbus *Ohio State Journal* for the time being refused to allow further discussion of it in its columns. During the following months, the enthusiasm of the abolitionists increased, with the result that societies were organized to oppose their efforts and that the matter was agitated in elections, particularly upon the Western Reserve.

Soon the question of freedom of speech was involved. Only Charles Hammond, among the Cincinnati editors, published announcements of abolition meetings. At the same time, Senator Thomas Morris, of Ohio, was presenting in the Senate petitions from certain citizens of Ohio asking for the abolition of slavery in the District of Columbia, and was raising his voice against Calhoun's efforts to prohibit the circulation of anti-slavery material from the United States mails.

James G. Birney, a native of Kentucky, who had become an anti-slavery leader and who had settled in Cincinnati, began to express views of a more extreme type than were generally countenanced; and at length a mob, in July, 1836, did violence to the property of Mr. Pugh, who was engaged in printing Birney's paper, the *Philanthropist*. Efforts were made after this incident to persuade Birney to cease the publication of the newspaper, particularly because Cincinnatians were interested in the stimulation of trade with the South and in the development of a Charleston and Cincinnati railroad.

The purposes of Birney and his colleagues were at this time primarily nonpolitical, being principally "religious" in their implications; yet their paper urged that in political matters abolition principles should be superior to ordinary partisan loyalties. Birney's zeal for the cause soon led him again into difficulties. A mulatto girl named Matilda Lawrence escaped from a steamer on the Ohio River anchored at Cincinnati and was harbored in Birney's home for several months. At length, in the spring of 1837, he was brought to trial and found guilty, under an Ohio law of January, 1804, of secreting a Negro.

An important aspect of the anti-slavery movement was the so-called "Underground Railroad," an organization that functioned in Ohio, as well as in other states of the North, and that utilized surreptitious methods in spiriting escaped slaves from the South to the freedom that was assured beyond the Canadian border. Often, under cover of darkness, the fugitive would be ferried to the north bank of the Ohio River and then directed or guided by friends to a route along which stations offered shelter and refreshment to the weary Negro. Quaker settlements, Methodist communities, and Scotch Covenanters invariably gave assistance, as did certain college centers. With at least twenty-three ports of entry along the river front and five important outlets along the Lake (Toledo, Sandusky, Cleveland, Fairport Harbor—near Painesville—and Ashtabula Harbor), Ohio was the most important state in the activities of the organization, and Levi Coffin, long a resident of Cincinnati, was responsible for the dispatch of as many as three thousand persons across Ohio and Indiana.

One of the most important episodes associated with the slavery controversy in Ohio occurred during the latter part of 1838. John B. Mahan, a Brown County clergyman, was accused of assisting fifteen slaves on their way to Canada from Kentucky. In connection with the Fugitive Slave Law, Governor Clark, of Kentucky, issued a request to Governor Vance, of Ohio, for the surrender of Mahan, that he might stand trial in the former state. The request was honored, but Vance soon regretted his ready compliance, for it was evident that Mahan had not been in Kentucky for many years, hence could not be answerable to her laws. He was found not guilty, and subsequent criticism of Vance's part in the incident contributed to his defeat for reëlection in October.

In view of Senator Morris's decided stand in Congress in connection with the slavery controversy, much interest was manifested in the choice of the Ohio Legislature for that office in December, 1838. Morris was questioned by a Democratic committee in regard to his views, and in general indicated a position satisfactory to the members of his party. On the slavery question, however, he took a very advanced stand, declaring it to be his constant belief that slavery was "wrong, in principle, in practice, in every country and under every condition of things." He asserted that slavery was so radically wrong, that no time, place, or circumstance could palliate it, or give it even the appearance of being right, and that American slavery was the most obnoxious of its kind, a libel upon our republican institutions. Morris stated his belief in the unconstitutionality of the Fugitive Slave Law and in the legality and desirability of the prohibition of slavery in the territories, but denied the right of Congress to interfere with slavery within a state. Such an unequivocal expression of opinion made his reëlection a virtual impossibility, but the Democrats, not wishing to alienate the good will of the anti-slavery element in the party, finally chose Benjamin Tappan in his stead. The latter, long a radical leader in party councils, although definitely not an abolitionist, was a brother of Arthur and Lewis Tappan, the anti-slavery leaders of New York.

The senatorial question was only one of several associated with slavery that troubled the members of the Ohio Legislature during the session of 1838–1839. Benjamin Wade, then a state senator who represented the point of view of the abolitionist Whigs of the Western Reserve, presented a memorial asking resolutions by the legislature asserting the right of Congress to abolish slavery in the District of Columbia and in the territories. When it was proposed that the memorial be laid on the table, Wade stated his determination to have it referred to a committee, and declared that he would, if necessary, make such a motion every day during the session.

At about the same time, a petition from certain colored persons in relation to the law prohibiting them from testifying in courts of justice was introduced into the house. Several Whigs spoke in favor of receiving it, while it was opposed chiefly by Democrats. The number of these petitions increased as the matter became one for animated discussion. At length, the Democrats introduced a series of resolutions dealing with the powers of states over such matters (as a rebuke to the abolitionists), which were forthwith passed by the house of representatives.

Growing out of the Mahan affair was the increasing dissatisfaction in Kentucky as to the relations with Ohio in regard to slave property. Accordingly, the legislature of the former state designated two commissioners to confer with the Ohio Legislature in regard to this matter. The communication of these commissioners was included in a special message of Governor Shannon to the legislature, and a bill providing for a more effective manner of securing the return of fugitive slaves than that provided for in the Federal law of 1793 was later enacted, although only after considerable opposition from the Whigs in the senate.

During 1839 and 1840, the air was full of discussions of abolition, which included a series of debates at Cincinnati between an agent of the American Colonization Society and the pastor of the Sixth Presbyterian Church on the subject: "Is the American Colonization Society worthy of the confidence and charities of the American People?" Interest increased with discussion and tended to arouse concern on two points: that Southern trade might be diverted from Cincinnati as a protest against abolitionist sentiment, and that the Whig Party might find itself embarrassed in attempting to meet the demands of both abolitionists and anti-abolitionists within its ranks.

Not only business interests but churches and colleges as well were severely shaken by the abolitionist influence. A few years earlier (1833–1834) Lane Seminary, a Presbyterian theological seminary at Cincinnati, had been the scene of much discussion and animosity over a series of debates on the slavery controversy. Many students did welfare work among the colored people of the city and at times even conducted them to the campus of the institution. At length the trustees of the seminary voted to suppress further discussion of slavery as "a political subject." Many students then left the seminary, and one trustee (Reverend Asa Mahan), one faculty man, and about thirty students eventually moved to Oberlin College, which had been founded in 1833. Mahan became the president of this new educational venture (in 1835) on condition that colored students as well as whites would be accepted, and the college became a center of Western anti-slavery influence. In February, 1839, the venerable and conservative pastor of the First Presbyterian Church of Cincinnati delivered two sermons on the "Relations and Duties of Servants and Masters," defending the lawfulness of existing civil relations from the standpoint of religion, only to call out severe rebukes from anti-slavery circles.

Undoubtedly sentiment against slavery was being rapidly welded into an organization. Atwater's new *History of Ohio* (1838) declared that there were seventeen thousand abolitionists in the state. Then, in Trumbull County alone there were 2,249 enrolled members with several hundred more who were not officially affiliated. In May, 1839, at a meeting of the state abolition society, there was adopted a resolution urging that persons who favored the abrogation of all distinctions in rights based upon color should be favored for public office. Many anti-slavery men, however, were distinctly partisan on questions other than the slavery controversy, and hesitated to declare themselves independent of the major parties. Hence the American Anti-Slavery Society at Cleveland late in October, 1839, decided that for the time being a bargaining with the candidates of the existing political organizations was preferable to a separate party alignment.

The elections of 1839 were far from satisfactory to the abolitionists. A large proportion of the new legislature was favorable to the continuance of the fugitive slave legislation of the previous session, and Wade, head of the Whig abolitionists in the senate, had been defeated by over three hundred votes in his contest for reëlection. Early in 1840, at the annual Democratic state convention in Columbus, strong resolutions against abolitionist agitation were introduced, and when ex-Senator Thomas Morris attempted to speak in opposition, he was termed "a rotten branch that should be lopped off," a designation that was so thoroughly applauded by the other delegates that Morris withdrew from the convention.

At the state Anti-Slavery Society meeting at Massillon in May, 1840, the majority of the delegates agreed that the organization should not be turned into a political party, but subsequently a definite feeling arose that Harrison's utterances were not satisfactory to the abolitionists, and a second convention at Hamilton, in September, resolved to support Birney for the Presidency on the Liberty ticket. Some difficulty was encountered in securing a list of electors, and the casting of only 892 votes for the Presidential candidate was not encouraging, but the *Philanthropist* found consolation in the declaration that at least "a nucleus" had been established for the new party.

National Politics in Ohio during the Forties

Upon the elevation to the Presidency of William Henry Harrison, Justice John McLean, the United States Supreme Court jurist from Ohio, was offered the position of secretary of war in the new Cabinet. He declined the post, but the position of secretary of the treasury was accepted by another Ohioan, ex-Senator Thomas Ewing, of Lancaster.

Although the election had been won largely by the demagogic appeal of the worth of the "plain farmer of North Bend" over the "aristocratic" Van Buren, during Harrison's brief month of office and, following his death, under Tyler's administration, the Whigs represented the conservative point of view in both national and state politics. In the arena of national affairs, they generally supported Clay's plans for the party, and two Ohio Congressmen played an active rôle in the meeting of indignation at Washington following Tyler's second veto of a proposed scheme for a new national financial institution.

Disappointed further on account of the method of Tyler's distribution of Federal appointments, and unenthusiastic over Webster's political ambitions, in 1844 the Whigs of Ohio rather naturally turned to Clay as their favorite candidate for the Presidency. As the anti-slavery movement grew in influence and received the support of such men as Salmon P. Chase, Samuel Lewis (Ohio's first Superintendent of Common Schools, and an able leader), and Edward Wade, the Whigs were considerably alarmed, for they well knew that, if the movement continued, defections from their ranks would be greater than from those of the Democrats. During 1844, however, the Whigs maintained that Clay's ideal was an emancipation to be achieved by gradual process, a contention that for the time being held such ardent anti-slavery men as Joshua R. Giddings within the Clay ranks.

The Democrats found difficulty in reconciling the differences of their radical and conservative factions. Lewis Cass, of Michigan, whose desire for support from both sides led him into a rather equivocal position on financial matters, was more conservative than Van Buren; but the latter, who had been well received on a trip through Ohio in 1842, became the favorite of the delegation from Ohio to the national convention. When Polk, a dark horse, was eventually nominated, his famous letter to Senator Kane, of Pennsylvania, indicating a viewpoint satisfactory to Ohioans on the tariff question made it clear that that problem would not be a vital issue, and so the annexation of Texas and the creation of a national bank became the storm centers of controversy.

In regard to Texas, the Ohio Whigs opposed annexation, realizing the dangers to Northern political control and to the continuance of the Union, although, like the Democrats, they insisted upon expansion through the securing of definite title to the Oregon country. The Democrats frankly favored annexation, and, as a party, were less friendly to anti-slavery principles than the Whigs, although Edwin M. Stanton and former Senator Thomas Morris were notable exceptions. Many Ohioans attributed the prosperity of the period to the Whig tariff of 1842, business men reacted against the Democratic financial policy in the state, and some even accused the Democrats of being "levellers," committed to principles such as had produced the Dorr Rebellion in Rhode Island. These factors, together with the nomination of James G. Birney, the Liberty Party's Presidential candidate, for the General Assembly of Michigan by the Democrats (a fact that kept anti-slavery Whigs within their old party), the unpopularity of the Democratic plea for the annexation of Texas, and the lack of enthusiasm on the part of radical Democrats for Polk, assisted Clay in carrying Ohio.

With the Democrats once again in control of the national administration, leaders of the party in the Northwest began to demand a more considerable share in the councils of the nation, and urged Samuel Medary, an aggressive Columbus editor, for the post of postmaster-general. Division among Ohio Democrats and Polk's inability to see the need for conciliating that section of the country prevented a realization of this hope, and quarrels between the hard-money and paper-currency elements of the party hindered the granting of other appointments to Ohioans.

In relation to annexation, the Whig general assembly had "instructed" the Senators and "requested" the Representatives from Ohio to oppose the securing of Texas, but the Democratic Congressmen from the state supported the joint resolution that sanctioned its acquisition.[2] Both

---

[2] When Calhoun's treaty for annexation had been secretly put before the Senate (in 1844), through the agency of Senator Tappan, of Ohio, it was

Whigs and Democrats urged the "reoccupation" of all of Oregon, though the former condemned the belligerent, bluntly imperialistic attitude of the latter. William Allen, one of Ohio's Democratic Senators, who was chairman of the Foreign Relations Committee of the upper House, was emboldened by the tone of leaders and newspapers in his home state and insisted upon the Russian Line (54° 40′) as the northern boundary. Polk felt suspicious that Allen was bidding for popular support for the Presidency in the nominating convention of 1848, and referred the British offer of the forty-ninth parallel to the Senate—an act that induced Allen's resignation from the Foreign Relations Committee.

Shortly afterward, the Oregon question came to an end by a treaty with Great Britain, but a war with Mexico was not avoided. Ohio was not especially enthusiastic over the contest, and although only five Whig Representatives from Ohio voted against the declaration of hostilities, the Whig press denounced the war as one "commenced by James K. Polk, as president, for personal, political and sectional aggrandizement, and not to redress national wrong and vindicate national honor—to acquire territory for the use, benefit, and extension of Southern Slavery and the augmentation of the Slave power in the councils of our General Government."

In December, 1846, a series of resolutions, introduced in the Ohio house and pledging hearty support to the administration, were rejected by a strictly party vote, and in their stead were passed others condemning the war and the course of the President. The Democrats accused the Whigs of giving comfort to the enemy, but the opposition to the war continued, climaxed by the memorable speech of

---

published in the New York *Evening Post*. Tappan apologized to the Senate, but was censured by that body. The treaty was later rejected by the Senate.

Thomas Corwin, of Ohio, in the Senate of the United States (in February, 1847). In this oratorical effort, which was generally considered as a bid for the Presidency in 1848, Corwin denounced the war as wrong, as actuated by motives of conquest, and urged that the United States troops be withdrawn from Mexico. Refusing to vote for any further appropriations for the armed forces, he cried, "If I were a Mexican, I would tell you: Have you not room in your own country to bury your dead men? If you come into mine we will greet you with bloody hands, and welcome you to hospitable graves." Although Corwin was branded as a traitor by the Democratic press and deserted by some of his Whig friends, such men as Joshua R. Giddings urged him for the Presidency, many of his constituents agreed with his point of view, and the judiciary committee of the state senate refused to act upon petitions for his removal.

Most of the Whigs and Democrats of Ohio alike opposed any extension of slavery, but the Whigs objected to any territorial expansion to the southwest, while the Democrats demanded the acquisition of territory, declaring that slavery could not exist in any of the area that might be acquired from Mexico until legalized by positive enactment. It was a Richland County Democrat, Jacob Brinkerhoff, who framed the resolution proposed in Congress refusing to grant any money for territory where slavery would be permitted, a resolution actually introduced by a Pennsylvanian and named, after him, the Wilmot Proviso. Southern Democrats wished to make opposition to the Proviso a test of party loyalty, but such a criterion of partisanship was vehemently resisted by the Ohio Democracy.

During 1847 the Whigs continued their opposition to the war, a Columbus organ of the party urged a great anti-war state convention (that failed to materialize), and the party in the fall elections gained control of both houses of the legislature. The Whig convention in 1848 declared the war to be an "unjust, unnecessary and bloody war with a sister republic," compared our attitude with the greed of Russia, Austria, and Prussia toward Poland, and called upon Congress to terminate the conflict.

In all, Ohio raised seven thousand men to fight under the national colors in the struggle, and among others Brigadier General Thomas L. Hamer, a former[3] Democratic Congressman from Brown County, who was serving under General Zachary Taylor, gave up his life in the war.

In the Presidential contest that came in the year of peace (1848), the Whigs of Ohio probably preferred Corwin to any other candidate, but the impossibility of support for him in other states raised the question as to whom they should indorse for the nomination. The opposition to Zachary Taylor was overwhelming on the Western Reserve, but the Ohio delegation, after hard work for Winfield Scott, eventually acquiesced in the selection of the former. Cass's candidacy and nomination in the Democratic camp was generally well received by the party men in Ohio, except for some radicals who identified him as an ally of the slave power.

The anti-Southern elements in both of the major parties were not satisfied with these nominations, hence Salmon P. Chase penned a call for a People's State Convention to meet in Columbus to consider the political situation. Assembling in June, this body, which proved to be "a large and harmonious" one, adopted resolutions recommending a national convention of those favoring free soil in the territories. As a result, such an assemblage met in Buffalo

---

[3] He had been elected to the Thirtieth Congress (1847–1849) also, but died before it convened.

in August, was presided over by Chase, and presented Van Buren for the Presidency. This candidacy thereupon was supported by some radical Ohio Democrats, but most of the "Free Soilers," as the new partisans were called, had been anti-Southern Whigs. In the fall elections, Van Buren carried only six Ohio counties—all in that former Whig stronghold, the Western Reserve. This vote was primarily a protest against Southern dictation, but it enabled Cass to secure a plurality of sixteen thousand votes over Taylor in the state and well-nigh wrecked the Whig Party in Ohio.

The loss of the state by the Whigs prevented Ohioans from securing much recognition in the appointments of the administration of Zachary Taylor, although Thomas Ewing was placed in the Cabinet as the head of the newly organized Department of the Interior.

State Politics during the Forties

In state politics, in spite of the divisions among the Democrats on financial matters, the Whigs were the especial guardians of vested property rights. In 1839, the Democrats had passed the Banking Commissioner Law, and in 1842, as a result of the reaction against Whig policies and of the discontent caused by the closing of a Cincinnati bank in January, 1842, they were in a position to enact more drastic legislation. The Latham Act of 1842, a general banking law that provided for individual liability of stockholders and officers of banks, was the result. The severity of the measure did not attract capital to comply with the terms of the law, hence no new banks were chartered, and in February, 1843, the Act was modified to satisfy the conservative Democrats. By December, 1843, Governor Shannon, who had been elected over Corwin in 1842 at the same time that the Democrats were continued in control of the legislature, declared a belief in a "well-guarded and well-restricted system of local banks," a material concession to the Whig program. Early in 1844, the legislature passed a bill granting special privileges to the Bank of Wooster—a procedure that marked a definite breakdown in the united front of the Democrats. It was believed by many that the Tyler Whigs had supported Shannon and were in collusion with him; at any rate the Governor was appointed Minister to Mexico in April, 1844, the position of acting governor being assumed by Thomas M. Bartley.

In the fall of the same year, David Tod, a son of George Tod, the Ohio jurist who had been involved a generation before in the struggle between the legislature and judiciary in Ohio, was the Democratic candidate for governor. He ran on a strong anti-bank platform against Mordecai Bartley, of Richland County, a veteran of the War of 1812, who had served in the state senate, and in Congress (from 1823 to 1831). Disaffection among the Democrats, the flooding of the state with currency from other localities, and the lack of enthusiasm for the national (Polk) ticket led to a Whig victory, both the governorship and the control of the legislature being won by that party. Incidentally, this victory involved the succession of a Whig father to the position occupied by his Democratic son.

Whig success was promptly expressed in the Kelley Bank Act of 1845, named for Alfred Kelley,[4] long a prominent figure in Ohio's political and economic life. This law provided that, in addition to the old banks already in existence, two new types of financial institutions might be created: (a) independent organizations; and (b) a "State

---

[4] Kelley was a dominant and constructive influence in the development of Ohio's canal system. His old home, once a show place in Columbus, is now occupied by St. Joseph's Cathedral School.

Bank of Ohio." The total amount of all new bank stock was not to exceed $6,150,000, the state being divided into twelve districts with a limitation as to the number of banks and the capitalization in each district. There were provisions for maximum and minimum capitalization, with all applications for charters to be passed upon by a board of commissioners.

There was no central bank in connection with the state bank: branches were to be established, and when seven had been organized, each could appoint a representative to a board of control. To this central organization, each branch had to surrender ten per cent of the amount of its circulating notes for a safety fund to be invested in state or United States securities or in first mortgages. The independent banks, on the other hand, were required to deposit state or United States securities equal to their capital with the state treasurer, to be used as a fund for the redemption of notes.

By July, 1845, the seven branch banks required for the formation of the state institution had been incorporated, eight independent banks had been organized, and this banking system, which was to last in its essential features for twenty years, had begun to function.

In 1846, the conservative Democrats desired to have Thomas L. Hamer as the nominee for the governorship, but David Tod, whom the radical Democrats supported, was named on a platform declaring for an exclusive gold and silver currency and a prohibition of all bank charters— a stand that alarmed many conservative Democrats. Another question that commanded much attention was the proposed repeal of the Black Laws, which placed restrictions upon the Negroes denying them the right to testify against a white man and requiring bond from them against becoming public charges. The Liberty Party urged the repeal of this legislation, but both Whigs and Democrats experienced difficulty in meeting the issue. Tod at first ignored the question but finally came out definitely against the proposed change. William Bebb, the Whig candidate, tended to favor repeal, but his position aroused so much antagonism that he modified it. Bebb was successful in the election, but southern Ohio Whigs objected so much to the abrogation of the laws that they remained on the statute books.

Two years later, the discontented classes of the state, interested in both political and economic reform, showed a tendency to embrace the Free Soil Party. This attitude impelled the Democratic leaders to become more liberal, and John B. Weller, their candidate for governor, approved the policy of the National Reform Association—an organization that aggressively advocated free homesteads for actual settlers. Nevertheless, they lost to the new party important individuals such as Jacob Brinkerhoff and ex-Senator Benjamin Tappan, while the Whigs lost men of the type of Joshua R. Giddings.

The Free Soilers, however, offered no candidate for the governorship, and Seabury Ford, the Whig nominee, tended to curry their favor by maintaining a studied silence on Taylor's nomination for President, and by indorsing unreservedly the repeal of the Black Laws. The increasingly large number of people of foreign birth augmented the Democratic vote against the Whigs, who were tinged with anti-foreign or nativist tendencies, but Weller lost the office to Ford by a margin of slightly more than three hundred votes. As to the legislature, the outcome was so close that the Free Soilers held the balance of power both in the house of representatives and on a joint ballot of the two houses.[5]

---

[5] For further details, see the next chapter.

The Second Constitutional Convention

The Democrats and Free Soilers coöperated in a movement for a new constitution, and in 1849 the legislature passed a bill to refer the question of a new constitutional convention to the voters. Much of the dissatisfaction with the existing constitution arose from the wholly inadequate judicial system, which placed upon the shoulders of four judges the task of holding court each year in all of the counties, which in 1849 numbered eighty-five.[6] Then, the constitution of 1802 had concentrated authority in the hands of the legislature, which was empowered to choose all state officials of importance except the governor. This situation had led to considerable logrolling and to the control of the body by special political and economic interests. As a result, a demand had arisen for the popular election of all public officials, for a prohibition of charters that granted exclusive privileges, and for the limitation of the power of the legislature to create a state debt (which at that time, through canal appropriations, aid to railroads, and other grants, amounted to almost twenty million dollars, largely held outside the state).

At the polls in 1849, the voters favored a constitutional convention by a vote of 145,698 to 51,161, and the legislature in February, 1850, called for the election of delegates in April to meet in convention in May. The Democrats held a clear majority among the delegates chosen, there being more members of their party than of the Whig and Free Soil Parties combined. Forty-three of the delegates were lawyers by vocation, and thirty of them were farmers. Among the leaders were William Medill, of Fairfield

---

[6] There are now eighty-eight counties in the state. Fulton and Vinton Counties were organized in 1850, and Noble County in 1851.

County, a Democrat, who was chosen president of the convention; Peter Hitchcock, of Geauga County, who was a member of the Supreme Court of Ohio for almost a generation (from 1824 to 1852); Joseph R. Swan, of Franklin County, a noted lawyer and later a judge of the supreme court of the state (from 1854 to 1859); Charles Reemelin, who represented the viewpoint of the German "radicals" of Cincinnati; William S. Groesbeck and Henry Stanbery—the former of Hamilton County, the latter from Franklin County—both of whom achieved renown as members of President Johnson's counsel in the famous impeachment trial;[7] ex-Governor Vance, of Champaign County; and Samuel J. Kirkwood, of Richland County, who later became Governor of Iowa, United States Senator from that state, and Secretary of the Interior under Garfield.

The new constitution did not materially change the power of the governor, still withholding from him the right of veto. The number of supreme court judges was increased to five,[8] and they, like other members of the judiciary, were to be chosen by popular vote instead of by the legislature. The courts intermediate between the supreme court and the courts of common pleas were designated as district courts, served by common pleas and supreme court judges and possessing the same original jurisdiction as the supreme court and such appellate jurisdiction as might be fixed by law.

The legislature, members of which were to be chosen biennially, was prohibited from creating any county of less than four hundred square miles, and it was required that any laws for the creation of new counties or for the changing of existing county boundaries should be referred

---

[7] Stanbery became a resident of Cincinnati in 1853. He was President Johnson's Attorney General, 1866–1868.

[8] By an act of 1892 the number was increased to six.

to the people of the counties affected. The aggregate debt of the state was limited to seven hundred fifty thousand dollars, and all appropriations were to be used only for the specific purpose designated. The state was prohibited from contracting debts for internal improvements, and only general acts, and not special ones, could be passed for the conferring of corporate powers.

A board of commissioners of the sinking fund was created for the purpose of extinguishing the state debt. The voting franchise was granted to all white male adult citizens of one year's residence—the Negro being counted in the apportioning of representatives, but not granted the ballot. Lotteries were prohibited, as were poll taxes. Taxation was to be based upon the "uniform rule"—the principle that all classes of property should be subject to the same rate. No license to traffic in intoxicating liquors was to be granted in the state.

Amendments might be made by the approval of three-fifths of each of the houses of the legislature—a sanction to be ratified, after six months of publication, by a majority of the voters actually casting their ballots at the election of state representatives and senators. A two-thirds vote of each house of the legislature and the approval of a majority of those voting at the polls in the next contest for the legislature were to be necessary for the calling of a constitutional convention. At the regular general election of 1871, and in each twentieth year thereafter, the question of holding a constitutional convention was to be submitted to the voters.

The constitutional convention of 1850, which had assembled in May, in Columbus, adjourned in July because of an epidemic of the cholera. Meeting again in Cincinnati, beginning in December, it continued its deliberations until March 10, 1851. Provision was made for the submission of the new document to the voters at a special election on June 17, with a separate submission at the same time of the proposition to prohibit the license of the sale of intoxicants. Both proposals were accepted by the voters—the constitution by a vote of 125,564 to 109,276.[9] Thus, approval was secured for the second constitution of Ohio, which was to become effective on September 1, 1851, and which has remained until the present time essentially the fundamental law of the commonwealth.

SELECTED BIBLIOGRAPHY

The political narrative of the period comprising this chapter is related in a detailed and accurate way by Edgar A. Holt in "Party Politics in Ohio, 1840–1850," *Ohio Archæological and Historical Quarterly*, Vols. XXXVII and XXXVIII; also printed separately. Several of the biographies cited in Chapter VII are also valuable for this period, especially McGrane, *William Allen*, pp. 57–135, and Mrs. Dorothy B. Goebel, *William Henry Harrison*. The career of Senator Thomas Morris, the first abolitionist Senator, is interpreted by his son, B. F. Morris, in *The Life of Thomas Morris* (Cincinnati, 1856). Josiah Morrow, *Life and Speeches of Thomas Corwin* (Cincinnati, 1896), is inadequate. Brief but satisfactory sketches of Thomas Corwin (by H. C. Hockett) and of Thomas Ewing (by R. C. McGrane) may be found in the *Dictionary of American Biography* (in progress), edited by Allen Johnson and Dumas Malone. This series is especially helpful in the case of many lesser lights, accounts of whose careers are not easily accessible elsewhere. Biographies of anti-slavery leaders who spent at least part of their careers in Ohio are: Geo. W. Julian, *Life of Joshua R. Giddings* (Chicago, 1897); Albert G. Riddle, *The Life of Benjamin F. Wade* (Cleveland, 1886); A. B. Hart, *Life of Salmon P. Chase* (Boston, 1899); Jacob W. Schuckers, *The Life and Public Services of Salmon Portland Chase* (New York, 1874); and R. B. Warden, *An Account of the Private Life and Public Services of Salmon Portland Chase* (Cincinnati, 1874).

---

[9] The returns of two counties, Defiance and Auglaize, were not counted, since they were not received within the twenty days specified.

The beginnings of the anti-slavery movement in Ohio are related in Chaddock, *op. cit.*, pp. 78–109, and Galbreath, Vol. II, pp. 153–212. The authoritative work on the Underground Railroad is W. H. Siebert, *The Underground Railroad from Slavery to Freedom* (New York, 1898). Of interest in the same connection are the *Reminiscences of Levi Coffin, the Reputed President of the Underground Railroad* (Cincinnati, 1876). A scholarly monograph on Free Soil political alignments is Theodore C. Smith, *Liberty and Free Soil Parties in the Northwest* (New York, 1897).

C. C. Huntington, *A History of Banking and Currency in Ohio before the Civil War* (previously mentioned) explains the financial problems of the period. A significant contribution in the same general field is Ernest L. Bogart, "Financial History of Ohio," *University of Illinois Studies in Social Science*, Vol. I (Urbana, 1912).

The movement for a second constitution of Ohio is discussed in detail in Galbreath, Vol. II, pp. 39–67. The text of the constitution is given in Isaac F. Patterson, *The Constitutions of Ohio* (Cleveland, 1912), pp. 117–160.

CHAPTER X

Slavery and Politics in the 1850's

The Great Compromise and its Aftermath, 1848–1853

*T*HE immediate result of the election of 1848 was a bitter party struggle for control of the general assembly. The Free Soil movement had shattered the Whig Party in the Western Reserve and had given the balance of power in the assembly to the third-party radicals. A United States senatorship, two supreme judgeships, and a number of lesser state offices, all chosen by the assembly, were the stakes for which the parties struggled. The Free Soilers were in an admirable position to secure both offices and favorable legislation by bargains with the major parties for support.

A further complication appeared in the form of two contested seats from Hamilton County in the lower house. The preceding Whig assembly had divided the county for electoral purposes into two districts, one of which would elect a senator and three representatives, the other a senator and two representatives. In this way, the Whigs hoped to overcome the large Democratic majorities when the county voted as a unit, and thus secure at least part of the delegation to the assembly. The Democrats claimed that the constitution did not permit the division of a county, and refused to abide by the law. At the election of 1848, they voted as usual with the entire county as the unit, and chose five Democrats to the lower house. The Whigs, voting by districts according to the law, carried one of the districts, and sent two Whig representatives to

Columbus to contest the claims of two of the Democrats.[1]
Upon the eight Free Soil members of the house fell the
responsibility of a decision.

No session of the assembly has occasioned greater excitement or more intrigue. All three parties wanted the great
prize at stake—the United States senatorship—while, in
addition, the Free Soilers saw an opportunity to secure the
repeal of the Black Laws, which for many years had placed
the Negro legally in an inferior position, even though
having slight practical effect. Both major parties were
willing to bargain with the third party, but the Whigs soon
found themselves at a disadvantage. Six of the eight Free
Soilers were former Whigs and were favorable to that party,
but the two remaining ones, John F. Morse and Norton S.
Townshend, who held the real balance of power, showed an
inclination to make terms only with the Democrats.
Influencing their actions was Salmon P. Chase, the Cincinnati Free Soil leader, who was ambitious to secure the
United States senatorship.

After a bitter struggle, the house finally seated the
Democratic claimants from Hamilton County by the votes
of the two independent Free Soilers, after which seating
the Black Laws were repealed, both Whigs and Democrats
assisting the Free Soilers to this end. But in the vote
for the United States senatorship, the Democrats and the
two independents joined forces to elect Chase—the two
supreme judgeships going to the Democrats. Whigs and
Free Soilers both sharply criticized this bargain, though they

---

[1] No senator was elected by this district in 1848, as its turn was not to
come until 1849. Senators, unlike representatives, were chosen for two-year
terms, half of them being elected each year. After the election of 1849, however, this problem came up in the senate when a Whig, elected by the district,
contested the claim of a Democrat, chosen by the whole county. Eventually
the Whig was given the seat, but the apportionment law itself was repealed
by the assembly, so that final victory rested with the Democrats.

had been unable themselves to agree on a satisfactory candidate—Giddings, the choice of the latter, proving unacceptable to the Whigs. The friends of Chase acclaimed the result as a great anti-slavery victory and Chase went to Washington to achieve national eminence, ranking with Seward, Hale, and Sumner as an outstanding leader of the anti-slavery cause. But the bargain convinced many people that he was ambitious for himself rather than his cause and aroused antagonisms that haunted him to the close of his political career.

The great problem of the Whigs in Ohio at the beginning of the 1850's was to win back the anti-slavery element that had deserted the party when Zachary Taylor became the Presidential candidate in 1848. Without this element, their chances would be slight, for the two major parties were too evenly balanced to permit any losses to the third party without serious effects at elections. When President Taylor, in an attempt to settle the slavery issue, declared for the immediate admission of California and New Mexico as states without any conditions attached, the Whigs were jubilant, for this admission would mean two more free states and would give proof that the slaveholding President was not pro-Southern. Taylor's opposition to Henry Clay's compromise proposals strengthened the President greatly in Ohio, and the Whigs were quite hopeful of winning back their former supporters in the Western Reserve. At this juncture, Taylor's sudden death (July, 1850) threatened to destroy these bright prospects. Would the new President adhere to his predecessor's plan, or would he adopt Clay's compromise proposals?

President Fillmore appointed Ohio's best-known Whig, Thomas Corwin, then in the Senate, as his Secretary of the Treasury, leading many Ohioans to hope that Corwin might influence the President in the right direction. "A change of policy would not leave a grease spot of us in Ohio at all events," wrote one prominent Whig to Corwin. But Fillmore was a conservative, fearful over the safety of the Union and anxious to end the slavery controversy. He supported the viewpoint of Clay and Webster; Corwin silently acquiesced, and the great Compromise of 1850 passed Congress and went into effect.

The October state election showed that the fears of the Ohio Whigs were well founded. For the first time since 1842, a Democrat was elected Governor, Reuben Wood defeating William Johnston, a Whig, by nearly twelve thousand votes. A Free Soil candidate had more than thirteen thousand votes, while a little group of Free Soilers from the Western Reserve again held the balance of power in the legislature. The third party, which had seemed on the verge of dissolution early in the campaign, had revived with the passage of the great Compromise and again was in a strong position in the Reserve. Both major parties had avoided the slavery issue and had emphasized the familiar banking and currency question, now especially important as the constitutional convention was in session. But the fact that a Whig President was responsible for the passage of the Compromise measures drove anti-slavery radicals away from that party and was sufficient to give the Democrats the victory, regardless of other issues.

The most hated feature of the Compromise of 1850 was, of course, the new Fugitive Slave Law. All through the North, in the fall of 1850, public meetings were held to denounce the act, and were only partially counteracted by "Union" meetings of business men and other conservatives, alarmed at the agitation against the Compromise. In northern Ohio and particularly in the Western Reserve, the Fugitive Law "rekindled all the fires of fanaticism," as one observer put it, "and they are burning with more fury

than ever." At public meetings resolutions urging people
to disobey the law were passed, while the *Ashtabula
Sentinel* advised the fugitive to receive the slave catcher
"with powder and ball, with dirk and bowie-knife, or
whatever weapon be most convenient. Slay the miscreant
. . . . wait not to determine whether it be Daniel Webster
or the editor of the Cleveland Herald, if he comes to
re-enslave you or your wife or child furnish him with a
speedy and hospitable grave."

In the face of such utterances, conservative Whigs and
Democrats grew alarmed, and public meetings at Dayton
and Cincinnati urged all good citizens to uphold the laws.
Leading newspapers, which had been opposed to the passage
of the law, now urged its acceptance as the only solution.
Governor Ford, a Whig, and his Democratic successor,
Reuben Wood, wanted Congress to repeal the hated law,
but neither advocated nullification. The general assembly
took the same position, and the agitation presently died
down. Yet the radicals were unreconciled, and when in
the succeeding years fugitives were seized by Federal
officers, serious trouble occurred.

The last Whig triumph of any importance in Ohio came
in the election of a United States Senator by the legislature
of 1850–1851. The Free Soilers, still holding the balance
of power, found it impossible to elect Giddings or any other
Free Soiler, as both the old parties refused to bargain with
them. Conservative Democrats as well as Whigs were
angry over the election of Chase in 1849 and would not
permit a third-party man to be chosen. After a long
deadlock, both Whigs and Free Soilers threw their votes
to Judge Benjamin F. Wade, of Ashtabula County, in the
Western Reserve, and he was chosen. Wade was a staunch
Whig, but his bitter criticism of the Fugitive Slave Law
and his anti-slavery radicalism made him acceptable to the

third party. Thus, within two years Ohio found itself represented in the United States Senate by two anti-slavery radicals, though the majority of the people were very far from accepting their viewpoint. The Western Reserve had brought about both these results by its control of the balance of power in the assembly.

The new constitution, adopted in June, 1851, provided for a state election for governor and several other officers in October of that year and every two years thereafter, thus making the odd years the important ones in state politics instead of the even-numbered, which had been the important ones in the first half-century of statehood. The Democrats, enthusiastic over their success in securing the adoption of the new frame of government, swept to an easy victory over the Whigs in the fall election. The Free Soilers, dismayed by the defection of Chase, who now avowed himself a Democrat, made little headway in the campaign. The Democracy was supreme in all departments of the state government.

The next two years saw a continuation of Democratic successes. The Whigs had some hope of carrying the state in 1852, as their Presidential candidate, General Winfield Scott, was a popular figure and much more satisfactory to Ohio Whigs than the leading statesmen of the party, who were generally involved in the Compromise measures. But the Free Soilers, now calling themselves Free Democrats, refused to accept Scott, and carried several of the Western Reserve counties for their Presidential candidate, John P. Hale. As a consequence, the Democrats won the election, and Ohio's electoral vote was given to Franklin Pierce. The state election of 1853 marked the disappearance of the Whig Party in Ohio. The temperance question now displaced all the old issues, but the Whigs could not present a united front on it and

suffered a disastrous defeat. The Free Democrats declared
for the destruction of the liquor traffic and greatly increased
their vote, while the Democrats, though not officially
committed, were more unfriendly to temperance than their
rivals and profited by the pronounced "wet" tendencies
of the majority of the voters.

Thus, the old political alignments seemed about to
disappear, and Ohio was ready for a reorganization of
parties. The failure of the Whigs to recover the anti-
slavery element that had deserted them in 1848 had proved
fatal. They could not win without the Western Reserve.
Yet the Whig Party seemed out of touch also with the
prevailing tendencies of the age. As the faithful Whig
Ohio State Journal aptly described the national contest of
1852: "We have been fighting against the destructive
tendencies of Dorrism, Anti-rentism, Filibusterism, Native
Americanism, Abolitionism and Loco-focoism. Our triumph would have been the triumph of conservative and
healthy influences." But the United States of the early
1850's was ready for experiment and change, whether
"healthy" or not. Whig negation could not suffice.
The term "radical" was the password to political success,
but to propertied Whiggery the very word was dangerous.

On the other hand, the Democrats, with a radical
program on state issues and an aggressive foreign policy
for the nation, could proclaim that they represented the
ideas of "Young America" as opposed to "Old Fogieism."
The third party in Ohio was also quite conscious of the
ferment of the age when it declared in its platform of
1853 for a variety of democratic reforms besides anti-
slavery. It even hoped to assume the place of defunct
Whiggery as a major party. But conservative Whigs,
living in central and southern Ohio and dominant in the
party, while admitting that their organization was dead,

were not ready to become Free Democrats. It remained for the events of 1854 and 1855 to determine their course.

The Political Revolution, 1854–1856

When Senator Stephen A. Douglas, of Illinois, introduced his Nebraska Bill in Congress in January, 1854, he set in motion a train of events almost as significant in American history as those that grew out of the famous "Boston Tea Party," for the Douglas measure opened to slavery a section of the old Louisiana Purchase that had been reserved for freedom ever since the great Missouri Compromise of 1820. At once a wave of indignation swept over the North, encouraged by Chase, Giddings, and other anti-slavery leaders, who saw a golden opportunity to further their cause. Public meetings of protest culminated in Ohio in a great state-wide mass convention, held at Columbus in March to voice the sentiment of the state against the Douglas proposal. Whigs, Democrats, and third-party men all attended, for the meeting was nonpartisan in character, though it was evident that the politicians were well represented. Probably nothing further would have happened had the Nebraska Bill failed; but, after a long and bitter struggle in Congress, the measure carried and President Pierce signed it. At once the three leading Whig papers suggested a state convention to unite the opponents of the act. With the Whig Party practically extinct, it seemed possible to build a new party from the various elements opposed to the opening of the territories to slavery. Whigs, Free Soilers, and anti-slavery Democrats in large numbers approved of the movement, and July 13, the anniversary of the passage of the Ordinance of 1787, was selected as the date for the convention.

This state convention of Anti-Nebraska men was the beginning of a great reorganization of parties. To it came anti-slavery men of all parties, and of no party, as well as shrewd politicians drawn thither by the promising possibilities in such a movement. Enthusiasm ran high, and the harmonious character of the proceedings surpassed the expectations of the most hopeful. While the radicals would have preferred to make the Fugitive Slave Law as well as the Kansas-Nebraska Act an issue, the moderates wisely held to the latter point, and the platform merely demanded that the territories be made free and that no more slave states be admitted. This policy satisfied conservative Whigs who were aroused over the repeal of the venerated Missouri Compromise, but who had no desire to go over to abolitionism. Even as it was, Corwin, Ewing, and other old Whig leaders did not take part in the movement, though they were sympathetic with its main purposes. On the other hand, the radicals, while not satisfied with the moderate temper of the majority, were too glad to have Whig and Democratic allies to cavil at the platform.

Although only two minor state offices were at stake in the coming election, the convention decided to run candidates to show the strength of the Anti-Nebraska cause. Judge Joseph R. Swan, of Columbus, at that time probably Ohio's greatest legal authority, who had taken the lead in the early stages of the Anti-Nebraska agitation, was named for supreme judge, with Jacob Blickensderfer, a former Whig, as the candidate for the Board of Public Works. Swan was a Democrat, but he had voted for Van Buren on the Free Soil ticket in 1848 and so satisfied the old third-party men. Thus the two candidates seemed to represent all three parties.

Unlike the movement in Michigan and other Northwestern states, the Ohio convention did not adopt the name Republican, though the *Ohio State Journal* referred to the nominations under that designation. Indeed, such terms as "Democratic Republican," "People's Democratic," "Anti-Nebraska," and "Reform" were used in different parts of the state. However, the term "Fusionist," applied to them by their opponents, probably best described the character of the movement.

At the very moment when the Democratic Party seemed about to pay the penalty for its folly in reopening the slavery issue, a new danger of a very different character suddenly appeared. This was "Know-Nothingism." Starting in the East as a secret society directed against foreign-born and Roman Catholics, it spread rapidly westward, entering Ohio in the spring of 1854. Outside of Cincinnati, nearly half of whose population was of foreign birth, the Germans and Irish constituted no problem for the natives in Ohio. Yet thousands of people in the small towns and rural districts joined the Know-Nothing lodges, drawn by the lure of secrecy and the clever appeals of organizers to the anti-Catholic prejudice ever present in most Protestant communities. Because the foreign-born were usually Democrats, the secret society drew in many Whigs who, despairing of their party's future, saw in this new movement an opportunity to combat their old opponents with a new weapon. Even many sincere anti-slavery men became Know-Nothings, as this seemed to be one way of rallying the forces hostile to the Nebraska Bill. Giddings, later a sharp critic of the secret order, declared that he at first looked upon it in a friendly spirit as "a screen—a dark wall—behind which members of old political organizations could escape unseen from party shackles, and take a new position, according to the dictates of judgment and conscience." Thus, largely because of the disturbed political situation,[2] the new secret society received a warm welcome in Ohio.

---

[2] An exception should be made, perhaps, in the case of Cincinnati, where anti-foreignism had existed before Know-Nothingism made its appearance.

Although a little fearful of the effect upon the Germans, the Fusion leaders quietly accepted Know-Nothing support, and the latter became an active element in the Anti-Nebraska movement. The Democrats, anxious to get away from the slavery issue, emphasized the anti-foreign tendencies of the opposition, in the hope of retaining their Irish and German supporters. But their opponents refused to be led away from their strongest argument and continued the war upon the Kansas-Nebraska Act. Occasionally, a Fusion paper would contain anti-Catholic propaganda, but since the majority of the Germans were Protestants and many were freethinkers, this position was satisfactory to them: their vote was important, while the less numerous Irish could be sacrificed to the demands of Protestant prejudice.

The election, singularly quiet—considering the importance of the issues—was a Fusion landslide. Judge Swan had a majority of over seventy-seven thousand, carrying all but ten counties, while a complete Anti-Nebraska slate of Congressmen was chosen—an astonishing reversal of the sweeping Democratic triumph of the preceding year. Unquestionably, Ohioans were bent upon punishing the party responsible for the repeal of the Missouri Compromise.

Yet other factors had had a share in this outcome. The radical tendencies of the Democratic Party had been revealed in state policies after the new Constitution was adopted, particularly in a drastic tax law designed to place heavier burdens on the banks. The law failed in this purpose, as the banks appealed to the United States courts to protect their charters against this interference.[3]

---

[3] The United States Supreme Court held in this case as in earlier cases that corporation charters were contracts not to be altered except with the consent of the corporation. Laws attempting to tax by some other method than that prescribed in the charter violated the provision of the United States Constitution forbidding a state to impair the obligation of a contract.

On the other hand, business men were angered because the tax law, as interpreted by the Ohio courts, placed a heavier load of taxation on their shoulders. Many of them, especially at Cincinnati, voted the Anti-Nebraska ticket to show their resentment. This situation and the Know-Nothing agitation contributed to turn a certain Democratic defeat into a disaster that almost destroyed the party. The slavery issue alone could not have caused such a result. As Rutherford B. Hayes, a young Cincinnati lawyer, put it in his diary, "Anti-Nebraska, Know-Nothings, and general disgust with the powers that be, have carried this county by between seven and eight thousand majority." The voters were voting their resentments.

Whether this almost unwieldy Fusion movement could be transformed into a party was the great problem for the Anti-Nebraska leaders. Their success had been almost too overwhelming, for it produced a struggle on the part of two powerful factions to control and direct this new force in Ohio politics. One of these, the radical anti-slavery element, was fearful that the conservatives would gain control and make the organization into a mild form of Whiggery. Chase, Giddings, Judge Spalding, James M. Ashley, the Wades, and other staunch anti-slavery men, mostly from northern Ohio, were of this view. They were generally of Free Soil or Democratic origin, with a few radical Whigs included. Opposed to them were the Know-Nothings, mostly former Whigs, who wanted to keep the movement from becoming abolitionized and who desired anti-foreignism and anti-Catholicism made a part of its program. Lewis D. Campbell, Congressman from the Dayton district, and Thomas Spooner, president of the Ohio Know-Nothings, led this faction, though they had the sympathy of many well-known Whigs who were not openly affiliated with the secret society.

The hostility of these factions reached such a pitch that it seemed likely, shortly before the state convention met in July, 1855, that the Fusion movement would break into two parties. The chief bone of contention was the governorship. The leading aspirant for the nomination to this office was Salmon P. Chase, who had failed to be reëlected to the United States Senate by the Democratic legislature, but whose leadership in the fight on the Nebraska Bill had won him great acclaim in the whole North. Chase had the support of the ardent anti-slavery men but was opposed by many former Whigs, who could not forget the "bargain of 1849," by conservatives, who regarded him as an abolitionist, and by the Know-Nothings, who felt that Chase was too friendly to the Germans and hostile to nativism. The candidate of the Whig-Know-Nothing faction was Jacob Brinkerhoff, once a Democratic Congressman of anti-slavery views and now a member of the secret order.

The Know-Nothing element was numerous enough to control the Fusion convention and defeat Chase if the members had presented a united front, but this they were unable to do. Many of the Know-Nothings, especially in northern Ohio, were more interested in the anti-slavery cause than in native Americanism and gave their support to Chase. Furthermore, the Know-Nothing leaders came to realize that Chase's defeat would wreck the Fusion movement, for the anti-slavery radicals were openly planning to hold an independent convention and run him regardless of what the July 13 convention did. So, after unsuccessful proposals for a compromise candidate, the anti-Chase element yielded.

On July 13, 1855, in the Town Street Methodist Church at Columbus, the "Fusion" or "Anti-Nebraska" movement became the Republican Party of Ohio. Chase was nominated by a large majority and the brief platform that was adopted had as its central feature opposition to the spread of slavery into the territories. Not a suggestion was there in any plank that a majority of the delegates were members of a secret order of nativists. However, as the anti-slavery men had the gubernatorial candidate and the platform, the Know-Nothings had to be compensated with the rest of the state offices. Eight of the nine candidates belonged to Know-Nothing lodges, Chase being the solitary exception. Yet the real victory rested with the anti-slavery element. It had preserved the original purpose of the Anti-Nebraska movement against any contamination from nativism or anti-Catholicism and had given the leadership of the new party to a man of its faith. The Know-Nothings had sold their principles for offices and anti-slavery votes at the coming election. The secret society had been swallowed up in the Republican Party and its force dissipated.

Yet a small group of "die-hards" refused to be bound by the action of the July 13 convention. Though Thomas Spooner, head of the Ohio Know-Nothings, issued a circular urging support of Chase by all members of the order as a mark of good faith, the dissatisfied, nevertheless, held a state convention in August and nominated former Governor Allen Trimble for governor. It was clearly an anti-Chase movement, as no candidates were named for the other state offices. The venerable ex-Governor was not a Know-Nothing but was nevertheless satisfactory to the bolters, as he represented old Whig traditions, and most of the delegates were of that political faith. Republican success was greatly endangered by this third nomination, as no one could foretell how much support southern Ohio conservatives might give to Trimble. The Scioto Valley and Ohio River Counties could thus defeat Chase.

The Democrats had already renominated Governor William Medill early in the year and were hoping that Republican dissensions might work to their advantage. While previously very critical of nativism in order to retain the German and Irish votes, they now began to encourage the seceding Know-Nothings in the Trimble movement in the hope that Chase might be defeated and the new party wrecked.

The campaign proved to be one of great bitterness. Chase was subjected to a cross fire from both Democrats and "Trimblers" who charged him with favoring Negro equality, abolitionism, and disunion. The Republicans attempted to counteract these tactics by appealing to the business classes for support against Democratic policies on banking and taxation and by urging the Know-Nothings to keep the bargain made with the anti-slavery element at the state convention. Chase emphasized the situation in Kansas and the dangers of slavery extension—safe themes in all parts of the state.

The result was a complete Republican victory, though Chase had a plurality of less than sixteen thousand votes over Medill, as Trimble polled over twenty-four thousand votes, preventing the Republican candidate from having a majority. The legislature and the rest of the state ticket were Republican by a large vote, as there were no third candidates for these places. Cincinnati showed itself as the center of hostility to Chase. Here the business interests feared a loss of Southern trade if Ohio chose an abolitionist Governor, while the Germans distrusted Chase because of his association with Know-Nothings. The result was that the successful candidate was a poor third in his home city.

It seems safe to conclude that the election of 1855 insured the permanence of the Republican Party in Ohio.

Had Chase been defeated, it would probably have divided into Know-Nothing and anti-slavery factions, for the latter would have charged his defeat to the failure of the secret order to give him a loyal support. The result in Ohio also strengthened the new party in the whole North at a time when the Democrats were recovering a part of the ground lost in the Anti-Nebraska uprising of the year before, and when it seemed doubtful whether an anti-slavery party could maintain itself. With the prestige and the patronage that went with success in Ohio, the new party could look forward with a degree of confidence to the national election of 1856. At least nativism had been largely absorbed and rendered harmless without poisoning the political atmosphere with race or religious prejudice.

In the new assembly, the twofold character of the Republican Party speedily became apparent. Economic conservatism and anti-slavery radicalism worked hand in hand. Legislation favorable to the banks and business classes was enacted, while the anti-slavery men were satisfied with the reëlection of Wade to the United States Senate and the passage of strong anti-slavery resolutions on the Kansas situation as well as measures to hamper the execution of the Fugitive Slave Law. In the words of the hostile *Statesman*, the Democratic state organ, the work of the legislature combined the "oft rejected measures of the old Whig party now defunct, and the impracticable and incendiary isms of the abolition faction."

The Presidential year was less significant in Ohio than the preceding year had been, for the result in 1856 had been forecast by the vote of 1855. The Democrats could succeed only by absorbing the Trimble votes. Though their Presidential candidate, James Buchanan, was sufficiently conservative to appeal to many former Whigs and Know-Nothings, the bolting Know-Nothings of fifty-five generally supported Fillmore, Presidential candidate of the third party, now known as the American Party. The great majority of the nativists, as in 1855, remained loyal to the Republican Party, however, and its candidate, John C. Fremont, carried the state by much the same vote as that for Chase the preceding year. Ohio had had two candidates for the Republican Presidential nomination, Governor Chase and Judge John McLean, of the United States Supreme Court, but the national convention had decided that the California explorer and "Pathfinder," Fremont, was more likely to win. McLean was particularly disappointed, as he had strong support outside Ohio, but probably no Republican could have won in 1856, and Fremont made as good a showing in the whole North as any man who might have been chosen.

The years 1854–1856 may be regarded as a period of political transition from the old alignments of Whigs against Democrats to the newer divisions of Republicans and Democrats. The older issues of banking and currency and economic radicalism had been largely displaced in the public mind by slavery and sectionalism, with nativism causing a temporary interest. The old Free Soil Party had been absorbed by the Republicans along with the majority of the Whigs and many Anti-Nebraska Democrats. The Democratic Party had lost its anti-slavery element but had won some conservative Whigs and was appealing to the remnants of the American Party on a Union-saving platform. From 1856 to 1860 the Democrats regarded themselves as the defenders of the Union and white supremacy against Republican sectionalism and race equality. On their part, the Republicans declaimed against Southern control of the Government and the dangers of slavery extension. Neither party paid much attention to state matters, though banking, taxation, transportation, and other economic problems were of more direct significance to most Ohioans than events in Kansas, the fate of Dred Scott, or the exploits of John Brown. Then, as today, the politicians appealed to the emotions: sectionalism and race prejudice inflamed the voting masses, and the Civil War became inevitable.

Republicans versus Democrats, 1857–1860

The Dred Scott decision of the United States Supreme Court, opening the territories to slavery, was bitterly denounced by the Republican press of Ohio, by resolutions of the assembly, and in the platform of the Republican state convention of 1857. The last named condemned the decision as "anti-constitutional, anti-republican, anti-democratic, incompatible with State rights and destructive of personal security." The Democrats upheld the decision as merely recognizing white supremacy and attacked the Republicans for favoring race amalgamation. Thus the two candidates for governor, Chase and Henry B. Payne, based their campaigns largely upon different aspects of the slavery issue.

But the political waters were greatly muddied by a new and most unexpected problem that suddenly appeared in the early summer of 1857. State Treasurer William H. Gibson was forced to disclose to the auditor that a deficit of some five hundred fifty thousand dollars existed in the state treasury. His explanation was that his Democratic predecessor and brother-in-law, John G. Breslin, had embezzled state funds during his term in office, but that the deficit had been covered up in the hope that Breslin might eventually repay it. With interest payments due on state bonds on July 1, the shortage could no longer be concealed, and so Gibson was compelled to make it public. Governor Chase at once demanded and received the

Treasurer's resignation, took steps to secure money for the interest then due, and appointed an investigating commission. The political effect of this action, however, was bad. Regardless of Gibson's own guilt or innocence, the fact that he had concealed the shortage placed the Republican administration in a bad light and seemed to discredit the party as a reform organization. The Democrats charged that Gibson was as guilty as Breslin, that other prominent Republicans were involved, and demanded a complete separation of the state treasury from the banks, for misuse of state funds in banking operations apparently had caused the defalcation.

The great Panic of 1857 burst on the country in August with the failure of the Ohio Life Insurance and Trust Company. The wreckage of banks, railways, and business houses prostrated economic life and revived for a time the anti-bank feeling of earlier days. Coupled with the treasury fraud, it furnished a good argument for an independent treasury system to take care of state funds. Most of the Ohio banks weathered the storm; but this fact was not at once evident, and the immediate effect of the Panic was unfavorable to the Republicans.

Chase and most of the Republican state nominees were successful at the October election, but the votes of the two major parties were so close that the result was in doubt for several days. The Democrats carried the assembly— a doubtful gain, however, as it placed on them the burden of legislation for the next two years. The American Party again held the balance of power in the popular vote, but its poor showing was its death knell. Having failed to defeat Chase—its chief purpose in the election—it now ceased to function as a state organization.

The course of party history in the United States in the closing years of the decade largely centers around the factionalism that appears in the Democratic Party. The question of the admission of Kansas as a slave state with a constitution adopted as the result of an unfair election in which free state voters took no part was the rock on which the Democratic Party split. The Buchanan administration, with the support of Southern Democrats and a few conservative northerners, favored this Lecompton constitution, while the followers of Stephen A. Douglas, the author of the original Kansas-Nebraska Act, opposed it and demanded a fair election in Kansas on the slavery question. In the end, a compromise measure, the English Bill, was passed by Congress to provide for another vote on the Lecompton constitution. This vote resulted in its rejection, but the bad feelings between the Douglas, or anti-Lecompton, Democrats and the Southern wing remained and led to the party split of 1860.

In Ohio, the great majority of the Democrats followed Douglas, and a great state-wide mass convention, held in Columbus in March, 1858, passed resolutions denouncing the Lecompton fraud and criticizing the Buchanan administration for trying to make the matter a test of party loyalty. Henry B. Payne, Stanley Matthews, and other prominent Ohio Democrats addressed the assemblage, while in Congress the brilliant young Columbus Representative, Samuel S. Cox (better known as "Sunset" Cox), made a name for himself as an anti-Lecompton leader. Only a small group of Ohio Democrats, consisting largely of Federal officeholders, supported the Buchanan administration. They were led by former Governor Wood and Samuel Medary—the latter once a partisan of Douglas but now bound to the administration by ties of office.

The English compromise measure was generally acceptable to Ohio Democrats, and the party seemed reunited when the congressional election of 1858 occurred. Yet this harmony was rather superficial, for the outcome of the election indicated that many dissatisfied Democrats had either refrained from voting or had supported Republican candidates. Only six Democrats were elected to Congress in the twenty-one districts—a clear indication of the effect of "the leaden load of Lecompton," as one of the defeated expressed it. It foretold the probable result in 1860.

Meanwhile, the Republicans, enjoying the discomfiture of their opponents, rested secure in the belief that Republican supremacy in Ohio was assured for some time to come. Even the remnants of the American Party had voted with the Republicans in 1858. But actually there were two divisions in the ranks of the victors, needing only some specific issue to reveal their differences. The radicals, decidedly anti-slavery and anti-Southern in viewpoint, were uncompromisingly hostile to compromise and concession. The veteran Reserve Congressman, Joshua R. Giddings, particularly held to these ideas, and to a lesser degree Governor Chase, Senator Wade, and the most prominent Republicans were in agreement with him. On the other hand, especially strong in southern Ohio were the conservatives, who believed in a policy of conciliating moderate Southerners and advocated other measures besides opposition to slavery—a protective tariff, for example—in an effort to build up a Republican, or opposition, party in the South devoted to upholding the Union. Tom Corwin, brilliant Whig orator of other days, returned to politics in 1858 and was elected to Congress from a southwestern Ohio district to become the mouthpiece of conservatism in the Republican Party. A protective tariff, rather than slavery, was his theme, and he found much support in the Ohio River counties. But this division in the party would have had slight importance had not the question of the

Fugitive Slave Law become a matter of violent controversy in 1859.

Prior to 1859, while unpopular in the state, the Fugitive Slave Law aroused concern only for a few weeks after its passage in 1850. Cases involving the law were not frequent enough to attract attention. The "Underground Railroad" was operating efficiently and quietly enough to enable hundreds of slaves to reach freedom, and no great excitement was engendered by it.

Nevertheless, in Governor Chase's administration, beginning in 1856, came a series of cases involving clashes between state and United States courts that threatened to become serious. In the first of these, the Margaret Garner case, the Federal court triumphed and a family of slaves was sent back to slave soil despite an indictment by a state grand jury against one of them, Margaret Garner, for murder. This poor woman, in a frenzy over the prospect of being returned to slavery, had killed one of her children with a butcher knife. The case involved some peculiar legal technicalities, but the Federal judge upheld the Fugitive Law, and the prisoners were hurried to Kentucky before the state authorities could intervene. Efforts of Governor Chase to secure their return proved unavailing.

In May, 1857, came the Champaign County rescue cases. In this instance, a United States marshal and his posse had arrested four Champaign County citizens for assisting a fugitive to escape and had attempted to take them to Cincinnati despite the efforts of local officials of two counties to stop them. Finally, the sheriff of Greene County, after an exchange of shots with the marshal's posse, took possession of the prisoners on a writ of habeas corpus and arrested some of the deputy marshals on charges of assault with intent to kill. Both state and United States courts claimed jurisdiction, and a difficult legal

tangle resulted. Federal District Judge Leavitt ordered
the release of the deputy marshals, but the matter was not
finally settled until Governor Chase had a personal inter-
view with President Buchanan and Secretary of State Cass.
The outcome was that prosecutions were dropped on both
sides.

The question of state and Federal relations over fugitives
had been made more complex by acts of the Republican
assembly of 1856–1857 usually known as "Personal Liberty
Laws." These measures were designed ostensibly to
prevent slaveholding in Ohio and the kidnapping of free
Negroes, but it was clear to any fair-minded person that
their real purpose was to nullify an act of the Federal
Government, the Fugitive Slave Law. One of the laws
specifically forbade the use of jails for the confinement of
fugitives. However, this legislation was of short duration,
for the Democratic assembly of 1857–1858 speedily repealed
it and even went to the other extreme of enacting a new
type of "black law." Hitherto all persons more than
half white by blood had been regarded as entitled to vote
under the term "white" in the constitution. Now the
assembly enacted that all persons having "a distinct and
visible admixture of African blood" should be forbidden
the franchise. The law had slight practical significance
and was presently declared unconstitutional by the state
supreme court, but it illustrates the tendency of the
Democratic Party as well as the Republican Party to make
political capital out of the "nigger question."

The climax of the slavery issue in Ohio came in 1859 in
the form of a dramatic struggle over the enforcement of the
Fugitive Slave Law in the "Oberlin-Wellington Rescue
Cases." A fugitive named John Price, living at Oberlin,
the very citadel of abolitionist sentiment, was seized by a
United States deputy marshal and carried to the neighbor-

ing village of Wellington to be taken south by train. A group of Oberlin citizens, on learning what had occurred, came to Wellington and, aided by a mob there, rescued the slave and sent him away. This was in September, 1858. As a consequence, a Federal grand jury indicted thirty-seven citizens of the two villages for violating the Fugitive Slave Law, and they were tried in the Federal district court in April, 1859. The first two tried, Simeon Bushnell and Charles Langston, were found guilty, but on a writ of habeas corpus, the cases were heard by the Ohio Supreme Court to determine whether the men were legally held.

The point at issue was whether the Fugitive Slave Law was constitutional or not. That a law of the United States, repeatedly held constitutional by the Federal courts, should now be in question before a state court appears an absurdity at first sight. But the Republican radicals were much embittered against the United States courts over the Dred Scott case and the fugitive cases already referred to, and were willing to assert the final authority of the highest state court even in interpretation of Federal laws. "The fact is," wrote one prominent Republican lawyer to Chase, "we have got to come to Calhoun's ground. It is the only sound logical and tenable position, unless we give up everything to the sweep of centralization. . . . What Hamilton failed in in the Convention, he accomplished through Congress and the Courts." The Cleveland *Herald*, once a staid Whig paper, quoted with approval the Kentucky Resolutions of 1798, which had first set forth clearly the theory of a State's right to interpret the United States Constitution for itself. Some ten thousand people at a great public meeting in Cleveland late in May heard various Republican leaders voice their disapproval of acts of Federal authorities.

Resolutions were passed expressing an extreme State-rights viewpoint and criticizing the life tenure of Federal judges. With but slight encouragement from the leaders, the crowd would have rushed to the jail and released the Oberlin prisoners by force.[4]

With excitement at a fever heat, the state supreme court, composed of five Republicans, handed down its decision in the Oberlin cases. The majority of the judges voted to uphold the constitutionality of the Fugitive Slave Law and refused to interfere with the proceedings of the Federal court. The vote was three to two, two northern Ohio judges dissenting and two from southern Ohio and Chief Justice Swan, of Columbus, constituting the majority. It was a victory for conservatism, and it saved the state not only from a bitter legal struggle with Federal authorities, but possibly from an armed clash, for the Governor would have been bound to uphold the proceedings of the state court to the point of using force.

But Judge Swan's courageous act cost him his official position. The Republican state convention, meeting three days after the court's decision, refused him a renomination. The northern Ohio radicals, bitterly incensed at him as "a cowardly and miserable sham conservative," as one paper put it, arranged a deal with a group of Cincinnati and southern Ohio delegates to name a Cincinnatian, Judge William Y. Gholson, for Swan's position. The city of Cincinnati, it was argued, needed representation on the supreme court bench, and Gholson was a man of high legal attainments. The radicals, eager to defeat Swan, joined with the most conservative section of the state and

---

[4] Only Bushnell and Langston were convicted, and their jail sentences were light, 60 and 20 days respectively. Proceedings against the other defendants were dropped.

accomplished their purpose. They were somewhat chagrined later to discover that Gholson was an ex-slaveholder
from Mississippi with a son still residing there, but they
supported him in good faith. The rest of the Republican
ticket, headed by William Dennison, of Columbus, an
ex-Whig banker and railroad president, for governor, gave
general satisfaction to both elements in the party, while
the platform, though critical of the Federal courts, evaded
the issue of nullification by declaring for the repeal of the
Fugitive Slave Law. Nevertheless, this was the most
radical position the party had yet assumed, and it received
the blessing of the veteran radical, Giddings, who exultantly
exclaimed, "Lord, now lettest thou thy servant depart in
peace." His work seemed done. On the other hand,
Abraham Lincoln wrote from Illinois his disapproval of the
repudiation of Judge Swan and of the demand for the
repeal of the Fugitive Slave Law.

The Democrats seized upon Swan's defeat as proof of the
extreme radicalism of their opponents, and appealed to
conservatives for support. They upheld the authority
of the Federal courts—a strange position for the party of
Jackson—and declared for popular sovereignty in the
territories. Their candidate for governor, Judge Rufus
P. Ranney, was a strong and able man and had held anti-
slavery views—which fact seemed proof that his election
would not be a pro-slavery triumph.

The campaign was exciting and hard fought. Dennison
and Ranney aroused much interest by engaging in a series
of joint debates with honors apparently even. Ranney
was a more skilful popular speaker, but Dennison, better
known as a business man and party campaign manager,
surprised his supporters by his effectiveness as a cam-
paigner and held his own quite well. From Illinois came
Stephen A. Douglas and Abraham Lincoln to aid their

respective parties, thus renewing on Ohio soil their famous rivalry of the year preceding.

The Republicans carried the state, electing their candidates by majorities of twelve to thirteen thousand. Despite its radical position, the party had held most of its conservatives in line, and seemed stronger and better organized than ever before. The influence of Corwin was quite important in holding southern Ohio Republicans loyal.

Soon after the election came John Brown's Raid with all its attendant excitement. For the moment, it seemed that the Democrats had a dangerous weapon to use on their opponents. Was not Brown's exploit the logical outcome of the radical teachings of Chase, Seward, Giddings, and other Republican leaders? Slave insurrections, armed outbreaks of fanatics, and disunion—these would be the consequences of Republican success in 1860. The newspapers of the Republican Party hastened to repudiate Brown and tried to belittle the importance of the whole affair. The party was radical enough in Ohio without being weighted down with fanatical abolitionism. Yet old Brown's noble bearing began to arouse admiration, and while careful to distinguish between the man and his acts, many Republicans expressed their sympathy, and the more radical, especially in the Western Reserve, held public meetings on the day of his execution. Even at Cincinnati, on the following Sunday, a memorial meeting in honor of the "new saint" was held by some fifteen hundred German and colored residents of the metropolis.

In the assembly, some conservative Republicans supported a measure to prevent the fitting out of armed expeditions on Ohio soil against another state, but this gesture of friendliness to Virginia received cold comfort from the majority, who felt that the measure implied a confession of guilt by the State of Ohio because some of its citizens had taken part in the Brown affair. Governor Wise, of Virginia, had already written Governor Chase expressing his alarm over rumors of a proposed invasion of Virginia to rescue Brown, but Ohio's executive refused to credit such reports, though he promised that the laws would be enforced in every way. Later, when Governor Letcher, of Virginia, issued requisition papers for the return of two members of Brown's force who had escaped and taken refuge in northern Ohio, Governor Dennison refused the request. The matter was then dropped, though the Virginia executive expressed his indignation and Ohio Democrats generally agreed with him.

The Republicans approached the campaign of 1860 with a great feeling of confidence. Indeed, no less than three Ohioans were being given consideration as Presidential possibilities. Governor Chase, elected United States Senator early in the year, had the indorsement of the state convention and hoped for support from other states. Judge McLean, despite his advanced years, was favorably regarded by conservatives who felt that Chase was too radical to carry Pennsylvania, Indiana, and Illinois. Furthermore, old Whigs regarded the Governor with disfavor, while protective tariff advocates charged that he was a free trader. An even more dangerous rival was Senator Ben Wade, who had the secret backing of a number of Ohio delegates to the national convention. Wade, a former Whig, was more available than Chase, and his friends had promises of strong support from other states. The natural consequence of these rivalries was that the Ohio delegation was too badly divided to have much influence in the national convention, but it did have the honor at the close of the third ballot of transferring to Abraham Lincoln four votes that gave him the necessary majority. In general, Lincoln was quite satisfactory to

Ohio Republicans, who had come to know him through his speeches in the state the year before.

The Democratic delegates to the national convention at Charleston, South Carolina, were solidly for Douglas, and two Ohioans, Henry B. Payne and George E. Pugh, had a prominent part in upholding the Northern viewpoint of popular sovereignty against the Southern demand that Congress protect slavery in the territories. After the Charleston convention, unable to agree upon a nomination, adjourned to meet later at Baltimore, there was some talk in Ohio of offering former Senator William Allen as a compromise choice. However, nothing came of this talk, the Ohio delegation continuing to support Douglas. The latter's nomination by the Northern Democrats and the naming of John C. Breckinridge by the Southern wing compelled Ohio Democrats to make their choice.

The state convention supported Douglas, backed by most of the party press, but a small minority, composed chiefly of supporters of the Buchanan administration, held a separate convention and named a Breckinridge electoral ticket. It was not a proslavery group but a conservative element who had opposed Douglas in 1852 and 1856, and who felt that he was responsible for the party's troubles. Nearly all the Federal officeholders were in this group.

The nomination of John Bell, of Tennessee, at Baltimore by the newly organized Constitutional Union Party resulted in a Constitutional Union electoral ticket in Ohio also. A few old Whigs and some members of the defunct American Party constituted its principal support, with Cincinnati as their headquarters.

Despite the efforts of the Democrats to arouse enthusiasm by bringing Douglas into the state, the odds were very much against them. Matters were made even worse by the Republican use of the tariff question in southern Ohio.

The coal and iron counties, still feeling the effects of the Panic of 1857, were joining with Pennsylvania iron interests

Presidential Election of 1860

Republican	Lincoln	231,610
Democratic	Douglas	187,232
Constitutional Unionist	Bell	12,193
Southern Democratic	Breckinridge	11,405

in demanding a protective tariff. The Republicans were thus able to use the rather vague tariff plank of their national platform as an argument for Republican votes in a region that was quite conservative on the slavery question. The *Ohio Statesman* charged that two of the Democratic congressional candidates in southern Ohio were defeated because of the pressure put upon the workingmen by the "Pig-Metal Aristocracy" and their allies, the coal dealers. In general, the Republicans were less radical on slavery than in 1859, little being said about the fugitive slave question. Success in the neighboring states of Pennsylvania and Indiana was too important to be endangered by radicalism in Ohio.

The October state and congressional election was a great Republican triumph, even Judge Brinkerhoff, against whom all the opposition had united, being reëlected to the Supreme Court. After the result in October, attempts were made to arrange a fusion electoral ticket to be supported by both wings of the Democrats and by the Constitutional Unionists, but no agreement could be reached. Defeat was certain in any case. In November Lincoln carried Ohio by a plurality of over forty-four thousand over Douglas, and a majority of more than twenty thousand over all three opponents. Ohio seemed thoroughly converted to the Republican cause, even the once Democratic stronghold of Cincinnati giving Lincoln a plurality. The German element in the "Queen City" had finally been won over to Republicanism and furnished the votes to defeat the party they had once so strongly supported.

The Democratic Party, shattered by slavery and sectionalism, presented a striking contrast to the victorious party of that name in the early fifties. Its radicalism submerged and its Jacksonian principles hardly more than traditions, it had become the refuge for conservatives, who saw in it a means of combatting anti-slavery fanaticism and sectionalism. Its center of strength had shifted from the "backbone" counties of northern Ohio (south of the Reserve) and the thinly populated, pioneer northwest to the southern half of the state, where anti-slavery doctrines were not popular. Its Republican rival, on the other hand, had not only built up great majorities in the once Whig Western Reserve, but controlled a considerable part of the entire north. Its strength in the south was confined chiefly to the old Whig strongholds in the Miami Valley and adjacent counties, but its majorities here could not equal those of Whig days. Its success in capturing some of the southern and southeastern counties in 1860 had depended on its tariff appeal primarily, excepting only the old Ohio Company Grant, where New England traditions made Republicanism take quick root.

The success of the Republicans may well have been the despair of their enemies. That a sectional party should control a state that was by no means radical on the slavery issue was due both to skilful politics and to the blunders of the opposition. As a consequence, Germans and nativists, abolitionists and conservatives, anti-bank radicals and bankers, farmers and manufacturers, all found a place in the party that called itself Republican. The old Liberty Party veterans of the 1840's, with their enthusiasm for reforming humanity, might well have marvelled at the company in which they found themselves.

Selected Bibliography

The histories of Ohio cited for other chapters are unsatisfactory for this period. Of the monographs mentioned for the preceding chapter, Smith, *Liberty and Free Soil Parties in the Northwest*, goes to 1854, while Holt, *Party Politics in Ohio, 1840–1850*, covers the legislative session of 1849–1850 and the senatorial election. McGrane, *William Allen*, deals briefly with the 1850's. Albert Bushnell Hart, *Salmon Portland Chase* (Boston, 1899, *American Statesman Series*), gives much space to Ohio

politics in covering Chase's career.   Briefer on Ohio matters is
A. G. Riddle, *Life of Benjamin F. Wade* (Cleveland, 1886).
George H. Porter, "Ohio Politics during the Civil War Period,"
*Columbia University Studies in History, Economics and Public
Law*, Vol. XL (New York, 1911), begins with the election of
1859.   Much material on the slavery issue in Ohio, though from
a decidedly anti-slavery point of view, appears in William C.
Cochran, "The Western Reserve and the Fugitive Slave Law,"
Western Reserve Historical Society Collections, No. 101 (Cleveland,
1920); the "Oberlin-Wellington Rescue Cases" are treated in
great detail.   Accounts of Republican state and national conventions with platforms, brief biographies of candidates, and
votes at all state elections are given in Joseph P. Smith, *History
of the Republican Party in Ohio* (2 vols., Chicago, 1898).   The
author is decidedly partisan in viewpoint.

Much material on this period may also be found in "The
Diary and Correspondence of Salmon P. Chase," *American
Historical Association Annual Report*, 1902, Vol. II, and in
biographies cited for the preceding chapter.   John Sherman,
Recollections of Forty Years (2 vols., Chicago, 1895), and Samuel
S. Cox, *Three Decades of Federal Legislation* (Providence, 1885),
deal chiefly with national affairs.   *The Diary and Letters of
Rutherford Birchard Hayes* (Charles R. Williams, ed., 4 vols.,
Columbus, 1922), is of some use for this period, though more
valuable when Hayes becomes a more important figure.

Much of the material in this chapter is taken from an unpublished Harvard doctoral dissertation (1932), Eugene H. Roseboom, *Ohio in the 1850's.*

CHAPTER XI

THE CIVIL WAR YEARS, 1861–1865

The Period of Compromise and Concession

AS soon as Lincoln was elected, South Carolina took steps to institute the process of secession from the Union, and the lower South, it was evident, would follow her lead. The victorious Republicans, accustomed to belittle the threats of Southern "fire-eaters," were unprepared for such action. The influential Cincinnati *Commercial* had argued before the election that the slavery question would subside with Republican success, and that political peace would follow, while the *Ohio State Journal* declared that Lincoln's victory would "effectually and forever silence this nauseating disunion twaddle that has been spawned continually ever since the slavery question has entered fully into our politics." That secession would be actually attempted seemed incredible. Consequently, when South Carolina announced her withdrawal from the Union, the party of Lincoln had no policy to meet the crisis, nor was public sentiment at all united on a course of action.

The *State Journal*, official voice of Ohio Republicanism, questioned whether it would be worth while to hold the Union together by force, and radical anti-slavery men took the same position. Southern Ohio, bound by ties of trade, blood, and social relations to the slave states, wanted anything but war. Cincinnati business men, alarmed at reports of Southern boycotts, were anxious for peace and good relations at any price. Railway capitalists, interested in connections with Chattanooga, Atlanta, Charleston, and other Southern centers, had been receiving delegations from various Southern roads in the fall of 1860 in an effort to determine the most favorable routes. More than ever before, the "Queen City" was looking southward to offset the losses of markets resulting from the rapid development of east-and-west railroads to the north of the Ohio metropolis. War would be fatal to such projects. The leading Presbyterian minister defended the South in his sermons and placed the blame for the existing troubles upon Northern aggressions.

Strangely enough, it was the official state organ of the Democratic Party, the *Ohio Statesman*, that first attacked the idea of peaceful secession. Quoting Madison, Webster, and Jackson against such a doctrine, it charged the Republicans with making common cause with the Southern disunionists in an effort to create two republics. It urged the repeal of all nullifying measures in the Northern states against which the South had complained, as a first step toward conciliation, and hoped that compromise might yet save the day. Thanks to a small group of conservative Republicans in the assembly, Ohio at least had no "Personal Liberty Laws" to repeal, for an attempt to reënact them had failed in the assembly session of 1860.

On the broader issue of conciliating the South, the state was generally favorable. The legislature passed conciliatory resolutions in January, 1861, and appointed delegates to the Peace Convention called by Virginia. Chase and Thomas Ewing were the best-known Ohioans in the delegation, the former leading the "no-compromise" element in the convention. However, the majority supported a proposed compromise constitutional amendment, the chief feature of which was the establishment of the line

36° 30′ as the boundary between slave and free territories. No action resulted from this proposal.

Congress was already considering various schemes for compromise, Thomas Corwin in the House being chairman of a "Committee of Thirty-three" to deal with the crisis. His old Whig conservatism was reflected in the committee's proposal that the Constitution be amended so as virtually to guarantee the existence of slavery in the slave states. Under Corwin's leadership, the proposal passed both Houses and was submitted to the states for their approval. The Ohio Legislature ratified, the Senate adopting the proposal even in the midst of the patriotic outbursts following the firing on Fort Sumter, with only eight negative votes. Such was the hold of conservatism among Ohioans. War was to be the last resort.

The First Year

The roar of guns at Fort Sumter settled the fate of conciliation and compromise in both North and South. The war fever swept both sections, and to the god of battles was left the solution. Few indeed were there bold enough to oppose the popular frenzy. The American people had become war-mad and the most deadly civil war in modern history had begun.

In Ohio the enthusiastic response to the President's call for volunteers and the quick action of Governor and assembly in adopting war measures were proof of the fierce flaming of the patriotic spirit. Not only was Ohio's quota of thirteen thousand volunteers speedily filled by the response of some thirty thousand in a few days, but the adjutant general declared that Ohio could have furnished the entire seventy-five thousand requested for the whole country if all who volunteered had been accepted.[1] Four days after the President's call had been received, two regiments left Columbus for the defense of the National Capital, cheered by the excited onlookers and possessed with enthusiasm for their patriotic mission, if not with arms and uniforms. Thus the first Ohioans went to war.

The assembly acted promptly in appropriating funds to put the state on a war basis. The senate, within twenty-four hours after Lincoln's call, passed a bill, with but one dissenting vote, appropriating one million dollars for war purposes. The House held up the measure for two days until the Democrats could consult as to their policy, but when the vote was taken it was unanimous. This act was followed by one introduced by James A. Garfield in the senate punishing treason against the state, and presently a series of war-time laws appeared upon the statute books. Partisanship had played no part in their enactment.

The gravest problems in these exciting weeks of preparation, however, were administrative. Upon Governor Dennison, better known for the correctness of his social deportment and the excellence of his business and political connections than for his executive ability, fell the burdens and the blame for the difficulties that arose. The old militia system, long in disrepute, had been partially reorganized by Governor Chase, and one hundred and fifty companies were reported in existence by the adjutant general in 1859. Indeed, military companies became a kind of fad among young men of good families, the Chicago Zouaves furnishing a model for such organizations. But while Ohio's militia system was probably superior to those of her neighbors, it was far from adequate for the sudden

---

[1] When the men called for three months' service were replaced with three-years men, under Lincoln's second call, Ohio furnished 77,844 men, though her quota was 67,365 of the total of 500,000.

emergency in which the state found itself. The whole nation was rushing to arms, and no amount of preparedness could have met such a situation in a satisfactory manner. Ohio's sleepy little capital city was overwhelmed with hordes of eager volunteers, for which the state had not even quarters or food, much less arms and equipment. As for the Governor's staff—inherited from the Chase administration—a competent authority has described it as a group "in which it seemed as if the capacity of bad selection had been almost exhausted."

The difficulties, however, were gradually overcome. Camp Jackson, at Columbus, and the hotels and boarding houses temporarily cared for the recruits until better provision could be made for them. Presently Camp Dennison, near Cincinnati, was established as a training camp for the prospective soldiers as well as a means of defense for the metropolis, then exposed to attack in case Kentucky seceded. Ultimately a number of camps in different parts of the state took care of the recruits of their sections, while the United States Government used Camp Dennison and Camp Chase (near Columbus) for troops mustered into Federal service.

The problem of equipment and supplies at first was bungled like everything else. Contracts were made at extravagant prices, and large profits went into the pockets of those mercenary patriots who are ever ready to take advantage of their country's necessities. Add to this the manifest inefficiency of the quartermaster's department and the natural proneness of soldiers, just transferred from civilian life, to grumble at every discomfort encountered, and it is not surprising that the state administration found itself overwhelmed with criticism. At this juncture, the Governor's unruffled poise stood him in good stead, and the situation gradually improved as new appointments infused order and energy into the system, and equipment and supplies—from the East, from Illinois, and from Europe—began to relieve the most pressing needs.

The choice of officers for the Ohio regiments was complicated by the ambitions of military-minded politicians to secure their share of gold braid and glory. Since some of these had been active in enlisting men for the service, it was difficult to refuse them. Indeed, at first officers were elected, even up to the rank of colonel. Governor Dennison was anxious to be relieved of much of the burden of military administration, and, learning that generals could be appointed by the governors of the states from which the troops came, he named Captain George B. McClellan, a former army officer, to be major general in command of all of Ohio's troops. Young McClellan was a Pennsylvanian but was then an official of the Ohio and Mississippi Railroad and was living at Cincinnati. The influence of prominent citizens of that place brought about McClellan's appointment over Irvin McDowell, an Ohioan on General Scott's staff, who was the Governor's first choice. Presently the new major general was further honored by an appointment by the President as a major general in the regular Army, apparently through the influence of Chase, now Secretary of the Treasury. The three brigadier generals, appointed by the Governor, had more political than military training, though one of them, Jacob D. Cox, was satisfactory enough to be retained when the three-year enlistments replaced the three-months men of the President's first call. .

In the actual fighting of 1861, Ohio's chief contribution was the occupation of the western counties of Virginia, soon to become the state of West Virginia. Desirous of protecting the loyalists of this area, to whom he had pledged his support, as well as of defending Ohio against possible invasion, Governor Dennison urged the reluctant McClellan to invade western Virginia as soon as possible. The latter, naturally slow to act and more concerned in whipping his raw recruits into trained and disciplined soldiers, at first refused to undertake such a campaign. However, when Virginia troops entered the region late in May and the loyal convention at Wheeling was in danger, McClellan, with the approval of the War Department, acceded to the Governor's wishes and invaded this section. His forces, at first Ohio militia not yet in Federal service, occupied the strategic points along the Baltimore and Ohio Railroad. Then, in a well-managed campaign, McClellan drove the Confederates over the mountains, and the western counties were saved for the Union. Ohio troops had comprised an important part of his army. This campaign had no vital significance in a military sense, as the number of Confederate troops was not great, and an invasion of Ohio from this direction highly improbable, but it placed an important railroad in Union control and was a ray of consolation in a summer made memorable by the great disillusionment of Bull Run.

Ohio's Governor was equally ready to invade the "neutral" state of Kentucky as a measure of defense for the great city of Cincinnati and to prevent the movement southward of recruits and supplies for the Confederacy. He had the support of Governors Yates, of Illinois, and Morton, of Indiana, in this suggestion, but the broader wisdom of President Lincoln prevented any precipitate action. Kentucky, allowed time to decide upon her own course, remained loyal to the Union. An invasion by Northern troops in May, 1861, would only have strenghtened the secessionist element, while delay did not prevent the later occupation of the state when the military and political situation warranted it.

In the enthusiasm that followed the surrender of Fort Sumter, it seemed that politics had been adjourned for the war. Desirous of retaining Democratic support, Governor Dennison was careful to give full recognition to members of that party in making military appointments, and occasionally he made use of prominent Democrats for special missions involving heavy responsibilities, thus insuring their coöperation in the common cause. With a state election at hand in the fall of 1861, the question naturally arose as to whether this party truce could be continued. The Republican State Central Committee attempted to solve the problem by inviting the Democratic Committee to join in a call for a nominating convention representing all those in favor of prosecuting the war. No reply was given, but a number of leading Republicans and Democrats issued a call for a "Union" convention of nonpartisan character to meet at Columbus on September 5. Thus, as far as the Republican Party was concerned, the war was not to be a party matter.

This convention inaugurated that coalition of Republicans and War Democrats, known as the Union Party, which dominated Ohio politics during the war years. Presided over by the veteran ex-Whig leader, Thomas Ewing, whose vote for Lincoln in 1860 was given as an independent and whose conservatism harked back to Clay and Webster, the convention showed its disregard of party by refusing even to indorse the existing Federal and state administrations and by confining its platform to the one question of supporting the war in order to maintain the Constitution and the Union. Slavery was not mentioned. Disappointing as this was to radical Republicans, it was accepted as the only basis on which Democrats would coöperate. In naming a candidate for governor, it seemed wise to select a Democrat to insure the largest possible support from that party. The choice of the convention was a well-known Douglas Democrat, David Tod, a Youngstown capitalist with important coal, iron, and railroad interests, who had been twice an unsuccessful candidate for governor in the 1840's and who had served as Minister to Brazil in Polk's administration. The rest of the ticket was divided between Republicans and Democrats.

Meanwhile, the regular Democratic organization had held its state convention and nominated Hugh J. Jewett, of Muskingum County, for governor. Its platform was critical of the administration, and while not clearly opposed to the war, favored peace through a constitutional convention. The candidate was more warlike than the platform and polled 151,774 votes to Tod's 206,997, after a very quiet campaign. The result indicated that the majority of the Democrats were not willing to give up their organization, though the Union Party was able to improve upon the prewar Republican majorities.

The Reaction of 1862

Upon Governor Tod's administration fell the most serious problems of the war. Governor Dennison's difficulties had been largely administrative—the organization of the state for war purposes, a task of no slight proportions, but not impossible of solution. He had had the loyal and enthusiastic support of the great majority of Ohioans, and there had been no lack of men or money, but his successor faced a far more difficult situation—the natural cooling of patriotic fervor, the discouragement over military failures of the Union armies, the problem of recruiting the unwilling, and the growing boldness of critics of the war. Lacking the even temperament of his predecessor, Tod was a more vigorous and forceful figure, who made enemies but whose courage and unselfish loyalty to the Union could not be questioned. No Ohio governor has faced a more trying situation than that produced by the war years of 1862 and 1863.

Recruiting became a serious matter in the summer of 1862, when, in the face of the growing war-weariness, the Federal Government continued its demands for men. The alarm over Stonewall Jackson's threat against Washington late in May was sufficient to enable the Governor to secure five thousand volunteers for three months' service in the emergency, but the later calls for six hundred thousand, of which Ohio was to raise seventy-four thousand, presented real problems. Unless the quota was filled, drafting would be resorted to in accordance with a recent act of Congress. Accordingly, the counties were assigned their proportions, and upon each locality was placed the burden of securing the necessary volunteers or submitting to the draft. Local pride, plus the payment of bounties, and the efforts of recruiting agents—promised commissions for securing volunteers—sufficed to fill the quotas in twenty-six counties. Of twelve thousand drafted from the others, 2,900 were excused for various reasons and 1,900 ran away. Strangely enough, most of the twenty-six counties in which the draft was unnecessary were in southern Ohio. The conservative lower Scioto Valley, though containing more people of Southern blood than any other portion of the state, was the first section to fill its quotas. On the other hand, not one county in the anti-slavery Western Reserve escaped the draft, while the counties just south of the Reserve, where the conservative Democrats were particularly strong, were most laggard of all.[2]

---

[2] Crawford, Hancock, Holmes, and Stark, in this area, and Noble and Montgomery, in southern Ohio, ranked high in their percentages of drafted men. Mahoning and Medina led the Reserve counties in this respect.

Support of the war in terms of enlistments was strongest in that part of Ohio where abolitionism had the weakest hold.

In keeping with the decline in enthusiasm was the growing volume of criticism. From the beginning of the war, Clement L. Vallandigham, Congressman from the Dayton district in southwestern Ohio, had attacked the war and the Lincoln administration in Congress and out. Eloquent and logical, endowed with a strong will and great courage, Vallandigham was admirably fitted to lead the cause of the Peace Democrats. Blind to any other viewpoint but his own, he had the Scotch-Presbyterian's narrowness and strength—an uncompromising devotion to the cause in which he believed. Despite storms of criticism and abuse, he advocated the idea of a peace by conciliation—what a later Scotch-Presbyterian President termed "a peace without victory." Believing that a Northern triumph would mean the destruction of the old Union, the end of State rights, and the establishment of a centralized despotism, Vallandigham and his followers tried to bring about the defeat of the Union armies and the overthrow of the Lincoln administration. Thus only, they argued, could a restoration of the Union be effected on terms fair to both sections. On the other hand, they were not desirous of complete Southern success, for that would utterly destroy the Union. Despite the charge of treason hurled at them, the Peace Democrats, popularly termed "Copperheads," held to their belief that the war was wicked, unnecessary, and unconstitutional and should be ended, if need be, by revolutionary means.

A number of Democratic newspapers voiced the views of this element, and it became increasingly difficult to distinguish between partisan criticisms of the administration and utterances that might be regarded as treasonable.

Samuel Medary, veteran Democratic editor and politician, whose career dated back to Jackson's time, was one of the most violent critics of the administration through the columns of his war-time paper, the *Crisis*, but Medary was too important a man to be dealt with summarily. Nor could Vallandigham, Member of Congress, be silenced. But others, less conspicuous, seemed more directly active in discouraging enlistments, and the process of suppressing these objectors began. At Governor Tod's direct instigation, United States officers arrested Dr. Edson B. Olds, of Lancaster, former Democratic Member of Congress, and imprisoned him for several months, while a number of other Democrats, mostly editors, were given similar treatment. According to a later investigation by a legislative committee, only eleven persons were arrested and imprisoned, but probably others were curbed in their utterances by these examples. That this policy of suppression helped the cause of the Union may well be doubted, judging by the occurrences of 1863.

The military events of 1862 gave Ohio citizens their first real taste of what war meant. The terrible battle of Shiloh, in April, one of the bloodiest of the war, resulted in nearly two thousand killed and wounded among Ohio troops alone. Surgeons and nurses were rushed on steamboats to the battlefield, and the wounded were removed to Ohio hospitals as speedily as possible. In other engagements, medical relief was sent where needed, as the Federal authorities were often unable to meet the sudden emergencies created by great battles.

Twice in the summer of 1862, the war approached Ohio's own soil. The first was a cavalry raid by John Morgan into the Blue Grass region of Kentucky in July, threatening Lexington and alarming the citizens of Cincinnati, who momentarily expected the bold raider to dash into Newport and Covington, just over the Ohio from the "Queen City." But Morgan's forces were too small to constitute a serious danger, and it remained for General Kirby Smith's invasion of Kentucky with some twelve thousand men to furnish a genuine cause for alarm. He captured Lexington on the first of September and might have taken Cincinnati by a quick march, though it is unlikely that he could have held it. Under General Lewis Wallace, the city was speedily placed in a state of defense, with the slogan, "Citizens for labor, soldiers for battle." All business was suspended, while rich and poor alike helped fortify the Kentucky hills, assembled supplies, constructed a pontoon bridge over the Ohio, and engaged in other war labors.

Meanwhile, at Governor Tod's call, men from all parts of the state were hurrying to the rescue of the "Queen City." Often armed with ancestral guns and powder horns, these "Squirrel Hunters" presented a picturesque, if not very military, appearance. Together with the regiments being recruited for long service, which were hastily sent to Cincinnati, and the local citizenry, they furnished a defensive force far outnumbering Smith's invaders. Smith made no serious effort to approach the city, as his advance depended in part upon General Bragg's progress, and the latter was already being pursued by Buell with a large Union army from Tennessee. This was the ultimate factor in saving both Louisville and Cincinnati, though the latter was in good position to resist immediate attack.

The political campaign of 1862 reflected the prevailing discouragement. Military failures, arbitrary imprisonments, mismanagement and blundering in the national administration, and, shortly before the election, the issuance by the President of the preliminary Emancipation Proclamation combined to create a revulsion of feeling against the Union Party. The Democrats carried fourteen of the nineteen congressional districts and elected their state ticket for supreme judge and some other offices by majorities of around 5,500. The Union Party claimed that the absence of the soldier vote accounted for the result, but it was quite evident that many War Democrats had rejoined their old party. In fact, the outcome was not so much a repudiation of the war as it was a vote of lack of confidence in the national administration, for several of the successful Democratic congressional candidates were supporters of the war. The peace element was not yet dominant in the party. The Union Party achieved one notable victory in this campaign in electing General Robert C. Schenck over Vallandigham in the Third Congressional District. A legislative gerrymander which had added a strongly Republican county to the district was responsible for the result.

The Crisis of 1863

The year 1863 marked the military and political crisis of the war. Gettysburg and Vicksburg settled the ultimate fate of the Confederacy, while the state elections in the fall wrecked the hopes of the peace party. Ohio's rôle was a conspicuous one, for here the anti-war element made its most dramatic stand.

Growing bolder with the failure of the Union armies to make any headway in the early months of the year, the extremists began to encourage desertions and resistance to the draft. In Noble County, Republican in its politics but containing in its hills a considerable number of Peace Democrats, occurred a case of forcible resistance to a deputy marshal, who was seeking to apprehend a deserter. Nearly a hundred armed men had organized at Hoskinsville to resist Federal authorities. However, this opposition evaporated with the arrival of troops, and in several cases fines and imprisonment were meted out to the guilty by the Federal court.

A more serious example of this nature developed in Holmes County in June. This county, unlike Noble, was a Democratic stronghold, one of the few counties in northeastern Ohio to resist the spread of Republicanism in the 1850's. Here the objectors to the draft were strong enough to require the sending out of a force of four hundred and fifty soldiers against them. Some nine hundred armed men with four howitzers had gathered in a fortified camp, but after firing one volley at the approaching soldiers, they fled to the woods and resistance ended. Leading Democrats persuaded the ringleaders to surrender peaceably, and bloodshed was avoided except for the wounding of two men in the fighting around the camp.

However, these were minor affairs compared with the Vallandigham case. That individual, made more defiant by his defeat, closed his congressional career with speeches demanding peace by conciliation and bitterly opposing what he charged were unconstitutional measures of the Lincoln administration. Though breathing a spirit of unflinching devotion to the Union and the Constitution, Vallandigham's utterances were regarded by Union men as akin to treason and as an incitement to forcible resistance to the war and the draft. Returning to Ohio, he continued his peace campaign in public speeches designed to strengthen the peace element in the Democratic Party. He was aided by the overzealousness of General Burnside, commander of the Department of the Ohio at Cincinnati. That officer, in General Orders No. 38, announced his intention of arresting persons declaring sympathy for the enemy. Treason, expressed or implied, the Order stated, would not be tolerated. Vallandigham responded to this challenge, and in a bitter speech, delivered at Mt. Vernon, not only denounced the war in terms such as he and others had used often enough before this, but attacked General Orders No. 38 as a base usurpation of arbitrary authority. "He despised it, spit upon it; he trampled it under his feet." His authority, he declared, was "General Orders No. 1—the Constitution."

This was too much for General Burnside. When two officers, who had taken notes on Vallandigham's speech, reported his remarks to the commanding general, the latter ordered the arrest of the offender. Hurried away from his Dayton home after midnight, Vallandigham was taken before a military commission at Cincinnati and tried for violation of General Orders No. 38 in declaring disloyal sentiments. The prisoner, however, refused to recognize the right of such a body to try him, as he was not a soldier and could be tried only by a jury in a civil court and according to the forms of the common law. Furthermore, he denied that he was guilty of any offense known to the Constitution and declared that he had appealed to the people to use the ballot-box, not forcible resistance, to right their wrongs.

Vallandigham's defense was a strong one, and his position was later upheld by the United States Supreme Court in a similar case, *Ex parte Milligan*, when it declared that military tribunals could have no jurisdiction in territory not actually being fought over and where the civil courts were still open. But this decision was made after the war was over, when passions had subsided somewhat. In Vallandigham's case, the United States courts would not interfere. Consequently, the military commission found the prisoner guilty and sentenced him to confinement for the rest of the war. But President Lincoln changed the sentence to exile to the Confederacy, and accordingly the leader of the Peace Democrats was sent to Tennessee, where he was transferred under a flag of truce to the Confederate lines.

The whole affair was a colossal blunder on the part of the military authorities. Vallandigham, the arch-enemy of the war, was far less dangerous making bitter speeches in Ohio than Vallandigham in exile, a martyr to his convictions. The reaction in his favor was pronounced. An enraged mob in his home city had seized control and burned the office of the Dayton *Journal*, a Union newspaper, on the day of his arrest. Martial law was necessary to restore order. Public meetings in New York City and other places protested against his seizure. The President himself regretted the action of General Burnside but felt constrained to uphold him.

The effect upon the Democratic Party was evident when the state convention met on June 11. Swept away by the enthusiasm for the exiled leader, the delegates ignored the advice of conservative leaders and nominated Vallandigham for governor by an almost unanimous vote, with ex-Senator George E. Pugh, his attorney and defender, as the candidate for lieutenant-governor. Pugh's speech to the convention was even more contemptuous of Order No. 38 than Vallandigham's at Mt. Vernon. The Peace Democrats now had complete control of the party. Acting by authority of the convention, a committee asked President Lincoln to permit Vallandigham to return to Ohio, but the President would agree to do so only on condition that the members of the committee pledge themselves to support the war—a condition they could not accept. Meanwhile, soon after his nomination, the candidate for governor left North Carolina on a blockade runner for Bermuda, from which place he sailed for Canada, eventually making Niagara Falls on the Canadian side his headquarters for the campaign.

Faced with such formidable opposition, and with dissatisfaction with the war growing on every side, the Union supporters at their state convention decided to put aside Governor Tod, and named for the governorship John Brough, a staunch Democrat of other days, at one time State Auditor but now a railroad president and retired from politics. A strong Union speech he had recently made at Marietta had been given much publicity by Cincinnati newspapers, and almost at once a movement had been launched to make him the candidate of the Union element for governor. The movement had spread rapidly and he was named on the first ballot. Tod was rejected for a second term because by his vigorous policies he had aroused enmities that rendered him less available than a new man.

The campaign was exciting and attracted Nation-wide interest. Vallandigham's supporters declared they would march to Niagara Falls and escort their hero home by armed force, if he were elected. Indeed it seemed that civil war would break out in the whole Northwest, as the peace element was strong in Indiana and Illinois, and Vallandigham's election would be the signal for action. Realizing the danger, the Union men strained every nerve to elect Brough. There was not complete unity in the Democratic Party, as was shown by the silence of Judge Jewett, Henry B. Payne, and Judge Rufus P. Ranney, all three former candidates of the party for governor, while a group of War Democrats held a bolting convention in September.

The election result was really determined by the two great Union victories of Gettysburg and Vicksburg. The war, after all, was not a failure, and the Union leaders now had a strong argument to prove the fact. Despite the seeming enthusiasm for Vallandigham, Brough had a majority of 100,882 votes,[3] a surprising change of sentiment from that of the preceding year. The vote of the Demo- crats was a little larger than in their victorious campaign of 1862, but the enormous increase in the Union total was unexpected. The crisis had brought out a great silent vote which had decided the contest. Eighteen counties voted for Vallandigham—twelve in the northern half of the state, where (excluding the Western Reserve) many old centers of Democratic strength had remained lukewarm toward the war.

Unionists all over the North rejoiced at the great victory in Ohio. "Glory to God in the highest; Ohio has saved the Union," telegraphed President Lincoln. He told Gideon Welles, Secretary of the Navy, that he was more anxious about the state elections of 1863 than he had been over his own election in 1860. But he thought the large vote for Vallandigham "a discredit to the country."

The same year that marked the passing of the political crisis gave Ohio its only taste of war. This taste was the midsummer plundering raid by General John Morgan across the southern part of the state. Of slight military impor- tance, it was rather an exhibition of the skill and daring of the Confederate cavalry leader than an indication of Ohio's defenseless condition. Crossing the Ohio River into southern Indiana with 2,460 men, he dashed into Ohio a few miles north of Cincinnati before the militia, called out by the Governor, had had time to assemble. Then, avoiding the cities and foraging from the country, he passed through the southern counties in an effort to reach the Ohio River at an available crossing place, while Union cavalry was in hot pursuit with the state militia unsuccess-

---

[3] The soldiers in the field were allowed to vote by an act of the legislature of this year.   The totals were: Civilian vote—Brough, 246,907, Vallandig- ham, 185,204; Soldier vote—Brough, 41,467, Vallandigham 2,288.

fully attempting to intercept the bold raider. On July 18, nine days after he had crossed the Ohio, Morgan was again on its banks in Meigs County at the ford opposite Buffington Island. Delayed overnight by a little body of men behind some earthworks, the Confederate raider found himself next day almost surrounded by his pursuers. A brief battle ended in a rout, but some twelve hundred escaped with their undaunted leader to seek a crossing farther up the river. When they found such a place twenty miles from Buffington, only three hundred were able to cross before the gunboats were on them, and the rest were forced to continue the flight. The race continued up the river, to end on July 26 at Salineville in Columbiana County, where the exhausted and demoralized Confederates surrendered after a final battle, fought, strange to say, in northeastern Ohio, even farther north than Lee's advance into Pennsylvania the earlier part of the same month— July, 1863.

Morgan's raid, trivial enough in the military sense, was nevertheless an expensive proposition to the State of Ohio. The damages inflicted upon its citizens amounted to $576,225, while the expense of keeping the militia in the field raised the total cost to well over a million dollars. But it gave Ohioans some of the thrills of war without its horrors, and the experiences of those in the path of the raiders were related and magnified with the passing years until Morgan has become one of the immortals of Ohio's history. The final dramatic touch was furnished by his daring escape with six of his officers from the Ohio penitentiary in November, 1863, apparently by tunneling beneath the walls.

Brough's Administration

Governor Brough possessed an energy and a love of action that demanded immediate results and that overrode obstructionists with a relentless vigor, leaving a trail of criticisms and enmities in his wake. Disgusted with evidences of official incompetence and governmental and military red tape, the Governor struck straight from the shoulder at the individuals he regarded as responsible, and generally secured results. Deeply concerned over the treatment of the private soldier, whether in the hospital or in the field, he listened to every complaint and hastened to remedy the trouble, if it was in his power to do so. He incurred the hostility of many of the higher officers by his disregard of their recommendations in matters of appointments and promotions of lower officers, and by his outspoken censures of their conduct when he deemed censure necessary. At times he acted too impulsively and was accused of meddling with matters that did not concern him, but the state has never had a more honest, conscientious, and fearless executive.

Recruiting again became a serious problem in 1864. The previous year had been less difficult than 1862, for the demands had not been so heavy and were met rather easily despite the rather exciting cases of draft resistance already referred to. But in 1864, Ohio was asked to furnish in four calls 148,879 men. Several drafts were required to fill these quotas in spite of the continued use of the vicious bounty system to induce enlistments. Desertions and bounty-jumping were all too common, but it was too late then to change the system. Governor Brough wrote that, of 30,000 men raised by Ohio under one call, over 10,000 failed to reach the front, and that at Camp Chase on that very day 263 out of 1,100 were absent without leave.

> The State swarms with bounty-brokers, bounty jumpers, and mercenaries of every description. Men take contracts to fill 'quotas' as they would to furnish

hay or wood.   They take the largest share to themselves, and frequently the recruit deserts because he says he has been swindled in his bounty.   Patriotism and love of the cause are supplanted to a large degree, as a motive of filling our armies by the mercenary spirit of making money out of the operation.

This was the situation when the war ended, with materialism at flood tide and patriotism becoming increasingly a channel for profits.

In addition to the recruits furnished under the President's calls, Ohio put 35,892 men in the field for one hundred days in the summer of 1864.   These were the state militia, recently organized by acts of the assembly for state defense, but now, at Governor Brough's suggestion, used for garrison duty, guarding railroads, and other work, mostly behind the lines, that would release men for the front. It was hoped that these reinforcements would enable General Grant to bring the war to a speedy end.   The plan did not accomplish its purpose and it took men from the farms and other productive occupations at an inconvenient time, but at least the attempt was worth making, and the thoroughness with which Ohio carried out its part was a tribute to the energy and resourcefulness of its war Governor.

Copperheadism, crushed politically by the defeat of 1863, took the form of secret societies to foment an armed uprising in 1864.   These societies, existing before this time under different names, were generally known in 1864 as the "Sons of Liberty."   Vallandigham became "Supreme Commander" in February, and the military aspects of the organization came to be emphasized.   Its numbers in Ohio were estimated at from 80,000 to 110,000 by the state adjutant general, but it seems probable that only a minority of extremists would have engaged in an

armed uprising. Furthermore, by a well-organized system
of spies, the Governor was able to keep in close touch with
the plans of the leaders and to take steps to counteract
them. The date for the rising of the Sons of Liberty in
the Northwest, after being postponed several times, was
set for the meeting of the Democratic national convention
in Chicago late in August; but the Federal Government
was fully informed and strengthened the garrison at Camp
Douglas, and the conspirators abandoned their plan.

A daring scheme of Confederate agents to release the
prisoners on Johnson's Island in Sandusky Bay was foiled
by the arrest of Captain Charles H. Cole, leading con-
spirator, as he was about to attempt the seizure of the gun-
boat *Michigan*. However, he could have accomplished
little in any case, as his fellow-conspirators, who were
supposed to seize a passenger vessel and come to his aid,
grew frightened and abandoned the project after securing
the boat. The madness of the proposed scheme is evident
from the fact that it was to include also the seizure of a
railroad train by the released Confederate prisoners and a
descent upon Camp Chase, at Columbus, to free the Confederates confined there. It was the height of folly to
think that this could be done without the arousing of an
alarm.

The political events of 1864 were rather an anticlimax
after the bitter struggle of 1863. The outcome of that
election made the result in the Presidential campaign
almost certain. The only question in the Union Party
ranks was whether Ohio would favor Lincoln's renomination or not. Chase, whose Presidential ambitions warped
his entire career, was anxious for the support of his home
state, but early in the year the Union Members of the
legislature declared for Lincoln, and the Secretary of the
Treasury reluctantly accepted the verdict. In the Demo-

cratic Party, the moderates controlled the state convention, and both Vallandigham and Medary were defeated for delegates-at-large to the Chicago national convention. The former, quietly returning home from Canada, was elected a delegate from his home district, however, and played a significant part at the convention. The Presidential nomination of McClellan, a war hero, did not suit the Peace Democrats, and Medary would not support him in the columns of *The Crisis*. Vallandigham was dissatisfied with McClellan's letter of acceptance favoring the prosecution of the war but went on the stump for him, nevertheless. A convention of Peace Democrats from the Northwestern States, held at Cincinnati in October, attempted to nominate Alexander Long, Cincinnati Congressman, for President, but he would not accept.

Although even the Union Party newspapers seemed lukewarm toward Lincoln in the discouraging summer of 1864, the military victories of the early fall rallied their spirits, and Lincoln carried Ohio by a majority of 60,055 votes, while seventeen of the nineteen Members of Congress were of his party. Many War Democrats had supported McClellan, making the Union majority smaller than in the preceding state election, but the result was decisive enough.

Ohio's contribution to the war had been a considerable one. The list of generals of Ohio birth or residence is an imposing one, including Grant, Sherman, Sheridan, McClellan, McDowell, Rosecrans, McPherson, Buell, and others, but Grant must be shared with Illinois, the state of his residence; McClellan lived in Ohio but a short time; while the army careers of some of the others carried them far from their native state. In any case, Ohioans may be content with less than a monopoly of the military glory of these figures. War records contributed to the later political importance of Hayes, Garfield, McKinley, Foraker, and a host of lesser figures, including several governors. Ohio contributed Chase to the Treasury Department, though his political ambitions marred his administration and brought about his resignation in 1864. Ex-Governor Tod was offered the vacancy but declined it. Ohio also shared in the honor of furnishing the head of the War Department, for Edwin M. Stanton was Ohio-born and Ohio-reared, though he had become a resident of Pennsylvania some years prior to the war. Wade and Sherman were conspicuous figures in the Senate, but the former was a constant critic of the President and an extremist from nearly every viewpoint.

On the Democratic side, George H. Pendleton and S. S. Cox were conspicuously able leaders in the House of Representatives but attracted far less attention than Vallandigham. The latter's prominence gave Ohio the doubtful honor of furnishing the outstanding "Copperhead" of the war.

In war relief work, Ohio's part was an honorable one. Not only did the state government play an important rôle through its "State Agencies," established in various cities, but civilian organizations furnished money and supplies of all kinds for soldiers and their dependents. The women of Cleveland claimed the honor of forming the first soldiers' aid society in the country (April 20, 1861), an organization that later became a branch of the United States Sanitary Commission, which centralized relief work in the North and was the predecessor of the Red Cross of today. Private charity gave money, bandages, food, clothing, and other supplies, with women doing a large part of the work. The use of fairs to raise funds for the Sanitary Commission proved particularly effective, both Cincinnati and Cleveland having very successful ventures of this type. At the former place, the net profits were $235,406.

The religious and moral, and to some extent the physical, welfare of the soldiers was the particular province of the United States Christian Commission, which had branches at Cincinnati, Cleveland, and Toledo. Its work is comparable to that carried on by the Y. M. C. A. in 1917–1918. In their pulpits the clergy thundered against the rebellion and in general gave a whole-hearted support to the war. The evangelical ministers at Cincinnati in June, 1861, joined in a resolution declaring their belief that the Government represented "the cause of God and man against a rebellion threatening the Nation with ruin," while the Catholic Archbishop Purcell raised the American flag over the Cincinnati cathedral as an indication of his sentiments. The peace element had almost no support from the clergy.

In the field, Ohio contributed, all together, 346,326 soldiers, including both volunteers and drafted men. Of these, 11,237 were killed or mortally wounded, and 13,354 died of disease. Unfortunately, Ohio had 18,354 desertions, ranking third among the states in this unenviable distinction. This number does not include drafted men who failed to report, of whom, according to Governor Brough's statement cited earlier, Ohio had a large number.

Perhaps the finest exhibition of the state's patriotism was in the field of finance. The amount of $10,410,240 was spent for war purposes, and, at the same time, the state debt was reduced by $1,985,259. A small increase in taxation, a large increase in property valuations, and the fact that tax delinquencies were smaller than at any time in Ohio's history explain this phenomenon.

SELECTED BIBLIOGRAPHY

Whitelaw Reid, *Ohio in the War* (2 vols., Columbus, 1893), is the most complete account of all phases of Ohio's part in the Civil War. G. H. Porter, *Ohio Politics during the Civil War Period*, cited for the preceding chapter, covers the political aspects of this subject. King, Galbreath, and Randall and Ryan have sections on the war. *Ohio Archæological and Historical Quarterly*, Vol. VIII, pp. 107–131, and Vol. XIII, pp. 40–70, contains articles on David Tod and John Brough by George B. Wright and O. C. Hooper, respectively. The same publication (Vol. XXXIV, pp. 548–589) has an article by Elizabeth F. Yager, "The Presidential Campaign of 1864 in Ohio." J. L. Vallandigham, *A Life of Clement L. Vallandigham* (Baltimore, 1872), is a biography of Vallandigham by his brother. The story of the rôle of the Ohio Peace Democrats may be read in Elbert J. Benton's excellent study, "The Movement for Peace without Victory during the Civil War," *Western Reserve Historical Society Collections*, No. 99 (Cleveland, 1918).

The biographies and memoirs cited for the preceding chapter continue through this period. Financial matters may be found in E. L. Bogart, *Financial History of Ohio, University of Illinois Studies in the Social Sciences*, Vol. I, No. 1, pp. 5–358. Daniel J. Ryan, *The Civil War Literature of Ohio* (Cleveland, 1911), is a good bibliography, especially for pamphlets, speeches, and histories of military units.

CHAPTER XII

The Post-Bellum Years, 1865–1872

Reconstruction Politics, 1865–1867

*T*HE close of the war in the spring of 1865 marked the achievement of the great goal of the Union Party—the preservation of the Union. Before the year was over, the slavery question was also settled by the passage and ratification of the thirteenth amendment to the Constitution. Although abolition was expressly excluded from the Union Party program early in the war, it had come to be generally accepted as the only solution, even by the War Democrats. But with the war issues cleared away, what was to become of the Union Party? Would the Republicans and Democrats divide as before the war, or would the changed situation, created by the great struggle, evolve new parties suited to new conditions? Already the knotty problems of restoring the seceded states and defining the relationship of whites and blacks had created divisions in the Union majority in Congress, a radical group led by Senator Wade, of Ohio, and Representative Henry Winter Davis, of Maryland, being opposed to the mild policy of President Lincoln. John Wilkes Booth's fatal shot left the solution to Andrew Johnson.

Johnson's continuation of Lincoln's policy soon aroused the opposition of the radicals, but they were not in a position to check the President until Congress met in December, 1865. Thus, for a few months Johnson had his way, and his moderate measures had the commendation of Democrats as well as Republicans. In Ohio, both party conventions indorsed the President's policy, though a radical minority in the Union convention was not satisfied with the platform as adopted. Both parties also chose military candidates: the Union Party, General Jacob D. Cox, a capable officer who had had no military experience before the war, and the Democrats, General George W. Morgan, who had served in the Texas Revolution, the Mexican War, and the Civil War. The Union platform was silent on Negro suffrage, and the Democrats unequivocally opposed to it.

General Cox soon made his position clear. In answer to a committee of colored students from Oberlin, he declared his belief that separation of the two races was the only solution of the Negro problem. He would have a special territory constructed for the Negroes out of parts of Southern states, in which they could enjoy rights not otherwise possible. In 1860, Governor Dennison had suggested a tropical colony for the Negroes, in Central or South America, but the question then was only a theoretical one. Now the race problem was of major importance, and to the Union leaders a source of great embarrassment. Wade, Garfield, and other Western Reserve politicians were insistent on Negro suffrage. But central and southern Ohio thought differently. Furthermore, most of the soldiers, fresh from direct contact with the Southern Negro, believed him unfit to exercise the franchise. General Cox had come to this view despite the fact that he was a resident of the Reserve and an Oberlin graduate and had been a radical before the war. As a consequence of Cox's attitude, his party fought the campaign with a noticeable lack of unity on the Negro suffrage question. The Democrats vigorously opposed both Cox's position and Negro suffrage, and reduced the Union majority to 28,843 votes.

The new Governor, in his inaugural, counselled moderation in dealing with the South and warned his party
against yielding too far to popular impulse:

> A victorious majority, flushed with its triumph, finds
> it easy to forget the rights of minorities, and it remains
> for us to prove whether in our day the old cry of "Woe
> to the conquered" may be silenced by a truly republican
> determination to administer the government for the real
> advantage of all—of the defeated rebels as well as of the
> loyal victors.

This wise and statesmanlike advice was followed later
by a letter to the Ohio Members of Congress urging them
to support the policies of the President, but the appeal
fell on deaf ears.   The radicalism of Wade was permeating
the party in Ohio, and Cox found himself more and more
out of sympathy with this tendency.   Some of the conservatives either joined the Democratic Party or coöperated
with it in support of Johnson's policies, but in the main the
Union Party held its forces together in Ohio, and by
denying that there was any great difference between the
plans of Congress and those of the President, succeeded in
electing sixteen out of nineteen Members of Congress in the
fall of 1866.

By the spring of 1867, the radicals in Congress were
forcing through their program of military rule in the South
followed by a restoration of civil government on the basis
of Negro suffrage.   This program had its counterpart in
the Ohio Legislature.   Here the fourteenth amendment
to the United States Constitution, on the recommendation
of Governor Cox, was ratified by a party vote.   Yet this
was not enough for the radicals, for the amendment
conferred citizenship and civil rights, not suffrage, on the
Negroes.   It remained for the assembly to take the
final step.   This took the form of a proposed amendment

to the state constitution eliminating the word "white" from that document, and thus giving the Negro the right to vote. This proposal had to be voted on at the October state election.

The Union Republican Party, as the former Union Party now called itself, was thoroughly under radical control. Its state convention, after listening to a violent attack upon the President by Congressman Robert C. Schenck, adopted resolutions indorsing the radical policy of Congress and favoring impartial manhood suffrage for Ohio. The convention then named as its candidate for governor Rutherford B. Hayes, Cincinnati Representative in Congress, a radical in votes rather than in speeches, whose gallant conduct in the war gave him an appeal to the soldier element. Governor Cox, despite a successful administration, was too far out of harmony with his party to permit of his being suggested for a second term.

The Democratic Party had already accepted the issue at its January convention. There three of the ablest leaders in the party's history are supposed to have divided the spoils. To Allen G. Thurman, of Chillicothe, for many years one of the safest and most intelligent, if not most striking, of the personalities directing the Democracy, went the nomination for the governorship. To Vallandigham was to go the United States senatorship in case a Democratic assembly was chosen. George H. Pendleton, former Peace Democratic Congressman from Cincinnati, a shrewd politician of great personal popularity, was to have his state's support for the Presidential nomination. The party's program included a bitter hostility to radical reconstruction and Negro suffrage.

With the issue so clearly made between the parties, the campaign aroused great interest. The Democrats appealed to the voters to save the state from "niggerism," and political processions contained floats bearing young girls in white with banners inscribed, "Fathers, save us from negro suffrage." Here was an emotional appeal to popular prejudice as effective as the Republican counter-appeal, "Honest black men are preferable to white traitors." The Republican state ticket was saved by a majority of less than three thousand, but control of the assembly was lost and the Negro suffrage amendment went down to defeat by fifty thousand votes. Despite their failure to elect Thurman governor, the Democrats had won a real triumph, for the state had repudiated the central feature of radical policy, Negro suffrage.

Furthermore, the Democratic success in winning the assembly meant the defeat of Wade for reëlection to the Senate after eighteen years of service there. That bitter old radical was surprised and much disappointed at the action of his home state. He had not realized the essential conservatism of Ohio. The state had supported a war for the Union and, under stress of that war, a program of abolition, but it reverted to its old conservatism when the radicals attempted to apply in the state the suffrage principle they were forcing on the South. Wade was further disappointed when the Senate failed to convict President Johnson after the House had impeached him, for the removal of Johnson would have placed the Ohioan in the Presidency. Wade was President *pro tempore* of the Senate, and by the law in existence then would have succeeded Johnson.

Vallandigham, who by the bargain of the preceding year was supposed to have Wade's place in the Senate, also suffered a humiliating disappointment. The Democratic assembly, influenced by Pendleton and other leaders, elected the more conservative Thurman instead. Vallandigham represented too well the party's unpopular war record, and his election would have furnished fuel for Republican orators to prove the "rebel" character of the Democrats. Thus, in its hour of triumph, the party denied him the vindication that he desired, though he had fought its battles against great odds and had been the target for the most venomous attacks of its enemies for years.

Political Instability, 1868–1872

Shrewd politicians were now becoming aware of new issues, of an economic rather than emotional character, that demanded attention. War-time financial legislation in particular had raised problems of no slight importance. Large Government issues of paper money, popularly called "greenbacks," without gold backing, had caused a depreciation in the value of this currency and a corresponding rise in prices. Together with the issues of bank notes by the newly created National banks, they furnished the country with a large supply of currency that encouraged borrowing and much speculation. The war-time demands for goods speeded up industry and agriculture, and with the large amount of money in circulation, created a period of great prosperity that continued for two years after the war. To the conservative business and financial interests, it seemed desirable to eliminate the paper issues and return to the gold standard, and the Secretary of the Treasury began to call in the greenbacks. However, a slackening of prosperity in 1867 was attributed by many to this withdrawal of paper from circulation, and Congress by law forbade any further contraction.

This problem of the greenbacks attracted the attention of George H. Pendleton, already assured of Ohio's backing for the Democratic Presidential nomination but anxious to attract support from other states. It happened that

Government bond-holders were in a particularly enviable position, as they were paid their interest in gold and were expecting the principal in the same medium when the bonds became due. As these bonds had been generally purchased with paper, this seemed an unfair advantage, now that the gold dollar was worth so much more than the greenback. Pendleton suggested in 1867 that, where gold was not specified in the bond, the face value should be paid in new issues of greenbacks. This action would further inflate the currency, but Pendleton would have the bank notes eliminated from circulation, as they were not popular and the banks were regarded as profiteering monopolies by many people. Paying the bonds in this fashion would reduce the debt and lower taxes, and would give the bondholders as good currency as they had paid for the bonds. With war prosperity threatening to come to an end in 1867, this idea speedily became popular and was christened the "Ohio Idea."

Republicans as well as Democrats, outside Eastern centers of wealth, could see no harm in giving bondholders the same kind of money the masses of the people had to accept. The State of Ohio was doing this very thing to its debt-holders and continued to do so to 1879. Senator John Sherman was of this viewpoint, though he wanted to give all forms of money the same value as soon as possible, thus putting an end to the question. The Republican state convention of 1868 declared in favor of paying the bonds in whatever kind of money might be the currency of the country when they were due, approved the action of Congress in stopping the withdrawal of greenbacks, and favored the taxation of Government bonds thereafter to be issued. These planks were less direct than the Pendleton demand, but they leaned strongly in the same direction.

Pendleton's hopes of securing the Democratic nomination were blasted, however, by the hostility of conservative easterners to his "Ohio Idea," and by the efforts of Alexander Long, Vallandigham, and other Ohioans for Chief Justice Salmon P. Chase, who, having failed three times to secure the Republican nomination, was now willing to look with favor upon the Democracy. But, in the end, neither Ohio candidate was nominated, the honor going to Horatio Seymour, of New York, though the "Ohio Idea" was included in the platform.

The nomination of General Grant by the Republican convention enabled that party to submerge all issues in an emotional appeal for the "Hero of Appomattox." Ohio was safely Republican at the election by a large majority, though seven of the nineteen Congressmen elected were Democrats.

Without the prestige of Grant's name heading their ticket, the Republicans were less fortunate in Ohio. Despite a successful administration, Governor Hayes was barely able to secure reëlection by a plurality of 7,500 votes over Pendleton in 1869. Again the Democrats attacked the bondholders and the National banks—a popular appeal— and again they used the Negro suffrage issue to advantage, for the Republicans had indorsed the proposed fifteenth amendment to the United States Constitution. The new assembly, by a majority of one in the Senate and two in the House, ratified the amendment, however, thus ending the Negro question as far as Ohio was concerned. It was soon ratified by the necessary number of states, and in 1870, for the first time colored delegates attended a Republican state convention in Ohio.

With the settlement of this question, the reconstruction issues seemed to have worn themselves out. They had served the Democratic Party well, for only by emphasizing the suffrage and financial problems had the party been able to overcome the cry of "Copperheadism" that had buried Vallandigham under an avalanche of votes in 1863. Many War Democrats and conservative Republicans had been added to the party, and it was in a strong position despite its failure to carry its state tickets.   Its leadership— the great triumvirate of Vallandigham, Pendleton, and Thurman—was probably the ablest in its history.   Yet after the assault upon radicalism in 1867, it had been losing ground.   There seemed little more to be gained by stirring up race prejudice or attacking banks and bondhold- ers.   The Negroes were voters now, and the country seemed inclined to accept Eastern "sound money" principles.

The best opportunity for the Democrats seemed to lie in an alliance with the growing number of Republicans who were becoming dissatisfied with the Grant administra- tion.   Former Governor Cox, who had been Secretary of the Interior under Grant, was now in this group.   Attempt- ing to carry out reforms in his department, he had quickly found himself out of sympathy with the crowd of corrupt politicians surrounding and influencing the inexperienced President, and resignation was his only recourse.   In the spring of 1871, Cox, Stanley Matthews, George Hoadly, Frederick Hassaurek—a distinguished leader of the German element in Ohio—and a number of other Cincinnati Republicans formed a "Reunion and Reform Association" having as its objects a more liberal policy toward the South (then afflicted with carpetbag rule), civil service reform, a sound currency, and revenue reform.   Cox was in touch with the great German leader, Carl Schurz, who was leading a similar "Liberal" movement in Missouri with much success. Democrats were becoming interested, but it remained for the most radical of all the Civil War leaders to herald the new day.

Clement L. Vallandigham, silent for the most part since Pendleton had assumed the party leadership, now emerged from his tent with a new program for his party, called the "New Departure." This program involved acceptance of the results of the war, including the three constitutional amendments, universal amnesty, economy in government, rapid payment of the public debt, a revenue tariff, and civil service reform. The spectacle of the "arch-Copperhead" eating his own words, as it were, and inviting his party to forget the past, aroused the derision of the Republicans; but it was accepted by the Democratic state convention, was acclaimed as a statesmanlike move by Liberals in other states, and for the moment seemed to have restored to him the control of his party's fortunes. But he never lived to see the "New Departure" tried out. Two weeks after the party convention, he accidentally shot himself while demonstrating to a friend how a pistol apparently had been discharged in a brawl in which a man had been killed. He was one of the attorneys in the trial of a man accused of the killing.

The Democrats showed little enthusiasm for the new issues after Vallandigham's untimely death. Thurman, Pendleton, and other leaders thought the move too radical, and the Democratic campaign languished. The Republicans named another military candidate for governor, General Edward F. Noyes, and rather easily elected him over George W. McCook, a member of a famous family of Civil War soldiers, the "Fighting McCooks." The legislature also reëlected John Sherman to the United States Senate despite the opposition of some of the "Liberal Republicans."

The Presidential election of 1872 saw the defeat and dissolution of the Liberal movement. All its hopes of defeating Grant were shattered when Horace Greeley, the

erratic and partisan editor of the New York *Tribune,*
was named by the national convention at Cincinnati.
Greeley was honest and well-meaning but unfitted to lead
a reform movement of this character. Cox, Hoadly,
Matthews, and other prominent Ohio Liberals either
remained silent or repudiated Greeley. The Democrats
saw no hope of defeating Grant except by supporting
Greeley, even Senator Thurman, who was averse to "new
departures" and insistently Democratic, acquiescing.
However, the regular Republicans carried the state
for Grant by a large majority. Even combination
with the Liberals had been of slight assistance to the
Democrats.

But, at least, the war issues were no longer matters of
importance to be settled at the polls. Republican orators
still waved the "bloody shirt" and appealed to the soldier
voters to vote as they had shot, but the appeal was emotional and sentimental and decreasingly effective. Political
corruption could not be concealed nor economic and governmental problems disposed of by a waving of the Flag. State
issues, obscured as never before by the prevalence of war
emotionalism, began to demand attention. The state
convention of a "Labor Party" at Columbus in 1871 and
the regular appearance of Prohibition Party candidates
from 1869 on were indications of a new spirit in politics.
Railway regulation, education, taxation, and other state
problems were arousing the interest of people without
regard to politics. The great industrial changes (dealt
with in the following chapter) were undermining the old
order and creating a host of new problems—economic and
social ones primarily. Ohio was becoming more and more
industrial, conservative, and Eastern in viewpoint. Tariff
and currency issues were to bring these tendencies to the
fore in the next decades.

The sixties and early seventies saw the generation that
had participated in the slavery controversy and that
remembered the struggles of Whigs and Democrats as
far back as Jackson's time disappear from the political
arena.   Corwin had died in 1865 and Ewing six years later.
They had carried the ideals of Clay and Webster into the
war period.   Giddings, the anti-slavery veteran, had ended
his career by serving as consul at Montreal, dying there in
1864.   Wade ceased to be active in politics after his retirement from the Senate in 1869.   Chase became Chief
Justice of the Supreme Court in 1864, but never lost touch
with politics to the time of his death in 1873.   In the
Democratic camp, Samuel Medary, the veteran editor, did
not survive the war he so bitterly opposed.   David Tod
and John Brough, once his party colleagues, closed their
political careers as war governors, Brough dying before
his term expired and Tod in 1868.   William Allen, retired
save for an occasional political speech even before the
war began, was to prove the exception among his political
contemporaries by a triumphant return to high office in
1873 at the age of seventy.   Lewis D. Campbell, Whig,
Know-Nothing, Republican, Unionist, and finally Democrat, returned to Congress for a single term in 1871 after
a long absence and concluded his career as a member of
the constitutional convention of 1873.

Overlapping the careers of the above in many cases, but
more important in the post-war period, were such Repub-
licans as Sherman, Hayes, Garfield, Cox, and, a little later,
McKinley, Hanna, and Foraker.   All but Sherman and
Hanna had served in the war.   On the Democratic side,
Thurman, Pendleton, Henry B. Payne, Hugh J. Jewett,
George Hoadly—converted from Liberal Republicanism—
Thomas Ewing, the younger, and Durbin Ward were
prominent figures.   Vallandigham was a contemporary

of these, being but fifty-one at the time of his death and apparently destined for further political activity.   Nevertheless, his passing was a fitting end to the period of slavery and civil strife, and his last work a recognition that a "New Departure" was necessary for all parties.   The war-time animosities could now be placed on the shelf with the figure who more than any other Ohioan had been the embodiment of them.

Selected Bibliography

Most of the references for Chapter XI are useful for the Reconstruction period, particularly Porter, *Ohio Politics during the Civil War Period.*   C. H. Moore, "Ohio in National Politics, 1865–1896," *Ohio Archæological and Historical Quarterly,* Vol. XXXVII, pp. 220–427, develops the national aspects of local politics.   Charles R. Williams, *Life of Rutherford Birchard Hayes* (2 vols., Boston and New York, 1914), and Theodore Clarke Smith, *Life and Letters of James Abram Garfield* (2 vols., New Haven, 1925), are useful biographies for the post-war period. The biographies, memoirs, letters, and diaries cited for earlier chapters should be consulted also, since most of the men prominent in the 1850's were active in post-war politics.

CHAPTER XIII

ECONOMIC PROGRESS, 1850–1880

Agriculture in Transition

*O*HIO was unsurpassed as a farming state in 1850. First in the production of corn and wool and in the numbers of horses and sheep, second in wheat and cattle, and third in oats and potatoes, the Buckeye State's supremacy as a diversified farming area was generally conceded, though the much older states of New York and Pennsylvania could boast of higher land values. A virgin soil, a favorable climate, the absence of mountain barriers, and river and lake outlets were nature's contribution, but Ohioans themselves were responsible for their canal and road systems, while both the East and the South furnished the growing markets for Ohio's agricultural surplus. The rush of immigration had done the rest.

Yet the tide was already turning in the 1850's. Except in the northwestern counties, where drainage difficulties incident to the "Black Swamp" retarded settlement, most of Ohio's agricultural area was occupied. Immigrants seeking cheap lands, and even many native Ohioans, were being attracted to Illinois, Iowa, and other Western states. The period of exploitation of virgin soil was coming to an end, and Ohio was beginning in the fifties to feel the competition of Western products grown on the rich prairies of the upper Mississippi and sent east by railroad. Despite great progress between 1850 and 1880, Ohio lost ground relatively and in the latter year had dropped to third in wheat production and to fifth in corn, while its live stock, though far more numerous and valuable than in 1850, gave it only fourth place in 1880 in contrast with its place as second thirty years before. The prairies were the agricultural center of the nation. Thus the real explanation is not Ohio's decline, but the more rapid growth of Illinois and Iowa.

The agriculture of the whole country was undergoing revolutionary changes in these decades, and Ohio was as striking an example of change as was any state in the Union. The use of machinery, the advent of scientific agriculture, the revolution in transportation wrought by the railway, and the Industrial Revolution with its far-reaching effects were fundamental factors in the transformation of agriculture. While the tremendously rapid development of manufacturing was not paralleled in farming, the changes between 1850 and 1880 were, nevertheless, of striking significance.

Nowhere were these things more noticeable than in the application of machinery to the farm. The Buckeye farmers of the 1880's had reapers, mowing machines, cultivators, corn planters, wheat drills, and other labor-saving machines unknown or little used in the 1840's. Even steel plows had not by 1848 taken the place of the old cast-iron and wood combinations of the pioneer generation. Not until a Gambier blacksmith began to make them in the state did steel plows become at all common. Stationary threshing machines existed in 1850, but the portable variety was only just coming into use, and steam power did not displace the horse in operating the machine until the 1860's. Greatly improved tools made of steel added to the efficiency of the farmer of the eighties as compared with his father of the forties. The reaper, as invented and improved upon by Hussey, McCormick, and others, was the most revolutionary piece of farm machinery

in its saving of labor. In 1840, to cut and bind twelve
acres of grain in one day required the labor of twelve men.
By the 1870's, this number was reduced to three. While
the more important kinds of modern farm machinery were
being widely used in the late 1850's, it was the Civil War
period, with its great scarcity of labor and its demand for
farm products, that made machinery almost a necessity.
Skepticism disappeared after the demonstration of the
reaper.

Next to interest in machinery, perhaps the most striking
evidence of progress lay in efforts to improve breeds of
domestic animals. As early as 1833, a group of Scioto
Valley cattle raisers had formed a company to import
English stock—a venture that not only proved financially
profitable but made the shorthorn cattle of southern
Ohio the finest in the West. Similar undertakings, particularly after 1850, continued this improvement. The
sales of imported stock were largely attended, and high
prices were paid for fine cattle, horses, and sheep. At a
Clinton County sale in 1854, one bull brought $3,700, one
sheep as high as $120, and a female shepherd dog, $51.
At first the improved stock was owned by wealthy gentle-
men farmers, such as the Renicks and the Worthingtons
of the Scioto Valley, but their example created a widespread
interest in scientific stock breeding. Fairs and public
sales stimulated this interest further until the ownership
of fine shorthorn and Devon cattle and merino sheep
came to be regarded as the mark of a successful farmer.

Both in production and in marketing there were significant changes between 1850 and 1880. To a considerable extent, Ohio agriculture had become sectionalized in
the early decades of the nineteenth century. Wheat
belonged to northern Ohio—particularly that row of
counties extending halfway across the state south of the

Reserve. This "backbone" region, settled chiefly from Pennsylvania, had become the wheat center of the West by the 1840's. Corn, on the other hand, was the great crop of the south, especially of the Miami and Scioto Valleys, where climate and soil were equally favorable. Cattle and hogs naturally were associated with the corn counties. Up in the Western Reserve, where grassy meadows and plenty of hay provided provender for animals, dairy farming was practiced to such a degree that the Reserve became popularly known as "Cheesedom." Sheep were also plentiful in this region, but were even more so farther south in the hills of eastern and east central Ohio adjacent to and north of the National Road. Harrison County was the wool capital of the state.

While wheat, sheep, and dairy cattle were associated with the northeastern quarter of the state, and corn, hogs, and beef cattle with the southwestern quarter, southeastern Ohio and the northwestern counties were backward areas. Though settled early, the southeast was too hilly and broken, except for some favored valleys and level uplands, to offer the attractions of other sections. Difficulties in reaching markets were a further retarding factor. In the northwest—the "Black Swamp" region—problems of drainage and malarial diseases, together with the absence of canal transportation until the middle forties, were great obstacles to the pioneer farmer, and this region was but thinly settled prior to 1850.

By 1880 much of this sectionalism had disappeared. The farmer was much less the creature of his environment and new methods of transportation had opened new markets. Northwestern Ohio had become a wealthy farming area crossed by canal and railroad. Its good soil, once drained, produced large crops, thus spreading the corn area over the entire western half of the state, while the old wheat belt had extended westward and southward until it overlapped most of the corn region. In the Reserve, dairy products were still important, but cheese making had left the farm by 1880 to become a factory enterprise.

In 1850, Ohio cattle and hogs were being driven over the mountains to the Eastern markets in large numbers after a period of fattening at the eastern edge of the corn belt or in the meadows of the Reserve. With the advent of the railroad, droving speedily came to an end, and long trains of cars carried Ohio live stock to the New York, Philadelphia, and Baltimore markets. No longer were breeds of animals selected for their endurance. The day of the "razorback" hog was over. Unlike other live stock, sheep had increased in numbers during the war years, owing to high prices for wool, which reached a climax in 1867. Despite tariff assistance, prices were less encouraging to sheep raisers in the seventies, and the number of sheep declined. Ohio was still an important state in respect to sheep raising, being surpassed only by California, but her days of supremacy were over by 1880.

Agricultural progress was more than a matter of crops and markets. New ideas began to make headway through a number of channels. One of the most important of these channels was the farm journal. Although not the first attempt of its kind, the *Ohio Cultivator*, established by M. B. Bateham at Columbus in 1845, was the first Ohio farm paper to enjoy a prosperous existence. Disseminating information about every phase of farm life—there was even a "Ladies' Department"—it attacked the lethargy and inertia of the masses of farmers and helped arouse a spirit for betterment. Rivals soon appeared, but only one, the *Ohio Farmer*, begun by Thomas Brown in 1852, lasted. Absorbing the *Cultivator* in the trying days of the Civil

War, it has maintained itself as a useful and prosperous farm journal down to the present day.

At the suggestion of the *Cultivator,* a state convention of friends of agriculture met in June, 1845, and organized the Ohio State Board of Agriculture. With the support and official sanction of the legislature, there were organized in the different counties agricultural societies whose delegates, meeting annually at Columbus, debated matters of interest to farmers and elected the state board. The local societies also held county fairs. Such fairs had appeared sporadically before this, but they now became permanent institutions in nearly every county. Exhibits of farm products, fine stock, machinery, and local manufactures, as well as of needlework, canned fruits, cakes and pies, and other household products aroused interest and gave an incentive for improvement, while horse races, "ladies' equestrian exhibitions," shows, and other lighter features furnished entertainment and amusement. Under supervision of the Ohio State Board of Agriculture appeared the greatest of these expositions, the State Fair, first held at Cincinnati in 1850 and thereafter held for many years at other important cities in different parts of the state. Beginning with the year 1874, the fair ceased to be an itinerant exposition and was permanently located at the capital city, though for several years the wisdom of this policy was debated by the state board.

Local farmers' clubs, active in the winter months, served a social as well as educational purpose in many communities around 1850. These organizations had no central organization, however, and often died of inanition. Not until after the Civil War, when the Grange came into existence, was a really effective organization established for the welfare of the farmer. Although the Ohio State Grange for a time experimented with coöperative buying and selling, its chief benefits were social and educational.   It helped break down the isolation of rural life and, through the mutual exchange of ideas, extended the farmer's intellectual horizon and made him a more important and better-appreciated figure in the life of his community.

Although a widespread prejudice existed against "book farming," the teaching of agriculture had its beginnings in this period.   Two or three academies offered courses in agriculture, though few students would take them and attempts at a work-and-study arrangement in one or two colleges were not successful.   At Oberlin in 1854, the "Ohio Agricultural College" was launched by a group of enthusiasts—among them that pioneer in this field, Dr. Norton S. Townshend, who served on the faculty. The project lasted only three years, however, dying for lack of support.   The advocates of agricultural education were not discouraged but turned their efforts to securing the establishment of a state-supported college.   Michigan started such a school in 1857, and Governor Chase recommended in 1858 that the Ohio Assembly take a similar step.   But that body was averse to such action, nor was there any general demand for such an institution on the part of the farmers themselves.   Hopes of Federal aid in the form of land grants were dashed when President Buchanan, a strict constructionist, vetoed the Morrill Bill in 1859.   The prejudice against a state-supported institution was expressed by the *Ohio Cultivator* in approval of the veto: "The success of Morrill's College Land Bill would have been to build up the most stupendous literary hospital for political invalids and sap-rotted theorists the world ever saw."

The success of the Republican Party in 1860 removed the obstacles to Federal aid, and the Morrill Bill became a law in 1862.   By its terms, each state was to receive thirty thousand acres of public land for each Senator and Representative in Congress, the income to serve as an endowment to support and maintain a college whose leading purpose should be instruction in agriculture and the mechanical arts. Other subjects were not to be excluded, however, and military science was to be offered. Buildings had to be erected and maintained by the state, as the endowment could not be used for such purposes.

Though both Governor Tod and the Ohio State Board of Agriculture favored accepting the grant, the legislature delayed two years before acting. Then, in 1864, Ohio received some 630,000 acres of public land and proceeded to sell it. Prices were low, the bulk of the land being sold at fifty-three cents an acre and the total return amounting to only $342,450.80. If the land had been retained and sold at a later period, a far larger sum could have been realized.

Years of delay ensued before the project was finally carried out. A number of difficult questions had to be settled. Sentiment was divided as to whether a new college should be created, or whether the money should be given to one or more of the existing institutions. The more active agricultural reformers held to the former view, and in the end this plan was adopted. Then the question of location and curriculum caused much debate. After a sharp rivalry with several other places, Columbus was given the college, a farm two miles north of the capital city being adjudged the most desirable location. Dr. Norton S. Townshend, expressing the farmers' viewpoint, wanted the new institution to be purely agricultural and mechanical in its curriculum and opposed the inclusion of such subjects as languages and literature. But a broader viewpoint prevailed in the board of trustees, and though called the "Ohio Agricultural and Mechanical College," the new college was much like other institutions except that it included a department of agriculture.

For years it was looked upon with suspicion by the farmer element, and its board of trustees was often the football of party politics. Though opened in 1873, it had, after an existence of a decade, only a dozen students in agriculture out of an enrollment of more than three hundred. Critics charged that its agricultural work was unsatisfactory, that its entrance requirements excluded most farm boys, that the president and faculty, except Dr. Townshend, were opposed to agricultural education (a charge made plausible by the change of its name to Ohio State University in 1878), and that it offered no religious training. A former trustee declared that it had gotten "as far as possible away from God and Agriculture." The instruction in agriculture was indeed quite elementary. Upon Dr. Townshend fell the duty of teaching all the courses in agriculture and veterinary medicine as well as that of operating the experimental farm. Under such conditions, and sadly neglected by the legislature, the new university was far from satisfactory to the farmers, though its academic work was increasingly successful. It had not by 1880 demonstrated that agricultural education was practicable, nor had it overcome the mountain of prejudice against a college education for farmers. It was not until the 1890's that it began to achieve the hopes of the agricultural reformers of the previous generation. Then, with larger appropriations from the assembly, more adequate equipment, and better teaching, the value of its work came to be slowly appreciated.

The Industrial Revolution, 1850–1880

In these changing years, when the farmer was learning his business anew, the roar of machinery and the smoke

of the factory announced the coming of the Industrial
Revolution to the Buckeye State. Cities grew by leaps
and bounds, railroads stretched their bands of iron to the
most isolated counties, and the old way of life disappeared forever. Not that Ohio was purely an agricultural
commonwealth before 1850, for it ranked fourth in the
Union in the value of its manufactured products by the
census of that year. Particularly in the Ohio Valley from
Steubenville to Cincinnati, thriving centers of industry
manufactured for the growing down-river markets, while
in many localities the county seat supplied an important
part of the goods needed for the area around it. But
outside Cincinnati the establishments were generally
small and the factory almost unknown. Ohio was essentially rural in 1850, even though its metropolis had become
the nation's third most important manufacturing city.
The bulk of the state's population either lived on the farm
or in the small town but a step removed from it.

But the 1850's, with their railway building, saw modern
industrialism raise its head. Despite the setback occasioned by the Panic of 1857, the production of coal and
iron—the basis of industrial progress—increased rapidly,
Lake Superior iron ore began to arrive at the lake ports,
and petroleum was discovered in some parts of the northeast. By the opening of the Civil War, the era of industry
was at hand, and the stimulus of that conflict speeded the
day of its domination. By 1880, the value of Ohio's
output of manufactures had reached $348,298,390, as
compared with an estimated value of $156,777,152 for
farm products. The former total was five and one-half
times the value of manufactures in 1850.

The leading cities of the state furnish a picture of its
varied industrial life in 1880. Cincinnati, as in 1850, was
the metropolis, though its rate of growth was smaller each

decade. No longer was it entitled to the proud name of "Porkopolis," for its meat-packing establishments were excelled by those of three other American cities. Its leading manufactured product was men's clothing, but it did not in this case hold as high a rank compared with other centers as it did in the carriage and wagon business, for no city surpassed it in the latter respect. In the production of malt liquors, it held second place, and in saddlery and harness third. But a prosperity that depended so largely on liquor and horses could not compete with the industrialism of iron and steel. Cincinnati was not well located with respect to iron ore and coke, the meat-packing centers had moved west, and the railroads had deprived the Ohio River of much of its importance. A steady growth of a stable sort was to be Cincinnati's portion rather than the exuberant spreading over the landscape that characterized Chicago and Cleveland.

Cleveland was the city with a future. A commercial, rather than a manufacturing, center in 1850, deriving its importance from its water connection with the East and from its location at the head of the Ohio Canal, it improved its transportation facilities in the early years of the railway era until by 1853 it had rail connections with the more important Eastern cities as well as with Cincinnati and Chicago in the West. The settlement of the upper Northwest and the flow of Lake Superior ore to the Pittsburgh district added to Cleveland's commerce, but its newspapers complained at first that manufacturing was slighted by its capitalists in favor of trade, banking, and real estate investments. But its admirable location with reference to coal and iron ore made its industrial development inevitable, and the sixties and seventies saw the "Forest City" become a city of iron and steel, the third in the country in this respect and ranking thirteenth in the total value of its manufactures. Owing in great measure to the astute leadership of John D. Rockefeller and his associates, Cleveland by 1870 had also become the greatest oil-refining center in the United States. Its population had grown from 17,034 in 1850 to 160,146 in 1880. Twenty years later, it passed Cincinnati, to become the metropolis of the state.

Columbus, after a period of economic stagnation in the 1850's, when it seemed that its destiny was to become a quiet provincial capital, developed rapidly as an industrial and market center, between 1860 and 1880, to pass the fifty-thousand mark in population, almost trebling its total of 1850. Its railroad connections with the southeastern coal fields contributed much to its industrial development, while its central location aided its commercial growth. Toledo, a mere village in 1840, grew, with the settlement of the northwestern counties, into an important city. Its location with reference to Lake Erie and the Miami Canal System gave a great impetus to its economic life that the railways furthered until it became a rival of the capital city for third place among Ohio's urban centers. Dayton, the fifth city in 1880, and its neighbor, Springfield, the sixth, were in the heart of a wealthy farming section and possessed good transportation facilities. Both were centers for the manufacture of agricultural implements, Springfield leading the cities of the nation in this field in 1880. Dayton ranked higher industrially than Columbus and Toledo despite its smaller population.

Yet more significant for the state's industrial future was the rapid growth of a number of little cities in the Cuyahoga and Mahoning Valleys and the adjacent areas. Except for Cleveland, the northeastern counties had not, in 1850, contained a single city with a population of four thousand. This region of wheat and sheep and dairy farms gave no hint of the smoke-blackened landscapes and crowded cities of the twentieth century. But by 1880 the rapid growth of Akron, Canton, and Youngstown foreshadowed the fate of this section. The Mahoning Valley was becoming one of the great iron and steel areas of the nation, for ore and coke were finding Youngstown a convenient meeting place. Farther south, East Liverpool was already one of the country's most important pottery centers, rivalled only by the Trenton (New Jersey) area. At Akron, Dr. Benjamin F. Goodrich was just getting a successful rubber industry under way after a decade of difficulties. The northeast was ready to realize its industrial destiny.

For a time, it seemed that the southern mineral counties, particularly Lawrence, Jackson, and the Hocking Valley area, would share in this great industrial development. Iron ore and coal both existed here, and a number of furnaces were in operation before 1850, though charcoal was then used as fuel. The lack of railroads held back the region until the 1860's, when it underwent a rapid growth. Ironton enjoyed for a time a national reputation, especially in the seventies, when one of the largest furnaces in the United States began to operate there. But the Cleveland-Youngstown region, with access to the finer Lake Superior ores, outstripped the southern counties, and Lawrence, which had led in iron production in 1860, had dropped to fifth in 1880, though still ranking first in the mining of the crude ore. The decline was to continue, for the handicaps were too great to be overcome.

Coal mining also reflected the growing industrial character of the state. While coal was known to exist in large quantities in the eastern and southeastern sections, the lack of a demand and the difficulty in reaching markets prevented any real development before 1850, though here and there mines existed, as in Meigs County, where a considerable quantity of coal was shipped down the river from Pomeroy. The growing use of coal by railroads and for industrial purposes and the improved means of transporting it gave the Hocking Valley and many of the eastern counties a mining industry of major proportions after the war. So many mines were opened that by 1880 some thirty counties were producing coal, with Perry ranking first, followed by Trumbull, Columbiana, Belmont, and Meigs. In the nation, Ohio enjoyed the honor of third place among the bituminous coal states.

Yet this development had its drawbacks. Too many mines were placed in production by eager capitalists, and in the sharp competition that resulted, prices were often too low for profit. Alternate periods of prosperity and depression led to labor difficulties and much part-time employment. Coal mining in Ohio was a chronically "sick" industry, subject to trade and seasonal fluctuations and with wage disagreements and strikes almost the rule.

Next to coal mining, the iron industry best reflected the economic condition of the country. Attempting to compete with the older and better-established British industry in the 1850's, American iron interests naturally demanded tariff assistance. After the Panic of 1857, this demand was more vigorously pressed, and the iron masters of Pennsylvania and Ohio were an important factor in securing the Republican victory of 1860 and the favorable tariffs that followed. Despite a large amount of protection, the industry could not withstand the rigors of the hard times after 1873, and the great majority of Ohio furnaces were out of blast by 1876. By 1880, business had revived, and iron and steel again became a basic factor in the state's industrial progress.

The Republican policy of protection had greatly strengthened the party in 1860 in the coal and iron counties of southern Ohio, where little anti-slavery feeling existed. This policy after the war contributed to the party's development in the Cuyahoga and Mahoning Valleys and adjacent areas, long after its early principles had lost their significance. Marcus A. Hanna and William McKinley were fit representatives of the industrialized northeast in politics, just as earlier Wade and Giddings had represented its anti-slavery viewpoint.

Some of the older centers of the state were but little affected by the new industrialism. Located in the southern half of the state, where settlement came first, but without the distinct advantages for the development of manufacturing that existed elsewhere, they saw themselves outstripped by their younger rivals after the 1850's. In the first half-century of Ohio's growth, such towns as Marietta, Chillicothe, Zanesville, and Lancaster were important places, seemingly destined to become the great cities of the state. But the gods of industry decreed otherwise, and a modest growth—perhaps a kinder fate—rather than great wealth and a congested population, proved to be their portion.

The Revolution in Transportation

One short decade, 1850–1860, saw transportation and communication undergo changes more immediate in effect and far more striking even than those of industry and agriculture. Indeed, without the railroad and the telegraph, economic progress would have been seriously retarded. Canal, river, and highway had played no slight part in the rapid development of the state between 1815 and 1850, but their possibilities had been largely realized by the latter year. Better roads, before the era of motor transport, could produce no revolution in commerce, however much isolated localities might benefit. The canals were limited in capacity, while the Ohio River could do little more for Ohio's progress than its steamboats had already accomplished. There was a need for a swifter, surer, and more generally available method of transport not dependent on seasons and water supply, and one that could reach every part of the state. The railway fulfilled this need.

Ohio's first railroad corporation was the Ohio and Steubenville, and was chartered in 1830, but the road was never constructed. In fact, of twenty-four railroads chartered between 1830 and 1840, but one was actually built, while even in later decades the great majority of those incorporated had only a paper existence. The first road to be placed in operation was the Kalamazoo and Erie, finished in 1836, from Toledo to Adrian, Michigan. The most important of the early lines was the Mad River and Lake Erie from Sandusky to Springfield. At the latter place, it connected with the Little Miami from Cincinnati, thus giving rail transportation from Lake Erie to the Ohio River by 1848.

Progress was slow, as railroads were found to be more costly than at first estimated, and funds were hard to obtain. By 1850 Ohio had only about three hundred miles of railway, though a great many projects were under way. The 1850's, however, were the great years of construction, the total miles of rail in 1860 being ten times that at the beginning of the decade. Most of this work was accomplished by 1857, as the panic of that year effectually stopped work on nearly all the roads for several years. The Civil War further complicated the situation so that the increase in mileage by 1870 was only four hundred miles. However, the succeeding years saw much activity, and by 1880 Ohio had 5,654.62 miles of railway. Only Morgan County lacked rail connection entirely in this year.

Combinations of short lines began in the fifties as the value of Eastern connections came to be realized. By various agreements and alliances, trunk lines appeared, so that presently at least four different systems reached Ohio from the important seaboard cities. This fact made local roads more or less subsidiary to and dependent upon the larger Eastern roads for their outlets. The process after the war became one of absorption and consolidation, resulting in the emergence of the Pennsylvania, New York Central, Baltimore and Ohio, Erie, and Chesapeake and Ohio systems, all of them reaching or crossing Ohio, now more than ever the highway of the nation. The state railway commissioner listed seventy-three separate roads in the state in 1880, but nearly all of these were directly or indirectly dependent upon, if not actually owned by, a few great lines.

At first the great problem was that of raising money for construction. State aid, lavishly granted in 1837 not merely to railroads but to turnpike, canal, and slackwater navigation companies, burdened the state treasury heavily, for the speculative character of these enterprises and the looseness of financing them were not evident at first. Counties, townships, and municipalities, eager to enjoy the benefits of rail transportation, had loaned their credit in one form or another to the extent of $7,542,600 by 1851. Then the new constitution put an end to such assistance, greatly to the dissatisfaction of some counties that were hoping to secure rail transportation by the use of their credit. But those that had given such aid in most cases came to regret it, particularly after the Panic of 1857, for the rosy dreams of the railway promoters ended in the general collapse of speculative enterprises. Less than seventeen per cent of the total mileage had paid dividends by 1868. Athens County, for example, lost one hundred and fifty thousand dollars by its subscriptions to the Marietta and Cincinnati Railroad. Individuals who had bought stock to have roads built in their neighborhoods not only received no dividends in many cases, but found their stock almost worthless and the railroad often left unfinished many miles away.

Other difficulties added to popular disillusionment. Rates were utterly lacking in uniformity, large shippers were being favored over small, and places dependent on one line were paying higher charges than those where competition existed. Local business paid disproportionately higher rates than through traffic, and the larger Eastern roads quite early began to control or dictate the charges of their Ohio connections.

Yet regulation by the state made slow headway. Chiefly in the interest of the canals, maximum rates had been established by the assembly in 1849, while a later act of 1852 required railroads to publish rates to and from points intersecting canals, with the additional provision that higher rates should not be charged between places not on the canals. This effort to effect uniformity of rates accomplished little, and the very existence of the law was soon forgotten. Governor Chase in 1857 suggested the possible establishment of a railroad commission, but the legislature took no action. Perhaps the viewpoint of the Cincinnati *Commercial* was that of a majority of Ohioans in 1860:

> The people have never delegated to their representatives in the Legislature the power to prescribe what they shall eat and drink, how much they shall pay for it, or

what price they shall pay for a ride for themselves, or for freight on their property.

This *laissez-faire* doctrine began to give way before the evident fact that unregulated private business in the field of transportation was seriously detrimental to the public interest. An investigation by a Senate committee in 1866 revealed abuses and discriminations of various kinds and led to the enactment in 1867 of a law creating a state commissioner of railroads and telegraphs to investigate violations of the laws and recommend prosecutions, to examine defective tracks, bridges, and equipment and compel repairs, and to collect statistics on railways and telegraphs and issue reports. This first step was not followed by any significant legislation, though every assembly made some changes in the railway code. The maximum rates of the 1850's—three cents per mile for passengers and five cents per ton for freight—remained unchanged but of little practical use. The laws made exceptions for distances under thirty miles and required "reasonable" charges for loading and unloading, which, with other loopholes, permitted the roads to do virtually as they pleased.

The commissioner was an investigating official with no power to act. He could report violations of the laws to county prosecutors, but these officials showed no desire to antagonize the railroads. Shippers were afraid to place their complaints in writing for fear of what the road might do to them in the future. Even a successful suit might cost more in legal expenses than the damages secured, while the penalties on the company were too small to occasion any fear of the law. The commissioner's opinion of the existing legislation in 1880 is worth quoting: "Had they [the laws] been passed solely in the interest of the railway corporations, it is scarcely possible that they could have been better constructed."

Yet even more drastic laws and a powerful regulating body to enforce them would hardly have solved the problem. Ohio was peculiarly at the mercy of the great trunk lines, much of whose business was interstate in character and whose controlling interests lay outside the state. As in the field of business corporations, state regulation was inadequate where huge economic units of national character were involved. But neither the state nor the Federal Government was ready to undertake a consistent policy of regulation of business until the turn of the century. The generation of the eighties and nineties, despite agrarian discontent and Populism, was too much controlled by the ideals of the successful business man to wage war against the dominant economic forces.

Railroad taxation was as unsatisfactory in Ohio as was regulation. By an act of 1862, the various county auditors along the line of the railway evaluated its property for taxation. This arrangement came to mean a junketing trip over the road by the auditors at its expense, at the end of which they accepted the company's own valuation of its property, usually after a royal entertainment by railroad officials. By this method, railways paid lower taxes than almost any other kind of property, yet the practice remained until well into the twentieth century.

The great changes wrought in Ohio's economic life by the railways have been suggested in other parts of this chapter with one important exception: namely, the effects upon water transportation. For the canals, the advent of the new method of transportation was the beginning of the end. In 1851, the gross receipts from the state canal system broke all records, yet five years later, for the first time, receipts did not equal expenditures. By the close of the decade, deficits had become chronic, and the wisdom of the state's retaining its canals was being questioned. Despite repeated reductions in tolls, the board of public works found that competition with the railroads was almost impossible. Matters were made worse by the fact that the board was a partisan body that made appointments accordingly, thus making the state system of public works a huge political machine. Contracts were let for repairs in 1855 with such unfairness and favoritism that the procedure became a political scandal, involving prominent men of both parties.

Sentiment turned, by the close of the decade, in favor of disposing of the state canals to private interests. After much debate and one unsuccessful attempt at a lease, the assembly enacted a measure in 1861 to lease the public works to the highest bidders. Under this law a lease was arranged at an annual rental of $20,075. Until December 1, 1877, the state canals were in private hands. But the lessees found the experiment too expensive and returned the waterways to the state two and one-half years before their contract expired. From this time on, the canal system remained a kind of derelict on the hands of the state. Branches were abandoned or sold, owners of adjacent property encroached on the canal lands, and the state itself granted valuable rights of way to railroads and municipalities.

Under Governor Foraker in 1888 a canal commission was established to determine the correct boundaries of the canals and their reservoirs and to recover land illegally held. This commission was active for many years and restored to the state much valuable property. The property thus restored was then leased or sold, where it was not needed. In 1898, the policy of making the reservoirs into state parks was inaugurated, providing recreation facilities for thousands of Ohioans on the shores of these artificial lakes.

But the canals themselves were beyond redemption. For a time, in the early 1900's, when much resentment existed against the railroads for unfair practices, the legislature attempted to improve the canals and there was much discussion of schemes for using electrically drawn barges and of increasing the size of the waterways. But the advent of the motor car and the great improvement of highways ended any expectations of restoring the canals. Indeed, some parts of the old canal bed are now fine state roads. In recent years there has been some agitation to have the Federal Government join the Ohio River and Lake Erie by a great inland waterway, but this would hardly be a restoration of the old system.

Ohio River transportation at first was favorably affected by the development of railways, for the first roads from the East and from the interior of Ohio served as feeders for the commerce of the great river. The early years of the 1850's were the golden age of river traffic, with palatial steamers, elaborately painted and decorated and luxuriously equipped, crowding the landing places and yet scarcely able to take care of all of the business that these prosperous years brought forth. The decline in the latter half of the fifties was amazingly sudden. It was brought about by the development of through lines of railways from the East to the Mississippi Valley combined with interruptions of navigation due to ice and low water— unusually severe in this period. The Civil War, with the Mississippi closed, almost paralyzed river traffic, and even war business did not restore its former importance.

The years following the war saw a recovery, as Southern business still depended to a considerable extent upon the

Mississippi and its branches. This fact, with high railway rates and the fact that many river towns had no rail outlets, kept a certain amount of traffic for the Ohio. The growing coal business, which required barges towed by steamboats, was a further factor, while the great industrial development of the Middle West meant business for the river as well as for the railroads, particularly in carrying commodities of great bulk. The river traffic reached a new peak in 1880, and, despite setbacks, carried over to the close of the century.

A number of factors, with railway competition playing its part, contributed to a decline since 1900, but the increased business incident to the World War and a great expenditure of money by the Federal Government in recent years to improve navigation and insure an adequate stage of water at all seasons seem to have arrested this decline and instituted another revival. At least, the Ohio, unlike the canals, is far from obsolete as a medium of transportation for the great interior. The great industrial area from Pittsburgh to Wheeling, the coal and other natural resources of the Ohio Valley, and the location of such cities as Pittsburgh, Cincinnati, and Louisville along the river seem to insure the permanence of river commerce.

The Problems of Labor

The growing power of organized capital in the industrial commonwealth produced a consciousness on the part of labor that it must fight for its rights and that organization was a necessity. Associations of mechanics and working-men for benevolent and fraternal purposes had long existed in Ohio, but not until the 1840's did the labor element develop a very definite program. Then, imbued with humanitarian ideals, labor reformers talked of coöperative establishments that the workers would control and operate, thus eliminating capitalism. At the same time, they urged a homestead policy on the part of the Federal Government that would give every man the opportunity of becoming an independent farmer. Horace Greeley, editor of the New York *Tribune*, advocated such a program and did much to influence the Republican Party of the 1850's to adopt the homestead principle.

Cincinnati, with its large foreign-born population, was a center of radicalism, the German political refugees being especially interested in reform movements of a democratic and socialistic character. A labor newspaper existed for a time, around 1850, to voice agrarian, socialistic, and anti-militaristic ideals. But in a material way, little was accomplished. The average workingman wanted higher wages and shorter hours, rather than a transformation of society, and presently labor unions appeared to secure these aims.

Except for the printers, few trades had developed organizations capable of dealing with employers on equal terms. But in the early fifties a number of local unions appeared at Cincinnati, resulting in an epidemic of strikes in 1853 and 1854. Most of these unions were of a temporary character, and, having achieved wage increases, soon disappeared. Following the Panic of 1857 came depression and unemployment, and little was left of the budding labor movement.

By 1860 the movement began to revive, and the protests of the workingmen were sufficient to defeat an anti-strike bill that certain astute coal operators were attempting to slip through the assembly. The prosperity of the war years and after gave a great impetus to the labor movement, and in 1864 there was organized at Cincinnati a trades assembly that kept a rather watchful eye on legislation at Columbus. Among the various unions organized at this time, the Brotherhood of Locomotive Engineers proved the strongest and most efficient, Cleveland becoming its national headquarters. Attempts at organizing the miners offered the greatest problems and resulted in slight success down to 1880.

In 1873 came another disastrous panic, and the black years that followed brought out the harshest features of the new industrialism. Never before had so much unemployment existed. Facing actual starvation, workers found themselves accepting drastic wage cuts, estimated by the commissioner of labor in 1877 at fifty per cent. In Mahoning County, one of the new industrial centers, workmen claimed that wages were averaging not over seven dollars per week, in contrast to twenty dollars in 1872. In general, conditions were at their worst in the coal-mining districts. Strikes and disorders characterized these years, as the mine operators attempted to reduce expenses by lowering wages, requiring employees to buy from company stores, often at higher prices than elsewhere, and frequently paying wages in scrip, redeemable only at these stores. The diagnosis of the general economic situation by the commissioner of labor deserves to be quoted: "The wealth and wealth-producing power remain intact, the brains and muscle are eager for employment, and nothing prevents a new era of prosperity but the poverty of the masses. Their wants are unsupplied, and their inability to supply them is keeping the workshops of the state closed, or nearly so." The wonder is that the greenback inflationists did not sweep the state.

Legislative remedies for the more pressing ills of labor received considerable support, and a number of laws presently appeared on the statute books. A state bureau of labor statistics was established in 1877, followed by acts the next year to prevent the use of scrip or other certificates of indebtedness in place of money wages, to stop the practice of charging more than the regular retail rates for goods sold to employees by employers, and to exempt three months' wages from attachment for debt in the case of heads of families. These laws were not well enforced, and the return of prosperity at the close of the decade did more to help the cause of labor than legislation could do.

Far more fundamental problems were presented by the growing numbers of women and children entering the industrial field and by the displacement of skilled labor by the use of machines. An act of 1852 limiting women and children under eighteen to a ten-hour day was the sole regulation of its kind, except for a provision forbidding the employment of children under twelve in mines. Otherwise, there were no restrictions, and the evils of exploitation were becoming all too evident. In many trades, boys and girls were displacing men, particularly where little skill was required. As for the women workers, the woes of the seamstresses had become a familiar story in the 1850's as hundreds of almost destitute women attempted to support themselves with the needle in their homes or in the "sweatshops," the capitalist supplying the materials and paying on a piecework basis. The seventies saw little improvement in their condition. Most of them now used sewing machines, but in many cases these were being paid for in installments that cut deeply into their small earnings. The benefits of the machine had not accrued to them.

For men, the ten-hour day had been established by law in 1852, but only where it was not otherwise specified in the contract. After the war, agitation for an eight-hour day began and continued intermittently for many years. The depression of the seventies furnished a strong argument for the shorter day in that such an arrangement would provide work for the unemployed—a growing problem with the increasing use of machinery and the general decline in buying power. Most employers were hostile to the eight-hour day, but not all were as frank as a carriage manufacturer who declared: "It would be ruinous to workmen, it would curtail their wages and increase their habits of idleness. Never reduce labor to less than ten hours per day, twelve would be better, for when they are at work they are out of mischief." Not until 1886 was the eight-hour day legally established, and even then it was scarcely more than an ideal, for it applied only in the absence of a contract specifying a longer day.

The better times beginning in 1879 improved the status of labor and resulted in increased wages. The legislature began to enact sanitary and protective legislation, hitherto confined to mines, and factory conditions improved. Restrictions on child labor and stricter school laws were also put on the statute books in the decade of the eighties. Thus Ohio began to counteract some of the evils that had come with the industrial era, and the cause of labor improved. Strikes continued to be regarded as the normal method of settling labor disputes, but employers were showing a greater willingness to arbitrate than earlier. The idea of labor's equality as a bargainer was gaining ground.

Selected Bibliography

There are no satisfactory general accounts of economic changes in Ohio, as the histories of the state neglect these aspects. Roderick Peattie, *Geography of Ohio, Ohio Geological Survey, Fourth Series, Bulletin 27* (Columbus, 1923), touches upon the more significant aspects of Ohio's economic development.

For changes in agriculture, see W. A. Lloyd, J. I. Falconer, and C. E. Thorne, *The Agriculture of Ohio, Ohio Agricultural*

Experiment Station Bulletin 326 (Wooster, 1918). The *Annual Reports of the State Board of Agriculture* and the files of the two leading farm periodicals, the *Ohio Cultivator* and the *Ohio Farmer*, contain much information on agriculture and farm life. A brief account of the Ohio State Grange appears in Galbreath, Vol. II, pp. 340 et seq.

On transportation and, to a lesser extent, industrial change, the volumes by Bogart, Gephart, and Huntington and McClelland, cited for Chapter VI, are still useful, though less extensive for the period since the Civil War. The volumes of the United States census since 1850 show the extent of economic changes from decade to decade. Early railway progress is sketched in Frederic L. Paxson, "The Railways of the Old Northwest before the Civil War," *Transactions of Wisconsin Academy of Sciences, Arts and Letters*, Vol. XVII (1914), pp. 243–274. The *Annual Reports of the State Commissioner of Railroads and Telegraphs*, beginning in 1867, contain much information on railroads. Ohio River transportation and its relation to economic changes is admirably treated in Charles H. Ambler, *A History of Transportation in the Ohio Valley* (Glendale, Cal., 1932).

The history of labor in Ohio has not been written. There is much material in the *Annual Reports of the Bureau of Labor Statistics*, beginning in 1877. The national aspects of the labor movement, in which Ohioans have played a part, may be studied in John R. Commons and associates, *History of Labour in the United States* (2 vols., New York, 1918).

CHAPTER XIV

POLITICAL TRENDS, 1873–1885

The Constitutional Convention of 1873

AS the "New Departure" idea of Vallandigham and others in 1871 paved the way for a reconsideration of national issues and policies within the Democratic Party, the end of twenty years of operation of the state constitution of 1851 meant an opportunity, as provided by that instrument, for a reëvaluation of the fundamental law of the state. Various considerations contributed to a desire for a new constitution—among them, the need for an alteration of the judicial system (the supreme court was four years in arrears with its docket), the demand for a more effective control of corporations, and the zeal of those advocating a license system for the liquor traffic. Members of both parties expressed their approval of a demand for a constitutional convention, and at the general election of October, 1871, the voters of the state gave definite sanction to the convening of such a body for the revision, alteration, or amendment of the state's basic instrument of government.

In January, 1873, the legislature provided for the election of delegates in April, at which time one hundred and five persons were chosen—fifty Republicans, forty-six Democrats, and nine Liberals or Independents. The convention assembled in Columbus on May 14, and organized, with Morrison R. Waite as president. The gentleman thus honored was a distinguished Toledo lawyer who had been a member of the counsel representing the United

States in the Alabama Claims before the Geneva Tribunal; other prominent members included two future governors, George Hoadly and Richard M. Bishop, both Cincinnatians; Lewis D. Campbell, a former Whig and Republican Congressman from Hamilton, who had just finished another term as a Democratic Member and was now chosen vice president of the convention; and Thomas Ewing, Jr., of Lancaster, who had formerly been Chief Justice of the Supreme Court of Kansas and was later to be a candidate for the governorship of Ohio.

The sessions were protracted. The convention adjourned on August 8, reopening in Cincinnati on December 2 and concluding in May, 1874. Shortly after the opening of the adjourned session, the president of the convention was appointed to fill the vacancy in the office of chief justice of the Supreme Court of the United States caused by the death of Salmon P. Chase. Thereupon, Rufus King, of Cincinnati (a grandson of the noted national statesman of the same name), was chosen to succeed Waite as the presiding officer of the convention.

The proposed constitution contemplated numerous changes in the basic law of the state. Among them was a provision that, although state elections for the legislature were to be held biennially as had been the case previously, there were to be annual sessions of that body, the members to be paid on an annual rather than a *per diem* basis. Legislators were given the right to demand a separate vote on each item of appropriation bills; the governor was granted a veto power (that could be overridden by a three-fifths vote of the legislature); and important changes were to be made in the organization of the judiciary, including the establishment of circuit courts—intermediate between the court of common pleas and the supreme court—with a separate set of judges. Women might be elected to any school offices except the office of state commissioner of schools, and might be appointed to any office except an elective one. Municipal corporations were to be restricted in their taxing power and in their ability to assume debts, and restrictions were provided as to railroads and other private corporations. County officers were to receive fixed salaries, and these were not to be augmented by fees or other compensation.

In addition to the main body of the proposed constitution, three separate propositions were submitted to the voters at the special election of August, 1874. One provided for a means of minority party representation on the supreme and circuit benches of the state; another permitted legislation authorizing local political subdivisions to aid in the construction of railroads; while the third provided for the introduction of a license system for the traffic in intoxicating liquors.

Various considerations contributed to the defeat of the new constitution by a vote of 102,885 in favor and 250,169 against. County officers opposed the abolition of the fee system; opponents of the license system for the liquor traffic voted against the constitution in order to defeat the separate proposal; corporations resisted the proposed restrictions upon them. Finally, a general lack of enthusiasm for the changes in the constitution was a determining factor. At the same time, the voters rejected each of the separate proposals.

The Greenback Era, 1873–1879

The period during which the convention was in session was one of financial uncertainty and economic discontent. In Ohio, this condition, in combination with the scandals of the Grant administration, placed the Republicans upon the defensive and made doubtful the reëlection in 1873 of Governor Edward Follensbee Noyes, a Cincinnati lawyer and Civil War officer who had lost his left foot as a result of fighting in Georgia in 1864, and who had actively entered politics upon his return to civilian life. The Democratic Party in the state, however, was not without its own problems. Members of the organization in Allen County had called upon state political leaders to meet in convention on July 30 in Columbus "to take such action as the exigencies of the time" might demand, and were thereupon joined by Liberal Republicans in the formation of a "People's Party,"[1] which declared "that both the Republican and the Democratic parties have outlived the issues in which they had their origin, and have outlived their usefulness, and a new organization of parties is demanded in the interests of the public welfare."

With their own candidate for the governorship, these malcontents obviously created consternation in Democratic ranks and stimulated careful efforts to prevent serious defections from that party. Dissatisfaction, however, was rampant, and a possibility existed that the state Democratic Party might join with the "People's" group in the ensuing campaign. Allen G. Thurman, of Columbus, who was looking forward to a reëlection to the United States Senate, refused to countenance such a proposal, and instead suggested that the leadership of the party be intrusted to his uncle, William Allen, of Chillicothe. The latter, a former Congressman and Senator, at this time seventy years of age and surrounded with something of the glamour of a half-forgotten past, was nominated for the governorship. There followed an aggressive campaign in which the Democrats stressed the abuses of the Grant administration and succeeded by the narrow margin of

---

[1] This party should not be confused with the People's Party or Populists of the late eighties and early nineties.

817 votes in electing Allen, the first Democratic Governor
in Ohio since the birth of the Republican Party.

In the meantime, the temperance question had become
important in state political and social circles. As early
as 1869, a prohibition candidate had run for the governorship, and some increase in the strength of this party
had been noted in subsequent elections. Much more
spectacular, however, was the movement that orginated in
Hillsboro in the closing days of 1873. A lecturer, Dio
Lewis, speaking in that community, suggested that the
women endeavor to suppress the liquor traffic of the town.
As a result, under the leadership of Mrs. Eliza J. Thompson,
the wife of a judge and the daughter of a former governor, Allen Trimble, seventy-five women gathered at a church,
sang and prayed, and then marched in double columns to
the saloons of the town, where they appealed to the
liquor-dealers to relinquish their business. Similarly at
Washington Court House, a meeting was held at which the
wives of three local clergymen presented an appeal directed
to the liquor-dealers of the place to abandon their traffic.
There was then formed a committee of sixty women who
went with their petition to several drinking establishments,
where they sang hymns and offered prayers. One proprietor offered his stock of liquors to the women, who rolled
the barrels into the street and set fire to the contents.
The movement continued, and within a few days, eleven
liquor-stores in the village had been closed. Other communities witnessed the spectacle of women parading
through the streets, singing and praying in the saloons. In
some places the liquor traffic was suspended for a time, but
a reaction inevitably set in, and after disturbances at
Cincinnati, Columbus, and Cleveland, municipal laws were
enforced against the obstruction of the streets. By the
end of 1874 the excitement had largely subsided.

During this period, the hardships endured as a result of the Panic of 1873 served to intensify the demand of many westerners for greenbacks as a solution for low prices and unemployment, hence it was not to be expected that the state that had nurtured the "Ohio Idea" of 1868 would escape the repercussions of the greenback issue.

The Resumption Act, which had passed Congress in January, 1875 (and whose authorship was formerly erroneously attributed to Senator John Sherman, of Ohio), gave the Republicans specific legislation to uphold, and their partisans in Ohio soon indicated their intention of supporting the plan for the resumption of specie payment by which greenbacks "without unnecessary shock to business" would be redeemable in gold. The attitude of most of the party in the state toward suggestions of further inflation was probably well represented by ex-Governor Hayes, who considered such schemes "a wretched business," wrong in every way.

The Democrats were divided upon the money question but in 1875 renominated Allen, an ardent champion of inflation, for governor. At the same time, they adopted a platform that declared that a further contraction of greenbacks would be disastrous and insisted "that the volume of currency be made and kept equal to the wants of trade, leaving the restoration of legal tenders to a par with gold to be brought about by promoting the industries of the people, and not by destroying them." Pendleton and Thurman were not wholly in accord with Allen and Samuel F. Cary (the candidate for lieutenant-governor), and Thurman, in a speech at Mansfield, took care to assert that the platform did not specifically indorse inflation or oppose resumption.

The former Liberal Republicans were alarmed, however, by the trend of the Democrats toward inflation and summoned Carl Schurz, the noted German-American reformer, to give addresses throughout the state in English and in German. It was hoped that he might assist in turning voters to the Republican standard, again carried by ex-Governor Hayes, who had been called from retirement to seek a third term as governor. The Democrats, on their part, were not inactive, and mottoes declaring, "We prefer the rag-baby to the Golden Calf," "Greenbacks saved the Union and let them avert starvation," were much in evidence.

The issues were complicated by the injection of the element of religious prejudice, since it was charged that the Democrats were unduly favorable to the Catholics in passing a proposal known as the "Geghan Bill," sponsored by a representative from Cincinnati and permitting "ample and equal facilities" for religious worship and instruction for persons of all denominations in public jails and asylums.

In the largest vote ever cast in the state up to that time, Hayes carried the election by a margin of 5,544 votes. The result was of national significance, for it helped party leaders to determine what should be their attitude toward the money question (since Ohio was a pivotal state), and thereby tended to settle the position of the two major parties upon this controversial problem. Hayes, moreover, began to be considered as a Presidential possibility.

Accordingly, at the Republican National Convention the next year, from the first he received the loyal support of the delegates from Ohio, with some scattered votes from other states. Then, as the bitter conflict between Blaine and his rivals prevented any of the major candidates from receiving a majority of votes, the delegates gradually turned to Hayes, who received the necessary votes for the nomination on the seventh ballot.

Allen was considered for the Democratic nomination, and had the support of his home state; but he was unsatisfactory to the Eastern conservatives, and Tilden, of New York, became the choice of the party.

In the ensuing election of 1876, Ohio's vote was cast for her native son, though nationally the outcome (dependent upon disputed returns from Louisiana, Florida, South Carolina, and Oregon) was not definitely determined until March 2, after an especially created Electoral Commission[2] had ended its work and Congress had accepted Hayes the successful candidate. So protracted had been the contest that the incoming President learned only that the result had been decided in his favor after his personal party had reached the vicinity of Harrisburg, Pennsylvania, en route to Washington.

The oath of office was administered to the new President by a Toledoan, Chief Justice Morrison R. Waite, while John Sherman, of Ohio, became the new Secretary of the Treasury and ex-Governor Noyes and James M. Comly, ministers to France and Hawaii respectively.

Hayes, now fifty-four years of age, was a man of "sterling character and solid attainments," who "without the brilliancy of Blaine or the audacity of Conkling" gave the country an administration characterized by a scrupulous regard for public trust amidst a host of difficulties. Following his resignation as Governor, that office fell into the hands of the Lieutenant Governor, Thomas L. Young, a native of Ireland who had served as an officer in the Civil War and as a member of both the Ohio House of Representatives and the Ohio Senate.

---

[2] Four of the fifteen members were Ohioans: Representatives James A. Garfield and Henry B. Payne, Senator Allen G. Thurman, and Associate Justice Noah H. Swayne.

The period of the late seventies in Ohio was a time of great suffering and unrest. The farmers of the state smarted under the sting of decreased prices for agricultural products, with oats dropping in price from 59 cents to 22 cents a bushel in the four years subsequent to 1875, and wheat dropping from $1.07 to 89 cents. At the same time, labor was suffering from unemployment and other economic grievances. The miners of eastern and southern Ohio in particular were complaining of high living costs and low wages, and forty thousand of them earned on an average less than three hundred dollars a year (in 1878), with living costs approximately one-fifth higher than at the opening of the war.

Such a situation created hopeful prospects for the party of discontent represented in the greenback movement. In June, 1877, a state convention of the party met in Columbus, expressed its despair of any hope of relief from the Democratic Party, and nominated Stephen Johnson, a retired lawyer and farmer, for the governorship. In the meantime, the great railway strike that spread westward from Pennsylvania in the summer of 1877 as wages were being reduced created disturbances in Columbus, Newark, and other points along the lines of the Baltimore and Ohio and Pennsylvania Railroads. In July, Governor Young, on application of the Sheriff of Licking County, sent militia to avert threatened violence, and volunteer policemen were organized in Cleveland to cope with strikers there. Loss of property and life was averted, but discontent continued.

Accordingly, a call was issued for workers to unite with the greenback men, a union was partially accomplished, and Johnson ran on a ticket known as that of the National Party, though a separate "Workingmen's" ticket remained in the field.

The Republicans nominated Judge William H. West, of Bellefontaine, over Alphonso Taft, of Cincinnati (the father of the later President), who had been Secretary of War and Attorney General under Grant and was later, in Arthur's administration, to be the American minister to Austria and to Russia. West, popularly known as "the blind man eloquent," made a definite appeal to the strikers and discontented classes, declaring that as a youth he had known the strain of manual labor and that he had never owned railroad stocks or bonds or served as a railroad official. He demanded a just compensation for workers, with a minimum wage, and he advocated a scheme by which the profit of employers would be shared with the workers.

Such an advanced program was interpreted as "communistic" by conservative Republicans, and, together with opposition from other quarters in regard to the resumption policy of the party[3] and to the moderate policy toward the South of President Hayes, it insured the election of the Democratic nominee, Richard M. Bishop. Bishop had been mayor of Cincinnati and a member of Ohio's third constitutional convention and was now running on a platform demanding the repeal of the Resumption Act and the remonetization of silver.[4]

Though the elections of the next year (1878) merely concerned the choice of Congressmen and certain state officials (not the Governor), the contest was an important

---

[3] This policy was a fact even though the Ohio Republican platform of 1877 did not mention resumption, while that of 1878 designated "further agitation of the question at this time as injurious to business and devoid of other than evil results." The Republicans also favored the remonetization of silver in 1877.

[4] Standard silver dollars were not provided for in the coinage act of 1873. This act, accordingly, was termed the "Crime of 1873" by inflationists and mine operators when the opening of new mines helped to precipitate a marked decline in the price of the metal.

one in Ohio because it marked the crest of the greenback movement. A national organization of this group, now called the National Party, composed of inflationists and laborites, had been effected in February at a convention in Toledo attended by hundreds of delegates from twenty-eight states. Their platform called for a supply of money "adequate to the full employment of labor," the suppression of national bank notes, legislation reducing the hours of labor, and steps for the exclusion of oriental workers from the country.

The Democrats looked upon this movement as one that was infringing upon their preëmpted ground, and they made every effort to show themselves as the real greenback party. Hence, they declared themselves in favor of a gradual substitution of greenbacks for national bank notes and in favor of the establishment of the greenbacks as the sole paper money of the country, receivable for all government dues and "of equal tender with coin." The remonetization of silver was also indorsed.

A startling event of the convention was the speech by Senator Thurman in which he declared: "I stand squarely on the platform. I have advocated its principles hitherto, and shall continue to advocate them." Then he endeavored to demonstrate his consistency by pointing out that he had always opposed contraction of the currency, had voted against the Resumption Act when it was passed, and had later voted in favor of the attempt to achieve its repeal. This expression of principle hardly coincided with Thurman's well-known stand against inflation in 1875 and caused many greenback men to consider it an evidence of Democratic insincerity. One Cleveland newspaper asserted that this was the utterance of "a new Thurman with the presidential bee buzzing in his ears, inconsistent, time serving, and truckling to the false notions which he once combatted with zeal and fearlessness." On the other hand, the powerful Cincinnati *Enquirer*, which was ardently in favor of inflation and had been sharply critical of Thurman's position in 1875, now declared that it was "better to be right than to be consistent" and indicated the proper reaction to Thurman to be implied in the couplet:

> What care I if he loved before
> So that he loves me last.

The same paper declared the Democratic Party of the state to be "the famed and potent Greenback Party," and that no reason existed why a "greenback Democrat should abandon it in the hour when the first notes of the jubilee are heard in the distance."

These assurances failed to convince the "Nationals" that Thurman was not "a political acrobat" and that the Democratic Party was to be trusted to carry out their promises. The result was that the National Greenback Labor Party cast over thirty-eight thousand votes in the state, and the Republican Party was enabled to secure a victory by a narrow margin. The Democrats, nevertheless, secured eleven of twenty congressional seats.

The currency question was carried over into the campaign of the next year (1879) when the Democrats once again bid for greenback support by the nomination for the governorship of Thomas Ewing, Jr., of Lancaster, an avowed inflationist, upon a greenback platform that was drafted by Thurman. Ewing, who was a son of the former Whig Senator of the same name and at the time a Representative in Congress, was characterized by President Hayes as "an able man, a good popular debater, and of excellent character," one who was "the ablest and most consistent of the Greenback leaders."

The attitude of the Democrats was deemed satisfactory by many of the National Party, hence when the latter's state convention met in Columbus, a large group, led by Samuel F. Cary, who had run for the Vice Presidency upon the greenback ticket in 1876, and Isaac R. Sherwood, an editor-politician of Toledo, left the organization to support the Democrats. Although the National Greenback organization continued for another five years, the carrying into effect of the resumption policy without disastrous consequences, the stimulation of agricultural and industrial activity in the fall of 1879, and the division within the party as to the wisdom of fusion with the Democrats and later with the Prohibitionists, caused it henceforth to be an insignificant factor in the politics of the state.

While the Democrats were supporting Ewing in 1879, the Republicans were urging the election of Charles Foster, whose father was a pioneer merchant at Fostoria, which took its name from him. The son had accumulated a considerable fortune in the dry goods business, had increased it by favorable investments in banking and in gas and oil companies, and at the time of his nomination had just completed four terms in Congress.

As a candidate for the governorship, he introduced modern methods of campaigning, organizing the state in an effective way and expending large sums of money in districts where support was weak. He had not served in the Civil War, owing to the wishes of his family, and this fact was seized upon by the Democratic newspapers, which declared that he was "a man who knew no higher occupation during the war than measuring calico." His followers turned this description to good account, however, as ardent Republicans wore neckties and their wives donned garments made of the fabric to boost the candidacy of "Calico Charlie."

The return of prosperity was a factor favorable to the Republican candidate, who won by a margin of over seventeen thousand votes. Foster's success was considered by President Hayes to be "a valuable victory" by which "inflation and State's rights" were badly beaten and a verdict rendered "in favor of a sound and honest currency" and "of the perpetuity of the Union, the supremacy of the national government, and the enforcement of the laws."

The Early Eighties

At the same time, Ohio Republicans looked with considerable interest to the Presidential contest of the next year. All but ten of Ohio's forty-four delegates were favorable to John Sherman, of Mansfield, then Secretary of the Treasury and prior to that time for over twenty years a Member of the National House or Senate. The lack of unanimity among the delegation from his home state, however, was a damaging factor to his prospects. The deadlock between Grant and Blaine in the convention might otherwise have paved the way for his nomination. This situation, however, presented an unexpected opportunity for another Ohioan—James Abram Garfield, whose participation in the work of the convention made a favorable impression upon many delegates—who at length received the nomination.

At the Democratic national convention, Senator Allen G. Thurman was a prominent candidate for the nomination, but he failed to enlist the support of the entire Ohio delegation (some of whom were favorable to Henry B. Payne, of Cleveland) and his equivocation upon the currency question made him unacceptable to the country at large.

In the elections of that year, Garfield easily carried the state over Hancock, the Democratic nominee, and, with similar success in other states, for the fourth term in succession a native of Ohio made ready to serve as Chief Executive of the nation. The new President was a striking example of the self-made man. Born near Cleveland, he was left fatherless at the age of one; hence, his early years were those of genuine poverty. Having served as a towboy on the Ohio Canal, he managed to attend Williams College, where he later became a professor of ancient languages and literature, and when only twenty-six years of age he became head of the institution now known as Hiram College, in northeastern Ohio. In 1859 he was elected to the Ohio Senate and later served with distinction for two years in the Civil War. Possibly at the behest of Lincoln, who needed administration support in Congress, he relinquished his major-generalcy in December, 1863, and entered the House of Representatives, where he served continuously until his election to the Presidency necessitated his resignation from the House and also from the Senate, to which he had been elected but in which he had never taken his seat. He was a man of distinguished ability, but he was sometimes too easily swayed in his judgment by the appeal of opposite sides of a question, and his Presidential career was cut short so soon by an assassin's bullet that little can be said about the character of his administration. The uncertainty of the suffering President's condition during the summer of 1881, and the period of mourning that followed his death in September, together with the paucity of vital issues, greatly tempered the contest for the governorship of Ohio in the fall of 1881. The Republicans had renominated Governor Foster by acclamation, and in the subsequent election he won easily over the Democratic candidate, John W. Bookwalter, of Springfield, who was better known as a manufacturer of turbine wheels and engines than as a politician.

Foster's administrations were characterized by the same business efficiency that he had utilized in his political campaigns. Thus, he advocated bipartisan boards of control for public institutions, as well as mine inspection, forest protection, and a revision of the tax system.

The liquor question became more and more a matter for public discussion and legislative debate. During 1881, the legislature had hotly considered a state constitutional amendment, local option bills, and a tax upon liquor; but nothing was accomplished except the passage of a bill that restricted dramatic musical entertainments on Sunday when associated with the sale of liquor.[5] The next year (1882), when the Republicans comprised two thirds of each house of the legislature, Governor Foster called attention to the agitation for additional liquor legislation, which had resulted in two leading proposals: one for a total prohibition of the manufacture and sale of intoxicating and malt liquors, and the other for a tax upon the traffic, coupled with restrictions upon the sale, of liquors. Each of these potential lines of action was of doubtful constitutionality; hence, it seemed desirable to submit to the voters proposed amendments to the constitution dealing with local option as to the sale of liquor, state prohibition, and a taxing of the liquor traffic. The legislature considered these proposals at the suggestion of the Governor, but the two houses could not agree upon the form of the amendments and adjourned without coming to a satisfactory conclusion. Nevertheless, legislation was passed providing for the taxation of saloons at a rate of from one hundred to three hundred dollars per year, depending upon the population of the locality in which they were

---

[5] In similar spirit, at the same session, a law was enacted prohibiting the recording of wagers "upon the results of any trial or contest of skill, speed, or power of endurance of man or beast."

situated,[6] and requiring a bond of one thousand dollars to insure the payment of the assessments. This act, known as the Pond Law, was declared void within two months as a violation of the prohibition in the constitution of 1851 of a license system. Governor Foster appealed to the legislature a second time on the subject of the liquor question, stating in his message that "the enormity of the evil" was admitted by all, as sixteen thousand places in Ohio carried on an "unrestrained traffic," at a cost exceeding seventy million dollars annually; that Sunday was being turned into "a day of rowdyism and carnivals"; and that a burden was being thrust upon the state through "the crime and pauperism" resulting from the liquor trade. As a result of the Governor's appeal, two amendments were adopted for submission to the voters: one granting the legislature power to regulate the liquor traffic, and the other "forever" prohibiting "the manufacture of and the traffic in" intoxicants. A new act was also passed (in 1883), the Scott Law, so devised as to avoid the constitutional objections to the previous legislation; but, although it was at first upheld by the state supreme court (in 1883), a partisan change in the personnel of that body later (in 1884) resulted in the tax feature's being declared contrary to the fundamental law of the state.[7]

The aggressive attitude of Foster and the Republicans upon the liquor question aroused much antagonism in certain sections of the state, especially among the Germans of Cincinnati, who were whole-heartedly opposed to liquor legislation. In view of these conditions, the Republicans

---

[6] Another act passed at the same session, the Smith Law, prohibited the sale of liquor on Sundays under heavy penalties. In many places enforcement was practically impossible.

[7] This action resulted in considerable confusion in local taxes, which had been assessed with an anticipation of considerable revenue from the saloons.

naturally turned to Cincinnati for a gubernatorial candidate in 1883, when they selected Joseph Benson Foraker, a lawyer in his late thirties who, following service in the Civil War, had served upon the superior bench in his home city. Running upon a platform advocating a high protective tariff in national legislation, favoring the taxation and regulation of the liquor traffic, and commending the general assembly for submitting to the voters the two proposed constitutional amendments upon the subject, Foraker opposed George Hoadly, also a Cincinnati lawyer.[8] Although a native of Connecticut, Hoadly had grown to manhood in Cleveland and had later served as Judge of the Superior Court of Cincinnati and as attorney for Tilden before the Electoral Commission of 1877. His party declared in favor of a tariff for revenue only and for the regulation of the liquor traffic by a license system.

The proposed amendment granting the legislature power to regulate the liquor traffic was considered by the prohibition forces of the state as likely to lead to the license system, of which they disapproved. Hence, they urged a concentration upon the other proposal—prohibition. Over 323,000 votes were cast in favor of this amendment in contrast to about 241,000 against it; but since the constitution required a favorable vote by a majority of all those casting votes at the election, many "wets" had shown their opposition by not voting at all on the proposals, and the failure to secure a majority of the 721,310 votes cast at the election defeated the proposition. The other amendment was also rejected, and the Democrats scored an easy

---

[8] Hoadly had originally been a Democrat, but as a young lawyer in the office of Salmon P. Chase, he had been drawn into the Republican Party. Its harsh reconstruction policy brought him into the Liberal Republican movement, though he refused to accept Greeley for the Presidency in 1872. Shortly thereafter, he rejoined the Democratic Party.

victory over Foraker for the governorship and captured both houses of the legislature.

During the next year (1884) Ohio saw three episodes worthy of mention: a destructive flood, a noteworthy riot, and an important strike. The first, which occurred in February, was due to the break-up of the ice in the Ohio River and its tributaries, accompanied by unusually heavy rains and an extraordinary rise in the river. The damage was greatest at Cincinnati, where many homes were wrecked, lives were lost, and thousands found themselves in a plight approaching destitution. Relief poured into the stricken communities to alleviate the suffering.

During the next month, public sentiment was aroused in Cincinnati by a jury rendering a verdict of manslaughter in the case of a man who had confessed his guilt in a particularly atrocious murder. About twenty untried persons, accused of homicide, were then in jail in the city, and the indignation resulted in a public meeting in Music Hall. When advocates of violent measures expressed themselves, the meeting was adjourned, but a mob gathered outside the jail and forced its way into the building—only to find that the convicted man had been spirited away to Columbus. Some militiamen were ordered out, and on the next day additional troops were called out by the Governor. The rioting continued, however, and the courthouse was set on fire, with considerable damage. At length, troops were called from all parts of the state, and barricades were thrown up for the protection of public buildings. The excitement gradually died down, but only after about forty-five persons had been killed and scores had been wounded.

A strike resulted in the Hocking Valley area from a disagreement over wages between miners and operators in that region. A general discharge of laborers took place;

a temporary cessation of labor followed; and finally imported laborers were employed at lower wage scales. The operators employed troops to guard their property—but with much suffering among the miners, at which stage violence developed and seven mines were set afire, three railway bridges were burned, and other property was destroyed. At length, state troops were called out, but they were soon removed and the following spring the workers capitulated to the terms prescribed by their employers.

In the meantime, the Democratic hold upon the state proved to be of short duration. The air was filled with a host of ugly rumors in connection with the circumstances attending the election by the Democratic legislature of the state of a new United States Senator in January, 1884. Senator George Hunt Pendleton, of Cincinnati, popularly called "Gentleman George," because of his dignified appearance and suave manner, was a candidate for reëlection. His name had been attached to the noted Federal civil service act of 1883 (often designated as the Magna Carta of civil service reform), but powerful opposition had arisen against him in Cincinnati—at least partly owing to dissatisfaction with his handling of the senatorial patronage. Durbin Ward, of Warren County, was also a candidate; but the office went to Henry B. Payne, of Cleveland, a millionaire capitalist then over seventy-three years of age. It was asserted that Payne's son, Oliver H., who was treasurer of the Standard Oil Company, had spent as much as one hundred thousand dollars to secure the success of his father. Large numbers of Democratic papers denounced the procedure; the lower house of the next legislature, which was Republican, demanded an investigation, and scores of witnesses were examined; but the Senate of the United States, to whom the evidence was submitted, refused to take action in the matter.

At the national conventions of 1884, the names of Allen G. Thurman and George Hoadly, both of Ohio, were presented to the Democrats, and that of John Sherman to the Republicans. Cleveland and Blaine, however, received the nominations of their respective parties for the Presidency. The contest in Ohio was largely fought over the tariff issue, though abusive attacks upon personal reputations were extensively made. Blaine carried Ohio, though he failed to capture the coveted prize in the nation as a whole.

The next year (1885) Foraker defeated Hoadly in the contest for the governorship. The election of this new chief executive was of more than ordinary importance, for it marked the rise to high position of one who for the next quarter of a century was to be a conspicuous leader in state and national political life.

SELECTED BIBLIOGRAPHY

The unsuccessful attempt to revamp Ohio's constitution in 1873 and 1874 is discussed in Galbreath, Vol. II, pp. 68–90; Randall and Ryan, Vol. IV, pp. 317–326; and Isaac F. Patterson, *The Constitutions of Ohio* (Cleveland, 1912). Considerable light upon Ohio politics can be secured from C. R. Williams, *The Life of Rutherford Birchard Hayes* (2 vols., Boston, 1914), from *Diary and Letters of Rutherford Birchard Hayes* (C. R. Williams, ed.) (already cited), and from H. J. Eckenrode, *Rutherford B. Hayes, Statesman of Reunion* (New York, 1930). Somewhat less valuable for the student of Ohio history are T. C. Smith, *The Life and Letters of James Abram Garfield* (previously mentioned), and Robert G. Caldwell, *James A. Garfield, Party Chieftain* (New York, 1931). The career of Joseph B. Foraker is given with extensive detail in his *Notes of a Busy Life* (2 vols., Cincinnati, 1916). Biographical sketches of Governors Foster and Hoadly (by Homer C. Hockett) and of Governor Noyes (by Francis P. Weisenburger) appear in *The Dictionary of American Biography*.

Various aspects of partisan politics of the period are analyzed in R. C. McGrane, *William Allen* (Columbus, 1925), pp. 188–263;

R. C. McGrane, "Ohio and the Greenback Movement," *Mississippi Valley Historical Review*, Vol. XI, pp. 526–542; F. W. Clonts, "The Political Campaign of 1875 in Ohio," *Ohio Archæological and Historical Quarterly*, Vol. XXXI, pp. 38–95; C. H. Moore, "Ohio in National Politics, 1865–1896," *Ibid.*, Vol. XXXVII, pp. 220–427; and C. B. Galbreath, "Ohio's Contribution to National Civil Service Reform," *Ibid.*, Vol. XXXIII, pp. 176–204. The influence of corporation officials upon political events in Ohio is indicated in Ida M. Tarbell, *The History of the Standard Oil Company* (2 vols., New York, 1904).

CHAPTER XV

THE HANNA-FORAKER ERA

Party Characteristics, 1885–1900

*T*HE eighties and nineties witnessed the growing influence of business on government and politics as Ohio's economic life became more and more intertwined with the interests of the capitalistic and industrial Eastern states. The nationalizing effect of big business made state boundaries lose much of their former significance. Consequently Ohio's political life was concerned primarily with national issues—tariff and financial problems and the situation created by the Panic of 1893. After the great silver struggle of 1896 came the Spanish-American War with the blazing up of the martial spirit and the revival of the patriotic urge. Thus did the nineteenth century come to an end fittingly with industrialism fortified by the prestige of a successful war and the prospects of larger foreign markets and better openings for capital than ever before. Political conservatism had reached high tide.

As Ohio became more industrialized and wealthy, its political parties grew more conservative. The business interests had to be conciliated or success would be impossible. For the Republicans, this was comparatively easy. The party had opposed paper money inflation and had prevented any reduction of the high tariffs inherited from the Civil War. In power in Ohio most of the time since that war, it had done little to regulate railways or interfere with business development. Though not unsympathetic toward the widely popular free silver movement of the nineties, it was able to present a united front against it when evasion was no longer possible. Its success was largely due to its ability to preserve the alliance with business so well typified by ex-Governor Foster, railway speculator, capitalist, and business man; Marcus A. Hanna, the Cleveland iron manufacturer, who was by 1890 a power in the party; Joseph B. Foraker, governor and United States Senator, with an extensive law practice as a corporation attorney; and William McKinley, Congressman from industrial northeastern Ohio and high tariff advocate.

The Democratic Party struggled to make itself as safe for business as was its Republican rival. Forgotten were the greenback heresies of the seventies. Even the revenue tariff views of President Cleveland had only mild support from Ohio Democrats, who preferred to oppose Republican extremes of protectionism—such as the unpopular McKinley Act—rather than to advocate any reductions supposedly injurious to business. Henry B. Payne, who defeated Pendleton for the Senate in 1884, fitly represented the growing conservatism of the party. Though a veteran in politics, his seat in the Senate came to him because of his wealth and business connections—particularly his connection with the Standard Oil Company. Likewise, his successor, Calvin S. Brice, was chosen under circumstances that suggested the questionable use of money. Brice was a railway promoter and Wall Street speculator besides being an adept in political manipulation. John R. McLean, wealthy Cincinnati newspaper owner and a growing power in politics, was generally conservative except on the silver question. The Democratic Party until 1896 remained very much like its Republican rival. Then, with the West and South in revolt for free silver, it abandoned conservatism and temporarily tried to follow the radicalism of Bryan.

Sherman, Thurman, and Pendleton were honored and admired national figures in their respective parties, but the party leaders in their home state dealt the cards with little regard for their past services. Money and a good organization meant more than a great name or a long and honorable record. Thurman, at the time of Payne's election to the Senate in 1884, protested against the growing power of bossism and overgrown wealth in the Democratic Party which would sacrifice men like Pendleton and Durbin Ward, who had long fought the party's battles. But his protest was unavailing. In the Republican Party, Sherman was removed from the Senate by a "promotion" to the State Department in 1897 to make way for Mark Hanna. The methods employed were a little more devious in this case than in Pendleton's, but the effects were the same. The dollar sign was never more potent in Ohio politics than in this period. For the reformer and the independent voter, the eighties and nineties were the dismal decades.

State issues varied from one campaign to another with neither party inclined to consider the more pressing economic problems of corporation and railway regulation. The temperance question retained a perennial interest, to the embarrassment of both parties, though it could not be said that temperance made much headway. The saloon was an important influence in city politics and the liquor interests were usually allied with the city bosses, of whom George B. Cox, of Cincinnati, was becoming the outstanding example. Cold, secretive, unscrupulous, he established such control over the "Queen City" that he became a power in state politics for more than twenty years and acquired a notoriety that transcended the boundaries of his home state. He was a typical product of that unholy union of business and politics that long made American cities the worst governed in the world.

The Foraker-McKinley Period, 1885–1895

Joseph B. Foraker's administration began with a bitter struggle in the assembly over the seats of four senators and ten representatives from Hamilton County. The poll-books had been tampered with in one precinct to give the Democratic candidates a majority and the county clerk had given them certificates of election, which entitled them to seats in the assembly until the two houses could pass upon the question. The Republican house of representatives soon solved the problem by unseating the ten Democrats and declaring the Republican contestants entitled to their places.

But in the senate, the four disputed seats involved control of that body, and neither side would yield. The four Democratic claimants with certificates of election insisted on the right to vote on their own cases, while the Republicans naturally refused to permit them to do so, as there was a Republican majority of one vote without the four. A long wrangle ensued with the Republican lieutenant-governor ruling in favor of his party on points of parliamentary law. Finally, to prevent a quorum, all of the Democrats but one absented themselves, and to escape arrest by the sergeant-at-arms, fled from the state. Though constituting only a minority of the senate, the Republican members proceeded to act as if a quorum were present and voted in the four Republicans, thus insuring their majority. The Democrats eventually carried the case to the supreme court, but the decision was against them. The senate journal was the only evidence that could be officially considered, and it contained no roll-calls on the question of seating the Republicans, for the members present had voted *viva voce*. Thus, there was no proof that a quorum was not present. Early in the session John Sherman had been reëlected to the United States Senate, as the Republicans had a majority on joint ballot, regardless of the disputed seats. Had the senatorship been at stake, the struggle would probably have been far more heated.

In 1887 Foraker was reëlected Governor over Thomas E. Powell by a somewhat larger plurality than in 1885. A Union Labor candidate polled 24,711 votes and a Prohibitionist 29,700 to hold the balance of power.

Foraker's administrations were marked by some rather significant measures. The Dow Law was passed in 1886 at the Governor's suggestion, beginning the policy of taxing the liquor traffic. This was in line with Republican platforms as opposed to the Democratic advocacy of a licensing system. Legislation was enacted to regulate elections in the larger cities to prevent fraud and corruption, the Ohio State Board of Health was established, a board of pardons was created, and a canal commission was instituted to recover for the state canal lands illegally occupied by private individuals. Foraker proved to be an energetic and vigorous administrator, though no great emergencies occurred in his governorship. A secret organization of "White Caps" in southern Ohio, a Ku Klux Klan kind of organization, was taking the law into its own hands in dealing with local offenders, but it was forced to disband by the Governor. At the time of the Johnstown (Pennsylvania) flood, Ohio supplies and relief workers were first on the scene—a tribute to Foraker's ability to act quickly in emergencies.

In 1888 came the year of centennials to celebrate the one hundredth anniversary of the beginnings of organized settlement in the state. Marietta held two such celebrations, with a galaxy of national figures present to deliver addresses. Cincinnati held an industrial exposition for the Ohio Valley and the Northwest, while Columbus displaced the State Fair with an exposition of its own in the fall. In connection with the latter was held the National Encampment of the Grand Army of the Republic, one of the most brilliant and picturesque occasions in the capital city's history. Some seventy thousand veterans of the Civil War marched in a parade lasting nearly all day, with General Sherman, ex-President Hayes, and the governors of several states, as well as other notables, present. Never had Columbus seen such crowds. The power and glory of the G. A. R. was at its zenith, for death had not yet taken great toll from its ranks.

Foraker himself fitly symbolized the ascendancy of the soldier influence. A partisan of partisans, he could never forget his own and his party's rôle in the great sectional conflict. He neglected no opportunity to "wave the bloody shirt." When President Cleveland innocently suggested the return of certain captured Confederate battle flags stored at the War Department in Washington, Ohio's Governor declared that "no rebel flags" would be returned from Ohio while he was Governor. At the Republican state convention of 1887, Foraker's remarks about the President were vindictively partisan and personal.

> We know he [Cleveland] had enough of that kind of courage to hire a substitute and stay at home from the war; enough courage to veto the Dependent Pension Bill, and to word his veto in language insulting to those who fought and died for the Union; had courage enough . . . to return to what he calls the Confederate States the captured battle flags, and is so lacking in courage as to cower before the storm of indignation which swept down upon him from the North because of this act.

His fiery campaign speeches gave Foraker the nickname of "Fire Alarm," and endeared him to the soldier element and the average Republican voter though it disgusted the more independent, such as ex-President Hayes.

Foraker's ambitions and his tendency to develop his own following in the party aroused the distrust of Sherman, McKinley, Hanna, and other leaders, who felt that the Governor was not thoroughly loyal to Sherman's Presidential candidacy in 1888. This feeling crystallized under Hanna's leadership into a powerful organization that eventually took control of the party, but in 1889 the friends of Foraker had their way and triumphantly nominated the Governor for a third term.

The Democrats, with the "no third term" cry and the dissatisfaction with Foraker in his own party, were in a strong position to wage a successful campaign, but they further improved their chances by the character of their nomination. James E. Campbell possessed an engaging personality, a skill in organization, and an ability as a popular speaker that had three times secured his election to Congress as Representative from the Dayton district—the last time in the face of a Republican gerrymander which had supposedly insured the district for that party. Campbell, like Foraker, had a fine Civil War record, so that his party seemed to have chosen wisely in naming him. With bands playing "The Campbells are Coming," Democrats flocked to hear their new champion assail the Republican administration with sarcasm and ridicule as effective as Foraker's own weapons.

The Governor, in conjunction with Murat Halstead, of the Cincinnati *Commercial Gazette*, charged that Campbell was urging ballot reform because of his own interest in a patented ballot box. Proof was offered by the publication of a contract with Campbell's name attached. The Democratic candidate presented evidence that it was a plain case of forgery and that the supposed contract also contained the names of McKinley, Sherman, and other prominent Republicans—a fact that Halstead had not made public. The reaction was unfavorable to Foraker, who, unaware of the forgery, had permitted Halstead to use the paper.

Not only was Campbell elected, but likewise a Democratic assembly, though the rest of the Republican state ticket, except the candidate for lieutenant-governor, was successful. Foraker's enemies in his own party were elated at his defeat and hoped that it meant the destruction of his influence in the party. This did not prove to be the case, though he was eclipsed as a Presidential possibility by the rising figure of William McKinley. The new Democratic assembly chose Calvin S. Brice—a man of considerable wealth and better known to Wall Street than to the voters of Ohio—as Henry B. Payne's successor in the United States Senate, showing that the party was in conservative hands.

Probably the one outstanding achievement of Governor Campbell's rather uneventful administration was the passage at his recommendation of an Australian ballot law, a reform that did much to lessen corruption at elections and to insure secrecy and greater independence for the voter. Another recommendation was designed to secure greater home rule for cities—a principle especially emphasized by the Governor in the preceding campaign. This home-rule plan was only partially carried out by the assembly, the city of Cincinnati being an exception in that two important municipal boards were appointed by the Governor. Finding that his own appointments to these positions were unfit, the Governor courageously called the assembly into special session and, after considerable difficulty, succeeded in securing the abolishment of the board of public improvements and its replacement by another appointed by the city's mayor until the next election, when popular choice should prevail. Certain local politicians were angered at the Governor, and this feeling probably contributed to his defeat in 1891.

William McKinley, a national figure after the passage of his tariff law in 1890, was defeated for reëlection to Congress in that year by a Democratic gerrymander. Regarded as a martyr by his party and loyally supported by his faithful friend, the powerful Hanna, he was made the Republican candidate for governor by acclamation in 1891, Foraker himself placing him in nomination. Governor Campbell was renominated by the Democrats. In a campaign concerned almost entirely with national issues,[1] particularly the tariff, McKinley recovered the state for his party by a plurality of 21,511 votes, the legislature also being Republican. John Sherman and Foraker engaged in a sharp battle over the United States senatorship, but Sherman's prestige, based on his long years of service, and Hanna's support proved too much for the former Governor, and Sherman was chosen by the assembly. McKinley was easily reëlected in 1893 over Lawrence T. Neal, as the tide was then running strongly against the Democrats nationally. The support of the American Protective Association,[2] an anti-Catholic organization, denounced by his opponent, contributed to the size of McKinley's majority.

McKinley had few problems to solve in his first term, and his conservative temperament did not cause him to create any or to initiate policies of a reform character. His

---

[1] This election is referred to at greater length under the succeeding topic, "Ohio and National Politics."

[2] This was a secret, oath-bound order, founded in Iowa in 1887, but enjoying its greatest prosperity in the years 1893–1896. Its decline, as in the case of the later Ku Klux Klan, was even more rapid than its rise. Theodore Roosevelt and Dr. Washington Gladden, Minister of the First Congregational Church of Columbus, were leading critics of the movement.

second term coincided with the period of depression following the Panic of 1893, and strikes, unemployment, and the
disorders incident to a time of financial distress placed
heavy burdens on the executive. The Governor was
forced repeatedly to call out the state militia to preserve
order, once, in June, 1894, when the coal miners in all
parts of the state were on strike at the same time. Relief
work was necessary in the Hocking Valley in the winter of
1894–1895, when, with three thousand miners unemployed,
starvation threatened entire communities.

The turbulent summer of 1894 also produced Jacob S.
Coxey's attempt to solve the troubles of the unemployed
by leading an "army" of them to Washington to present a
statement of their grievances. His program of large
issues of paper money to employ men in building and
improving roads as a curative for unemployment was not as
fantastic as it seemed to the conservative-minded then,
but his methods and the nondescript character of his
supporters lost him the sympathy of the great majority of
the people. Coxey, a resident of Massillon, polled over
fifty thousand votes as the Populist candidate for governor
in 1895—a proof of widespread discontent in a state as
conservative as Ohio had become.[3]

McKinley, despite these difficulties, retained and even
increased his popularity, for it was easy to place the blame
for the economic distress upon the Democratic national
administration. The success of these tactics was evident
in 1895, when Asa S. Bushnell was triumphantly elected as
McKinley's successor by a plurality of 92,622 votes over
former Governor Campbell despite an energetic campaign

---

[3] Thirty-six years later, in another year of unemployment, "General"
Coxey was elected mayor of his home city, largely as a protest against existing
economic conditions, and in the following spring received seventy-five
thousand votes in the Republican Presidential preference primary.

by the latter. The way seemed clear for Republican success in 1896.

Ohio and National Politics, 1888–1900

Much of Ohio's political history in the late eighties and the decade of the nineties centers around national issues and national figures. State campaigns were fought over tariff and currency questions chiefly, and state leaders were conscious of the possible national significance of their actions. When President Cleveland emphasized the principle of tariff reform in 1887 as against the protective idea, Ohio Republicans were pleased by the prospect of a tariff campaign, for not only the industrial interests of the state but also the wool growers would stand faithful to the party of protection. Indeed, there had been much tariff sentiment among Democrats before this. Senator Payne was a conservative and a protectionist, while most of the Democratic Congressmen were only lukewarm toward tariff reduction. But party solidarity compelled approval of the President's viewpoint, and the state convention acted accordingly. Ohio was given the Vice Presidential nomination in 1888, the venerable Allen G. Thurman being chosen as Cleveland's running-mate.

The Republicans of Ohio were quite harmonious on the tariff issue and seemed to be at last united and enthusiastic for Sherman for the Presidency. Hanna was actively engaged in securing delegates from other states, and McKinley, despite his position in 1884, seemed thoroughly loyal. Foraker had declared for Sherman, but the latter was not certain that the popular Governor was not looking out for his own chances. The example of Garfield in 1880 was not easy to forget. Foraker's speech, seconding Sherman's nomination, was regarded in some quarters as an attempt to draw the lightning upon himself. However, despite overtures from some of the Blaine supporters, he remained loyal to Sherman, and the latter was defeated, not because of defections in his own state, but because he could not secure sufficient support from the East. McKinley had refused to permit any delegates to vote for him at one stage of the proceedings. Hanna himself was ready to shift to McKinley, but only with Sherman's consent, which was not forthcoming. Harrison, an Ohioan by birth if not by residence, was probably a more satisfactory nominee than one of the Ohioans mentioned would have been, for there were no personal or factional jealousies as an aftermath. He carried Ohio by a plurality of less than twenty thousand votes, neither candidates nor issues evoking any great enthusiasm.

Harrison's administration speedily became unpopular, and the Republicans in Ohio suffered from the reaction. The defeat of Foraker for a third term in 1889 was due to local causes already referred to, but the success of the Democratic congressional ticket in 1890, when fourteen out of twenty-one Representatives were Democrats, was almost entirely the result of national affairs. The McKinley Tariff Act was such an extreme example of protection that public opinion revolted against the party responsible for it.

However, Hanna saw in McKinley a Presidential possibility, and turned his attention to furthering the latter's cause. The first step toward this end was the nomination and election of McKinley as Governor in 1891. The nomination came without opposition, but Governor Campbell, running for a second term, was a formidable opponent. The tariff was the chief issue, with McKinley upholding the measure he had fathered. By this time, since the country was still prosperous, some of the resentment against the act was dying down, particularly since Ohio was normally protectionist. Hanna, who had plenty of funds available, saw that these funds were spent where they would do the most good. Campbell was probably injured by the presence of a Populist candidate. In any case, the Republicans succeeded in restoring their normal plurality.

Yet the renomination of President Harrison in 1892 was fatal to Republican national success and almost cost the Republicans Ohio's electoral vote. Harrison's frigid, colorless personality and the general dissatisfaction with the high-tariff policy and large expenditures of his administration caused his defeat by Cleveland by a large electoral majority. Hanna had tried to bring about McKinley's nomination, and 182 delegates had voted for him; but Harrison's friends, with the Federal patronage at their disposal, easily controlled the convention. Cleveland was not popular with the Democratic Party leaders, and Senator Brice, controlling the Ohio delegation to the national convention, had the majority of its votes cast for other candidates, but to no avail. Cleveland had too great popular support and was easily nominated. In this election, for the first time since the Republican Party was formed, Ohio cast an electoral vote for a Democrat. The result was so close that one Democratic elector had more votes than the lowest on the Republican list and was elected. The other twenty-two electors were Republicans.

The outcome nationally had slight significance. President Cleveland's tariff policy was balked by his own party in the Senate, where a low-tariff bill was changed into a protectionist one, with Gorman, of Maryland, Brice, and other prominent Democrats joining in checkmating the House and the President. The conservative character of the ruling element in the party was clear. But the tariff was losing its importance as the currency question pushed its way to the front.

Low prices for farm products, heavy mortgage indebtedness of Western and Southern farmers, and the declining price of silver produced a demand around 1890 for the free and unlimited coinage of the silver dollar at the old ratio of 16 to 1. The East, stronghold of the business and financial interests, opposed any movement to increase the quantity of currency in circulation, particularly since silver was falling in price and unlimited coinage would, it was feared, flood the country with cheap dollars. The debtor sections, suffering from a scarcity of money, were embittered at this attitude, and, controlling the United States Senate in 1890, they compelled the Republican majority in Congress to increase the quantity of silver purchased by the Government, but failed in their efforts to secure complete free coinage.

Both parties were divided on the silver question and took no definite stand in the Presidential election of 1892. However, there appeared a new party of discontent comprising the dissatisfied of the South and West and some of the Eastern workingmen, which not only adopted free coinage but drew up a generally radical and democratic program that aimed at breaking the hold on government of the industrial and financial interests. Though the national convention to organize the new People's Party met at Cincinnati in 1891, it had no great support in Ohio, for the state was outside the orbit of agrarian discontent. Nevertheless, the Democrats realized that even a small third-party vote might cost them the state, and their state convention made a bid for the radical vote by putting into their platform of 1891 a cautiously worded free-silver plank and a declaration for a graduated income tax. Even these resolutions aroused much opposition and were adopted by a rather narrow margin in the convention. The Republicans upheld the compromise silver measure of the year before to which Senator Sherman's name was attached, declaring that it added the entire production of the silver mines of the United States to the currency. Political expediency marked the action of both parties.

The silver question did not really become a significant issue in Ohio until the depression following the Panic of 1893 made itself felt. Then, with hard times, low prices, and much unemployment as arguments, the silver advocates began to urge an increase in the volume of the currency as the logical method of relief. In 1894 the Democrats came out flatly for free coinage by a convention vote of 468 to 320, an indication that conservatism was losing ground in the party and that the majority was ready to repudiate President Cleveland in his hostility toward silver. Even this declaration did not prevent the Populist vote in the state from being trebled in size over the preceding year, reaching 49,495. In 1895 the conservatives prevailed temporarily in the Democratic convention, and Senator Brice's influence secured the adoption of an ambiguous and meaningless silver plank.

But in 1896 the wave of silver sentiment, spreading over the party in the West, reached Ohio, though with diminishing force, and a new group of leaders took control away from Brice and aligned the Ohio Democracy with their brethren of the South and West. John R. McLean, owner of the Cincinnati *Enquirer*, Allen W. Thurman, son of the veteran leader of the older generation, General A. J. Warner, of Marietta, and others were the active silver supporters. Ex-Governor Campbell, a Presidential possibility, reluctantly accepted this viewpoint, though he urged that an international agreement for free silver be attempted before the United States should undertake the experiment alone. At the national convention, the Ohio delegation supported McLean for the Presidency and later for the Vice Presidency, but accepted the nominations of Bryan and Sewall with enthusiasm. A few of the friends of President Cleveland ran a separate electoral ticket supporting the so-called "Gold Democratic" candidates, Palmer and Buckner, but it had little support at the polls. The Ohio Democracy had joined the radical cause.

Hanna, guiding the destinies of McKinley, was quietly securing the support of Republicans in all parts of the country for his candidate long before the Republican national convention met. There was a danger that an attitude of hostility to silver might drive away Western support, and so emphasis was placed upon the tariff— McKinley's particular interest. Furthermore, Ohio Republican conventions for several years had been including in their platforms planks ambiguously worded to evade the free-silver principle but pledging the party vaguely to bimetallism. There was much sentiment for the use of silver as currency, and McKinley himself was favorable to silver until the time of his nomination. The national convention, however, was controlled by the conservative business elements, and with McKinley's nomination secure, Hanna was quite willing to have the gold standard indorsed. The currency resolution actually declared for bimetallism by international agreement with the retention of the gold standard in the meantime. However, there was little likelihood of other nations' accepting silver: the plank was merely a sugar-coated pill for the silver advocates. Actually, the Republican Party had cast its lot with the East.

Bryan had strong hopes of carrying Ohio and twice invaded the state for a number of speeches, drawing large

crowds and arousing much enthusiasm, even in his opponent's home city.   McKinley, though an effective speaker,
preferred the more dignified plan of remaining at his Canton
home and receiving delegations from all parts of the

Presidential Election of 1896

Republican	McKinley	525,991
Democratic	Bryan	474,882
Prohibition	Levering	5,068
National	Bentley	2,716
National Democratic	Palmer	1,858
Socialist Labor	Matchett	1,165
People's	Bryan	2,615

country. Addresses, carefully scanned by his advisors in advance, were read to the candidate by speakers for the delegations and appropriate replies received. The Republicans shrewdly emphasized the tariff and the prosperity that was sure to come if McKinley were elected, and gave as little offense to the silver Republicans as possible by talking about international bimetallism. Hanna, with the business and financial interests at his back, collected large sums of money and conducted a campaign of propaganda on a scale unheard of theretofore. Democrats charged that employers were putting pressure on employees to vote for McKinley, but Hanna answered that he would help prosecute any individual reported using such tactics.

The outcome was a clear-cut Republican victory, McKinley winning by more than fifty thousand in what was by far the largest vote ever polled in the state up to that time. While McKinley's Ohio residence and his personal popularity contributed to the result, the real basis for Republican success was the marshalling of the conservative industrial and financial interests for the party that upheld the gold standard and high tariff against agrarian radicalism. The great industrial centers turned in large majorities for McKinley, while in the rural districts the Democrats did no more than hold their own. Ohio was too industrialized to listen to a radical agrarian program, even in the midst of economic unrest when currency inflation had its strongest appeal. Considering the money and organization of the Republicans and the fact that Ohio was normally of their faith, it is surprising that the Democrats did as well as they did. Success under the circumstances would have been remarkable.

The elevation of McKinley to the Presidency paved the

way for Hanna's entrance into the United States Senate. Hanna's senatorship was brought about by the "promotion" of the venerable John Sherman to the position of Secretary of State, a place that he was unfitted to fill at his age, but the act created a vacancy in the Senate. Governor Bushnell was urged to give the temporary appointment to Hanna until the meeting of the next legislature. Bushnell was by no means desirous of pleasing Hanna, for he belonged to the Foraker faction of the party and had secured his own nomination in 1895 over the opposition of the Hanna following. By this time, however, the Cleveland leader was too powerful to be resisted, and the Governor finally with considerable reluctance made the appointment.

Hanna's troubles were by no means over. The legislature to be chosen in the fall of 1897 would decide whether he should continue to fill out Sherman's term to 1899 and would also elect a Senator for the full term beginning in that year. It was necessary then for Hanna to control the new assembly if he were to remain in the Senate. The Republican state convention of 1897 indorsed him for the place, while eighty-four of the eighty-eight county conventions took similar action. The state convention also renominated Governor Bushnell, but the Hanna faction was in complete control and even selected the campaign manager.

The Democrats were more hopeful than they had been for several years. Factional rivalries in the Republican Party, the hostility of silver Republicans to the state ticket, and the charges of bossism and corruption raised against Hanna made success seem possible. Their candidate for governor, Horace L. Chapman, was a business man with important coal and iron interests and had the support of all elements in the party. Bryan came to help, and Hanna was mercilessly assailed as the representative of big business in politics. Such accusations had been made in 1896, but then the Republican leader had been merely McKinley's campaign manager and could afford to ignore such attacks. Now he was a candidate himself and had to take the stump in his own defense. Without experience as a public speaker and facing large audiences curious to see how the much cartooned representative of the dollar mark in politics looked, Hanna was at first fearful of the outcome. But his embarrassment speedily disappeared, he developed unexpected power as an extempore speaker, and his audiences generally were attracted by his likeable personality.

The Republican majority of twenty-eight thousand was sufficient to elect both houses of the assembly as well as the entire state ticket, but Hanna here encountered another difficulty. Not all the Republican members were pledged to him, and some half dozen showed signs of making terms with the Democrats. Though Foraker remained neutral, some of his lieutenants aided the anti-Hanna elements, Governor Bushnell, among others, being apparently in sympathy with them. Mayor Robert E. McKisson, of Cleveland, led the dissatisfied Republicans, and the Democrats finally agreed to support him for the Senate in order to defeat Hanna. Columbus became a veritable theatre of intrigue when the legislature met in January. Both sides made desperate efforts to capture every vote, one poor assemblyman being captured and hidden by the McKisson men only to be recovered later by the Hanna supporters, who finally induced him to remain loyal after hiding him in the Neil House until the day of the election. Mass meetings of Hanna followers in different parts of the state demanded that the legislature vote the wishes of the party as expressed by the state convention. When the vote was finally taken, Hanna had just the majority required to elect.

Ugly charges that money had been corruptly used by the friends of Hanna to elect him led to an investigation by a committee of the state senate. This committee, controlled by the Senator's enemies, reported a case of attempted bribery with considerable evidence to support it and recommended to the United States Senate that Hanna be expelled. But neither the accused nor his friends would testify before the committee, and in the end the matter was dropped. It seems quite possible that money was used on Hanna's behalf, but it is unlikely that the Senator would have allowed himself to be directly involved. What his friends might do was another matter.

Hanna's triumph marked the end of all opposition to him and he dominated the Republican Party in the state as no man has done before or since his day. With George K. Nash replacing Bushnell in the governorship after the election of 1899, both state and Federal patronage were in Hanna's control, and the Foraker following was helpless.

The Spanish-American War in 1898 created scarcely more than a ripple in Ohio's history. The wave of patriotic enthusiasm that swept the state produced far more volunteers than could be used. The National Guard units, supplemented by volunteers, supplied 15,354 men in response to the two calls of the President. The total number of deaths was seven officers and 223 enlisted men, disease being the cause, as only three regiments reached the scene of fighting and these saw little service, since the war came to a speedy end in midsummer. Among the officers and enlisted men in the regular army, Ohio was well represented, General Henry W. Lawton playing a conspicuous part both in Cuba and in the Philippines, losing his life in the Philippine insurrection in 1899, while Colonel (later Brigadier General) Frederick Funston, Ohio-born but a resident of Kansas, won acclaim as the captor of Aguinaldo, the leader of the Filipinos in their war for independence.

In the McKinley administration, next to the President himself the most important figure during the war period was a little-known Ohioan, William R. Day, who conducted the State Department for the aging Sherman until the outbreak of war and after that as Secretary in his own right. Day later resigned to head the commission to negotiate peace. With that accomplished, he retired to the comparative obscurity of the Federal Bench, being appointed a Federal circuit judge by President McKinley and later to the Supreme Court by President Roosevelt.

The reëlection of McKinley over Bryan in 1900 placed the country's stamp of approval on the war and the administration's policies generally. Ohio was Republican by a larger majority than it had been in 1896. With the country prosperous, labor in demand, the business interests satisfied with the tariff and financial policies of the Government, and the majority of voters apparently enthusiastic over the war and the new imperialism, the McKinley-Hanna era reached high tide. Big business, undisturbed by governmental policies, was never more powerful. The forces of discontent, as represented by the Populism of the nineties, seemed to have entirely evaporated. It remained for the new century to shatter this great illusion and to end the golden age of political and economic conservatism.

Economic Problems of Government

The finances of the state were not in altogether sound condition through most of the period 1885–1900. The

growing demands of various state institutions plus the
irresponsibility and extravagance of the different legislatures, regardless of party, kept the treasury empty and
made deficits an almost annual occurrence. Most of the
increases in expenditures were probably necessary, but
no proper provision was made to meet them in the form of
new taxes, nor were business methods used in the management of state institutions. Twice, between 1885 and 1900,
loans of five hundred thousand dollars each were necessary
to care for running expenses.

A step in the direction of reform was taken in 1893,
when a bipartisan tax commission was appointed to
investigate the situation. It reported that real estate
was paying far more than its just share, that intangible
property was escaping almost entirely, and that railways
were far less burdened than banks and real estate. The
commission recommended, among other things, a franchise
tax on corporations, including railroads, and an extension
and increase of the inheritance tax. Some legislation
resulted in the direction of placing heavier burdens on
corporations, but the railways were still in a favored
position in 1900. The time was hardly ripe for any vigorous policy toward intrenched interests.

The assembly also enacted, in 1894, a direct inheritance
tax law exempting from taxation estates of twenty thousand
dollars or less but graduated to bear more heavily on large
estates. An earlier law had not applied to direct heirs,
such as a man's wife or children, and had brought in little
money to the state; but this new measure affected inher-
itances of every sort. It was regarded by the conservative-
minded as a radical enactment, the *Ohio Farmer* declaring
that "the state has no more right to tax the dead man's
estate than the live man's, if it descends directly to those
for whom he labored and saved." The old notion that

men became wealthy solely through hard work and thrift persisted in spite of the growing number of millionaires whose estates were evidence that speculation, shrewd investment, unfair practices, and other factors were far more important in the growth of their wealth.

But the state supreme court came to the rescue of the opponents of the tax by declaring it unconstitutional as a violation of the bill of rights of the state constitution, which declared that government is instituted for the equal protection and benefit of all. The large exemption—twenty thousand dollars—and the higher percentage on large estates made it unequal taxation, according to the court. The tax was not properly graduated and there was some basis for the court's objection, but its flat statement that exemptions should not exceed two hundred dollars and that the rate should be the same on all estates indicates what would have happened to a better-drawn law. "There can be no discrimination in favor of the rich or poor," said the court, ignoring the fact that an equal rate did not necessarily mean equal burdens on those who paid. But the court's position was characteristic of the legal logic of the nineties.[4]

In its handling of the trust question, the state government encountered its most serious economic problem. The most powerful large-scale business in the country was originally an Ohio corporation with an Ohioan, John D. Rockefeller, as its guiding force. When the various units in the great combination known as the Standard Oil Company were organized as a trust, an example was set for a number of other combinations. Public opinion

---

[4] An act passed in 1904 for a tax of two per cent on all estates over three thousand dollars, passing to direct heirs, was declared constitutional by the supreme court but was repealed in 1906. The new constitution cleared away all doubts in 1912.

became aroused against this monopolistic trend in the late eighties, and the enactment of the Sherman Anti-trust Law by Congress in 1890 was a consequence. But state action was also undertaken, for the various units in the Standard were state corporations, chartered under and responsible to state laws.

The Standard Oil Company of Ohio, one of the most important members of the trust, was the defendant in a suit brought by the attorney general, David K. Watson, in 1890 to compel a dissolution of the combination. Watson's suit was regarded with surprise and disapproval by the business interests, no less a person than Marcus A. Hanna remonstrating with him against such an action and warning him that it might affect his political future. Watson was unmoved, however, and the case was heard by the Ohio Supreme Court. The attorneys for the Standard denied that the Ohio corporation itself had violated any state laws, though admitting that the individual stock-holders had turned their stock over to the trustees in New York who managed the trust.

The supreme court in March, 1892, held that the acts of the stockholders were really the act of the corporation as a unit, and, more important than that, it declared the trust a monopoly in violation of the common law and ordered the Ohio corporation to withdraw from it. In words that harked back to the old-fashioned American philosophy of individualism and democracy, Chief Justice Minshall declared: "A society in which a few men are the employers and the great body are merely employes or servants, is not the most desirable in a republic; and it should be as much the policy of the laws to multiply the numbers engaged in independent pursuits or in the profits of production, as to cheapen the price to the consumer. Such policy would tend to an equality of fortunes among its citizens, thought to be so desirable in a republic, and lessen the amount of pauperism and crime."

It was not easy, however, to withdraw the Ohio corporation from the trust, and further legal proceedings were undertaken by Attorney General Frank S. Monnett in 1897 to determine whether the court order had been complied with. He charged that the Standard had not carried out its promises and wanted it adjudged guilty of contempt.

After long wranglings between attorneys, and testimony by a number of witnesses, including John D. Rockefeller himself, the case ended in 1899 in a deadlock. The Ohio Supreme Court divided, three to three, on the question of whether the Standard was guilty of contempt. But the trust heads were already changing the organization of the combine into a huge corporation, chartered under the laws of New Jersey, and owning all the companies of the Standard in the various states. This, it was supposed, would solve its legal difficulties, as a New Jersey corporation, unlike a secret group of trustees, could own the stock of an Ohio corporation and do business in the state. But Attorney General Monnett had discovered three other Ohio corporations, besides the original one, that were under Standard control and that were secretly fixing prices according to its dictates. This arrangement seemed to violate a newly passed state anti-trust law—referred to hereafter—and suits were instituted by the energetic attorney general accordingly. However, his term expired before they could be heard and his successor let the matter drop.

The epidemic of combinations that marked the closing years of the century in so many fields was exciting alarm at the time the Standard was under fire. In 1898 a senate committee of the Ohio Assembly investigated reports of evil practices of various business concerns in their efforts to destroy competitors. Seventy-eight witnesses were examined by the committee, assisted by Attorney General Monnett, and a great deal of information was secured. The railroad, insurance, coal, and oil businesses seemed especially affected, though there was some evidence of combinations to fix prices in certain cities among laundries, hardware dealers, plumbers, bakers, and others. The committee reported the existence of "various trusts and combinations of individuals and corporations organized for the purpose of controlling the price of many of the necessaries of life, as well as many other commodities of common sale in the state." It estimated that Ohioans paid seven hundred fifty thousand to one million dollars more for insurance annually than they would pay if open competition were permitted, while it cited a Hocking Valley coal combine as having raised prices and lowered wages at the same time. Railroad discriminations made the freight costs of coal as great from New Straitsville to Columbus as from the former place to Boston, Massachusetts.

The chief result of the investigation was the passage in 1898 of the Valentine Anti-trust Law, whose author, Senator H. E. Valentine, had been chairman of the investigating committee. The law forbade combinations to restrict trade, to limit or reduce production, or to prevent competition in the manufacture, transportation, and sale of any commodity. Agreements to fix prices were also made illegal. Like other anti-trust statutes of this period, the law was too sweeping in its terms to be enforced literally. It probably checked or drove under cover some of the worst practices of combinations, but it could not stop the tendency toward larger and larger units of business, which was a natural outgrowth of the Industrial Revolution. For example, if a group of companies could not legally fix prices, could they be prevented from amalgamating into one corporation to secure the same result? Furthermore, unless neighboring states adopted similar laws, one state could not effectively combat the growth of big business, which was becoming more and more a national problem. When President Roosevelt began his crusade against the trusts in 1901, interest shifted from the state government to the Federal Government as the responsible authority in regulating business.

Selected Bibliography

Moore, "Ohio in National Politics, 1865–1896," *loc. cit.*, continues to be useful through this period, as does Foraker, *Notes of A Busy Life,* though allowance must be made for the latter's personal and political bias. Herbert Croly, *Marcus Alonzo Hanna* (New York, 1912), is written in a spirit of fairness and moderation. Thomas Beer's *Hanna* (New York, 1930) presents an interesting picture. Charles S. Olcott, *The Life of William McKinley* (2 vols., Boston and New York, 1916), is rather eulogistic and partisan in tone. Governor Campbell's life is briefly and appreciatively sketched by Lowry F. Sater in *James Edwin Campbell, a Contemporary Political Study* (Columbus, 1932). For a delightful account of the gayer side of social life in the eighties and nineties, the reader should consult Mrs. Julia B. Foraker, *I Would Live It Again* (New York, 1932). The most sordid features of Ohio politics in the 1880's are portrayed in sensational fashion in Allen O. Myers, *Bosses and Boodle in Ohio Politics* (Cincinnati, 1895). Ida M. Tarbell, *History of the Standard Oil Company* (2 vols., New York, 1904), should be consulted for the Ohio activities of the company. The work of the Valentine Committee appears in a special volume, *Trust Investigation of Ohio Senate* (no place, no date). State finances and taxation are discussed in E. L. Bogart, *Financial History of Ohio, University of Illinois Studies in the Social Sciences,* Vol. I, No. 1, pp. 5–358.

CHAPTER XVI

CULTURAL PROGRESS SINCE 1850: LITERATURE, ART, AND SCIENCE

The Cultural Background

*I*N the first half-century of statehood, cultural development did not keep pace with material progress. The conquest of the soil and the hard struggle with nature characteristic of the frontier would not permit of an active intellectual life. The beginnings of a common school system, the emergence of an able group of lawyers and a smaller number of educated preachers, the appearance of a few struggling colleges, a large number of newspapers—many of them short-lived and few prosperous—and some feeble attempts at literary production constitute the chief intellectual contributions of the period prior to 1850. Yet as Ohio achieved economic maturity and wealth accumulated, urban life and culture developed, and with improved transportation facilities, closer contacts with Eastern centers of culture became possible. Furthermore, by mid-century the melting pot was transforming the New Englander, the Pennsylvanian, and the southerner, if not as yet the German or Irish immigrant, into something that could be called an Ohioan. A native culture seemed about to take root.

Between 1850 and the closing years of the century, Ohio could point with pride to its accomplishments in the field of education and to the excellence of its newspapers. But literature, after a rather promising beginning, had made but slight headway, while the fine arts, painting excepted, were in much the same state. Law, medicine, and the ministry were on a distinctly higher plane than that which they had occupied before 1850. Yet, considering the wealth of the state and its importance in the Union, cultural progress was rather disappointing. Ohio might boast of its generals, its politicians, and its captains of industry, but creative artists were all too few, and nearly all of these preferred the more congenial atmosphere of Eastern centers of culture such as New York and Boston, or were spending much of their time in Europe.

As Ohio was emerging, in the middle years of the century, from the backwoods stage of culture, it was swept by the new frontier of industrialism, which destroyed the budding native literature and provided no substitute. Great industrial development and the attractive opportunities offered for amassing wealth along many lines absorbed the energies of its people and left little leisure for the cultivation or appreciation of intellectual accomplishments. There was no stimulus for the artist in this atmosphere. James Ford Rhodes, the historian, said of Cleveland in the 1880's that "a writer of books walking down Euclid Avenue would have been stared at as a somewhat remarkable personage." Having made his fortune in the Forest City, Rhodes migrated to Cambridge, Massachusetts, to complete his historical work. William Dean Howells, though retaining fond memories of his early life in Ohio, preferred to live in the East, where his editorial and literary activities could be performed more satisfactorily.

In any case, a native culture would have had difficulty in making headway in a state exposed as Ohio was to every change in American life. It was too accessible to the world and its population was changing too rapidly in character to permit provincialism to mould its people and their customs into any particular type. The Buckeye State, sending

thousands of its sons westward and receiving new infusions
from the older states of the seaboard and from Europe,
growing rapidly in wealth, and concerned chiefly with
material progress, reflected a situation rather general in
the United States in the generation following the Civil
War. Marcus A. Hanna and John D. Rockefeller were
better-known and more admired figures than William
Dean Howells, the writer, or J. Q. A. Ward, the sculptor.
This was perhaps the penalty for rapid economic progress.

Literature

. Prior to 1840, literature's chief exponents were Timothy
Flint and Judge James Hall, who wrote both fact and fiction
for Western readers and on Western themes. Hall in
particular, a lawyer and banker of Cincinnati, did much to
preserve the history and legends of the West, concluding
his literary career, in the 1850's, with two volumes, *Legends
of the West* and *The Romance of Western History*. His
name deserves to rank high among those who attempted
to create a Western literature before the pioneer stage had
come to an end.

An outburst of Western periodicals in the forties and
fifties gave evidence of cultural stirrings that pointed
toward the emergence of a genuine Western school of
writers. By 1860 more than ninety such publications
had appeared in Ohio, the great majority in the quarter-
century preceding the Civil War. Yet, without exception,
those of a purely literary character were short-lived.
Only the *Ladies' Repository*, a religious as well as literary
periodical, published under the auspices of the Methodist
Episcopal Church, enjoyed a prosperous career, lasting
from 1841 to 1876. The failure of these projects was due
not so much to their inferior quality as to the fact that the
reading public was not large and those who read preferred

Eastern magazines and books, written by men with established reputations and less provincial in character than their Western counterparts. The earnest efforts of such Ohioans as William D. Gallagher, William T. Coggeshall, Moncure D. Conway, and others to create Western periodicals went for naught.

After the Civil War, the sweep of nationalism destroyed what little appeal local literary periodicals had possessed, and Eastern magazines held sway over the entire country. Yet the latter were divested of much of their earlier provincialism and cultural snobbishness, and Western and Southern writers received recognition in their pages as never before. No longer was an aspiring writer treated with contempt merely because he resided west of the Alleghenies. Bret Harte and Mark Twain were proof of the new era. Thus the occasion for regional periodicals seemed to have passed.

The 1850's also marked the high tide of the romantic and sentimental school of literature in Ohio. This was particularly noticeable in the poetry of the period. It is doubtful if there has been a time in the state's history when more of its citizens were writing poetry. William T. Coggeshall edited a large volume in 1860 entitled *The Poets and Poetry of The West*, in which he included one hundred and fifty-two writers of verse. Sixty of these writers were residents of Ohio—among them Governor Chase and Colonel S. D. Harris, editor of the leading farm paper, along with Alice and Phœbe Cary, William Dean Howells, William D. Gallagher, Coates Kinney, and other literary lights. Poetry furnished an easy outlet for the emotions, required only a certain skill in rhyming to satisfy the popular taste of the day, helped to fill the columns of the local newspapers, and was suitable for recitation in an age that prized the masters of eloquence. Most of the verse was the work of men and women of various occupations who found occasional leisure moments to indulge in a taste for writing. Hence it could be neither very artistic nor very profound.

Written in a sentimental strain accompanied usually by a touch of melancholy and a tendency to moralize, and emphasizing such themes as love, flowers, and death, the poetic output was singularly banal and conventional. There is little of the freshness, exuberance of spirits, humor, or crude manner of speech that is associated with frontier society. The writers, suffering from a literary inferiority complex, wrote according to New England standards and avoided any suggestion of crudeness. Coggeshall was even apologetic for including in his volume some rather clever parodies by Phœbe Cary, the only humorous touches in the entire book. Some of the verse dealt with Western themes but reflected little of the freshness and vigor of the West.

Yet the fault really lay in the cultural standards of the American people in this period. A generation that eulogized Longfellow to the skies and decried Whitman and Poe demanded the type of verse that the Cary sisters could do so well. Ohio could at least welcome comparison with most of the older states. With the frontier period scarcely past, the Buckeye State could offer Alice and Phœbe Cary, William Dean Howells, John J. Piatt, Coates Kinney, and William D. Gallagher as fit representatives of the poets of the period.

Of these, the Cary sisters have received widest acclaim. Their gentle domestic verse still has its appeal, though much that they wrote has been swept away with the passing of the sentimental, romantic era of American literature. Even in their day an occasional dissenting voice was heard. Coates Kinney, commenting on a book of

Alice Cary's poems, protested against the "distressing sameness" of the subjects and inquired whether four hundred pages of sorrow were not too much for one volume. "Does not one come out with a rather cloyed sensation of crossed love and sentimental death, after having agonized along these thousands of passion-dyed and fancy-spun lines of beautiful woe?" Yet Kinney's own attempts, though broader in theme and more vigorous in treatment, rarely rose above the level of mediocrity. William D. Gallagher at times caught the vision of the new industrialized civilization when he wrote of the

> Patient, pent-up man-machine
> At the loom and shuttle seen,

but the Celtic idealist in him saw the speedy emancipation of humanity and the approaching dawn of a better day.

The generation of Americans from the Civil War to 1900 was more interested in prose than poetry, and no group of Ohioans appeared on the scene to arouse particular interest in verse. Of thirty-four Ohio poets included in Emerson Venable's *Poets of Ohio*, published in 1912, twenty-three were born before 1840 and in nearly every case had begun to write before the Civil War. Only five were born since the war. Of the earlier group, Gallagher, living on a Kentucky farm, wrote little after the 1850's, though a volume of his earlier poems was published in 1881. The Cary sisters migrated to New York City in 1853 and rounded out their careers among the *literati* of the great metropolis. Howells likewise left his native state in 1861 and became an easterner in viewpoint as well as in residence. Abandoning poetry for prose, he achieved for himself a place in the front rank of American novelists and literary critics. Coates Kinney and John J. Piatt remained in Ohio and continued to write poetry, at times with a Western flavor and largely divorced from the sentimentality of the earlier period, but singularly lacking in life and spirit and little appreciated by the restless, rushing generation in which they found themselves.

One or two new voices made themselves heard in the eighties and nineties. Edith Matilda Thomas, born in Medina County in 1854, was the most important of these. Gaining recognition in the *Atlantic Monthly* and the *Century*, she found New York City more congenial than Ohio and moved there in 1888. Professor Fred Lewis Pattee's analysis of her work is worth quoting here:[1] "Only by birth and rearing was she of Ohio. To read her poems is to be transported into that no-man's land which so many poets have called Arcady. She is more Greek than American . . . She seems curiously out of place in the headlong West in those stormy closing years of the nineteenth century." The brief career of Paul Laurence Dunbar (1872–1906), of Dayton, a poet of Negro life, added a significant name to the list of those Americans of African birth who have achieved literary distinction. In both his short stories and his poetry, Dunbar showed great promise. Ohio had other writers of verse in this period, but not one gained more than a transient local fame. Ohioans who were interested enough to read poetry found Will Carleton and James Whitcomb Riley more satisfactory than any native writers.

A few of the early sentimental poems won popular acclaim for their authors. "Antony and Cleopatra" gave General William H. Lytle, of Cincinnati, a secure place in the hearts of the ante-bellum generation, while "O Were You Ne'er a School-boy" was read in the McGuffey

---

[1] Fred L. Pattee, *American Literature Since 1870* (Century Company, New York, 1917), p. 341.

readers by thousands of school children who probably forgot, if indeed they ever knew, the name of James H. Perkins, its author. The patriotic fervor of Civil War days was aroused by Thomas Buchanan Read's "Sheridan's Ride," written while the author was residing in Cincinnati. Coates Kinney's "Rain on the Roof" was another early favorite.

Closely akin to the poets were the song writers of the sentimental school. Benjamin Russell Hanby, a student at Otterbein, in 1856 wrote "Darling Nellie Gray," a song which achieved immediate popularity, combining as it did the theme of the grieving lover and a portrayal of the wrongs of the enslaved African. Daniel Decatur Emmet, minstrel singer and composer of popular songs, wrote "Dixie" in a New York City hotel in 1859, unaware that he was composing the "national song" of the South. Certainly there is nothing about the work to suggest that the author was an Ohioan, born at Mt. Vernon.

Until well after the Civil War period, fiction was in much the same state as was poetry. It was stilted and oversentimental, and the moral lesson was always in evidence. Not one Ohioan produced in this period a story or a novel that constituted a permanent contribution to American literature, though Alice Cary, Metta Victoria Fuller, William W. Fosdick, and others whose names are forgotten today were turning out a considerable quantity of fiction of a popular type. All were inferior to Hall and Flint of an earlier day. Ohio did, however, claim a share in Harriet Beecher Stowe's fame, for the materials for "Uncle Tom's Cabin" were collected during the author's eighteen years of residence in Cincinnati, adjacent to slaveholding Kentucky. The work was far more of an Ohio product than the stilted, artificial romances native Ohioans were writing.

Outside the fields of the novel and the short story, the prose writers of the fifties and sixties make a better showing. Genuine American humor came to light in the columns of the Cleveland *Plain Dealer* when Charles Farrar Browne, late in the 1850's, wrote of the experiences and adventures of "Artemus Ward." Browne, a transplanted Yankee, revealed himself as a master of drollery and burlesque of a peculiarly American sort. He mocked at the sentimentality, artificiality, and overseriousness of his contemporaries and engaged in a work in recent years denominated "debunking." Though not a native of Ohio, his genius first blossomed in the happy atmosphere of the Western Reserve, where the foibles and peculiarities of the transplanted New Englander furnished abundant material for the satirist. Sketches on such subjects as "Oberlin," "Among the Free Lovers," "Woman's Rights," and "Among the Spirits" reveal the character of his work. As his fame grew, the lecture platform attracted him, and he left Ohio in 1860 never to return, dying seven years later in London, England.

The war years produced "Petroleum V. Nasby," the creation of David Ross Locke, an editor of northwestern Ohio, whose satire of a northerner of secessionist sympathies soon had the interest of the entire North. The "Nasby" letters continued to have great influence through the war and Reconstruction years, though their coarse wit, grotesque spelling, and caricature of "copperheadism" have little appeal today. Locke was a New Yorker by birth but did most of his writing in Toledo, his home for many years.

The most brilliant and versatile Ohioan of his generation contributed to literature in the 1850's a popular book of travels entitled *The Buckeye Abroad*, which went through several editions. The author was Samuel S. Cox, who gained the sobriquet "Sunset" from an editorial in the *Ohio Statesman*, describing in florid terms the beauties of a particularly brilliant sunset. After a rather brief and financially unsuccessful newspaper career, Cox entered politics, was elected to Congress from the Columbus district, and was soon a national figure. Public life claimed most of his energies, though he later wrote *Three Decades of Federal Legislation*, as well as a volume on the philosophy of humor and some other books. In addition to his skill with the pen, Cox was a gifted public speaker.

The war and its aftermath were dreary years in American literature, but the seventies saw the emergence of a new generation of prose writers very different from the sentimentalists of the ante-bellum decade. Of the new school, Mrs. Mary Hartwell Catherwood, born in Licking County, gained real distinction. After various experiments in realism, she finally took up the historical romance, and, influenced by the historian Parkman, wrote brilliantly and with rare descriptive powers on the period of French colonization. *The Romance of Dollard* (1889), *The Lady of Fort St. John* (1891), and some excellent short stories constitute the best of her work. She was the forerunner of the modern school of historical novelists that enjoyed such vogue in the years around the turn of the century.

Three native Ohioans, Albion W. Tourgee, Ambrose Bierce, and William Dean Howells, did their writing far removed from the Buckeye State and were, for the most part, little influenced by their Ohio background. Tourgee's best-known novels were the product of his "carpetbag" career in the South after the war and were largely of a political character. Bierce—like Tourgee, a Civil War veteran—went to California and won eminence there as a journalist and writer of stories and finally as a literary critic of a peculiarly savage type. He has come to be somewhat more highly regarded since his death than he was in the days of his productivity. There is little of an Ohio flavor to the writings of Bierce and Tourgee despite their early years in this state.

Howells likewise seemed completely divorced from his native state, though occasionally he reverted to Ohio themes, as in *A Boy's Town*, really an account of his own boyhood, and in the autobiographical *Years of My Youth*, a charming picture of ante-bellum Ohio before the industrial era and colored with the romantic haze of reminiscent old age. But, for the most part, Howells wrote on themes far removed from his Buckeye background and in a style that a cultured New Englander might well envy.

As the nineteenth century closed, fiction writers were multiplying in Ohio, but the quality of their product was almost uniformly mediocre, none of it achieving the standard set by Mrs. Catherwood. James Ball Naylor in the first decade of the new century was typical of this period. He wrote a number of entertaining historical romances, based on incidents in early Ohio history, that enjoyed considerable popularity in his home state. But their literary qualities are hardly sufficient to give the author a permanent place even among Western writers of fiction.

The literary impulse that had moved the writers of the 1850's to imitate the New England School and to struggle with themes divorced from reality and beyond their powers nevertheless had indicated an intellectual stirring that promised well for the future. But by 1900, it must be confessed, the achievements were disappointing. The early promise had not been realized. The stirring years of change between 1865 and 1900 found but a pale reflection in the writings of the period. The literary impulse seemed to have worn itself threadbare in historical romances or to have found its chief outlet in journalism.

It is too early to pass judgment upon the present-day writers. Zane Grey has written a number of "best sellers" of the adventure type emphasizing the Wild West theme, but their popularity is no proof of permanence or even excellence. A similar judgment must be pronounced upon the popular fiction of Burton Stevenson, of Chillicothe. Mrs. Mary S. Watts, of Cincinnati, has produced some rather carefully worked-out novels that place her among the better women writers of the period since 1900. Her novel of Ohio life in the 1840's, *Nathan Burke*, is far superior to the tawdry romances that so many Ohioans have produced. She has not ignored modern themes, however, and has shown some skill in studies of present-day social problems. Careful workmanship and a sane realism characterize her work. Brand Whitlock, reform Mayor of Toledo and minister to Belgium during the Great War, produced fiction of a political and sociological flavor early in his career but deserves to be read rather for his reminiscences found in *Forty Years of It*, and for his account of his years in Belgium. These, with his excellent biography of La Fayette, reveal not merely a skilful writer but a genuine liberal of courage and sincerity.

The most unusual figure to attain literary fame from Ohio in the twentieth century is Sherwood Anderson. Gifted with imagination, sensitivity, and keen powers of observation, he has written in realistic strain of the sordidness, disappointments, and repressions of Middle Western life. In his early novels, *Windy McPherson's Son*, *Marching Men*, and *Poor White*, he has pictured the corroding effects of industrialism and the quest for material gain. No Ohioan has reflected so thoroughly in his writings the background of his native state in the rapidly changing industrial age. *Winesburg, Ohio*, and *The Triumph of the Egg*, volumes of short stories, *Tar, a Midwest Childhood*, and *A Story Teller's Story* (autobiographical) reveal this influence. His more recent works are less associated with his early environment. The fumbling futility of his characters, their sense of bewilderment, and the author's explorations—at times almost incoherent—of their emotions and dreams bewilder the reader in some places while revealing rare insight in others. Whatever the verdict of the critics of the future, at least Anderson's right to a place in the front rank of present-day writers cannot be questioned.

Among the growing numbers of clever young men and women who have sought to win fame and fortune in New York City, Ohio has a fair representation. Articles and stories in magazines, editorial work, columns in newspapers, and occasional books reveal the disillusionment, the cynicism, the "debunking," and the "wise-cracking" of the modern school. Their contributions to literature cannot as yet be determined. But there is no Ohio school of writers distinctively of the Buckeye State, nor can Ohio today, any more than in the nineteenth century, boast of the greatness of her literature. A few names have stood out, but the list is not an imposing one.

Historical Writers

To the field of historical scholarship in the nineteenth century, Ohio made only a modest contribution. There were in the state no great libraries or collections of historical materials or graduate schools to encourage the writing of history. Nor was there the cultural atmosphere and the stimulus that comes from contact with other scholars and critics. The individual who attempted anything except local history worked under serious disadvantages. Nevertheless, at Cleveland in the 1880's a scholarly inclined iron manufacturer set out to write the history of the United

States beginning with the Compromise of 1850. Retiring from active business, James Ford Rhodes (1848–1927) began his notable history. Before completing it, however, he removed to a more satisfactory center for historical research—Cambridge, Massachusetts. While criticized for ignoring the influence of many economic and social factors and for an overemphasis of the slavery and Civil War themes, Rhodes's nine volumes, which ended with the close of the Theodore Roosevelt administration, constitute one of the really important works of American historians.

Another Ohioan, Hubert Howe Bancroft (1832–1918), born at Granville in 1832, went to California during the gold rush to become a merchant and a publisher. He developed an interest in Pacific coast history, and prepared, with the help of a number of assistants, twenty-eight volumes on the history of western American from Alaska down to Central America, besides five volumes on the native races and several volumes of essays. For this work he assembled a remarkable collection of materials on Western history in his library. In the field of economics and economic history, John R. Commons, educated at Oberlin but long associated with the University of Wisconsin, has written much of great value, particularly on labor and related problems.

A list could be compiled of the Ohioans who contributed to American and European historical research in the years around 1900, but the names of Burke Aaron Hinsdale, William Milligan Sloane, Edwin E. Sparks, Elroy McKendree Avery, and Henry W. Elson are representative. Particularly well-known because of his textbooks was Philip Van Ness Myers.

In recent years the high degree of specialization in the social sciences and the large numbers of scholars engaged in research make the compilation of a list of important names connected with such work an impossible task. The development of graduate work in the universities and colleges and the presence on the faculties of the various institutions of men from all parts of the country have greatly stimulated research and have given Ohio a position of importance in the realm of scholarship. Likewise, Ohioans have gone in large numbers to the great universities elsewhere to become teachers and research workers in all parts of the nation. To evaluate the contribution of any state is quite difficult under these circumstances.

While the trained scientific historian has so largely supplanted the amateur in the broader fields of history, the latter has continued his activities in his special province, local history. This has been particularly true in Ohio, where, until recent years, most of the historical work has been done by enthusiastic amateurs imbued with a pride in the state's past and a desire that it should not be forgotten. The best-known of these was Henry Howe, whose methods were uniquely his own. First in 1846 and 1847 and again as an old man in 1886 and 1887, he traveled from county to county, collecting all manner of information about each locality, interviewing the old inhabitants, visiting historic spots, and compiling a miscellaneous, undiscriminating, and badly organized body of facts and legends about Ohio's past and its present known as Howe's *Historical Collections of Ohio*. But from his bulky volumes, found in thousands of homes, Ohioans learned much about their early history, and later historians have gleaned valuable information. In recent years, Howe's work has been largely superseded by E. O. Randall and Daniel J. Ryan's *History of Ohio* (5 vols., 1912) and C. B. Galbreath's *History of Ohio* (5 vols., 1925).

Much has been done for Ohio and Western history by the historical societies. The Ohio Archæological and Historical Society, at Columbus, and the Western Reserve Historical Society, at Cleveland, have been particularly active in collecting newspapers and manuscripts and now have excellent collections for historical scholars. The venerable Historical and Philosophical Society of Ohio, at Cincinnati, also has some valuable materials, while the Hayes Memorial Library, at Fremont, has the papers of Rutherford B. Hayes as its chief attraction. Libraries and local historical societies in many places have been active in collecting and preserving materials of historic value. No longer can Ohio be pointed out as a state that neglects to preserve the records of its past and offers few facilities for historical research.

The Fine Arts

Early art in Ohio was naturally utilitarian in character. Furniture, dishes and glassware, candlesticks, needlework, woven articles, and the like were expressions of this tendency and furnished the artistic impulse an outlet in an age when time and energies could not be spared for art as an end in itself. Thus the skilled craftsmen and the housewives were the artists of the pioneer era. Since Ohio was a meeting place for emigrants from all the older states and from Europe, such art as developed reflected the background of the settlers' former homes more than the influence of the new environment.

The types of buildings in a region, once the log cabin era was past, often disclosed the origin of the population. The Western Reserve and villages here and there in other sections revealed a New England background in the tall, pointed spires of the meetinghouses and in some of the domestic architecture, while in the Virginia Military Tract an occasional baronial mansion bespoke a Southern influence. Yet architecture was not a profession, and the builders were really carpenters who might copy but who could not create. Too often they produced unsightly dwellings and business structures that had little to commend them but sturdiness. In the rural districts, especially in southern Ohio, the landscape was frequently marred by ugly, unpainted farmhouses with their clusters of outbuildings, their unkempt appearance revealing the slovenliness or perhaps the hard conditions of life of the owners or tenants.

Toward the middle of the century, Ohio began to reflect the architectural styles that swept the seaboard states. Classical and Greek revival forms appeared in public buildings and churches, a notable example being the statehouse, constructed between 1839 and 1857. This massive stone structure, with its Grecian Doric columns, though often ridiculed for its "cheesebox" cupola, possesses a classic beauty that has won the approval of no less a person than Frank Lloyd Wright, most famous of modern American architects.

The generation following the Civil War saw Ohio, like the rest of the country, wallowing in Victorian Gothic and French mansard styles as the newly rich attempted to display their wealth and culture in copying and misusing styles that belonged to other lands. On the heels of this development, in the late seventies and eighties, came the Romanesque revival in the United States, started by the great Henry H. Richardson but turned by less competent imitators into a bastard form as ugly as its predecessors, particularly in the medley of styles that appeared in domestic architecture. The World's Fair at Chicago in 1893, with its classical revival, broke the hold of the Romanesque and paved the way for new types.

By the close of the century, the cast-iron dog, symbolic of the taste of the seventies and eighties, had almost disappeared from the lawns of the well-to-do Ohioans and a new period was ushered in. No one style predominated either for homes or for public buildings, but the skyscraper constituted the most significant American contribution to architecture. The use of a steel skeleton to support a tall building was an engineering accomplishment, but the great architect, Louis Sullivan, developed the modern design with vertical lines enhancing the appearance of loftiness and lightness in contrast with the heaviness and ornamentation of the old structures of heavy masonry. The Cleveland Terminal and the building of the American Insurance Union of Columbus are examples of modern architecture in Ohio. An Ohioan, Cass Gilbert, born in Zanesville, designed the great Woolworth Building in New York City. Church architecture, freed from conformity to any one style, has taken a variety of forms, while school buildings, though by no means standardized, have been constructed along more uniform lines to provide light and space and to satisfy other utilitarian ends. The idea that a building should express its purpose in its architecture, seemingly forgotten in the later nineteenth century, is clearly evident in present-day construction. The civic center idea, with a whole group of public buildings in harmonious relationship, started in Cleveland and has spread to other Ohio cities. With builders of residences, apartment houses, and even factories discovering virtues in beauty of design expressive of their purpose, Ohio seems to be recovering from the drab ugliness of the years of the Industrial Revolution and the equally distressing attempts to conceal actual ugliness of design with every style of architecture that blew across the Atlantic or that was adopted in the cultured East.

Ohio's contribution to architecture was negligible almost to the close of the nineteenth century. The state had

few architects worthy of the name, and the buildings that
showed any trace of the architect's hand were usually
inferior examples of the prevailing style. The few good
things were nearly all done by out-of-state architects.
Only in the last generation, with professional training
available in the universities, has Ohio developed her own
architects and begun to contribute to the cultural progress
of the nation along this line. There is no native architecture in the state and no prospect that there will be one.
But, at least, Ohio is in a position to share in the great
developments in American architecture that have come
with the twentieth century.

Painting is the only one of the fine arts in which Ohioans
have contributed greatly to the enrichment of American
art. Early in the nineteenth century, first at Cincinnati
and then in other cities, portrait painting became a flourish-
ing business, not to be displaced until the era of photog-
raphy. This occupation afforded an apprenticeship in
handling the brush as well as commercial opportunities, for
the talented. As Cincinnati developed into the most
important city in the West in the 1840's, it became a
cultural center that, if it was not the equal of the older
seaboard cities, at least offered some encouragement to
young artists. But fame could be achieved only in the East
or abroad, where an education in art could be obtained,
hence the aspiring beginners possessed with real talent
usually left Ohio as their art developed. The Cincinnati
Gazette in 1850 pointed to the number of artists who had
once lived there and sharply criticized the city for its lack
of appreciation, which had forced them to go elsewhere
to win recognition. Yet even in the East every student of
art looked forward to study in Europe to complete his
education, so that Cincinnati was not much worse than the
older centers.

Among the earliest of Ohioans to gain fame for his paintings was Thomas Cole, born in England in 1801 but residing for a time at Steubenville, where he first attempted to paint. From the latter place, he went east to become a member of a group known as the "Hudson River School," which emphasized the beauties of the American landscape.

Beginning about 1840, a number of rather talented painters made Cincinnati their headquarters, though most of them soon followed the beaten path eastward. The better-known among these painters were Thomas Buchanan Read, James H. Beard, William L. Sonntag, the Frankenstein brothers, and William H. Powell. Ohioans are not likely to forget the last named, for he painted "Perry's Victory," which hangs in the statehouse, an object of patriotic pride to the thousands who have viewed it if not a great work of art. It cost the state ten thousand dollars.

In the 1870's—dreary years in most respects in American history—came the heyday of a more important group of young Cincinnati artists, including Frank Duveneck, John Twachtman, Robert Blum, Joseph DeCamp, Kenyon Cox, and some others, while at Cleveland Otto Bacher and Max Bohm were beginning their careers. Duveneck led the way across the Atlantic, and presently established a school, first at Munich, in 1878, and then, by 1880, removed to Florence and Venice. Among the brilliant group working with him were several of the artists mentioned above.

Duveneck alone returned to make Ohio his permanent home, coming back to Cincinnati in 1888 and remaining there until his death in 1919. As dean of the faculty of the Cincinnati Art Academy and advisor for the Art Museum, he added to his wide reputation as an inspiring teacher and gifted painter, wielding the most talented brush, in the opinion of John S. Sargent, in his generation. He was given a special medal of honor for his impressive exhibit at the Panama-Pacific Exposition at San Francisco in 1915. Besides oil paintings and etchings, Duveneck showed marked talent in sculpture, particularly in the beautiful memorial to his wife, who died and was buried in Florence—a recumbent effigy in bronze. In the art museum at Cincinnati is the great collection of his works, a donation from the artist. While he looms large in the history of American art both as painter and teacher, Ohioans may well hold him in special esteem, for almost alone of the significant artists of the Buckeye State he made Ohio his permanent home and gave his influence to the development of the artistic life of his city and state.

Two of the best-known modern painters were Ohio-born. Robert Henri (1865–1929) was a native of Cincinnati, but his art education really began at Philadelphia in 1886. He spent much time abroad and became a significant influence in breaking with old traditions. He has pictures in more than thirty public art museums and at the time of his death was ranked near the head of his profession. One of his pupils was George Bellows (1882–1925), more of an Ohioan than Henri, for he was born and reared in Columbus and educated at Ohio State University. He went to New York in 1904 and speedily won distinction. He painted human beings, being particularly effective in dealing with groups and crowds. His war-time painting, "Edith Cavell," was widely commented upon, though Ohioans will prefer to remember him for his portrait of Dr. William Oxley Thompson—one of his masterpieces. His early death robbed American art of its most promising figure.

It would not be appropriate to criticize or pass judgment here upon the accomplishments of the many artists who once called Ohio their home. Their work lies in the broader field of American art. Were there a special school of Ohio painters, their relationship to their environment would require explanation. But while Ohioans have become important figures in American art, the state has developed no native art. It has been engulfed in the broad sweep of American life too completely to permit of provincialism.

Within the state, Cincinnati, though now rivalled by the great city on the lake, was long the cultural capital of Ohio[2] and, until the Civil War, of the entire West. The rapidity of its growth prior to 1850, its wealth, its cosmopolitan character, and its educational institutions gave it advantages in the early development of a cultured society. Particularly was the influx of the foreign-born a great intellectual stimulus. The skilled artisans who made watches, musical instruments, church ornaments, wood carvings, and the like were usually Germans, and their sons often aspired to become artists. The number of German names among Ohio painters is striking proof of this influence.

Sculpture developed slowly in Ohio. Unlike painting, sculpture produced no commercial demand for the artist who worked in stone save an occasional opportunity to make a bust of some local celebrity. Nevertheless, Ohio furnished the early inspiration for two of the best-known American sculptors. Hiram Powers (1805–1873) was not an Ohioan by birth, but as a young man, residing in Cincinnati, he was first attracted to an artistic career by working with a German artist. After acquiring a certain skill in making busts, he went east, for there was no opportunity for an ambitious sculptor to perfect his art or to increase his income in "Porkopolis" in the 1830's. Nicholas Longworth, Cincinnati's wealthiest citizen, assisted

---

[2] The famous Rookwood Pottery at Cincinnati is an illustration of that city's artistic supremacy in a unique field.

Powers financially so that he was able to study in Italy. As fame came to him, the sculptor preferred the more congenial atmosphere of the Old World and became a permanent resident of Florence. His statue, "The Greek Slave," was received with great acclaim and was long regarded as the finest work of art produced by an American. When exhibited in various Ohio cities, crowds thronged to see it, drawn, it must be conceded, as much by curiosity concerning the statue's daring nudity—much commented on in that age of prudery—as by a desire to admire its artistic lines. But with the decline of the cult of classicism, it has been overshadowed by the more virile work of later Americans. Powers did better work in some of his busts of important figures in American life.

A far greater artist was John Quincy Adams Ward, born at Urbana, in Champaign County, in 1830. Although showing an interest in modelling in clay as a boy, his artistic education really began with his removal to Brooklyn, where he came in contact with Henry Kirke Brown, a sculptor of some note, who taught him for several years. Ward returned to Ohio in 1860 and executed a bust of Dr. Lincoln Goodale, now in Goodale Park, Columbus. He was hoping for a contract from the legislature to do a statue of Simon Kenton, but he was disappointed in this expectation by the outbreak of the Civil War. The rest of his career was associated principally with New York City, Central Park possessing several of his works, including his favorite, "The Indian Hunter." His equestrian statue of General Thomas, at Washington, is one of his finest works. Thoroughly American in his viewpoint, he exercised a powerful influence on the development of a native product. He died in 1910.

Ohio had other sculptors in the post-bellum years, and the craze for soldiers' monuments supplied plenty of business. Their work, however, was generally mediocre. Levi T. Schofield deserves to be mentioned, for he created the one piece of statuary that nearly every Ohioan who comes to the capital city sees and remembers. In the statehouse yard stands the Roman matron, Cornelia, mother of the Gracchi, with seven distinguished Ohioans of Civil War days around her. She seems to be saying, "These are my jewels," symbolic of Ohio's war-time importance, but the group hardly represents the highest expression of artistic achievement.

To evaluate the present-day sculptors is even more difficult than to pass judgment upon recent literature and painting. It is enough to say that interest in this field is growing and that a number of Ohioans are doing creditable work. Indeed, it seems that Ohio's contribution to American sculpture is yet to be made, for only in recent years has it been unnecessary for her artists to become exiles to find training and inspiration for their work.

In general, the rapid development of the fine arts is one of the most encouraging signs of cultural progress in the twentieth century. With every large city possessing an art museum and more than a score of institutions offering special training in art, with numerous organizations existing to foster interest in the fine arts, and with improving standards of taste more and more evident, Ohio seems in a position to play a far more important part in American cultural life than the frontier and industrial state of the nineteenth century.

Progress in Science

Science in the United States, in the early years of its history, was a plant of slow growth. Few Americans could interest themselves in experimentation and in the formulation of theories when no material gain was involved in the process. Furthermore, educational institutions offered little encouragement for the study of science.

Not until the last quarter of the nineteenth century was there evidence of progress along scientific lines at all comparable to the achievements on the other side of the Atlantic. Several influences explain the interest that developed then. For one thing, the new industrialism was beginning to recognize the possibilities of practical usefulness in the advancement of science in the way of improving machinery and methods, testing raw materials and finished products, making new discoveries, and accelerating productive capacity generally. Trained engineers, chemists, and geologists became increasingly in demand for industrial purposes. In the educational world, the influence of the ideas of Darwin, Huxley, and Spencer and the decline of theological control of the colleges gave science an opportunity to establish itself as never before. The development of graduate study was of further assistance, while engineering and agricultural colleges and greatly improved schools of medicine applied science to practical ends. The establishment of the United States Geological Survey in 1879 was a final recognition of the importance of the one science that both Federal and state governments had for many years regarded as within their province and worthy of their financial support.

Ohio was affected by all of these influences. Prior to the Civil War, science had received scant attention in the educational institutions, and scientific knowledge was either a hobby of men whose occupations gave them leisure and opportunities to indulge in this luxury or the concern of the few who saw some practical end to be achieved through such knowledge, such as the improvement of agriculture or the discovery of mineral resources. It is not surprising that three of the half dozen men known outside the state for their accomplishments in science were physicians, for practitioners of medicine, more than any other class of professional workers, were required to have some knowledge of natural sciences and possessed opportunities to observe and experiment.

The most noted figure in the annals of early Ohio science was Dr. Daniel Drake (1785–1852), born in New Jersey but most of his life a resident of Cincinnati. Besides the usual apprenticeship in a physician's office, he studied at the University of Pennsylvania under Dr. Benjamin Rush and returned to Cincinnati imbued with a desire to elevate the profession in the West. His years of teaching in the Ohio Medical College and elsewhere were marred by bickerings with jealous colleagues, but his reputation grew. Besides writing for medical periodicals, he wrote several books, the best-known a two-volume work— *Principal Diseases of the Interior Valley of North America*— called by one writer "a mine of information on the topography, meteorology, character of population, customs and diseases of the interior of North America." It represented many years of travel and investigation and great labor in collecting materials. His name was long honored in the "Queen City" for his public spirit and his interest in almost every type of reform.

In northern Ohio, Jared Potter Kirtland (1793–1877) was a pioneer in the broadest fields of science. He was born and educated in Connecticut, studying medicine at Yale and at the University of Pennsylvania, and geology and mineralogy under the noted Silliman at the former school. He came to Ohio in 1823 and until his death was associated with the development of medical education in the Western Reserve, teaching for many years in the Cleveland Medical College, which he helped to found. His breadth of interest is shown by his contributions to medical, scientific, and agricultural periodicals in such different fields as medicine, zoölogy, botany, and scientific agriculture. He even edited a farm-and-home journal for several years. He was a correspondent of the great Agassiz and a member of several scientific and learned societies.

More nearly devoted to science as an end in itself was William S. Sullivant (1803–1873), a native Ohioan and a member of a well-known pioneer family of Franklin County. He was educated at Ohio University and Yale and became a surveyor and practical engineer. Botany, however, came to be his passion, and he gained the recognition of Asa Gray, of Harvard, the father of American botany, who incorporated Sullivant's work on mosses and liverworts in his famous manual. Sullivant also published two important books, both dealing with the mosses of eastern North America, which he had made his particular field of study. He was a member of the National Academy of Science and a contributor to scientific periodicals.

That Ohio should possess an astronomical observatory, the first large one in the United States, when the state was scarcely past the pioneer stage, was owing to the enthusiasm of Ormsby MacKnight Mitchell (1809–1862), a Kentuckian by birth but long a leading citizen of Cincinnati. Mitchell was educated at the United States Military Academy at West Point and taught mathematics there. He resigned from the Army in 1832, studied law at Cincinnati, and was admitted to the bar, but mathematics and astronomy constituted his chief interest. While professor of these subjects in Cincinnati College, he proposed to establish an observatory, and, largely through his own labors, raised the necessary funds. The apparatus was purchased in Europe, and the cornerstone was laid by John Quincy Adams in 1843. Mitchell was also an engineer in railroad construction work and later served with distinction in the Civil War, attaining the rank of major general. He died of yellow fever in the midst of the war. He had achieved a wide reputation as a popular writer and lecturer on astronomical subjects, receiving the degree of A. M. from Harvard. His observatory experienced many financial vicissitudes early in its history but remained a monument to his scientific interests and an indication of the public spirit of the city of Cincinnati.

Illustrating well the wide range of interest and the practical character of American men of science in the nineteenth century, Charles Whittlesey, of Cleveland (1808–1886), born in Connecticut, was, like Mitchell, educated at West Point, saw service in the Army, studied law, was a geologist for both state and Federal governments, was employed as a mining engineer for a time, and became an authority on archæology and Western history. He was also an officer in the Civil War. Colonel Whittlesey's most important work was in the field of geology—in helping to discover the mineral resources of his own state and of Wisconsin and the Lake Superior region, where he spent several years. A bibliography of some two hundred titles reveals the extent of his writings in the several fields in which he was interested.

The chief contribution of the state government to science in the nineteenth century was the establishment of the Geological Survey. First organized under W. W. Mather in 1837, it had functioned for only two years when the legislature discontinued it. Mather (1804–1850), like Whittlesey, was a native of Connecticut and a graduate of the United States Military Academy. He later taught at Ohio University and served as agricultural chemist for the state, while editing a farm paper. Not until 1869 was the survey revived with John S. Newberry (1822–1892) in charge. Connecticut-born, but educated in the Western

Reserve and at Cleveland Medical College, he practiced medicine for several years before his interest in geology and paleontology drew him into Government service and led eventually to a professorship in these fields at Columbia University. He retained this position while acting as head of the Ohio survey. Seven volumes of reports, chiefly scientific in character, had been published by 1882.

Edward Orton, the first president of Ohio State University, succeeded Newberry in 1882 and was responsible for some reports of an economic character dealing with the state's resources and their development. But the legislature, doubtful of the utilitarian value of the work of the survey, suspended appropriations from 1893 to 1899. Then, with Edward Orton, Jr., succeeding his father as state geologist, the department began to function as a permanent part of the machinery of state government. Associated with it in some way in the course of the nineteenth century were nearly all the prominent Ohioans who were interested in the advancement of science, the list including such names as Mather, Whittlesey, Kirtland, Sullivant, Newberry, and the two Ortons. The broad scope of geology attracted men with an interest in the natural sciences as well as those of a more practical bent who wished to discover and develop oil, coal, clays, and other mineral resources.

The outstanding Ohioan in the scientific world at the close of the nineteenth century was a lover of science for its own sake. Thomas Corwin Mendenhall (1841–1924), a native of Columbiana County, was the first professor of physics and mechanics at Ohio State University. In the course of a long career devoted to scientific pursuits, he taught in the Imperial University, Tokyo, Japan, was Superintendent of the United States Coast and Geodetic Survey, served as president of Rose Polytechnic Institute,

Terre Haute, Indiana, and later as president of Worcester Polytechnic Institute, Worcester, Massachusetts, was a member of several important Government commissions, and in 1889 had the honor of election to the presidency of the American Association for the Advancement of Science. His definitions of the ohm, the volt, and the ampere were accepted by the International Electrical Congress in 1893 with but slight changes.   Dr. Mendenhall closed his long and active career as chairman of the Board of Trustees of the Ohio State University.   In recent years another Ohioan has achieved international fame as a physicist. Professor Arthur H. Compton (1892–   ), of the University of Chicago, was awarded the Nobel Prize in physics in 1927.   He was born at Wooster and received his first degree at Wooster College.   His brother, Karl T. Compton (1887–   ), is president of Massachusetts Institute of Technology.

The science of medicine, in Ohio, has produced few great names in the field of research, but the general level of the profession has improved in a remarkable degree since the middle of the nineteenth century.   Medicine in 1850 was the paradise of the incompetent.   Early legislation requiring of men who wished to practice medicine three years of study with a physician or surgeon, or a degree from any medical institution in the United States, admitted to the profession all who cared to enter it, for there was little attempt at enforcement even of these lax regulations. Medical colleges, of which Ohio had no less than ten—at least so called—in 1860, with over eleven hundred students, competed with one another for patronage and granted degrees freely to all who attended their courses of lectures. As a result, a degree had little significance.   "Specialists" filled the advertising columns of the newspapers with their claims.   One at Cincinnati in 1860, "from the hospitals of

London, Paris and Baltimore," proclaimed his power to cure gonorrhœa in three days and syphilis in five, while in the hills of Hocking County two medical partners vouched "to extirpate the most difficult cases of Cancer in the short space of from thirty minutes to seven hours— almost in every case without the use of the knife."

Patent medicines, despite the protests of medical conventions and journals, flaunted their claims in the newspapers, whose ethical standards admitted any advertisements that added to the papers' revenues. Scrofula, syphilis, bronchitis, ulcers, tumors, consumption, rickets, asthma, St. Vitus's dance, and erysipelas constituted a partial list of the diseases to be cured by one well-known nostrum. The frankness of advertisements with regard to sexual matters is surprising in an age of prudery.

Progress in reforming medicine at first was very slow. For years the State Medical Society, organized in 1848 and displacing the older state medical conventions, attempted to elevate the standards of the profession as well as educate the public, but with rather discouraging results. A law passed in 1868 requiring two full courses of twelve weeks each at a medical college as a requirement for practicing medicine accomplished little, for there was no machinery to enforce it. Further legislation in the 1880's did not improve conditions, and Ohio became a refuge for incompetents from neighboring states, whose requirements were far stricter.

Not until near the close of the century did the much needed reforms come. An act of 1896 created the State Board of Registration to pass upon the qualifications of physicians, surgeons, and midwives, and established higher standards for entrance into the profession. This was amended in 1900 to require of candidates for licenses four years of study (at least twenty-six weeks were to constitute a year's work) and graduation from an accredited medical college, besides the passing of an examination to be given by the state board. Other regulations in these laws required those already practicing to present evidences of their fitness. When the law of 1896 was passed, in the words of the president of the state board, "it is probable that no equal territory contained so many vampires, charlatans, mountebanks and quacks as did Ohio." Within two years, four colleges had been closed, 369 applications to practice had been rejected, and a large number of practitioners, estimated at seven hundred, had left the state.

In the same period had come a similar elevation in the standards of pharmacy and dentistry, while a little later (1915–1920) nursing and optometry were subjected to stricter requirements. With the medical and dental colleges generally becoming affiliated with the larger universities, and requirements for entrance being raised to eliminate not merely the unfit but even the mediocre, the medical profession in Ohio seems to be firmly established on a new high plane.

One phase of the progress of science is its practical application in the field of invention. Here Americans made notable contributions in the nineteenth and twentieth centuries, with Ohioans playing a significant part. Since inventions and new discoveries have, until recent years, been so largely the work of individuals, the story of inventive genius becomes a recital of individual accomplishments. Of the familiar names in the list of American inventors, that of Thomas A. Edison stands at the top. Ohio claims a share in Edison's fame, for the inventor was born at Milan, Erie County, in 1847 and lived the first few years of his life in that place. His family moved to Michigan in 1854, and Edison grew up in that state. His later career took him to many different places, but eventually his laboratories at Menlo Park, New Jersey, became his headquarters. Since genius is not a matter of environment, Ohio cannot claim more than the honor of being his birthplace.

The Wright brothers, Orville and Wilbur, were Ohio products, and their early studies and experiments were performed at their Dayton home. The first successful, man-carrying airplane was their great work. Charles F. Brush, of Cleveland, a graduate of the University of Michigan, tried out in his home city in 1878 a system of arc lights for street illumination—the first practical demonstration of the use of electricity for public lighting. Obed Hussey, Massachusetts-born, was living at Cincinnati when he secured a patent for a reaper in 1833, six months before Cyrus McCormick's patent was granted. It was first demonstrated July 2, 1833, near Carthage, Hamilton County. Had he possessed more business acumen, his creation would have outstripped McCormick's, for it had certain superior features. However, Hussey would not adopt improvements as his rival did and was eventually forced out of business after years of competition. Elisha Gray, born at Barnesville, Belmont County, in 1835 and educated at Oberlin, disputed with Alexander Graham Bell the invention of the telephone and was denied the priority only after a long legal battle. He invented a number of other electrical devices, securing some seventy patents. Benjamin G. Lamme, born on a farm near Springfield in 1864 and educated at Ohio State University, was an inventor and electrical engineer of wide reputation with 162 patents to his credit at the time of his death. As chief engineer of the Westinghouse Electric Company, he was responsible for some of the most significant changes in the improvement of electrical machinery.

Invention in recent years has become more and more coöperative, with the laboratories of large industrial concerns the chief centers of investigation and experimentation. Science and invention are now in close relationship, and the age when enthusiastic individuals developed their ideas by haphazard experimenting seems at an end. Many Ohioans are contributing to the advancement of science along both theoretical and practical lines, but their individual achievements do not reflect the glory that came to Edison and the Wright brothers.

Selected Bibliography

William Henry Venable, *Beginnings of Literary Culture in the Ohio Valley* (Cincinnati, 1891), deals with early Ohio writers, but there is no later study to supplement it. Sketches and criticisms of the significant figures in Ohio literature may be found in such broader studies as Fred L. Pattee, *A History of American Literature since 1870* (New York, 1917), and Dorothy Anne Dondore, *The Prairie and the Making of Middle America* (Cedar Rapids, Iowa, 1926). William T. Coggeshall, *Poets and Poetry of the West* (Columbus, 1860), and Emerson Venable, *Poets of Ohio* (Cincinnati, 1912), include not only selections of verse but also brief biographical sketches of the writers selected. Randall and Ryan, Vol. V, pp. 3–84 (a chapter by W. H. Venable), summarizes the literary careers of a large number of Ohioans in uncritical fashion.

Ohio's contribution to the fine arts is covered carefully in *Ohio Art and Artists* (Richmond, 1932) by Edna Maria Clark. For a somewhat more critical appraisal of Ohio artists, the reader should consult the larger histories of American painting, sculpture, and architecture, and the *Dictionary of American Biography*. The latter work also contains biographies of the more significant figures in the field of science. Two important Ohio artists are dealt with in Norbert Heermann, *Frank Duveneck* (Boston and New York, 1918), and *George W. Bellows, His Lithographs* (Mrs. Emma Louise Bellows, comp., New York, 1927), which contains an appreciation by Thomas Beer. Otto Juettner, *Daniel Drake and His Followers* (Cincinnati, 1909), covers the career of the pioneer of Ohio scientists and physicians. An early account by a friend is Edward D. Mansfield, *Memoirs of the Life and Services of Daniel Drake* (Cincinnati, 1855). C. C. Baldwin is the author of a "Memorial of Colonel Charles Whittlesey," in *Western Reserve Historical Society Tracts* (Cleveland, 1887), Vol. II, No. 68. Wilbur H. Siebert, *Thomas Corwin Mendenhall* (no place, no date), is an interesting sketch. The history of medical progress is summarized in Randall and Ryan, Vol. V, pp. 161–227 (a chapter by Dr. D. Tod Gilliam). The *Annual Reports of the State Board of Medical Registration and Examination*, beginning in 1896, are valuable. The work of Ohio inventors may be found in Waldemar Kaempffert, *A Popular History of American Invention* (2 vols., New York, 1924). *The Dictionary of American Biography* may be used to advantage also, though it deals only with individuals who died prior to its publication.

CHAPTER XVII

CULTURAL PROGRESS SINCE 1850: EDUCATION AND JOURNALISM

Education

THE ideal of state-supported common schools was accepted in Ohio in the 1820's, but serious practical problems remained to be solved before this ideal became a reality. Such matters as the extent and character of state aid, the proper organization for the school system, the question of establishing public high schools, and an adequate supply of trained teachers could not be easily disposed of in a state but a step removed from the frontier period. The foundations for a great system of popular education were laid before the Civil War, but it required many years of discussion, experimentation, and legislation to complete the work and to eliminate its worst defects. Indeed, not until the reforms of 1914, in the administration of Governor Cox, could the state be said to have a genuinely modern system of public schools.

Samuel Lewis, educational as well as anti-slavery and temperance reformer, held the newly created position of state superintendent of common schools from 1837 to 1840, and stirred up interest in improving the system, but at his retirement the office he had held was abolished and a brief period of reaction followed. The late forties, however, were years of progress marked by the appearance of teachers' institutes, the publication of educational periodicals, and the organization of a state teachers' association, thenceforth a vital factor in educational progress. The association employed Lorin Andrews as its agent to travel over the state and spread the gospel of reform, while in 1852 appeared the *Ohio Journal of Education*, edited by A. D. Lord, as its official organ. This agitation was soon productive of new laws.

The most important legislative accomplishment in these years was the law permitting the organization of cities and incorporated towns into special districts by popular vote and authorizing them to establish systems of graded schools at their own expense. This "Akron Law," so named because it was first applied to Akron by a special act in 1847, became the basis for the city school systems of Ohio for many years and placed municipalities far in advance of the rural districts in educational advantages. Prior to this time, Cincinnati, wealthy and progressive, had had good schools, but most other cities had been as laggard as the rural areas. The rapid growth of many cities in population and wealth, a consequence of the Industrial Revolution, made special arrangements necessary in their case, and this condition has continued to prevail to the present day.

The reforming spirit connected with the movement for a new constitution in 1850–1851 affected education, and the assembly in 1853 responded with one of the important measures in the history of education in Ohio. Part of this enactment was really a collection and codification of existing laws in the interest of simplicity and clearness. Other sections, however, made important additions to the code. Township boards of education were to be organized to take over most of the duties of the old district boards, school libraries were established by a special tax, a state levy of two mills was provided for the benefit of the schools, and the office of state commissioner of common schools was created for the supervision of the system.

This official was to be elected by the voters for a three-year term.

Objectors speedily appeared, and for some years the fate of the new system was in doubt. Taxpayers felt the increased burden, and doubtless many agreed with the critic who wrote to the Zanesville *Courier* his objections to "being robbed to pay for the education of my neighbor's child" and to "robbing my neighbor to pay for the education of mine." To the objections of the conservative taxpayers was added the hostility of the Roman Catholic element, who felt a sense of injustice at being taxed to support public schools in addition to maintaining their parochial schools, of which Cincinnati in 1860 had seventeen. The presence of many Protestant ministers and former ministers in the teaching profession and the use of the Protestant Bible in the schoolroom gave some basis to the charge that the public schools were sectarian in character. However, most features of the system survived the attacks of its critics and became generally accepted.

The high school had the hardest fight to justify its existence, for many friends of common schools questioned the necessity of an institution that reached but a small proportion of the children of school age. The Cincinnati *Commercial* in 1860 referred to high schools as "educational luxuries in which a tax-ridden community can illy afford to indulge." The term "high school" had been first applied to some privately supported schools and came to have its present meaning around 1850, when Cincinnati and Cleveland were organizing their systems. It is possible that public high-school training existed in other places earlier, as it was entirely optional with the local boards and there was no very definite idea as to what constituted a high school. Advanced subjects might be offered in the higher grades without a formal organization of a secondary school. By 1860 the state had 161 high schools, confined almost entirely to the towns and cities. By 1880 the number had reached 567.

The rise of the high school coincided with the decline of the privately supported academies and seminaries. As early as 1854, the state school commissioner reported that "in no state have the higher departments of common schools so effectually taken the place of academies as in Ohio," while by the close of the decade, the latter were far outnumbered by the tax-supported secondary schools and ceased to offer serious rivalry.

The years from the Civil War to 1900 saw no revolutionary changes in the school system, but rather improvements and extensions to make the system function more efficiently. Improvements in organization, greatly increased expenditures for education, the spread of the high school to villages and country districts, the adoption of the principle of compulsory attendance of pupils, and improved standards for the training of teachers were the more significant trends.

With regard to the organization of rural schools, the act of 1853 transferred most of the authority of the district boards to township boards but did not abolish the former. As a consequence, considerable friction resulted, with the district authorities in practice asserting far more power than the law intended they should. For many years this situation continued. The old tendency to let each community go its own way, inherited from frontier days, was not easy to overcome. But the complaints of the various state school commissioners and the growing dissatisfaction with the condition of rural schools led in the 1890's to legislation that established the township board, chosen by popular election, as the sole responsible authority. In

1900 a system of graded schools was made compulsory for townships, while in the same law appeared the optional centralized school. Authority was granted to the townships to abolish the district schools and to set up one or more centralized schools to which pupils were to be transported at public expense. This action marked the beginning of the end for the "little red schoolhouses" in many parts of Ohio.

Outside the jurisdiction of the township in the 1850's were the city, village, and special districts. The last named consisted of small villages or rural communities that found it more convenient and more to their own interest to organize separately from the township and to develop a system of schools to suit themselves. As the cities grew in size, the old legislation proved unsatisfactory, and the legislature adopted the plan of classifying the municipalities according to population and of creating a special system for each class. This arrangement resulted after a time in a dozen different kinds of city districts—an absurdly complicated arrangement and really a way of evading the constitutional provision forbidding special acts applying to one particular place. This condition was swept away in 1904, when all cities were included in one classification and some special provisions were made to meet the needs of the largest municipalities. The village, township, and special districts were still retained.

In 1914 a general revision of the school laws was enacted, so fundamental in character that it produced almost a new system. Like the act of 1853, it followed in the wake of the adoption of a new constitution by which a state government of a progressive character was put into operation and much of the old machinery was overhauled or discarded. The time seemed ripe for a new school code, and educators pressed for reforms long discussed and long needed.

The law destroyed the old system for the rural districts by making the county, instead of the township, the unit of organization. A county board of education with large powers controlled the schools (city and village districts of more than three thousand population excepted) and appointed a county superintendent. He was assisted by district superintendents at first chosen by the districts, but after 1921 elected by the county board upon nomination by the county superintendent—a definite centralization of the system. The old township districts as well as the old "special districts" became mere subdivisions of the county with boundary lines subject to change—under certain restrictions—by the county board. Both types of districts were to be called simply "rural school districts." Thus, Ohio at last modernized her rural school organization and abandoned the traditional ideal of local control.

Down to 1880, the high school was a city or village institution. In that year, only thirteen townships in the entire state had separate high-school buildings, though parts of a number of townships were included in special districts. The tendency of the rural sections to make use of village and city high schools was encouraged by legislation in the last two decades of the century as well as by the alternative of the union of districts or townships for high-school purposes. If a centralized system was adopted, a two-year high school was required as a minimum. The spread of centralization meant the spread of the high school in the rural sections. In 1921, the Bing Act for compulsory attendance of pupils up to eighteen years of age forced the rural districts to pay tuition and transportation or provide high schools for pupils who had completed the elementary grades.

One of the curious facts in connection with the development of the high school is the absence of any clear-cut distinction between high schools and elementary schools for nearly half a century. Spelling, reading, writing, arithmetic, grammar, and geography constituted the fundamentals of the elementary school for many years, with history and physiology occasionally being taught there but more often studied in the high school. The curriculum of the latter in the 1850's included, besides the two subjects mentioned, such subjects as algebra, philosophy, chemistry, geometry, astronomy, and surveying, but by 1880 it was expanding to take in Latin, Greek, botany, bookkeeping, physical geography, rhetoric, and a variety of other subjects closely approaching work of a collegiate character. With no uniformity either in curriculum or in the number of courses or years of study, the high school was decidedly a variable quantity. Not until 1902 was the term accurately defined by law and the secondary schools classified. High schools of three grades were then described and minimum standards required of each. Those of the first grade were to offer four years of study for thirty-two weeks each year with sixteen courses the requisite for graduation. These standards were reduced for the others down to two years for the third grade with sessions of twenty-eight weeks. All schools below this category were classed as elementary schools. The curriculum might include history, composition, rhetoric, literature, algebra, geometry, natural science, political or mental science, languages, commercial and industrial branches, and such other advanced work as the board of education might direct. Upon the state school commissioner fell the burden of inspecting and classifying high schools.

The idea of compulsory attendance of pupils developed slowly in Ohio. Advocated as early as 1857 by School Commissioner Anson Smyth and considered at various times by the assembly, it lacked the popular support necessary to obtain legislation for many years. In 1877 came the first enactment—a mild requirement of twelve weeks' attendance in each school year for children between the ages of eight and fourteen. So many exemptions were permitted that the law accomplished very little. Not until 1889 was an effective law passed—one far more drastic in character than the earlier one. The provision for truant officers in every locality made the law's enforcement more than a formality, though it encountered in some places the hostility of factory owners desirous of using child labor. Gradually the requirements were made more drastic until in 1921, by the Bing Law, attendance was required between the ages of six and eighteen, unless, of course, the pupil had been graduated from a first-grade high school. An individual might be released to work at the age of sixteen provided he had completed the seventh grade.

Early requirements for teaching were quite simple. The applicant secured a certificate to teach by satisfying a local board of examiners as to his competence. A county board of three examiners was instituted by the act of 1853, and examinations became more formal. In 1864 a state board of examiners, appointed by the state school commissioner, was authorized to examine persons of unusual competence. Certificates by this board were to be accepted anywhere in the state. The subjects for examination and the types of certificates issued by the various city, county, and state examiners increased in number toward the close of the century until the system became unnecessarily complicated. The new code of 1914 and subsequent amendments strengthened the authority of the state board of examiners and brought about greater uniformity in the system. Requirements of training and experience had now reached the point where teaching was no longer a refuge for incompetents and failures in other walks of life, but a profession in itself.

To fit teachers for their work, teachers' institutes were organized in the late 1840's with some slight support from the counties. Counties were permitted to unite for this purpose in 1861, and in 1873 the system was placed upon a permanent basis by a law defining carefully the method of holding institutes and financing them. Cities, counties, or groups of counties might have institutes of their own. Until the early years of the twentieth century, the movement prospered, and the teachers of nearly every county had an opportunity to spend several days each year attending the sessions. But as the requirements for teacher training became more extensive and the colleges, universities, and normal schools offered summer sessions for teachers, the institutes lost much of their importance.

The early normal schools were privately owned, but in the 1850's the state teachers' association began an agitation for state aid. The association itself tried to operate a normal school, "The McNeely Normal School of Ohio," at Hopedale in Harrison County in 1855, but it was not a financial success and the association withdrew its support, though the school was continued under other auspices for many years. In southwestern Ohio in these years, a group of teachers projected a normal school that resulted in the "National Normal University" at Lebanon. The school was a pronounced success despite the absence of state aid. Altogether, seven normal schools were established between 1850 and 1875, while some of the cities were developing their own training schools. The state refused to act, even though most of the other states had such schools, until 1902, when two were created. One was to be operated in connection with Ohio University, at Athens, and the other, at Oxford, was to be associated with Miami University.

In 1910 Bowling Green State Normal College was founded for northwestern Ohio and in 1913 Kent State Normal College, for the northeast. With many counties and cities operating their own schools and with the various colleges and universities offering work in education, Ohio was well supplied with teacher-training schools.

In the field of higher education, the most significant development was the appearance of state-supported universities. Except for a nominal connection with Ohio and Miami Universities, the state had left the field of college instruction to denominational and private institutions. The organization of the "Ohio Agricultural and Mechanical College,"[1] which opened in 1873, was the first important step; but in this case a land grant from the Federal Government was the chief inducement. The college, renamed "Ohio State University," was under state control, however, and received aid from the state treasury. Not until 1891 was it given the benefit of a direct state tax levy making its income more regular. Ohio and Miami Universities were given this privilege in 1896 and became state institutions in fact as well as name. Wilberforce University, in existence since 1856 for Negro education, has received state aid since 1887 for its normal and industrial departments. It also received a special levy in 1900. Thus the state became responsible for four universities as well as the normal schools already referred to. Three cities, Cincinnati, Toledo, and Akron, also operated municipal universities, supported in part from local taxation.

This extension of public aid to higher education was not accompanied by the decline of the denominational colleges. In fact, the worst years for most of these institutions were the middle years of the nineteenth century, when they were

---

[1] This institution is dealt with in Chapter XIII.

just becoming established and endowments were too small to be of much help. Every denomination aspired to have its own college, and Ohio was dotted with many weak institutions of a narrowly sectarian character scarcely deserving the name of colleges. There were no large numbers of youths seeking a college education, and Ohio's twenty-two colleges and universities in 1859 had but 3,873 students, of which 2,105 were in the preparatory departments. Oberlin, with 181 students in its college department, was the largest. The Civil War years were difficult years for higher education, but the later years of the century saw the gradual growth of the more soundly established colleges as the state developed in wealth and the high schools increased the number of available entrants. Sectarianism received less emphasis, the curriculum was broadened, and the idea of a college education became less of a novelty. Not until the twentieth century, however, did the principle of higher education for the masses transform the enrollment of colleges and universities, both state and private, and make college degrees as numerous as high-school diplomas had been a generation earlier. With an industrial civilization demanding specialized training along so many lines and emphasizing the economic value of a college degree, the institutions of higher learning had no choice but to extend their facilities to all.

One of the striking tendencies of higher education in the nineteenth century was the spread of the idea of college education for women. Ohio institutions were pioneers in this respect, with Oberlin leading the way for the entire nation. Otterbein and Antioch, the latter under the guidance of Horace Mann in the 1850's, were equally liberal. But down to the Civil War, female seminaries, little more than high schools in reality, were still attracting girl students in considerable numbers, though feeling the competition of the public high schools. When Ohio State University opened its doors in 1873, women were admitted on an equality with men. The various denominations that had been maintaining separate seminaries for girls, often in the same towns as their colleges, began to accept the idea of coeducation until, by the end of the century, it had become the rule and exclusion the exception.

Among the great American educational leaders of the nineteenth century,[2] the name of one Ohioan has a conspicuous place. William Rainey Harper, president and creator of the University of Chicago and an accomplished scholar of Semitic languages, was born at New Concord, Muskingum County, in 1856, was educated at Muskingum College and at Yale, taught for several years at Denison and later at Yale, and in 1892 assumed the headship of the newly established University of Chicago. Here he broke new ground in emphasizing complete academic freedom, the importance of graduate study and research, university extension work, the division of the academic year into four quarters, and the concentration of students on a few subjects. Almost overnight a great university grew up under his guidance. His death at the age of fifty removed an important figure in American education. Among college executives, Charles F. Thwing, of Western Reserve, William Oxley Thompson, of Ohio State University, Henry Churchill King, of Oberlin, and many others have done much for the state's educational progress. Indeed, it seems that Ohio educators have found their energies chiefly absorbed at home by the problems of giving the state satisfactory schools and colleges and producing an educated body of citizens. In one respect, however, the

---

[2] Horace Mann belongs to Massachusetts rather than Ohio, though he spent the closing years of his life as president of Antioch College, Yellow Springs, Ohio.

state has claimed equality with, if not preëminence over, all of her sisters. William Holmes McGuffey (1800–1873), born in Pennsylvania but spending many years as a college teacher and president at Miami University, Cincinnati College, and Ohio University, compiled a series of school readers that, with many revisions, enjoyed great popularity from the late 1830's down to the early years of the twentieth century.[3] The edifying moral lessons and the numerous selections suitable for recitation were factors of prime importance in influencing the literary tastes and ethical standards of the generations that used them. In many rural homes, where books were marks of affluence, the Bible and the McGuffey readers were almost the only available roads to culture. The readers for the higher grades were particularly valuable, for they contained numerous selections from well-known literary masterpieces and orations otherwise unobtainable to the great majority. Almost as important were the arithmetics and algebras of Dr. Joseph Ray (1807–1855), born in Virginia but living most of his life in Cincinnati. Deserting medicine for teaching, he was for many years a teacher of mathematics at Woodward College. On its reorganization as a high school in 1851, he became its principal. His textbooks, later revised by others, retained their popularity for a half-century after his death. In the next generation, Thomas W. Harvey (1821–1893), state school commissioner from 1871 to 1875, was the author of grammars that made him almost as well-known as McGuffey and Ray. Despite the smiles of the more sophisticated youth of today and the criticisms of educational authorities, few of the older generation brought

---

[3] The readers for the first four grades were the work of McGuffey himself, but the reader for the fifth, later expanded into two, was the work of McGuffey's son, Alexander, a teacher who later became an attorney living in Cincinnati.

up on these familiar manuals will concede that Ohio schools improved their standards when the old textbooks were put aside.

The Newspaper

The modern newspaper was just emerging in the 1850's. The telegraph and the improved mail service resulting from the spread of the railway made a rapid dissemination of news possible and added freshness and variety even to the smaller county papers. No longer were they dependent for news upon week-old copies of metropolitan journals. Greater independence in editorial viewpoint toward events of national importance also resulted, as the Ohio papers could not await the arrival of the Washington party organs for expressions of opinion. For example, John Brown's Raid in 1859 was known in most parts of Ohio a few hours after it had occurred and long before the Eastern papers reached the state.

The development of the news aspect, the greater speed and cheapness in delivering papers to subscribers, the spread of common school education, and the growth of cities enlarged circulations and increased the value of newspapers as an advertising medium. The process was furthered by the use of the steam press by the larger papers. Politics ceased to be the primary concern of the press, nor was there such dependence upon party support as there had been in the past. Newspapers in the larger cities could exist without subsidies from the party organizations in the form of public printing contracts or postmasterships for editors. At Columbus, the state organs of the two parties were in a worse situation, as they were compelled to devote much space to political matters, while the public printing, once a rich plum, under the new constitution of 1851 had to be awarded to the lowest bidder. However, at Cleveland and

Cincinnati, while by no means oblivious to politics, the papers were emphasizing news and advertising and were not dependent on party appeal for support. The Cincinnati *Commercial*, claiming a larger circulation than any other Western paper, placed advertising first in importance, news second, personal and literary gossip and pleasant reading third, and editorials fourth, ranking below everything but letters from readers. Its frank statement that advertising was "indispensably necessary" was a clear indication that the modern era in journalism was at hand.

The Civil War gave a great impetus to newspaper reading. Accounts of battles and of movements of armies aroused tremendous interest, and there appeared a corps of war correspondents whose stories thrilled thousands of readers and aided greatly in popularizing the newspaper. In Ohio the press became in the latter half of the nineteenth century a significant factor in intellectual progress surpassed only by the development of the public school system. Despite the growing importance of the business aspect of the newspaper, the editor was usually the controlling voice, and not until the close of the century was his individuality submerged in the larger papers, which had then become great business corporations.

The Civil War generation gave to Ohio journalism a number of important figures. The last of the "old guard" of the Jacksonian era, Samuel Medary, lived long enough to carry on a bitter struggle for peace in the tempestuous war years, but not long enough to see the conflict's close. Editor of the *Ohio Statesman* almost continuously for nearly twenty years, Medary deserted journalism in Buchanan's administration to become Governor of the Territory of Minnesota and then Governor of Kansas. With the outbreak of the war, he returned to Columbus to edit the *Crisis*, an organ of the Peace Democrats. His hostility to the war placed his name under a cloud and obscured for later generations his real services to the state. Yet in the two decades preceding the war, he was probably more widely known than any Ohio editor and was an important national figure in his party. His influence was a potent factor in bringing about the meeting of the constitutional convention of 1850–1851 and the later adoption of the new constitution by the voters. He was also actively interested in agricultural improvement and served on the state board of agriculture for several years. Medary's methods were those of the old school of journalists: violent partisanship, free use of personalities, and skill at invective.

Of a different type was Murat Halstead, Ohio's best-known newspaper man in the post-bellum years. Associated for many years with the Cincinnati *Commercial* and the later *Commercial Gazette*, he was a powerful influence in the Republican Party and a writer of skill, vigor, and independence. His accounts of the party conventions of 1860 rank among the classics of journalism. His facile pen was not confined to newspaper work but produced a number of books on contemporary subjects, such as biographies of McKinley, Admiral Dewey, and Roosevelt, and accounts of the Spanish-American War, Cuba, and the Philippines. These books were written in popular style with little discrimination and have slight value today.

Whitelaw Reid began his newspaper career on a small Xenia paper before the Civil War but presently achieved the distinction of serving under Horace Greeley on the New York *Tribune,* and eventually succeeded that brilliant but ill-starred figure. Reid wrote several books, but for Ohioans his two-volume work, *Ohio in the War,* will remain his chief claim to fame. Written soon after the war's close, it contains much material of which the author had

first-hand knowledge and is still the chief fund of information for Ohio's part in the great sectional struggle. Reid's
services as ambassador to France and Great Britain in his
later years made him a figure of importance in American
diplomacy.

Joseph Medill began his newspaper career on a small
Ohio paper, the Coshocton *Republican*, but soon moved to
Cleveland to take control of the *Leader*, and then in 1855
to Chicago, where, until his death in 1888, he was either
editor of or a controlling factor in the Chicago *Tribune*,
and one of the well-known figures in American journalism.
Like Reid, he secured his start on a small Ohio newspaper
but left his native state to achieve fame.

Edward Deering Mansfield, a graduate of West Point
and Princeton, was editor of Cincinnati newspapers, correspondent of the New York *Times*, author of several books,
and the first state commissioner of statistics, in which position he compiled reports of great value on economic and
social conditions in the state.[4] Donn Piatt, of Mack-o-
chee, lawyer, editor, poet, and politician, was a picturesque
and interesting, if eccentric, figure to Ohioans of the Civil
War generation. Januarius Aloysius McGahan left a
Perry County farm at the age of sixteen to become eventually the Paris correspondent of the New York *Herald*
during the Franco-Prussian War and later the Russian
representative of the London *Daily News*. His accounts of
Turkish atrocities in Bulgaria aroused tremendous interest
in England, and when he died suddenly of typhus at
Constantinople in 1878, he had won international recognition. Albert Shaw, for many years editor of the *Review of
Reviews*, was born at Shandon, in Butler County. The
names of many others could be cited, but the above examples

---

[4] His first report appeared in 1857.

are typical of the contribution of Ohio to American journalism.

Among the cartoonists and makers of comic strips, the names of Richard F. Outcalt and Frederick Burr Opper deserve a high rank. Outcalt, born in Lancaster in 1863, studied art at Cincinnati, worked on the *Enquirer* for some years, but won fame in New York, where he drew for the New York *World* the "Yellow Kid" comic strips, the first of their kind. The "Buster Brown" series later contributed further to his popularity with readers of the Sunday supplements.

Opper, born at Madison, Lake County, in 1857, became a cartoonist of note on the New York *Journal* when that paper was the chief organ of William Randolph Hearst. Opper's cartoons of McKinley and Mark Hanna were particularly effective. He also enjoyed great popularity for his comic strips, "Happy Hooligan," "Alphonse and Gaston," and "Maud," the kicking mule.

The names of other Ohioans with reputations as newspaper artists would make a long list, but such names as William A. Rogers, once of *Harper's Magazine* and later of the New York *Herald*, Frank McKinney Hubbard, originator of "Abe Martin," with his homely philosophy, and Charles R. Macauley, who drew for the New York *Herald*, the New York *World*, and the Brooklyn *Eagle* and was awarded a Pulitzer prize in 1929, are representative of Ohio's contribution. Of those who remained in their native state, William Ireland, of the Columbus *Dispatch*, Claude Shafer, of the Cincinnati *Times-Star*, and J. H. (Hal) Donahey, of the Cleveland *Plain Dealer*, are perhaps the best-known.

The importance of the newspaper as a training school for other fields is evidenced by such names as Charles F. Browne, William Dean Howells, and Samuel S. Cox.

Browne, as has been seen, made "Artemus Ward" famous through the columns of an Ohio newspaper. Howells was reared in a printing office, as his father, W. C. Howells, was editor of the *Ashtabula Sentinel* for many years. The future novelist assisted his father and later was on the staff of the *Ohio State Journal*. He and Samuel R. Reed made this sober old party organ one of the most readable of newspapers, giving to it an ironical humor and facetious tone unlike the style of any other paper in the state in the years just prior to the Civil War. But Howells was not primarily a newspaper man, and literature presently claimed him for its own. Samuel S. Cox, though immortalized by his "Sunset" editorial, soon found politics far more to his liking and financially more remunerative than attempting to edit the *Ohio Statesman*.

Of the state's influential newspapers in the latter half of the nineteenth century, probably the most important were the *Commercial* (later the *Commercial Gazette*) and the *Enquirer*, at Cincinnati. The former, Republican but not blindly partisan, owed much to Halstead's guidance. The latter, controlled from the Civil War period by Washington McLean and his son, John R. McLean, held its place as the great organ of the Democratic Party in the Ohio Valley. In other large cities, several newspapers could boast of long and prosperous careers, particularly the *Ohio State Journal*, at Columbus, the *Blade*, at Toledo, the *Journal*, at Dayton, and the two Cleveland rivals, the *Leader* and the *Plain Dealer*. But if age constituted a valid claim to greatness, the venerable *Scioto Gazette*, of Chillicothe, could claim precedence over all.

For the Civil War generation especially, Ohio's newspapers possessed great cultural value. Libraries were few, books not so easily obtainable as today, and magazines scarcer and of more limited appeal. But the newspaper

was to be found everywhere and was read thoroughly—
news, editorials, poems, stories, advertisements, and all.
As an educational factor, it deserves high rank, and despite
certain crudities and imperfections, was probably a more
potent influence in the enlightenment of the masses than
its more finished, more sensational, and financially more
powerful successor of the present day.

In recent years Ohio has witnessed the consolidation process, common to the whole country, which has reduced the
number of city papers and has made the remaining ones
all the more powerful. At the same time, many of the
small-town papers have been dying out as the isolation in
which they had once prospered disappears. In the twentieth century there have also appeared the chains of
newspapers under one ownership with certain common
policies but with the individual papers adapted to the
interests of the particular localities. The Scripps-Howard
group, a national organization with units in the larger cities
(originally the Scripps-McRae League), has been particularly successful in Ohio. Some attempts have been made
by Ohioans to operate chains of newspapers in the smaller
cities, but these enterprises have not in all cases been
successful.

The teaching of journalism in the colleges and universities has become widespread, with Ohio State University
one of the pioneers in this field. The future of the profession may lie in the hands of the graduates of these schools
despite the criticisms of skeptics who question the value of
such training. However, the modern newspaper is largely
the product of the industrial age, and individuals can do
little to alter its tendencies or to give it new direction.
Uniformity and standardization are the order of the day
in journalism as in almost everything else in American
life.

SELECTED BIBLIOGRAPHY

The *Ohio Archæological and Historical Quarterly* contains two good studies of educational legislation: one by Edward A. Miller, "History of Educational Legislation in Ohio from 1803 to 1850" (Vol. XXVII, pp. 1–271), and the other by Nelson L. Bossing, "History of Educational Legislation in Ohio from 1851 to 1925" (Vol. XXXIX, pp. 78–397). Much briefer is Mary Hinsdale, "A Legislative History of the Public School System of the State of Ohio," *Report of the United States Commissioner of Education, 1900–1901,* Vol. I, pp. 129–159. An early account of Ohio's schools is James W. Taylor, *A Manual of the Ohio School System* (Cincinnati, 1857). A summary of education in the nineteenth century, from the administrative viewpoint, is found in Samuel P. Orth, "The Centralization of Administration in Ohio," *Columbia University Studies in History, Economics and Public Law* (New York, 1903), Vol. XVI, pp. 23–74. A stimulating sketch of educational developments is "Education in Ohio Today," by George W. Rightmire, in *Ohio State University Bulletin,* Vol. XXXVII, No. 1, Sept. 15, 1932. The *Annual Reports of the Commissioner of Common Schools,* beginning in 1854, are of much value. Institutions of higher learning are sketched in Galbreath, Vol. I, pp. 465–511. Most of these have their own histories, which should be consulted for details. Horace Mann's Ohio career is covered in *Ohio Archæological and Historical Quarterly,* Vol. XIV, pp. 12–27, "Horace Mann and Antioch College," by George Allen Hubbell. The story of the McGuffey readers may be read in Henry H. Vail, *A History of the McGuffey Readers* (Cleveland, 1911).

Randall and Ryan, Vol. V, pp. 10–16, lists and briefly characterizes the leading Ohio newspaper men. The *Dictionary of American Biography* includes the better-known figures. The larger histories of American journalism give little space to Ohio newspapers and editors. The character of the early newspapers and the changes that have come about can be understood only through an examination of the files of several in the collections of the different historical societies. Just published (December, 1933) is Osman C. Hooper, *History of Ohio Journalism.*

CHAPTER XVIII

THE PROGRESSIVE MOVEMENT

The Background of the Movement

A^N oligarchy of business bosses strangled Cleveland
and every other city in Ohio. Two million city-
dwellers were in servitude to three or four men who
stood astride of the State, who filled the State offices,
who selected members of the House of Representatives
and candidates for the courts as they would select clerks
in their offices. Cleveland, Toledo, and other progressive communities were compelled to have their crooked
bosses and their vice districts, because these conditions
contributed to the continued supremacy of the interests
that ruled the State. Cleveland could not achieve
itself, because in doing so it menaced the private interests of Senator Hanna and Senator Foraker, of John R.
McLean and lesser bosses.[1]

Thus, a political idealist (Frederic C. Howe), who as a
student at Johns Hopkins University had glimpsed a vision
of a better-ordered society from the lectures of James
Bryce, Woodrow Wilson, and others, recalls the difficulties
that beset him as an earnest young reformer entering the
Ohio Legislature in the early years of the present century.
Open corruption, he found, was seldom used, but there
were employed skillful and well-financed lobbyists who
permitted members of the legislature to win substantial
sums at poker or lured them into other forbidden pleasures,

---

[1] Howe, *The Confessions of a Reformer*, p. 158 (used by permission of the
author).

after which a fear of exposure tended to render them docile instruments of political manipulation. Throughout the state friendly presses and ambitious local politicians served to make the system an effective one: machine politics had reached the peak of its influence in Ohio.

The profits of large investments were, of course, involved in the success of well-planned and effective political strategy; hence in city, as well as in state, politics methods of the most unscrupulous sort were used as a means to the desired end. Washington Gladden, the nationally known pastor of a prominent church of Columbus (the First Congregational), after serving for two years (1900–1902) on the council of that city, declared that his experience had taught him "that a corporation, in dealing with a city, need not be expected to tell the truth." Men whose word in private life could have been relied upon implicitly he found as the representatives of a corporation dealing with the city to be apparently guided by a wholly "different rule of morality."

Aside from the obvious strength inherent in an alliance of political and economic forces that had tremendous sums to expend in achieving their ends and remunerative offices to bestow as rewards for loyal service, the existing political order probably found its greatest bulwark in the widely accepted doctrine of *laissez-faire*. This theory taught the desirability of allowing industry to develop without governmental restriction upon its freedom of action. Large groups of Ohioans, like others among their contemporaries, were inclined to believe in the efficacy of that fierce individualism which had spurred on the pioneer to the winning of a fortune from the resources of a virgin continent. True to the traditions of frontier America, many resented any considerable interference with the expression of personal initiative. If unusual success came to some, often it served rather as an inspiration to similar attainment on the part of others rather than as an incitement to envy.

Associated with these factors was a widely held impression that what was most profitable for "Big Business" in the state must of necessity form the foundation for the welfare of other economic classes. The prosperity of the wealthy and powerful, it was supposed, created economic opportunities that enabled the benefits of industry to percolate to the masses. The native ability of many associated with the régime of machine politics could not be doubted, and the large possibilities of statesmanship and the many admirable traits of character that were recognized in the personality of such a man as Mark Hanna caused many to prefer men of his type to persons whose generous promises and good intentions often far exceeded their capacity to perform.

Nevertheless, rumblings of discontent had for some time been heard as large corporations had increased to monopolistic proportions and tended to control to an enlarged degree the political destiny of the state and nation. The remedy for the evil, however, seemed difficult to determine. Long before, some had suggested that monopolies should be prohibited, state laws had been passed to deal with the problem, and an Ohio Senator, John Sherman, had lent his name and influence to the national anti-trust law of 1890, which declared illegal any combination in restraint of trade in interstate or foreign commerce.

The enforcement of such laws, however, had been extremely difficult. As has already been shown, an unusually conscientious attorney general of the state, David K. Watson, ascertaining that the creation of the Standard Oil Trust was apparently a violation of the laws of Ohio, had brought suit in the state supreme court in May, 1890, declaring that the Standard Oil Company of

Ohio had forfeited its rights to a charter and ought to be dissolved. The colossal difficulties attending the effective enforcement of existing statutes, however, became readily apparent as this case came up for consideration by the courts during the subsequent years.[2]

Moreover, in national politics, the absence of an express constitutional sanction, the fear of hampering the success of legitimate business, the ease of evading restrictions of various types, and the conservative attitude of the Federal courts, all contributed to the problem of formulating and enforcing effective anti-trust legislation. Clearly the regulation of "Big Business" lent itself to no easy solution.

A New Spirit in Municipal Affairs

As a result, many persons came to feel that new leaders and drastic remedies provided the only feasible method of restoring a reasonable equality of opportunity. One of the ablest and most courageous persons identified with this viewpoint was Tom Loftin Johnson, the son of a gifted but impoverished Kentucky family. Having reached a position of wealth and prominence as a steel manufacturer, street-railway magnate, and inventor of street car equipment, he was led by a chance introduction to the writings of Henry George to doubt the essential fairness of the system upon which his fortune was based. At length he was wholeheartedly convinced by what he considered George's unanswerable arguments in favor of the idea of a single tax, the proposal that all taxes should be levied upon the unimproved worth of land in order that society might thus reap the benefit of socially created value. Aflame with the zeal of the convert, he decided to test his ability in the field of politics. Although previous to this time he had not even concerned himself to the extent of voting, in 1890

---

[2] See Chap. XV.

and 1892 he was elected from the Cleveland district to Congress, where he showed himself to be an ardent supporter of the principle of free trade and endeavored to accomplish a more equitable distribution of the burden of taxation in the District of Columbia. After again turning his attention to street railways for a time, in 1901 he was elected Mayor of Cleveland, a position that for the next eight years was to serve as a medium for the expression of his conspicuous talents.

While Johnson's administrations "tried to give the people clear and well lighted streets, pure water, free access to their parks, public baths and comfort stations, a good police department, careful market inspection, a rigid system of weights and measures, and to make the charitable and correctional institutions aid rather than punish wrongdoers," contributions along these lines were not considered of fundamental importance. Johnson placed chief emphasis upon his attempts to lighten the burdens that he considered the masses were bearing while the more favored classes were escaping with a share that was relatively inadequate. He organized a "tax school" (with an able assistant, Peter Witt, in charge, and with Newton D. Baker as legal advisor) for the purpose of revealing by plats of local areas the inequalities of taxation. The work of this organization was ultimately halted by the injunction process, but not until the path had been opened for important changes in the taxing system.

An attempt to inaugurate municipal control over the street railways met with similar difficulties: over fifty injunctions were issued by the courts, the twelve-year-old charter of Cleveland was declared to be unconstitutional by the Ohio Supreme Court, and a new municipal code was adopted by the legislature—apparently for the purpose of reducing the mayor of Cleveland to a mere figurehead.

The struggle, however, was not without its victories, including the introduction of three-cent fare in the largest city in Ohio. In the fall of 1909, Johnson was defeated for another term, yet he could rejoice in the knowledge that his administrations had brought permanent benefits and that his able protégé, Newton D. Baker, had again been elected to the office of city solicitor.

Only less prominent than Johnson as a protestant against the existing order in municipal affairs was Samuel M. Jones, who in 1897 had been elected Mayor of Toledo. A native of Wales, brought to America as a child, he had eventually gained a fortune in the oil business and as a manufacturer of sucker-rods used in that industry. Originally nominated as one satisfactory to the business interests and as one who would assist the public utilities in securing lucrative franchises, he showed himself to be more interested in remedying the evils in civic affairs than in securing concessions for wealthy corporations. Large of stature, of sandy complexion, with "an eye that looked right into the center of your skull," he was richly endowed with humor and was zealous in carrying into official life those principles of the golden rule that had been his guideposts in private business.

The establishment of free kindergartens, public playgrounds, free concerts in the parks, and an eight-hour day for employees of the city indicate the direction of some of his efforts. Like Johnson, he believed in the public ownership of public utilities and labored to prevent the renewal of such corporate privileges as he considered unfavorable to the public welfare. Tolstoyan in his skepticism of the value of punitive measures, he relieved policemen of their clubs and employed every opportunity to exempt the unfortunate from serving workhouse sentences. He knew "no such thing as murderers, or even criminals, or 'good' people, or 'bad' people, they were all to him men and indeed brothers." Hence, on Monday mornings he customarily listened to the tales of drunkards, disorderly persons, and women of tainted reputation and dismissed them with a sermon directed not at them but at a social system that he considered responsible for the evil ways of individuals.

Society in general paid lip service to the golden rule but probably agreed rather definitely with a very successful evangelist who held meetings during this period, at one of which he declared, "I am for the golden rule myself up to a certain point, and then I want to take the shotgun and the club." Hence, the chamber of commerce, the press, and the churches were opposed to Jones, "good" people shunned him, and at times it seemed that "everyone was against him except the workers and the underworld." Yet he was four times elected mayor on a nonpartisan ticket and was serving in that office at the time of his death in 1904. Shortly afterwards, at the suggestion of Tom Johnson and others, Brand Whitlock, a disciple and former secretary of Jones, was urged to run for the position. The son of a Methodist clergyman of northwestern Ohio, Whitlock had gained experience as a journalist and as a lawyer that had given him an outlook similar to that of Jones. Elected to the office and supported by an able group of officials, Whitlock continued the same general policies, though doing so often meant that his social contacts were narrowed in the more favored circles of his city, and at the end of four successive terms, he was relieved to retire from a public life that had been full of strenuous combat.

Progressivism in State and National Politics

Simultaneous with the progressive movement in municipal politics was a corresponding trend, though not immedi-

ately attended with success, in state affairs. In 1899
"Golden Rule" Jones had run for the governorship on a
nonpartisan ticket against George K. Nash, a Republican
of Columbus, who had served two terms as attorney
general of the state under Governor Foster and who was in
thorough accord with the party leaders, and against
John R. McLean, the wealthy owner of the potent Cincinnati *Enquirer*, who had gained a fortune in the development
of public utilities in Washington, D. C. McLean represented the conservative business element in the Democratic
Party and exercised a tremendous influence on the policies
of that organization, though his position was neither so
secure nor so effective as that of Hanna in the Republican
Party. In the hope of capitalizing upon such a spirit of
reform as was manifesting itself against Hanna's organization, McLean strangely enough came forth with a relatively
radical program including the adoption of the initiative
and the referendum and opposition to boss rule. Jones's
platform was distinctly more socialistic, with provisions
for the abolition of political parties and the direct nomination of candidates, direct law-making, public ownership of
all public utilities, an eight-hour day for unskilled labor,
union standards for skilled employees, the abolition of the
contract system on public works, and state aid for unemployment. In view of the relative prosperity of the country
and the Republican claim to credit for the successful
termination of the Spanish-American War, the vote of
106,000 for Jones to 417,000 for Nash and 368,000 for
McLean can be interpreted only as an expression of considerable discontent with existing conditions in political
affairs.

The problem of corporation control at length seemed to
demand further attention, and during Nash's administrations the legislature (in 1902) passed acts requiring both

Ohio and outside corporations to file annual reports and to pay a fee on their capital employed within the state, and taxing foreign life and fire insurance companies for the privilege of doing business in Ohio. Another change of primary importance was the adoption of a constitutional amendment, effective November, 1903, giving the governor for the first time the power of veto—which might be overridden by a two-thirds vote of each house of the legislature.

The Republicans two years before (in 1901) had secured the reëlection of Nash over James Kilbourne,[3] a leading Columbus manufacturer and banker. Now, in 1903, they turned to Myron T. Herrick, a Cleveland attorney who had risen to financial power as an officer of the Society for Savings in that city, had become president of the American Bankers' Association (in 1901), and was to reach the climax of his career as United States Ambassador to France (1912–1914; 1921–1929). Herrick represented the conservative business men of the state and, even more particularly, the Republicanism of Mark Hanna, with whom he had been closely associated in politics since 1888. The Foraker wing of the party in this year had to be content with the nomination for lieutenant-governor, which went to Warren Gamaliel Harding. Hanna himself was looking forward to a reëlection to the Senate by the next legislature, so the contest was popularly called the "campaign of the three H's."

The Democrats accepted Tom L. Johnson, who during the previous year had toured the state in an imported automobile—popularly called the "Red Devil"—and had held meetings in a circus tent, pitched wherever an audience

---

[3] Kilbourne was a grandson of the New Englander of the same name who had founded Worthington, Ohio (in 1803), and who had later been a Member of Congress.

could be found for his expostulations of the dangers of corporation influence and the need for better tax legislation. As a candidate for the governorship, he declared for the valuation for taxation purposes of all property at its full value, a two-cent-per-mile rate for railroad passenger fare, measures beneficial to labor, and the nomination of senatorial candidates by state conventions. The rank and file of the Democratic Party, however, was unwilling to go to the lengths proposed by Johnson, the popularity of President Roosevelt worked clearly in favor of the Republicans, and Herrick was elected by a margin of more than one hundred thousand votes over Johnson.

In the meantime, the prominence of Mark Hanna in the Republican Party had caused Roosevelt considerable uneasiness, as the latter looked forward to a nomination in 1904. The matter was brought to a head by the action of Senator Foraker, who had his own Presidential ambitions for 1908 and, as a step in that direction, wished to displace Hanna as the acknowledged leader of Ohio Republicanism. Accordingly, Foraker summoned representatives of the press to his office in Washington in May, 1903, and referred to unimportant newspaper statements to the effect that the Ohio state convention, which would meet the next month, would refuse to indorse Roosevelt. Foraker then stated that he deemed it a mistake for the delegates not to vote such an indorsement and that the difficulty had been created by the friends of Hanna. The latter, practically forced to make a statement, told a newspaperman that he thought it unwise for the convention of 1903 to pass upon a matter that was properly the work of the national convention of 1904; but he also telegraphed to Roosevelt, intimating that Foraker's attitude was a reason for his stand. The President, however, peremptorily asserted that his real supporters would sanction his nomination, and Hanna felt obliged to telegraph him that he would not oppose Roosevelt's indorsement by the Ohio convention. Such action was taken by that body, and a year later, following his nomination by the national convention, Roosevelt received in Ohio almost twice as many popular votes as the Democratic candidate, Alton B. Parker.

In state politics, however, the long succession of Republican triumphs was about to be broken. Hanna, who only a month before had been reëlected to the United States Senate by an overwhelming majority of the legislature (115:25) and who was seemingly at the zenith of his political power, died after a short illness in February, 1904. Governor Herrick sincerely wished to avoid antagonisms, but he felt called upon to demand that the legislature make certain changes in a pending measure, the Brannock Bill, concerned with the establishment of local option on the question of the operation of saloons in the residential districts of cities. Herrick insisted that the alterations were necessary to insure its constitutionality and its reasonable enforcement, and the suggestions were in general included in the law as it was enacted, but his stand upon the question brought him the bitter opposition of the Anti-Saloon League.

Simultaneously, he incurred the animosity of an entirely different element. The Mayor of Bratenahl, a suburb of Cleveland, had decided to enforce the state law against gambling in connection with the race track in that vicinity that was well patronized by Clevelanders. As a result, the owners of the course secured the passage of the Chisholm Bill, specifically legalizing the selling of pools at race-meets. Herrick, believing that this was a direct violation of the state constitution, administered a veto, an act that at once brought down upon him the wrath of the "sporting crowd" in the state.

The Democratic nominee of 1905, John M. Pattison, of Clermont County, a former legislator and Congressman, on the other hand, agreed with the contentions of the Anti-Saloon League and had had no occasion to antagonize other groups in the state. In the midst of the campaign, Secretary of War Taft in a noted speech at Akron denounced "Boss" Coss and the local Republican ticket of Cincinnati —possibly as a means of expressing his sympathy with the reformist tendencies of President Roosevelt.

These various factors contributed to the election of Pattison as the first Democratic Governor in a decade and a half. The remainder of the Republican ticket, however, was elected, and when Pattison died in June, 1906, Andrew L. Harris, a Preble County lawyer-farmer, who had served in both houses of the legislature, succeeded to the governorship. A constitutional amendment had been ratified in 1905, providing for the election of state and county officers in the even-numbered years and extending the terms of those in office for an additional year. Thus the next contest for the governorship did not occur until 1908, when Judson Harmon, who had been a judge of the common pleas court and of the superior court in Cincinnati and had served as Attorney General of the United States in the second administration of President Cleveland, defeated Harris for reëlection. The dissatisfaction of "wet" Republicans with Harris's attitude on the liquor question was a contributing factor toward this result. Excepting the candidate for state treasurer, the remainder of the Republican state ticket was successful.

In the same year, another Cincinnatian, William Howard Taft, was the Republican nominee for the Presidency. A native of the city where he maintained his legal residence, Taft had served as Solicitor General of the United States, judge of the Federal circuit court in Ohio, Civil Governor of the Philippines, and was at the time Secretary of War in Roosevelt's Cabinet. The possibility of Taft's nomination had been looked upon with disfavor by a powerful conservative Republican of the state, Senator Foraker, who doubtless had his own Presidential aspirations. The Senator had long been a thorn in President Roosevelt's side, as he had opposed the latter's plans for railway regulation and more recently had been airing what he claimed was the injustice of Roosevelt's conduct in relation to the "Brownsville affair." Negro soldiers, stationed at Brownsville, Texas, on the Rio Grande, had been accused of engaging in a riot in the streets of that city in August, 1906, and since individual offenders could not be discovered, as a punishment Roosevelt had ordered three companies to be dishonorably discharged from the service. Foraker, perhaps inspired in part by a desire to court the Negro influence of the country and to prevent the nomination of Roosevelt's protégé, was able and ingenious in presenting to the Senate evidence that tended to vindicate the colored troops. By May, 1908, however, Taft's nomination was a foregone conclusion, prominent party leaders pointed out to Foraker that continued discussion of the matter at that time would be party disloyalty, and the issue was not further pressed during that session of Congress.

While Foraker doubtless had a better case than the President in regard to the Brownsville affair, his political fortunes soon declined rapidly. In the elections, Taft received the electoral vote of Ohio, and success in the nation as a whole brought him to the Presidency. At the same time, evidence of a damaging nature had been brought against Foraker. While campaigning at Columbus in September, 1908, the journalist-politician, William Randolph Hearst, had read to his audience certain letters that had passed between the Ohio Senator and John D. Archbold, of the Standard Oil Company. Previously sold to the Hearst interests by two employees of the oil company, these letters revealed that while in office Foraker had received from the company the sum of $29,500. Foraker insisted that the money was paid for legal services and not for his influence in preventing Federal legislation unfavorable to the oil interests. His reputation, however, was now under a cloud. Upon the completion of his senatorial term in 1909, Theodore E. Burton, of Cleveland, was chosen to succeed him, and he retired from public life.

Discontent with political tendencies was definitely in the air, and the spirit developed further as the essential conservatism of Taft's administration became apparent. In state politics, this added to the impression that the Republicans could not serve as agents of reform, and in 1910 the Democrats reëlected Harmon, by a plurality of one hundred thousand votes, over Warren G. Harding. The achievements of the new legislature illustrated something of the temper of the times, as the Federal income tax amendment was ratified, a one-per-cent tax limitation was adopted, the direct nomination of United States Senators was provided for, and the initiative and referendum for municipalities were established.

A noteworthy development was the adoption of a Workmen's Compensation Law (in 1911) that provided for a state-administered fund—of which ninety per cent was to be subscribed by the employers and ten per cent by the employees, with the overhead borne by the state—to be used in compensating workmen or their families for injury or death incurred as a result of industrial accidents. This legislation, formulated by a state commission appointed in 1910, did not make participation by employers compulsory, but it registered a notable advance in the state's solicitude for the workers of the commonwealth and in the establishment of fair compensation for injuries to workers without a tedious and often unavailing recourse to the courts.

Not the least significant of the acts of the legislature was the issuance of a call for a state constitutional convention.

Ohio's Fourth Constitutional Convention

For half a dozen years, the movement for significant changes in the fundamental law of the state had been under way, culminating in an approval of a constitutional convention by the voters in 1910, the election of delegates in 1911, and the actual convening of the body in January, 1912. A distinctly liberal trend was noted among the one hundred and nineteen delegates, and Herbert S. Bigelow, of Cincinnati, a minister and a special champion of the initiative and the referendum, was made president. Simeon D. Fess, then president of Antioch College and later United States Senator, was chosen vice president and Charles B. Galbreath, of Columbus, was chosen secretary. Other delegates were future Governor Vic Donahey; Walter F. Brown, of Toledo, Postmaster General in the Hoover administration; and George W. Knight, for over forty years a member of the Ohio State University faculty. A new constitution was not adopted, but forty-one propositions were submitted to the voters as prospective amendments at a special election on September 3, 1912. These propositions revealed a distinct distrust of the legislature and a corresponding trend toward confidence in direct legislation.

Upon reference to the voters, eight of the proposed amendments were rejected, including those providing for the abolition of capital punishment, for woman's suffrage, for the use of voting machines, and for the regulation of

out-door advertising. Oddly enough, the voters refused
to sanction an attempt to harmonize the state and Federal
constitutions by the omission of the word "white" from the
qualifications for the suffrage in the former, though, of
course, such rejection was of no consequence in regard to
the actual exercise of the suffrage by Negroes. Discontent
had expressed itself as a consequence of a feeling that the
judges were unduly conservative and that delays were too
long before cases were finally disposed of by the courts.
As a result, amendments were adopted providing for
changes affecting the judicial process by permitting laws
to be passed authorizing a decision by not less than three-
fourths of the jury in civil cases. Provision also was made
for the taking of the depositions of witnesses in cases where
they could not be present in person at a trial and for the
passing of legislation dealing with the bringing of suits
against the state.

Legislative power was placed more directly in the hands
of the voters by the adoption of the initiative and the
referendum. Under the initiative, ten per cent of the
qualified voters might petition for a proposed amendment
to the state constitution, which by the referendum would
then be passed upon by the qualified voters of the state.
Ordinary legislation might be proposed to the general
assembly by the initiative of three per cent of the voters,
and in the event that the assembly failed to act within four
months, an additional three per cent of the voters might
secure a referendum of the proposal to the electorate.

Legislation passed by the general assembly, except "tax
levies, appropriations for the current expenses of the state
government and state institutions, and emergency laws
necessary for the immediate preservation of the public
peace, health or safety," might be referred to the decision
of the electorate upon petition of six per cent of the voters

and might not become effective until such approval had been given.

In the event of the calling of a special session of the general assembly, the work to be taken up was to be strictly limited to the special business indicated by the governor, whose veto power was now curtailed by the provision that three fifths rather than two thirds of each house might override his objections to proposed legislation. Separate items in appropriation bills, however, were for the first time subject to his veto power. This provision obviously was of importance in enabling the chief executive to eliminate items that had been inserted as "riders" or for "pork barrel" purposes without, at the same time, endangering constructive measures.

The amendments also specifically permitted the adoption of varied types of social and economic legislation, including compulsory workingmen's compensation, mechanic's lien, the regulation of hours, health conditions, and minimum wages, and the conservation of natural resources, and provided for an eight-hour day on public works and for the abolition of the prison contract system.

The merit principle in the state civil service, the nomination of all officers except in the smaller communities by direct primary or by petition, municipal home rule for cities, a double liability for bank stockholders, and the inspection of private banks by the state were other notable provisions. In general, distinct progress had been made in adapting the constitution to the changing needs of the changing times.

Progressivism at High Tide

The same spirit of revolt had been gathering strength in the arena of national politics. On New Year's Day,

1912, the Ohio Progressive Republican League had been organized, supposedly to further the candidacy of Robert M. La Follette, but through the influence of Gifford Pinchot, of Pennsylvania, and James R. Garfield, of Ohio, actually inclined to Roosevelt. A few weeks later (on February 21) Roosevelt himself appeared in Columbus to address the Ohio constitutional convention, making on that occasion his famous "A Charter of Democracy" speech, which was variously termed "a new Declaration of Independence" and "a charter of demagogy" repudiating "the principles upon which American institutions were established." Indicating his advocacy of the initiative and the referendum, he favored as a substitute for the recall of judges, the recall of judicial decisions—an arrangement by which a decision of the supreme court of a state declaring a state law unconstitutional might be referred to a popular vote. He asserted: "The judge is just as much the servant of the people as any other official. . . . The question of applying the recall in any shape is one of expediency merely. Each community has a right to try the experiment for itself in whatever shape it pleases." En route to Columbus, at Cleveland he had told a reporter, "My hat is in the ring," and soon a battle royal ensued for the control of delegates to the Republican national convention. At the primaries held to decide this matter in Ohio, eight Taft delegates were chosen and thirty-four Roosevelt ones, while the state convention by a narrow margin instructed the six delegates-at-large to vote for Taft. At the national convention in Chicago, President Taft was placed in nomination by one of Ohio's delegates-at-large, Warren G. Harding, who eulogized him as "the greatest progressive of the age." The Roosevelt delegates from Ohio refused to vote for Taft (who was nevertheless nominated upon the first ballot), and joined in the movement that early in August tendered the nomination of the new Progressive Party to the ex-President.

Meanwhile the Democrats had chosen delegates to the Baltimore convention of their party. Governor Judson Harmon secured a majority of the delegates from Ohio, and on the first ballot he ranked next to Clark and Wilson as a favorite candidate of the convention. Progressivism stood forth as the hope of the party's success, however, and Harmon had revealed himself as fundamentally a conservative earlier in the year in his address before the Ohio constitutional convention, on which occasion he had expressed his opposition to the state-wide application of the initiative and the referendum. Some of the Ohio delegates, bound to cast their votes for Harmon under the unit rule imposed by the state convention, were accordingly eager to secure the setting aside of this time-honored regulation. The leader in the fight against the rule upon the convention floor was Newton D. Baker, of Cleveland, who spoke with such persuasiveness that his mention of Wilson brought forth a demonstration thirty-three minutes in length, and, upon a vote, his contention was supported by the convention. Thus, members of the Ohio delegation found it possible to join in the movement that produced the nomination of Woodrow Wilson.

The choice of these men was supported at the polls by the voters of the state, as the Democratic Governor of New Jersey, running on a progressive platform, received in Ohio a plurality of almost 148,000 votes. A momentous thing had happened: for the first time since the birth of the Republican Party in 1854 the electoral vote of Ohio was not to be cast for the Presidential nominee of that organization but for the Democrats, at a time when a native son and citizen of the state was the standard bearer of the "Grand Old Party."

SELECTED BIBLIOGRAPHY

Ohio Legislative History (James K. Mercer, ed., 6 vols., Columbus, 1914–1926) in Vol. I, covering the Harmon administrations, 1909–1913, presents material relating to the work of the legislature and the constitutional convention of 1912.

Various memoirs and biographies such as Herbert Croly, *Mark Hanna*, and Joseph B. Foraker, *Notes on a Busy Life* (already mentioned), are distinctly useful. Others that illuminate certain aspects of the period are: Washington Gladden, *Recollections* (Boston, 1909); Frederic C. Howe, *Confessions of a Reformer* (New York, 1925); Tom L. Johnson, *My Story* (New York, 1913); Carl Lorenz, *Tom L. Johnson, Mayor of Cleveland* (New York, 1911); Thomas B. Mott, *Myron T. Herrick, Friend of France* (Garden City, N. Y., 1929); *The Autobiography of Lincoln Steffens* (New York, 1931); Brand Whitlock, *Forty Years of It* (New York, 1914). Herbert S. Duffy, *William Howard Taft* (New York, 1930), the life story of a native-born Ohioan, does not realize in content or objectivity the possibilities of a biography of Taft. The life of Judson Harmon is summarized in the *Dictionary of American Biography* by Arthur C. Cole.

Some material relating to the constitutional convention of 1912 is in I. F. Patterson, *The Constitutions of Ohio*, pp. 299–312, and a full treatment is given in Galbreath, *History of Ohio*, Vol. II, pp. 97–112. "The Veto Power in Ohio," by R. C. McGrane, *Mississippi Valley Historical Association Proceedings*, Vol. IX, pp. 177–189, discusses the attitude of Ohio toward the veto power of the governor.

CHAPTER XIX

Progressivism Yields to the Martial Spirit

A New Democratic Administration

*T*HE triumph of Wilson at the polls in 1912 was accompanied by the election of another Democratic Governor of Ohio, James M. Cox, to succeed the retiring chief executive of the same political faith, Judson Harmon. The new leader was a native of Butler County who as a youth had worked on the farm and as a printer's devil and reporter on a daily newspaper. Subsequently, after service upon the staff of the Cincinnati *Enquirer*, he had become secretary to an Ohio Congressman and in 1898 the owner and publisher of the Dayton *Daily News*. Success in the new venture enabled him to acquire a second newspaper, in Springfield, in 1903, and at the time of his election to the governorship he was serving his second term in the national House of Representatives. His campaign for the highest state position against Robert B. Brown, of Zanesville, the Republican nominee, and Arthur L. Garford, an Elyria automobile manufacturer who was the Progressive candidate, was featured by an aggressive support of the amendments to the Ohio constitution.

There was a considerable portion of the people of Ohio who regarded many of the additions to the constitution as so detailed in their nature as to partake of the specific character usually found in ordinary laws. Nevertheless, it was generally conceded that much legislation was necessary to carry the constitutional changes into effect, and Cox's first term was to a large extent devoted to the accomplishment of that task.

Following his inauguration in January, 1913, Governor Cox, in his first message to the recently convened legislature, pointed out that some of the amendments went into effect automatically; that others granted the legislature discretionary authority in regard to placing them into operation; and that still others were of a mandatory nature and specifically charged the legislature with the responsibility of enacting detailed laws to put them into effect.

The legislature took a serious view of its duties and passed an almost unprecedented number of constructive enactments, many of which were of far-reaching importance. Some of these constituted rather bold innovations and caused one political scientist to report that "a radical constitution to which to conform, a radical legislature, and a radical governor, who demonstrated his ability to handle a legislature and who had a definite program laid out and insisted on its fulfillment, all have conspired to give the Buckeye State, according to conservative minds, a taste of that which populism, in its wildest vagaries, never dared to dream."

The legislation passed at this time to give effect to the new provisions of the state constitution falls logically into three groups: (1) changes in governmental administration; (2) reforms favorable to labor; (3) miscellaneous reforms. Laws affecting the administration of government provided for changes in the court and legal systems, for a carefully organized civil service, for reforms in municipal government, for the use of the direct primary, and for the carrying into effect of the initiative and the referendum.

The judicial changes included the addition of a chief justice to the personnel of the supreme court[1] and the

---

[1] Previously, there had been six instead of seven justices, and the members of the court served as chief justice in rotation, as none was specifically elected to that office.

alteration of the powers of the old circuit court so that it would no longer be merely a court of review, remanding cases to a lower court for retrial, but would have final jurisdiction in all but certain specifically excepted cases. Plans to have at least one common pleas judge in each county were also carried out. Other laws provided for a verdict in civil cases by the agreement of three fourths of the jury and for the removal of the limit of ten thousand dollars as a maximum amount of damages recoverable for wrongful death.

The amendment which provided that "appointments and promotions in the civil service of the state, the several counties and cities, shall be made according to merit and fitness, to be ascertained as far as practicable by competitive examination" resulted in the Friebolin Act, effective January 1, 1914. This act established a complete civil service system for the state, counties, cities, and city schools, supervised by a commission of three members, one of whom—the president—was to give his whole time to the work. Various exemptions from this classified service were specifically mentioned, including elective officials, teachers and directors of schools, and members of university faculties. In practice, the system has not been so effective as many reformers had hoped that it would prove.

In the carrying out of the provision of the amended constitution relating to the exercise of self-government by municipalities, optional plans were offered to the citizens of such communities, who might determine by popular vote the type of local government to be employed. The choices available were the commission plan, featured by three or five elective commissioners, the number dependent upon the population; the city manager plan, by which five or more councilmen made regulations for the city and a city manager enforced them; and the federal plan, by which authority was vested in an elective mayor and council. In all cases the initiative, the referendum, and the recall were parts of the machinery of government.

The "direct primary" amendment adopted in 1912 also made imperative certain additional legislation. Hence, provision was made for the nomination by direct primary or by petition, of all elective officials with the exception of Presidential electors, township officers, and officials of municipalities of less than two thousand people. In the latter cases, a petition of a majority of the voters would be necessary for a direct primary. Delegates and alternates to state and national conventions were to be similarly chosen by direct vote of the people, and those desiring to be selected as members of the national conventions were required to file a sworn statement expressing their first and second choices for President. The initiative and the referendum sections of the revised constitution were quite explicit, but detailed statutory enactments were passed to carry them into effect.

The legislature also provided for reform in taxation by the application of the "uniform rule" to "intangibles" as well as to real and personal property—a change directed by the amended constitution. The result was the Warnes Act, which provided for the setting aside of each county as a separate assessment district in which the governor would appoint at least one district assessor, who in turn was to select a suitable number of deputies and assistants. This system, it was hoped, would help to insure a more complete return of the taxable property of the state.

Among the acts passed to improve the lot of the laboring classes were laws limiting the hours of consecutive labor for railway or electric car employees; laws prohibiting the employment of boys under sixteen or girls under eighteen

years of age without an age and schooling certificate;
laws establishing safeguards against occupational diseases;
and laws prohibiting more than an eight-hour day on all
public works whether done by a contractor or directly by
the state. In accordance with the mandatory feature of
one of the amendments, there also was passed a compulsory
workmen's compensation act constructed largely, as had
been that of 1911, by State Senator William Green, destined
to become the successor of Samuel Gompers as president
of the American Federation of Labor. The operation of
the law was imperilled for a long time through the opposition and potential competition of private insurance companies, but through the initiative process there was passed
in 1917 a law eliminating the private companies from the
field. Such an effective and successful system of workmen's compensation was developed in Ohio that no less a
personage than Albert, King of the Belgians, upon a visit to
the United States in 1919 described the Ohio law as one
of the greatest pieces of social legislation upon the statute
books of any country. Many contributed valiantly to the
maintenance and extension of the operation of this important piece of social legislation, and it is difficult to single
out its many champions, unless one be Thomas J. Duffy, of
East Liverpool, who stands out as one of the law's staunch-
est defenders and most effective administrators. Another
measure that carried out the purpose of an amendment
adopted in 1912 and that was designed as an aid to labor
provided for the giving of liens in favor of contractors, sub-
contractors, and laborers for work done or material furnished by them.

Other miscellaneous reforms serve to indicate the
paternalistic tendency of many of the new enactments. To
comply with another new constitutional provision, a
license system for the liquor traffic was established for the

first time. To supervise this business, a state commission
of three persons, appointed by the governor, was created.
In each "wet" county the commission was empowered to
select two commissioners whose responsibility was the
licensing of saloons in that subdivision. Not more than
one saloon could be permitted for each five hundred people,
and a license fee of one thousand dollars plus a registration
fee of one hundred dollars was charged each proprietor.

To protect unwary investors, there was enacted a "blue
sky" law providing for the licensing of those dealing in
bonds, stocks, and other securities and in real estate not
located in Ohio, by the superintendent of banks, who was
to be designated a "commissioner." A fee of ten dollars
was required with all applications for licenses, and a statement giving the general plan and scope of the business,
the names of the officers and agents of the business, and
other pertinent details was made necessary. The purpose
of the law was to secure to investors information as to
the kinds of stocks and bonds offered for sale in the state.

Other legislative acts resulting from the new amendments changed the position of commissioner of schools from
an elective to an appointive office, henceforth to be known
as "superintendent of public instruction," and provided
for the appointment of a commission of three to survey the
educational agencies of the state.[2]

In addition to this imposing array of enactments, other
progressive measures passed by the legislature in the session
of 1913 include the provision for a state budget system, one
of the first created in any of the states of the Union. As a
member of the committee on appropriations of the national
House of Representatives, Governor Cox had been aston-
ished and disgusted by the unsystematic handling of the

---

[2] A more detailed analysis of changes in the school system is given in
Chapter XVII.

public funds. In the light of this experience, he energetically pressed the need for improved methods. The new law provided that all receipts of the state should go to the state treasury and remain there until appropriated in specific sums for definite purposes within a given department. In the even-numbered years, state departments and institutions were to report their needs as to appropriations to the governor, who would receive information from the state auditor as to their past expenditures and report a budget proposal to the legislature.

Another law, whose operation was eagerly watched by social workers throughout the nation, created a state industrial commission of three members, who were to be appointed by the governor. The new board was to undertake the responsibility for work formerly entrusted to at least half a dozen agencies and was given extensive powers over the regulation of the hours and conditions of labor of employees.

Much interest was manifested also in a new mothers' pension law which made the provision that a woman whose husband was dead, wholly disabled, or in prison or had deserted his family for three years or more might receive from the county treasury fifteen dollars a month for the support of one child and seven dollars for each additional child under the legal age of employment. Only women who were in such straitened circumstances that in the absence of a pension they would be forced to work outside the home were eligible, as the law was intended to preserve the integrity of the family by enabling poverty-stricken mothers to keep their children in their care as long as possible.

The legislature also created a public utilities commission and prescribed its powers, duties, and organization. This commission succeeded to all of the powers of the old

Public Service Commission of 1911 (which had supplanted the Railroad Commission of 1906) and was charged with ascertaining the value of all public utility and railroad properties in the state in order to determine the reasonableness of their rates.

Possibly actuated by the same zeal that prompted President Wilson to make his famous attack upon the tariff lobbyists at Washington in 1913, the Ohio Legislature required by statute that all lobbyists must register with the secretary of state, pay a fee of three dollars, and name their employers and the purposes for which they were employed. In practice, the law was not enforced in such a way as to eliminate the evils of the lobby system. In 1921, one hundred and sixteen lobbyists were registered, and in 1925, one hundred and ten; but all reported in their expense accounts, which were officially filed, that they had received no money and spent none in their lobbying activities.

The legislature also introduced the idea of indeterminate sentences to the penitentiary for felonies other than treason and murder in the first degree. By this arrangement, the state board of administration might discharge prisoners at its discretion any time after the expiration of the minimum term prescribed for their crimes.

Although the voters of the state had rejected an amendment to the constitution providing for bond issues not to exceed fifty millions of dollars "for the purpose of constructing, rebuilding, improving, and repairing a system of inter-county wagon roads throughout the State," Governor Cox expressed the belief that this fact did not indicate an opposition to good roads but rather a distrust that the money would be used for the building of highways in counties that had been extremely parsimonious in financing their own. Accordingly, he emphasized the need for improved road legislation, and the legislature responded with the establishment of a main market and inter-county road system under the supervision of the state highway commissioner. Under this arrangement, the state paid for all of the main market road improvements and for one half of the inter-county highway construction, thus stimulating the development of a fairly satisfactory highway system throughout the state. The legislature also ratified the seventeenth amendment to the Federal Constitution, establishing the direct election of United States Senators.

In spite of the many achievements of the legislature of 1913, certain matters required further study before satisfactory action could be taken, and these problems, along with new ones that developed during the year, created the occasion for the calling of a special session of the assembly in January, 1914. In convening the members of the legislature at that time, Governor Cox specified nine definite projects that should constitute the scope of their work. One purpose of the session was the enactment of new laws to carry into effect the recommendations of a commission appointed by the Governor at the previous session to investigate the school system of the state. Another was the alteration of the primary and election laws of the state by providing for the nomination at the primaries of candidates for United States Senators and by granting the governor the power to make a temporary appointment to fill a senatorial vacancy. These changes seemed desirable in view of the ratification of the seventeenth amendment to the Constitution of the United States.

Important also was the need, as Governor Cox pointed out, for a revision of the banking laws in order to adjust them to the operation of the newly created banking system of the country. By the terms of the Federal Reserve Act, which introduced many new features into the national banking system, twelve district banks were established, one of which (for the Fourth District of the country) opened its headquarters at Cleveland. State banks, according to the national law, could affiliate with this system; hence arose the necessity for adjustments in the Ohio law to enable Ohio banks to conform to the Federal requirements.

The legislature in general responded in a coöperative spirit to bring about the desired enactments. In addition to the measures already mentioned, the well-known Conservancy Law of February, 1914, was a product of this legislative session.

The Flood of 1913 and the Conservancy Program

The Conservancy Law was a direct result of one of the greatest tragedies that has ever visited Ohio—the flood of 1913. On March 23, which was Easter Sunday, a steady rain began to fall and continued through the night and all day Monday. By Tuesday, flooded districts had developed in several localities, and by Wednesday, the crest of the flood had been reached in every place except Cincinnati. The Miami River Valley was the scene of the greatest destruction, but other sections of Ohio (as well as parts of Indiana and other states) were severely affected. The great rapidity with which the swollen streams advanced upon unprepared districts caused a tremendous loss of life and property. In all, four hundred and twenty-eight bodies were recovered as the waters receded (two hundred and eighty-three of them in the valley of the Great Miami), and many more were never found. In Colmubus alone, over four thousand buildings were flooded, and in the state as a whole twenty thousand houses were destroyed and more than thirty-five thousand were damaged. The property loss probably amounted to three hundred million dollars.

At the helght of the flood, the need for relief measures was almost overwhelming. In a city like Columbus, where the loss of life and property due to the overflowing of the Scioto River was great, the problem of relief was simpler than at Dayton, in the Miami Valley. In Columbus the main portion of the community, including the business district, was not under water, while in Dayton the whole business district, as well as two thirds of the residential district, was flooded. In an effort to meet the requirements of protection in the emergency, eight thousand state troops were called out by Governor Cox, and to cope with the problem of food and shelter for the homeless, local relief committees sprang up in the various stricken communities. The Governor appointed a state relief committee, which was afterwards recognized by legislative act, and with this organization the Red Cross coöperated. For several days, at least two hundred and twenty thousand people had to be provided with food. As usual on such occasions of distress, large sums of money poured in from private sources for the work of the Red Cross, and the Ohio Legislature appropriated a quarter of a million dollars. Generally speaking, the emergency was met with admirable efficiency. In spite of the isolation of some of those needing aid, scarcely anyone was without food of some kind for over twenty-four hours, and, following the return of the waters to their regular channels, heroic efforts were made to avert the danger of disease.

In the Miami Valley the inhabitants refused to face the possibility of a recurrence of the calamity with a fatalistic philosophy. In Dayton, a civic committee was established and was headed by Edward A. Deeds, at that time vice president of the National Cash Register Company. As a result of its efforts, Arthur E. Morgan, a noted hydraulic engineer of Memphis, Tennessee, and more recently president of Antioch College, was employed to conduct an investigation of the problem of flood prevention. Beginning their work two months after the March disaster, Morgan and other engineers with their assistants (about sixty in all) made a thorough study of the storms in the Middle West, of the conformation of the river channels, and of methods of high-water control. Approximately two million dollars was raised by twenty-three thousand Dayton citizens to cover the cost of the research and survey. The experts reported that the entire watershed of the Miami Rivers must be approached as a single unit, and that the floods must be checked in the upper valleys by a reservoir system. It was determined, therefore, that six large earthworks should be constructed, five above Dayton and one upon a branch entering the Miami below that city. To insure against any possibility of a recurrence of the damage, the dams were to have a capacity to hold back a flood of water fifty per cent greater than that present in 1913. The cost of the work was estimated at about seventeen million dollars.

State legislation in the form of the Conservancy Law, already mentioned, had to be devised to deal with the legal aspects of the problem. The law, providing that the expense be borne by the property owners and the towns and cities that would receive the protection, was drafted under the supervision of John A. McMahon, a highly respected Dayton lawyer and one-time Congressman (1875–1881), who was a nephew of Clement L. Vallandigham. Much opposition to the projected legislation arose: some farms in the upper Miami Valley would have to be abandoned, although their owners would be compensated; a spirit of individualism arose to oppose the tendency toward coöperation; rumors spread that interests desirous of cornering the water power were seeking advantage for themselves; and politicians played upon unreasoned fears for their own selfish benefit. The Governor, however, was a Daytonian and had behind him sufficient strength in the legislature to pass the law. The measure that was enacted is a model of legal pioneering in its field. Although attempts were made to repeal the law in the next legislature, they were unsuccessful, and although attacks were made upon the constitutionality of the law, the Ohio Supreme Court upheld its validity in June, 1915, and the United States Supreme Court did likewise in 1919 (*Orr* vs. *Allen*).

A New Republican Administration

The aggressive attitude of Governor Cox in securing an extensive body of enactments during his first administration had inevitably created a large measure of opposition, and in 1914 he was defeated in his contest for reëlection by Frank B. Willis, who had been opposed also by a Progressive candidate, James R. Garfield, a son of the martyred President. At the same time were voted upon three proposed amendments to the state constitution, two of which, one providing for woman suffrage and another for state-wide prohibition, were rejected. A third, which made the township or municipality the unit for local option purposes in relation to the liquor traffic, was approved.

This was a period of experimenting in city government, and under the Ohio municipal home-rule amendment, which had become effective on January 1, 1913, twenty-five cities of the state considered the adoption of charters. In nine of these, Cleveland, Columbus, Dayton, Lakewood, Middletown, Springfield, Sandusky, Ashtabula, and Toledo, the change was approved by popular vote. Dayton, which adopted the city manager type of government, did so partly as a result of the satisfactory results that Daytonians had attained by dealing with experts on the problem of flood control. It was the first large city of the country to approve of that form of municipal government.

Willis, the new Governor, was a native of Delaware County and a graduate of Ohio Northern University, at Ada. Having studied law and having been admitted to the bar, he taught history, economics, and law at his Alma Mater for a period of sixteen years (1894–1910). He was a man of attractive personality and a teacher of real popularity, the students sometimes absenting themselves from other courses to line the walls and occupy the window sills of his classroom to hear his lectures. While retaining his professorial position, he served two terms in the lower house of the state legislature, and in 1911 he began the first of two terms in the national House of Representatives.

Willis's term as Governor marked a reaction from what he termed the "executive usurpation" of the previous administration. He stressed economy in government, and since he asserted that the volume of the laws of the state was already too great, his administration was not characterized by much new legislation. The latter part of his term saw the mobilization of the National Guard to protect American interests along the Rio Grande—an enterprise in which Ohio troops were conspicuous participants.

In 1915 four constitutional amendments were submitted to the voters: one fixing the term of county officers at four years, another exempting the bonds of the state and its subdivisions from taxation, and a third prohibiting the resubmission to the voters of the state of any twice-defeated constitutional amendment until a lapse of six years had occurred since its last rejection. The last-mentioned proposal was favored by the liquor interests, in view of the rejection of a prohibition amendment in 1914, and as it happened, again in 1915, but was opposed by labor unions, direct-legislation enthusiasts, and the Anti-Saloon League. The fourth amendment, which indicated the persistence of the "dry" element, again proposed state-wide prohibition. Large interests in the state were involved in the maintenance of the liquor traffic, as Cincinnati was then the largest distillery center and the third largest brewing center in the nation, and thirty thousand men paraded all of one day in that city in opposition to the acceptance of the proposal. All four of the amendments were rejected, but the majority against prohibition was considerably less than any of the majorities against the other three proposals.

The Coming of War

The outbreak of the World War in Europe in 1914 was of such significance as to tend to overshadow, in increasing degree, all local questions. Ohio's attitude when the war began may be described as essentially neutral. The population of the state, however, was a most heterogeneous one; many groups were drawn by their sympathies to hope for the success of either the German or the Allied cause; and manifestations of favoritism were probably inevitable. The German-language press, in spite of some criticisms of the "arrogant, dull and blundering" Junker class, which dictated Germany's foreign policy, was, of course, consistently and ardently pro-German. Especially in a city like Cincinnati with a large portion of its population of

German origin or descent, a considerable sentiment in favor of Germany was manifest. Hence the American "preparedness" movement of 1915 and 1916 made little headway in that city. When a Cincinnati manufacturer gave two hundred and fifty men in his office a chance to attend the Officers' Training Camp at Plattsburg, New York, only eleven accepted. Some definitely pacifistic sentiment showed itself, and when Herbert Bigelow, the Cincinnati minister-reformer, announced his intention of voting for Henry Ford, a peace candidate for President, in the preferential primaries, two thousand voters followed his lead in writing Ford's name upon the ballot.

In the Presidential contest of 1916, the problems of the war naturally played a part. Theodore E. Burton, of Cleveland, an internationally minded gentleman, who had served as Congressman and Senator from Ohio and whose scholarly capacities had caused him to be chosen as a biographer of John Sherman, had the unanimous support on the first ballot of the Ohio delegation to the Republican national convention. Senator Warren G. Harding, of Marion, who delivered the keynote speech, however, aroused more enthusiasm among many leaders of Ohio Republicanism, and a hope was fostered that he might secure the nomination of the party. Neither Ohioan, as it developed, was to have that distinction, and Charles Evans Hughes, of New York, became the party's leader against the Democratic candidate for reëlection—Woodrow Wilson.

Ohio's part in the campaign was a significant, even a decisive, one, for alone among the politically important states east of the Mississippi and north of the Mason-Dixon line and the Ohio River, its electoral vote assisted in giving a second term to Wilson. The only other state in the North, east of the Mississippi, whose vote was given to the Democratic candidate was New Hampshire, which was carried by the President by only fifty-six

Presidential Election of 1916

Democratic..................	Wilson	604,161
Republican..................	Hughes	514,753
Socialist....................	Benson..............	38,092
Prohibition	Hanly...............	8,080

votes. Wilson's Ohio plurality was almost ninety thousand. Among the reasons for Wilson's success were:

the desire on the part of millions of Ohioans to avoid war if peace were at all compatible with a preservation of the rights of the United States on the high seas; the friendly attitude of organized labor because of the President's advocacy of the Clayton Anti-Trust Law of 1914 (which contained sections especially desired by labor) and the newly-sanctioned Adamson Act (which granted unusual terms, including the eight-hour day, to the four railroad brotherhoods); the influence of the Tom Johnson tradition, in Cleveland, on independent voting; and the success with which the Democrats of the state had won the support of some who had formerly been associated with the Progressive Party. At the same time, Atlee Pomerene, a Canton Democrat, won reëlection to the Senate over Myron T. Herrick, and James M. Cox defeated Frank B. Willis for the governorship.

Earlier in the year, upon the resignation of Lindley M. Garrison, Ohio had for the first time gained representation in Wilson's Cabinet by the appointment to the War Department of Newton D. Baker, who had served as Mayor of Cleveland since 1912 and who previous to that time had been city solicitor for almost a decade.

The first legislature under the second Cox administration produced a number of important enactments. Provision was made for absent voting, for the acceptance of Federal aid for highway construction and for vocational education, for the reduction of the hours of labor for women from ten to nine hours a day (except on Saturdays in mercantile establishments) and from fifty-four to fifty hours a week, and for the appropriation of a quarter of a million dollars to be used in the event of the entrance of the United States into war. Presidential and municipal suffrage was granted to women, but through the use of the referendum, this proposal was rejected by a large majority.

Approximately three months after Governor Cox's second inauguration and about two weeks after the adjournment of the Ohio Legislature, the United States entered the World War (April, 1917). Although President Wilson had been reëlected in November, 1916, partly because of a feeling of hopefulness in the country that he could continue to avert American participation in the conflict, the situation for the United States, beginning late in January, 1917, rapidly became more acute. Earlier in the war, each side had severely tried the patience of the United States, and Wilson had sent pertinent "notes" demanding a safeguarding of neutral rights. Probably the heavy loans made to the Allies by Eastern bankers were not without an appreciable influence in turning public sentiment—particularly in the Northeastern States—rather noticeably in favor of Great Britain and her allies. On January 31, 1917, the pledge made by Germany in May, 1916, that she would refrain from submarine attacks upon merchant vessels "without warning and without saving human lives," was abruptly repudiated, and President Wilson promptly severed diplomatic relations. Wilson hoped to maintain American rights on the high seas by the arming of American merchant vessels, and on February 26, asked Congress to sanction such a policy. This proposal was passed by the House of Representatives with only thirteen dissenting votes, one of which was that of a Congressman of Ohio. A small group in the Senate, however, prevented congressional authorization of the plan by filibustering during the remaining days before the expiration of Congress on March 4. The President, thereupon, took upon himself the responsibility of carrying out the plan, under the authority of an almost forgotten law, and American merchantmen subsequently went to sea mounted with guns and provided with expert sharpshooters.

The one Ohioan in Congress who had voted against granting the President the authority that he had desired was the octogenarian, Isaac R. Sherwood, of Toledo, who had served four years in the Union Army during the Civil War, had been an aggressive advocate of pensions, and was the sponsor of the "Dollar-a-Day Pension Law" of 1912. In his advancing years, he had become a fervent upholder of pacifistic principles, and upon the occasion of a great peace meeting in Carnegie Hall, New York City, March 9, 1917, he had sent a telegram condemning the use of armed American merchantmen, which were "carrying munitions of war to England and her allies, because we are making millions of bloody dollars in the murder of tens of thousands of innocents abroad."

During the month of March, the loss of American lives on the armed merchantmen indicated the ineffectiveness of that policy, and with the downfall of the Czarist régime in Russia in the middle of the same month, the objection of Americans to championing the side of such a military autocracy was removed. Early in April the President appealed to Congress for a declaration of war. This was promptly granted with six votes in the Senate and fifty in the House in opposition. Again the only dissenting vote from Ohio was that of General Sherwood, who after the passage of the resolution at once declared his loyalty to the Government. Apparently Sherwood's constituents approved of the independence of his stand, for he was reëlected to his seat in 1918. The new alignment of the country in a common cause with other nations in 1917 was dramatically presented to the people of the state by the arrival of a French mission, including M. René Viviani and Marshal Joffre, who visited Ohio during the month of May.

As elsewhere in the United States, all activities in Ohio for over a year and a half were largely subordinated to efforts to win the war. Ohio's part in the mobilization of men, money, resources, and a sustained morale was similar to that played by other states, but deserves more extensive discussion.

Ohio as a Participant in the War

The National Guard of the state, which had been called out in June, 1916, to assist in policing the Mexican border, formed a substantial basis for Ohio's contribution of men to service in the World War. The call for volunteers to enlarge the Army in Ohio, as in some other of the older states of the Union, did not, however, produce a very enthusiastic response. During the month following the declaration of war (up to May 7), only 1,920 Ohioans enlisted in the Army in comparison with 3,995 from Indiana and 5,586 from Illinois. Ohio nevertheless furnished in all as volunteers (including those from the National Guard) 48,850 men to the Army and 16,908 to the Navy. In the air service, as perhaps befitted the state that had produced Orville Wright (who with his brother, Wilbur, had given the airplane to the world), many Ohioans were outstanding. Distinguished among them was Captain Edward V. Rickenbacker, of Columbus, who was popularly known as "America's Ace of Aces." Men from every walk of life entered the Government service. By the spring of 1918, approximately fifty members of the teaching staff of the Ohio State University had been granted leaves of absence to enter the governmental service, and four deans were serving as majors in the Army.

With the adoption by the National Government of the Selective Service Act in May, 1917, the registration of men between twenty-one and thirty-one years of age began, and later, that of men between eighteen and forty-five was started. In all, 1,389,474 registrations were made in Ohio and 154,236 were actually drafted into the service. Ohio's quota was found to rank high in physical fitness, the state standing in the next to the highest group of states in the percentage of drafted men who passed their physical examinations. Between sixty-five and sixty-nine per cent of the Ohioans examined were accepted, as compared with seventy to eighty per cent for prairie states such as Kansas and Nebraska and fifty to fifty-nine per cent for Michigan. Volunteers, National Guardsmen, and drafted men (distinctions that were soon ignored) from Ohio who entered service in the Army totalled 200,293 men (excluding officers), or 5.33 per cent of the whole.

The members of the Ohio National Guard were mobilized for further training at Camp Sheridan, near Montgomery, Alabama, beginning in August, 1917. At the same time, the National Army men (the draftees) were assembled at a great cantonment constructed near Chillicothe and known as Camp Sherman. The men at this camp constituted the Eighty-Third Division, composed chiefly of Ohioans but including also men from western Pennsylvania. Some difficulty was experienced with the Amish and Mennonites, conscientious objectors, largely from northwestern Ohio, some of whom even refused to work in the hospitals or till the soil and, rejecting any pay from the Government, spent a considerable portion of their time in religious services.

Ohio contributed the former Fourth Regiment of the Ohio National Guard, with Benson W. Hough as its colonel, to the Forty-Second or "Rainbow" Division, which was organized at Camp Mills, New York, and entered into active combat service in France early in July, 1918. The Eighty-Third Division, made up of drafted men, largely from Ohio, arrived in France in June, 1918, but saw service on the firing line only in November, when the war was nearly ended. One regiment, however, had been detached and sent to Italy for fighting along the Piave River.

It was the Thirty-Seventh Division, composed of Ohio National Guardsmen, that most definitely represented the Buckeye State upon the field of battle. Assembled at Camp Sheridan, Alabama, in August, 1917, it was commanded by various officers and finally by Major General Charles S. Farnsworth, who led the division in France and Belgium. After months of training at Camp Sheridan and at Camp Lee, Virginia, in June, 1918, the journey overseas from Hoboken, New Jersey, to Brest, France, was made. A few weeks later, the men entered the trenches in the Baccarat sector in the Alsace-Lorraine salient, a relatively quiet district where they received their baptism of fire. In the middle of September, the division started northward to the vicinity of Verdun for a real introduction to the experiences of war. Their efforts in this locality resulted in the capture of Montfaucon and the liberation of territory that had been under German control for four years. In October, the division was moved to the St. Mihiel sector and took over trenches near Hattonchatel. Later in the month, it was selected as one of two American divisions to represent the Americans on Belgian soil and assisted in the restoration to Allied control of more than twenty towns in the vicinity of the Lys River. On November 10, the division again went "over the top" in a region farther northward. With the proclaiming of the armistice on the next morning, the war came to a close.

In the absence of the former National Guard from Ohio's borders, Home Guard units were organized throughout the state. By the spring of 1918, their strength equalled that of the National Guard in 1913. In Cincinnati alone, there were thirty companies, comprising 2,577 men.

Various problems in relation to finance arose during the course of the war. The Ohio Legislature had adjourned in 1917 before the declaration of war, but in the expectation of such an event, it had appropriated for war purposes $250,000, of which $131,587 was expended by the Adjutant General in recruiting the National Guard and for expenses attending the mobilization of that organization.[3]

Ohioans of course were called upon to pay their share of the war taxes and to subscribe a proportionate part to the four "Liberty" loans and the Fifth "Victory" Loan. Moving-picture actresses came to the state to stimulate enthusiasm for the loans, civic pride was challenged through the introduction of quotas, and considerable pressure was exerted upon those who were considered able to make liberal subscriptions. Thrift stamps and war-savings certificates were disposed of to those of less abundant means, Ohio's share in 1918 being $106,000,000 out of a total of $2,000,-000,000. One Columbus woman even organized a Greek-letter society, Beta Tau Sigma (Buy Thrift Stamps), to arouse the interest of boys and girls.

Great efforts were made to raise funds for such organizations as the Red Cross, the Knights of Columbus, and the Y. M. C. A. An illustration of the methods employed is found in an auction for the benefit of the Red Cross at South Charleston in January, 1918, honored by the attendance of Governor Cox. On this occasion as much as sixty-eight dollars was paid for a pumpkin and eleven dollars for a home-made cake.

The various communities of the state attempted to raise large war chest funds to aid those who found their means of support inadequate owing to a bread-winner's having been drawn into the national service. Every

---

[3] The balance was used by the Ohio Branch of the Council of National Defense.

effort was expended to make the drives successful. In Columbus, for example, advertising was furnished by the erection on the capitol grounds of a large billboard on which were painted figures representing the Crown Prince, the Kaiser, and Field Marshal Von Hindenburg. A hit with a baseball against any one of them set off a gong, hence the board carried the injunction to passers-by to "swat the Hohenzollerns and ring the bell for our war chest."

The mobilization of the state's economic resources was stimulated by the Ohio Branch of the Council of National Defense, appointed by Governor Cox in June, 1917. Its main committees were Finance, Food Conservation, Labor and Industrial Relations, Publicity, Transportation, Americanization, and County and Community Council Organization. Unlike councils in most of the other states, it had no legal basis but acted as a war cabinet advisory to the governor. Its work is indicated by its employment service, which furnished thousands of men for the construction of the cantonment at Chillicothe without unduly interfering with industry in any part of the state; by its committee on mining, which established a State Coal Clearance to facilitate the production, transportation, and distribution of coal; by its food conservation committee, which stimulated the planting of war gardens and the canning of surplus vegetables. The Woman's Committee of the Council had in May, 1918, seventy-eight county units and four hundred and fifty township organizations that assisted in securing nurses and stenographers for the Government service and in educating women along lines of food conservation.

The state control of fuel supplies was discontinued in October, 1917, the supervision at that time being turned over to Homer H. Johnson, who had been appointed Federal Fuel Administrator for Ohio. Frederick C. Crox-

ton was made Federal food commissioner for the state.
Under Federal regulations, enforced under the direction of
Johnson in Ohio, over eight thousand industrial plants in
the state were practically closed for a period of five days in
January, 1918, as a means of conserving fuel, and theatres
and retail stores were also restricted in their consumption
of coal. To safeguard food supplies, hotels, clubs, and
restaurants observed "meatless" and "wheatless" days,
and the consumption of sugar even by private families was
strictly regulated. Bakeries were required to use substitute flours in certain proportions in place of the wheat
product, and the hoarding of flour and sugar often led to its
official confiscation. Hundreds of factories throughout
the industrial districts of the state were at the same time
rushing the production of munitions and other necessary
materials. At Lima, "Liberty" trucks were produced in
quantities for the use of the American Army abroad.
Ohio on the home front was straining every nerve for the
winning of the war.

To arouse the fighting spirit of the state to as high a
pitch as possible, the same methods that were employed in
other parts of the country were utilized. "Four-minute
men" were secured from among attorneys, educators,
ministers, and even school children in every community
to make brief speeches before public gatherings. On
other occasions, the theme of formal addresses naturally
turned to war aims and policies. Thousands were led to
believe that the struggle was really a "war to end wars,"
and they believed with President W. O. Thompson, of the
Ohio State University, that if Wilson would stand true
to his principles and the people true to him, "this greatest
war of twenty centuries" would result "in great good."
Sometimes the issues were approached from a different
angle, as at a convocation of the Ohio State University,

when the dean of the College of Agriculture declared that in Germany "business, agriculture, the press and even the church came under the power and instruction of the most hated man the world has ever known" and "school children were taught to play, not with the things which we teach our children to play with, but with bombs, airplanes and submarines." Even Herbert L. Bigelow, of Cincinnati, a pacifist and a Socialist, who during the early months of America's participation in the war had been spirited into Kentucky to be treated with physical violence because of his alleged pro-Germanism, in February, 1918, in a speech at Dayton urged all Socialists to join the colors because of the annexationist designs of Germany.

Speeches by veterans who sometimes capitalized upon their war experiences for pecuniary gains were made before interested groups. One address that illustrates well the use of extremely dubious propaganda was that of "Private Peat," the Canadian veteran, before the Ohio United Mine Workers of America at Columbus in January, 1918. He asserted that, with some of their comrades crucified, "with 95 per cent of the girls carrying babies in their arms, and many of these violated young mothers with only one arm left to hold their offspring," allied soldiers were naturally eager to see "some German legs and arms also flying through the air." For days in certain communities a free lecture, "Wake up, America," with movies to supplement it, was offered to an excited public, one of its features, according to the press announcements, being an exhibition of the Kaiser "in the days of his babyhood as he was raised in a gunroom of a nursery."

Earnest and sometimes fanatical efforts were used to suppress any manifestations of disloyalty. The Advertising Club of the Columbus Chamber of Commerce sponsored a "Yellow Dog Clubbers' Club," which demanded "the absolute starvation of German propaganda for lack of food to feed upon—for lack of tongues to pass the tale along." Governor Cox asserted that a group of men in Cleveland had repeatedly despoiled the American flag and sent the remnants to his office, and he suggested that a firing squad for traitors be organized.

Persons of alleged pro-German sentiments often met with summary treatment. A retired German minister of Woodsfield was interned for several months in a county jail for alleged unpatriotic utterances and at length paroled on drastic conditions. At a village near Wellington, a man accused of pro-German remarks was waited upon by a group of citizens and compelled to salute and kiss the American flag. At Delphos, where many Germans had settled, five business men were seized by a volunteer vigilance committee and taken to the brightly lighted downtown street and forced to pay respect to the flag under pain of being hanged from a nearby telephone pole. A shoe merchant exhibited a gun when the crowd approached his home, but the chief of police secured from him a salute of the flag.

At Toledo three musicians in a theatre were placed under heavy bond and discharged from their positions because they refused to play "The Star-spangled Banner" and used a "ragtime" selection instead. At Baldwin-Wallace College, at Berea, one hundred and fifty students petitioned for the removal of their president, who, it was asserted, had failed to denounce "German crimes and atrocities" and had avoided mention of the war. Nine bishops of the Methodist Church conducted an investigation, while the students staged a spectacular parade outside the buildings, and the president was removed from his position. Two Socialists in March, 1918, were ousted from the city council of Cleveland for alleged unpatriotic remarks. The war spirit also manifested itself in the banning of many things of German origin. Organizations in various communities soon demanded the abolition of German instruction in the schools, and at North Baltimore a group of people raided the high-school building and made a bonfire of the German textbooks. During the same period, numerous German-American banks dropped the Teutonic portion of their titles.

In November, 1918, Governor Cox was reëlected over ex-Governor Willis, the Republican nominee, probably in part because of the opposition of "wet" Republicans to Willis's "dry" pronouncements. The rest of the Republican state ticket, nevertheless, was elected, and the Democrats lost several Ohio seats in Congress. Less than a week later, the armistice was proclaimed, and the war had come to an end.

Governor Cox, however, maintained that the dangers of German "propaganda" were not yet at an end, and his third term as Governor was marked by certain measures that must now be viewed as products of a "post-war hysteria." In his message to the legislature on January 13, 1919, he asserted, in the spirit of the time, that "the man who doubts that a conspiracy was hatched in Germany to make of the rest of the earth vassal states, either lacks the intelligence of analysis, or the loyal mental attitude of an American." He urged that "every germ of Prussian poison" should "be squeezed out of the organic law of Ohio," and in a special message of February 20 advocated the banning of German instruction from the private and parochial as well as from the public schools. In a further message of April 1, he indulged in the extreme statement that the teaching of German to American children was "not only a distinct menace to Americanism, but it is part of a conspiracy formed long ago by the German Govern-

ment in Berlin." The result was the Ake Law, passed
by the legislature in May, 1919. It provided that German
should "not be taught below the eighth grade in any of
the elementary schools of this state" and that all instruction
in the first seven grades of public and private schools should
be given in English. The Supreme Court of the United
States, however, during the October term, 1922, in cases
involving similar statutes in Iowa and Nebraska declared
such legislation, in so far as it involved private and denominational schools, to be a violation of the liberty secured
to the teachers and students by the fourteenth amendment
to the Federal Constitution.

Other legislation passed at this time required all teachers
in public, private, and parochial schools of the state to take
a solemn oath to support the constitutions of the United
States and of Ohio and the laws enacted thereunder, and
to teach, "by precept and example, respect for the flag,
reverence for law and order and undivided allegiance to
the government of one country, the United States of
America."

Another manifestation of the same fear of foreign
influences was the passing in 1919 of an act that prohibited
the carrying or display of any red or black flag or any
banner or ensign having on it any inscription opposed to
organized government or that is sacrilegious or that may
be derogatory to public morals. In the same year, a
Criminal Syndicalism Act became law. This act provided
a maximum punishment of ten years' imprisonment and
a fine of five thousand dollars for anyone who "deliberately
justifies, by word of mouth or writing, the commission or
the attempt to commit crime, sabotage, violence or unlaw-
ful methods of terrorism" to secure industrial or political
reform. Many persons, including Newton D. Baker, have
justified this law as a reasonable measure of protection to

organized government, but others, both within the legislature and without, have urged its repeal as an un-American
curtailment of the liberties of the individual.

SELECTED BIBLIOGRAPHY

Ohio Legislative History (James K. Mercer, ed.) (previously
cited) is of distinct value for data on the work of the legislature.
Volume II covers the years 1913–1917.

Much of the material for this chapter was gleaned from
newspapers, magazines, and yearbooks. The *American Year
Book* (1910–1919; 1925–   ) and the *New International Year
Book* (1908–   ) are of genuine assistance. Articles in the
Political Science Quarterly (New York, 1886–   ) and the
American Political Science Review (Baltimore, 1906–   ) are
of unusual value. The *Literary Digest* (New York, 1890–   ),
the *Outlook* (New York, 1870–   ), and the *New Republic*
(New York, 1914–   ) give reflections of events in Ohio and
the opinions of Ohioans.

H. R. Mengert, "The Ohio Workmen's Compensation Law,"
Ohio Archæological and Historical Quarterly, Vol. XXIX, pp.
1–48, is a careful study of highly important legislation. The
Miami Valley Conservancy work is summarized by Arthur E.
Morgan and C. A. Bock in Galbreath, *History of Ohio*, Vol. I,
pp. 13–24.

A résumé of Ohio's part in the World War is included in C. B.
Galbreath, *History of Ohio*, Vol. I, pp. 633–710. Of unexcelled
value for Ohio's part in the war are the numerous files of contemporary newspaper clippings, collected by the Historical
Commission of Ohio and deposited in the Ohio Archæological
and Historical Society Library, at Columbus. Authoritative
material dealing with the World War can be found in Leonard
P. Ayres, "The War with Germany: a Statistical Summary," in
C. F. Horne and W. F. Austin, *The Great Events of the Great War*
(7 vols., New York, 1920), Vol. VII, Appendix. Special articles
include E. J. Benton, "The Cleveland World War Machine,"
Ohio Archæological and Historical Quarterly, Vol. XXXVIII,
pp. 448–474; Carl Wittke, "Ohio's German-language Press and
the War," *Ibid.*, Vol. XXVIII, pp. 82–95; Carl Wittke, "Ohio's

German-language Press and the Peace Negotiations," *Ibid.*, Vol. XXIX, pp. 49–79; Carl Wittke, "Ohio's German-language Press in the Campaign of 1920," *Mississippi Valley Historical Association Proceedings*, Vol. X, pp. 468–480.

The movements toward prohibition and woman suffrage are treated fully in the next chapter of this volume.

CHAPTER XX

SINCE THE WORLD WAR

Movements toward Reform

*D*URING the months of American participation in the
World War and for some time thereafter, Ohioans,
like others among their contemporaries, experienced the
exhilarating influence of a feverish idealism which was
responsible in part for the ratification of two new amendments to the Federal Constitution and for a strong movement in favor of the acceptance of a third. Each of these
proposals was the result of much agitation, the progress of
which deserves more extended analysis.

Prohibition

The protracted struggle between defenders and opponents of the liquor traffic in Ohio has been treated in part
in this volume in a consideration of social and political
forces during the various decades. Much of the story,
however, must be further discussed, especially that part
relating to the activities of the Anti-Saloon League since
the constitutional convention of 1912.

Following a preliminary meeting in the Spear Library
at Oberlin College, this league had been definitely organized
at a Sunday mass meeting at Oberlin in June, 1893. The
movement was largely a means of unifying sentiment
among religious organizations against the liquor traffic
so as to achieve results in a political way. Howard H.
Russell was its first state superintendent and figured so

prominently in its activities that he was soon chosen to a similar position in the national organization.

The adoption of a license system in the constitution of the state in 1912 ran counter to the wishes of the prohibitionists, who nevertheless capitalized upon the situation to secure in the new license statute of 1913 the furtherance of restrictions upon the liquor traffic. The adoption of the initiative and the referendum in 1912 also proved a stumblingblock to the "dry" forces. The power that the less populous rural counties (generally favorable to prohibition) had exercised in the legislature to secure the local option laws that they desired was checked by the restraining effect of the popular referendum. By this process of appealing to the electorate of the state as a whole, a "wet" majority in a single populous county like Hamilton might counterbalance the "dry" lead for a proposal, piled up in forty smaller counties. The adoption of the "home rule" amendment in 1914 also handicapped the anti-liquor forces by repealing the Rose Law, of 1908, which had made the county the unit for local option and which, within two years, had resulted in fifty-eight out of eighty-eight counties' deciding for prohibition. Following the acceptance of this amendment, some of the formerly "dry" counties reëstablished the liquor trade, and hundreds of new saloons were opened.

The referendum process, nevertheless, carried with it the possibility of making the whole state legally "dry," and the Anti-Saloon League was active in bringing the question of state-wide prohibition to the voters of the state in 1914, 1915, 1917, and 1918. As is explained elsewhere, the anti-prohibition forces soon wearied of continuous defense of their interests at the polls and attempted unsuccessfully in 1915 to secure the acceptance of a "Stability League amendment," which would have prevented another vote upon twice-defeated constitutional amendments for a period of six years following the adoption of the constitutional changes of 1912. In the vote of 1917, a "wet" majority of only 1,137 was recorded in a total of over a million votes, and in the next year state-wide prohibition was carried by a margin of 25,759 votes. In 1919, the manner in which proposals relating to prohibition were presented to the voters caused results that seemed strangely inconsistent. On the one hand, the electorate rejected a proposition to legalize the sale of 2.75 per cent beer and disapproved a proposed constitutional amendment to repeal state-wide prohibition. On the other hand, the Crabbe Act for the enforcement of state prohibition (passed by the legislature in 1919) was rejected by means of a referendum, as was the ratification of the eighteenth amendment to the national Constitution, which had secured the approval of the legislature on January 7, 1919.

It is interesting to note that in the elections of 1918, a new amendment to the state constitution, providing for the use of the referendum in the case of such proposed amendments to the Federal Constitution as had been ratified by the legislature, had been accepted by an overwhelming majority; and that the eighteenth (prohibition) amendment to the Federal Constitution was the first to which such a referendum was applied. The validity of this process as applied to the United States constitutional amendments was upheld by the Ohio Supreme Court but was denied by the highest United States tribunal in 1920 in a decision (*Hawke* vs. *Smith*) that held that the assent of the state expressed through the legislature was final.

In 1920 the voters of Ohio ratified a second Crabbe (state prohibition enforcement) Act, which had been passed by the legislature in that year and which was less drastic than the measure rejected in the previous year. In 1922 the electorate voted down a proposal to permit 2.75 per cent beer and light wines for home consumption. In the meantime, state prohibition had been made somewhat more effective by the establishment of a State Bureau of Enforcement (in 1921) and by the enactment of additional legislation to assist in the suppression of illicit business.

During these turbulent years, the Anti-Saloon League, with headquarters at Westerville, a few miles northeast of Columbus, was publishing a paper, *The American Issue*, which attained an extensive circulation. In the political arena, Wayne B. Wheeler, of Columbus, a most effective lobbyist, was active in Washington as the head of the legal and legislative department of the league. Tremendous power was exercised by the Anti-Saloon League in securing support for "dry" candidates. In November, 1924, the prohibitionists elected an overwhelming majority to the next Ohio Legislature and obtained nineteen out of twenty-two seats in the state's congressional delegation.

A change in sentiment on the prohibition question, however, soon began to assert itself. This change was due partly to a reaction from the idealism of the war period, which seemed too difficult for general acceptance over an extended period of time; partly to a feeling among many of an illusion-shattered generation that the gratification of the senses offered some recompense for the strain of existence in the machine age; and partly to a belief that the Anti-Saloon League had employed its powers to prostitute all other considerations in political life to a maintenance of prohibition.

The effective control of the liquor traffic in a state of such conflicting attitudes as are found in Ohio was at best a difficult problem. In their zeal to secure rigid enforcement, the prohibitionists in Ohio had secured legislation providing that mayors, justices of the peace, and other local magistrates should receive, in addition to their salaries, substantial fees when persons were convicted and fined in liquor cases. This legislation led to the extension by the magistrates of their jurisdiction, especially in the vicinity of the large cities—so as to make liquor cases profitable to the nearby smaller communities. A case (*Tumey* vs. *Ohio*) arising in North College Hill, Ohio, was carried to the United States Supreme Court, which in March, 1927, declared the Ohio law to be void as a violation of the fourteenth amendment to the Constitution. The Ohio Legislature, therefore, attempted to circumvent the objections to the old law by the passage of the Marshall Bill (in April, 1927), which was a new proposal that allowed compensation to magistrates on the basis of the number of cases tried (within a maximum figure) but assured payment whether fines were imposed or not. The bill was championed by the Anti-Saloon League but opposed even by some "drys" on constitutional grounds and on account of the need for a thorough revision of the justice and mayoralty courts. The proposal was neither vetoed nor signed by Governor Donahey and by the referendum process came before the voters in the fall of 1927. The result was a two-to-one vote against the measure. *The American Issue* attempted to lay the result to extremely light voting in the rural districts and insisted that the question at stake was not "a wet-and-dry issue." While the outcome could not be interpreted as a repudiation of prohibition, it was nevertheless a distinct rebuke to the Anti-Saloon League. In 1930, the election to the United States Senate of a "dripping wet" Democrat, Robert J. Bulkley, of Cleveland, over Senator Roscoe McCulloch, a "dry" (who had been appointed to fill the place of the deceased Theodore Burton), indicated a definite change in sentiment. This trend became apparent to all, following the

Ohio primaries of May, 1932, when anti-prohibition candidates for the senatorship, Bettman (Republican) and Bulkley (Democrat), were swept into the nomination of both parties and not one candidate recommended for an important state office by the dry organization received a nomination.

Following the triumph of the Democrats in the fall of 1932 and the accession to power of the Franklin D. Roosevelt administration, Federal legislation was passed in March, 1933, legalizing the manufacture and sale of 3.2 per cent (by weight) beer in states that were favorable to such a change. The Ohio Legislature quickly enacted the necessary state legislation in the form of the Ackerman Law, and beginning on April 7, legal beer, subject to a license system, with state and Federal fees and taxes, was again available in Ohio. In March the legislature also passed the Mosier Act, which provided for a convention of fifty-two delegates-at-large to consider the repeal of the eighteenth amendment to the national Constitution. The members of this body, nominated by petition, were to be pledged to the repeal or the retention of prohibition, or were to be wholly uncommitted on the subject. The Anti-Saloon League and the W. C. T. U. quickly organized a movement to postpone the proposed change by means of the referendum process. By June they had secured 242,060 signatures (about 87,000 in excess of the minimum required by law) to petitions that asked that the voter be given an opportunity to accept or reject the Mosier Law. A month later, however, the Ohio Supreme Court decided that this law was not subject to a referendum since it related to a Federal function and not to a distinctly state purpose. Accordingly, Ohioans voted on November 7 for delegates, who assembled in convention on December 5. At the polls those candidates pledged to repeal received about two and one-half times as many votes as those committed to the retention of prohibition (none being unpledged). Hence, on December 5, the Ohio convention followed similar action in other states in ratifying the first proposal of a change in the Federal Constitution that provided for the repeal of a previous amendment. In November, the voters of Ohio had also approved of a repeal of the prohibition amendment to the state constitution, but the task of rescinding the state enforcement acts fell to a forthcoming special session of the legislature.

Woman's Rights

Ohio played a part in the woman's rights movement perhaps only second in importance to that played by New York. Following the first woman's rights convention at Seneca Falls, New York, in 1848, a second gathering, which was a state convention, was held at Salem, Ohio, in April, 1850. At the latter assembly, in which no man was allowed to participate in any way, twenty-two resolutions were adopted for presentation to the second constitutional convention of the state. Subsequently, for a number of years, annual state conventions were held, at one of which at Massillon in 1852, the Ohio Woman's Rights Association was organized. The coming of the Civil War and the Reconstruction period that followed turned popular attention in large degree to other affairs. In the eighteen-eighties and early nineties, however, proposals that aimed at woman suffrage were considered in the legislature, and in 1894 a law was passed granting suffrage to women in school elections. This act was clearly constitutional without an amendment to the organic law, for the constitution gave full control over school affairs to the legislature.

During the same period, laws were passed to improve the civil status of women. In 1887 married women obtained control of their own property; in 1893 they secured the right to act as guardians and, in 1894, as executors and administrators; in the latter year they were granted the right to sue and be sued.

During the early years of the present century, the advocates of woman suffrage made unsuccessful attempts to secure from the legislature a state constitutional amendment for submission to the voters. Such a proposal, however, was approved by the constitutional convention of 1912, only to be rejected at the polls by the electorate in the same year. The liquor interests feared the effect of woman suffrage upon a continuance of their business and worked for its rejection, and at the elections of 1914 a proposed amendment was again lost. By means of municipal charters, however, women were granted the suffrage during the next few years in several cities, including East Cleveland, Lakewood, and Columbus. Early in 1917 the legislature granted Presidential suffrage to women and the measure was approved by Governor Cox. By the use of the referendum (in connection with which the suffragists charged that frauds were perpetrated on a wholesale scale), however, the question was submitted to the voters in 1917 and rejected by a majority of over 146,000.

During this decade, a national woman suffrage amendment was voted upon several times in Congress, and at the time of its successful passage in 1919, only two Ohio Congressmen[1] and one Ohio Senator, Atlee Pomerene, were recorded in opposition. In the state legislature, Ohio's ratification came quickly, Ohio being the fifth state to register its approval.

In 1923 the Ohio Legislature, taking cognizance of the trend toward civil and political equality of the sexes,

---

[1] Warren Gard, of Dayton, and A. E. B. Stephens, of Cincinnati.

provided for twenty-one years as the age of majority for women as well as men and extended to women the same rights as men in all respects as voters.

Women soon showed an ambition to hold office, and in 1922 the first of their sex was chosen to the legislature. In that year two women were elected to the state senate and four to the house of representatives. Four years later, the number had increased to three senators and eight representatives. In 1922 Florence E. Allen, of Cleveland, was elected to the Ohio Supreme Court, and the highest tribunal of Ohio had the distinction of being the first supreme court in any state with a woman on its panel of judges.

Some ardent feminists still felt, however, that certain laws that aimed at the protection of women were discriminatory and pointed to such legislation as that passed in 1919 by the Ohio Legislature. This statute forbade women to serve in almost a score of occupations, for instance as bell hops, taxi drivers, and gas or electric meter readers, and prohibited their employment in the handling of freight or at any task "requiring frequent and repeated lifting of weights over twenty-five pounds." The laws of Ohio still implied that the functions of members of the two sexes were not in all respects identical.

Child Labor Legislation

Another reform eagerly advocated for inclusion in the Federal Constitution was the granting to Congress of the power to legislate concerning the labor of children under eighteen years of age. Ohio had been a pioneer in the enactment of state child labor laws, having as early as 1852 limited working hours for children. Twelve years was the minimum age for work in mines. A law of 1885 had required manufacturers to keep a record of all minors in their employ and had provided for factory inspectors. The number of children employed in the state increased in spite of restrictions, and in 1905 further legislation prohibited the employment for wages of any boy under fifteen or any girl under sixteen during the sessions of the public schools. The competition with Ohio industry of factories in nearby states such as Pennsylvania and West Virginia, where the laws were less rigid, hampered the enforcement of Ohio statutes. This was especially the case in the eastern Ohio glass factories, in close proximity to states that permitted night work for children of twelve and thirteen years.

The agitation for the national regulation of child labor developed slowly, but in 1916 Congress passed a law prohibiting the transportation in interstate commerce of the products of child labor. Upon the Supreme Court's pronouncement of this statute as unconstitutional, Senator Atlee Pomerene, of Ohio, had introduced into Congress the second child labor proposal, based upon the taxing power of Congress. When this law in turn was declared unconstitutional by the highest court of the country, there was widespread expression of regret in Ohio. One Columbus paper deplored the lack of protection to youth "from capitalistic Simon Legrees who would coin their little lives into dollars." Many felt, nevertheless, that the powers of the National Government ought not to be stretched to extreme limits.

Federal statistics as to children gainfully employed showed a rather lax enforcement of the state statutes, and in 1921 the Ohio Legislature passed the Bing Act. This act raised the school age to eighteen years, required employment certificates for all children under that age who worked, increased the penalties for violations of the child labor or school laws, and established sixteen years as the minimum age (except under certain circumstances) in a long list of specified industries.[2]

Much sentiment developed in Ohio in favor of a national constitutional amendment against child labor. Scores of clubs passed resolutions urging action upon Congress, and Representative Israel M. Foster, of Athens, labored to secure such an amendment. When the proposal that would grant to Congress the power to regulate the labor of persons under eighteen years of age came to a vote, both Ohio Senators supported the amendment, as did all Ohio Representatives except two.[3]

Many organizations like the League of Women Voters and the American Federation of Labor promptly announced their support of the contemplated change, but the National Manufacturers' Association, the Ohio Farm Bureau, and the Ohio State Grange declared their opposition to the proposed Federal amendment. Farm groups constituted the most formidable opponents of the measure, criticizing it as an "invasion of the rights of parents." Louis J. Taber, of Columbus, Master of the National Grange, asserted that if the age limit had been lower and farm and home labor had been specifically exempted from congressional regulation, the opposition would have been negligible. Such concerted hostility developed that the state house of representatives rejected the amendment by a vote of 91 to 35, and it was not at that time brought to a vote in the Ohio Senate. A drastic, somewhat unexpected change in sentiment, however, had developed by March, 1933, when

[2] In 1923 the Bloom Bill, which sought to lower the age for school attendance from the Bing Act standard, was vetoed by the Governor, but in 1925 legislation was enacted to allow children who were over fourteen and were incapable of profiting by further schooling, to be employed under special working certificates.

[3] Charles Brand, of Urbana, voted "nay" and Ralph C. Cole, of Findlay, did not vote.

the Ohio Senate, by a vote of 26 to 2, followed similar action taken some weeks earlier by the house in approving the child labor amendment. Thus, Ohio became the eighth state to ratify the proposal.

Opposition similar to that at first expressed in Ohio, nevertheless, had developed in other states, so that the Child Labor proposal did not become the twentieth amendment to the Federal Constitution, as its advocates had hoped it would. Instead, the next amendment turned out to be the "Lame Duck" proposal, which sanctioned a change in the date of the President's inauguration from March 4 to January 20, and changed the date of the beginning of new terms of Congress from March 4 to January 3. The Ohio Legislature was tardy in ratifying this amendment, giving its assent during the evening of the day (January 23, 1933)[4] on which Missouri (the thirty-sixth state to ratify the proposal) had registered its assent and thereby insured the necessary three fourths of the States to make the amendment part of the Constitution.

State and National Politics, 1919–1933

The election of James M. Cox in 1918 as Governor for a third time of a state that is politically strategic in national contests marked him as a Presidential possibility in 1920. His vote-commanding ability was particularly significant, for never before had a Democrat been elected to the Ohio governorship for three terms. In 1918, moreover, his

---

[4] During the day, Georgia and Utah had also ratified, hence Ohio was the thirty-ninth state to act favorably. Ohio's official certificate of ratification, however, was sent to Washington with such expedition that its vote was the twenty-eighth to be recorded by the Secretary of State.

Census figures, released by the Census Bureau in July, 1933, indicated that Ohio ranked first among the states of the Union in the elimination of child labor. Only one out of every one hundred children between ten and fifteen years of age was gainfully employed.

victory was unusually noteworthy, for it had been accomplished in an election when the rest of the state ticket, both houses of the legislature, and about two thirds of the congressional districts were captured by Republican candidates.

In the national Democratic convention of 1920 at San Francisco, however, Cox won the Presidential nomination only on the forty-fourth ballot, after a heated contest with A. Mitchell Palmer and William G. McAdoo. Some observers felt that his selection was due to the delegates' becoming weary of the clamor for McAdoo; some considered that the "wet bosses" had worked for his success.

The naming of Cox made it certain that an Ohio newspaper man would be the next President, for the Republicans had already broken a deadlock in their convention by the nomination of Warren G. Harding, a native of central Ohio, who had risen as a "Foraker Republican" to the post of lieutenant-governor in 1903 and had attained business success as the publisher of the Marion *Star*. In addition, a minor candidate, Aaron Watkins, of the Prohibitionist ticket,[5] was an Ohioan, a Methodist minister of Cincinnati. Harding carried the state by a plurality of over 400,000 votes and the nation by an electoral vote of 404 to 127, but the "Ohio Gang" of unpleasant memory marred his term.

The reaction against the Democratic Party that characterized the post-war "return to normalcy" contributed at the same time to the election of Harry L. Davis, Republican, of Cuyahoga County, to the governorship over Vic Donahey, of Tuscarawas County, by a plurality of about 121,000 votes. The new Governor was a native of Cleveland who had gone to work in a rolling mill at the age of thirteen and had subsequently studied commercial subjects and

---

[5] Watkin's recorded vote in Ohio was only 294, while that of Debs, the Socialist candidate, was 57,147.

civil engineering. In 1909 he had been elected city treasurer and, beginning in 1915, to three terms as mayor of Ohio's largest municipality.

The chief problem attacked by the new Governor was that of the administrative reorganizaiton of the state government. The way had been paved for constructive achievement in this field by the work of a joint legislative committee that had been established in 1919 with State Senator Frank E. Whittemore as chairman. The findings of the committee had been published in about seventy-five pamphlets, and although no specific plans had been prepared, Davis in his campaign for the governorship had emphasized the need for reform in this direction. Upon Davis's accession to office, experts like George E. Frazer and Walter F. Dodd, of Chicago, and Clarence D. Laylin, of the Ohio State University, were engaged to draft appropriate legislation. The house and senate chairmen of the legislative committees, Senator Wallace W. Bellew and Representative Robert C. Dunn, rendered invaluable service, and the proposed bill received the Governor's approval in April, 1921. Davis felt that the possibility of delay in consummating the desired changes by means of an appeal to the referendum process should be avoided, so the legislation was passed as an emergency measure (and therefore exempted from a referendum). The opposition looked upon the law as a "ripper bill," tearing open the departments of the state government for the Republican spoilsmen and particularly criticized the employment of the emergency provision as an undemocratic procedure. The legality of the use of the procedure in this instance, however, was upheld by the state supreme court, and the Republican plans were carried into effect.

The new administrative code did not touch the constitutional offices of lieutenant-governor, secretary of state, auditor, treasurer, and attorney general, but organized the state administration into seven departments. The most distinctive features of the plan were: (1) the development, to a degree found at that time in the administration of no other state, of the idea that administrative work should be conducted by single heads of departments; (2) the granting to department heads, rather than to the governor, of the power to appoint heads of divisions within each department (except in the case of the head of the division of banks, who was to be selected directly by the governor); and (3) the bestowal upon the governor of complete command over the heads of his departments, who were subject to removal at his pleasure.

One of the defects of the existing system that Davis recognized as impairing the efficiency of the state administration was the short term of office of the governor (two years) and the consequent frequent changes in administrative heads. An attempt was made to remedy this in November, 1925, by a submission to the voters of a constitutional amendment increasing the terms of county and state officers to four years. This amendment failed to be adopted, but the movement for change continued, and in 1928 a nonpartisan organization in Cleveland, the Citizens' League, through its state committee publicly urged the extension of the governor's term.

During the Davis administration, in February, 1921, the legislature created a fund for the payment of a state bonus to Ohio's veterans of the World War, each service man to receive ten dollars for each month of enlistment up to a maximum of twenty-five months. Four-and-three-fourths-per-cent bonds, dated January 1, 1922, and maturing from April 1, 1922, to October 1, 1932, in a total amount of twenty-five million dollars, were to be issued, subject to a referendum of the voters. The decision of the popular

vote in November, 1921, was approximately three to one in
favor of the proposition. Later, it became evident that
about ten million dollars additional would be needed to
meet the applications that were being presented, but it was
found feasible to appropriate this money without the
floating of another bond issue. Such a measure was passed
by a session of the legislature called especially for the
purpose in July, 1922. Another concession to the war
veterans was a law approved by the Governor in May,
1921, that provided for a remission to ex-service men of all
tuition and matriculation charges at state colleges and
universities.

Davis had previously stated his intention to serve only a
single term, so in 1922 Carmi A. Thompson, of Cleveland,
became the Republican nominee. He was opposed on the
Democratic ticket by Vic Donahey, former state auditor,
who in that office had made a reputation as the "watch-dog
of the treasury." Donahey was victor by a plurality of
about 18,000 votes in a total vote of over 1,600,000. At
the same time, Congressman Simeon Fess, one-time professor at Ohio Northern University and president of
Antioch College, won an election to the United States
Senate over Atlee Pomerene.

Among the laws passed during Donahey's first term and
over the Governor's veto was a provision for the creation of
a judicial council of nine judges, headed by the Chief
Justice, to make a continuous study of the organization,
rules, and methods of procedure and practice of the judicial
system of the state. A well-known professor of law at
the Ohio State University declared this "a long step toward
closer coördination of the courts." One of the principal
objections that legal experts found to the operation of the
court system was in the manner in which one of the seemingly progressive constitutional changes of 1912 had

worked out in practice. The revised constitution had made a provision that no law should be held void by the state supreme court without the concurrence of all but one of the judges. An exception was made in the case of an appeal from the judgment of the court of appeals when the court had declared a law unconstitutional, in which case a mere majority of the supreme court could affirm the unconstitutionality of a law. The members of the constitutional convention of 1912 had hoped to prevent a bare majority of the supreme court from invalidating an apparently desirable statute. In 1930, after the constitutionality of a law had been sustained by the court of appeals in Ohio, five judges of the supreme court held the law to be void while two of them sustained its validity. The law in question, accordingly, continued to be considered valid (since all but one judge's concurrence was necessary under these circumstances to declare it void). Naturally, objections arose to the lack of uniformity in decisions in the state as a result of this situation, and the United States Supreme Court was called upon to pass judgment on the Ohio constitutional provision. The high court, however, held in the case of *Ohio* ex rel. *Bryant* vs. *Akron Metropolitan Park District* (1930) that the state by failing to establish uniformity did not "deny the equal protection of the laws" and maintained that it was not the Federal Supreme Court's business "to intervene to protect the citizens of this state from the consequences of its policy."

In August, 1923, the state was surprised and shocked by news of the death of President Harding, and the eyes of the nation were temporarily focused upon Ohio as the funeral train ultimately found its way to Marion, where later a costly Harding Memorial was erected and, after long delays, officially dedicated by President Hoover.

In 1924, Donahey was reëlected by a plurality of 176,842 over former Governor Davis at the same time that the Democratic Party carried only seven of the twenty-two congressional districts of the state. In the Presidential contest, Calvin Coolidge, a Republican, carried the state by a plurality of 698,242 over John W. Davis, Democrat, and by a larger margin over Robert M. La Follette, the Progressive candidate, who was also endorsed by the Socialists.

This was a period when a nativist movement, the Ku-Klux Klan, appeared in numerous American communities, including many in Ohio. As an example of their activities, on the Saturday following the death of Harding in 1923, about a hundred robed Klansmen (together with four hundred civilians) at Mt. Vernon, Ohio, marched to the local ball park, burned a cross at midnight, and knelt in silent prayer. The leader declared that they were merely paying tribute to a typical native-born American. More serious, however, was the outbreak of rioting between members of the Ku-Klux Klan and Knights of the Flaming Circle at Niles, Ohio, in November, 1924. About twelve persons were badly injured, and qualified martial law had to be established by the Governor in order to control the situation.

A somewhat different manifestation of Protestant nativism was the Buchanan-Clark Bible Bill, sponsored by the Ku-Klux Klan and certain other religious organizations. The bill required all public school teachers to read ten verses of the Scriptures to the pupils each school day, and for all students above the fourth grade, it prescribed memorizing the Ten Commandments. The bill passed the legislature in 1925 but did not become law, owing to a veto by Governor Donahey.

The difference in political affiliation between the Governor and the Republican legislature did not contribute to a ready coöperation on the part of the executive and legislative branches of the state government, and such a veto as that of the Bible Bill was a frequent occurrence during Donahey's terms as Governor. Thus, during the legislative session of 1925, forty-three bills and specific items in three appropriation bills were vetoed by the Governor, and thirty-three of the bills and items in two of the appropriation measures were enacted over his veto. This was, however, not so striking an example of the effectiveness of the Governor's power as was the case of the previous legislature, which had repassed only eleven bills out of seventy-four (excluding parts of appropriation bills) that the Governor, "Veto Vic," had returned to the legislature without his signature.

During the years following the World War, various changes were proposed in Ohio's election laws. In 1919 a revision and codification of the entire election legislation of the state was accomplished without the making of any drastic changes in the nominating system. The primary system was so expensive for the apparent benefits received from it that some leaders of public opinion, especially former Congressman Knight, of Akron (who was often a stormy petrel in Republican Party circles), actively championed an amendment to the state constitution to make possible a return to the convention system for nominations to public office. Such a proposed change, however, was overwhelmingly defeated at the polls in 1926, the people of Ohio evidently considering the primaries the lesser of two evils. In the same year, a legislative committee appointed to consider changes in election methods investigated the possible use of voting machines. The fact that the state supreme court had declared their use unconstitutional, however, was a deterrent to immediate

action, and although a bill was presented to the legislature
to secure an amendment to the constitution to permit
their use, it was not passed. A noteworthy change in the
state's election law occurred in 1929, when provision was
made for the removal from the ballot of the long list of
names of the candidates of the different parties for Presidential electors. Only the names of the candidates for
President and Vice President were to appear—a change
which so shortened and simplified the Presidential ballot
that this ballot has been merged with the state and local
ballot.

Governor Donahey, who had been elected for a third
time in 1926, defeating Myers Y. Cooper, of Cincinnati, a
banker, lumberman, and real estate operator, retired at
the end of the term from active political life to enter
private business.   In 1928 the Democratic standard in the
race for the governorship was carried by Martin L. Davey,
of Kent, then a Congressman and a member of the family
that had acquired a fortune as developers of a system of
"tree surgery." Davey was beaten, however, by M. Y.
Cooper, the Republican, whose party carried every seat in
the state senate and all but eleven in the house of
representatives.

In the preliminaries leading to the Republican national
convention of the same year, Senator Willis considered
himself a real contender for the nomination. Willis had
never attained to the higher levels of statesmanship, and
the characterization made of him as one who possessed
"the mental equipment of a Harding without his suave
lovableness, the good nature of a Taft without his bubbling
joviality, the serious-mindedness of a McKinley without
his quiet dignity" probably was very near the truth.
Many political observers considered the Willis delegates
who were selected to run for seats in the national convention

as really potential strength for Frank O. Lowden, of Illinois, the leading anti-Hoover contender for the Republican nomination for President. At all events, while campaigning for the Ohio primary of April, 1928, Willis died suddenly at Ohio Wesleyan University, at Delaware. Some anti-Hoover sentiment continued to display itself in Ohio, and Willis received posthumously over seventy thousand votes in the primary. Hoover's nomination on the first ballot at the Kansas City convention, where Senator Fess, of Ohio, was the keynote speaker, found a well-disciplined party ready to ride to victory largely on the strength of a supposedly substantial prosperity. The prohibition issue was also raised, and Mrs. Mabel Walker Willebrandt, Assistant Attorney General of the United States, speaking before the 2,500 pastors and laymen of the Methodist Ohio Conference, at Springfield, appealed to them to use "every day and every ounce of energy" in order "to rouse the friends of prohibition to register and vote."

The result in Ohio was an easy victory for the Republicans. Alfred E. Smith, the Democratic nominee, succeeded in carrying only two of the eighty-eight counties (Mercer and Putnam), and Hoover received a popular vote greater than in any state except Pennsylvania. At the same time, all but three of the Congressmen elected in Ohio were of the Republican Party.

In state affairs, one of the most important problems of the time was that of taxation. The state government depended entirely upon indirect levies—revenues derived from such sources as corporations, franchises, public utilities, and automobiles. The problem of taxation was more acute in local areas, where cities, counties, townships, and school districts were supported principally by the general property tax. The constitution of Ohio provided that all property had to be taxed at the same rate, so that in practice all but the scrupulously honest citizens generally refrained from making tax returns on their stocks, bonds, and deposits in financial institutions. As a result, inadequate revenues were received by the subdivisions. To enforce economy, the state legislature had passed a Smith Law which limited ordinary expenses of government to 1.5 per cent of the value of the property on the tax duplicate. This law still permitted local districts to run into debt and to borrow money by the issuance of bonds. Since the interest and principal of the indebtedness had to be paid out of the taxes, situations arose where, after the payment of interest and part of the principal, current expenses could not be met and local schools had to be closed. To relieve the situation, the Krueger Act was passed in 1925, requiring the voters who desired a bond issue to accept at the same time an extra levy of taxes (above the ordinary 1.5 per cent limitation) so as to provide for the payment of interest and the ultimate discharge of the debt. This action, however, did not correct difficulties arising out of old indebtedness, and such a critical situation developed in the finances of the city of Lima that in January, 1926, a special one-day session of the legislature met to permit one or two counties to levy additional taxes for operating expenses. Cities and counties had acquired such a habit of running into debt (forty-four counties in 1925 operating under a deficit) that the Vorys Budget Act was passed (in 1925) to require that expenditures should not be made in excess of the money in the treasury for meeting them.

To assist poor localities where the maintenance of proper schools seemed to be too expensive, the state began to extend financial aid and in 1929 voted four million dollars for the support of such districts. In 1933 a development of this state-aid system, under a complicated arrangement known as the Mort Plan, was urged upon the legislature, but the burden appeared too great for the state to undertake. Meantime scores of schools were closed and hundreds of teachers were unable to collect their salaries, owing to the continued depression. There was widespread criticism of a policy of spending more money on highway construction than on public education, and the state might well feel deeply chagrined at the Federal census of 1930, which placed it in forty-fourth place in per capita expenditures for education.

The levying of a state gasoline tax (two cents a gallon in 1925; three cents, in 1927; and four cents, in 1929)[6] carried with it the possibility of some improvement in the burden of local taxation, since a part of the tax was ultimately used for township and county roads. In 1929 the old and somewhat unfair assessments on abutting property-owners for state highway costs were abolished, and in 1933 a strong effort was made to secure a refund of taxes of this kind in earlier years.

Further assistance in the alleviation of the burden of local taxation was attempted by the adoption, in 1931, of an amendment to the state constitution providing that not less than fifty per cent of such income and inheritance taxes as the state might collect should be returned to the counties and other local subdivisions in which they originated.

Probably the most important change in Ohio's taxation laws in many years was accomplished by a popular referendum in 1929, when there was adopted a constitutional amendment providing for the abolition of the time-honored "uniform rule," which required the taxation of all property at the same rate. It was expected that this change would

---

[6] The United States Government assessed an additional Federal tax of one cent per gallon in 1932.

make the taxation of so-called intangibles more effective. Governor White, who entered office in January, 1931, expressed himself in favor of the carrying into effect of such a plan by the fixing of a rate lower than that upon real estate. In 1930 a commission of over one hundred and eighty members representing various sections of public opinion was appointed, and in 1931 the legislature adopted a low tax for intangibles, applied on three different schedules of rates according to the type of intangibles involved.

The need for additional revenues in 1931 for educational purposes resulted in a new tax upon the sale of cigarettes, one cent being collected for each package of ten. In the same session, as a result of decreased earnings and perhaps because of an efficient lobby, the steam and electric railroads received a reduction in their taxes of from four per cent to three per cent on their gross earnings after 1933, and the street and suburban railroads, a reduction on a different scale after 1932.

A disaster that seemed to indicate the imperative need for the expenditure of considerable money in the improvement of Ohio's welfare institutions was the penitentiary fire of April 21, 1930, which originated as a plot on the part of several inmates to effect an escape during a general prison "break." The building, in the city of Columbus, had been built to meet the needs of the nineteenth century and was shockingly antiquated and overcrowded. The loss of three hundred and eighteen lives among the prisoners, many of whom had been trapped in their cells, created a demand for improved facilities. Accordingly, in 1931, there was submitted to the voters a proposed constitutional amendment sanctioning the issuance of bonds to the amount of $7,500,000 for the construction and the repairing of penal and welfare institutions of the state. The financial stringency of the times and the fact that a board of control would have been empowered to manage the expenditure of the funds without supervision by the legislature were reasons contributing to the overwhelming rejection of the proposal.

The desire for a political change because of the altered economic situation in the state and in the nation was a factor in 1930 in the defeat for reëlection of Governor Cooper by George White, a Marietta Democrat. The latter had worked in the coal mines of Pennsylvania as a youth, and, after a Princeton education, had participated in the gold rush to the Klondike region. Later he had accumulated a comfortable fortune in the oil business and had served three terms in Congress.

Problems relating to the depression that gradually fastened itself upon the country with increasing severity after the stock-market crash of 1929 demanded a large amount of attention from the White administration. The difficulties relating to taxation as they confronted the legislature of 1931 have already been discussed. The same session also authorized a commission of nine members, appointed by the Governor, to investigate the possibilities of unemployment insurance and to recommend legislation suitable for enactment in Ohio. Dr. Isaac M. Rubinow, of Cincinnati, an expert in the field, was appointed the chairman of the commission, and a comprehensive plan was proposed, but widespread objections arose to imposing upon business an additional burden at a time when bankruptcy was almost imminent in many cases.

During 1932, the unusual circumstances of the time and the increasing suffering of hundreds of thousands due to the prolonged depression were responsible for three special sessions of the legislature. The first, which met March 29–31, passed legislation relating to five subjects: (1) the authorization of counties to issue bonds for economic relief; (2) the increase of excise taxes on public utilities with the stipulation that funds raised from this source should be applied to the retirement of county relief bonds; (3) the empowering of boards of education to supply clothing, medical attention, and other necessities to school children; (4) a provision that part of the revenues from gasoline taxes and motor vehicle licenses that already had been allocated to subdivisions of the state might be used for relief purposes during a limited period; (5) the creation of a temporary state relief commission with power to administer the relief laws.

The second special session met on May 16 and adjourned on the same day. Its work was limited to the amending of the state banking laws so as to permit the state superintendent of banks to borrow money from the Reconstruction Finance Corporation (a Federal agency established by the Hoover administration) for the purpose of liquidating or reopening and reorganizing those banks of the state whose "frozen assets" had resulted in their suspension of business operations.

In September, a third extraordinary session was summoned by the Governor. Its work was accomplished in less than a week and included the enactment of the Governor's recommendations with relatively unimportant changes. The essential parts of the new legislation provided: (1) for reductions in the salaries of state and county officials upon a graduated scale; (2) for housing corporations in Ohio, to be financed in part by the Reconstruction Finance Corporation, for the elimination of slum districts; and (3) for various means to enable local subdivisions to meet their obligations, in view of decreasing revenues. Joint resolutions were also passed providing for special commissions to investigate milk prices in Ohio and the highway assessment problem in the state.

The steadily increasing severity of the economic crisis carried with it a decided reaction against the Hoover administration, hence the impression that it was "a Democratic year" added to the interest in the national convention of that party in 1932. Governor White and Newton D. Baker were Ohioans who had been mentioned as possible nominees, and the former received the complimentary vote of the Ohio delegation on the first ballot. Upon the fourth and last ballot, however, a majority of the Ohioans joined in nominating Franklin D. Roosevelt as their Presidential candidate in opposition to Herbert Hoover. The campaign excited intense interest in the state as Roosevelt opened his campaign at Columbus, and Hoover and Norman Thomas, the Socialist candidate, each made a number of speeches within the borders of Ohio. The extent of the political change during four years in Ohio is suggested by the fact that in November, 1932, Hoover carried only thirty of the counties in contrast with eighty-six in 1928, although Roosevelt's plurality was far from exceptional—74,016. At the same time, eighteen of the twenty-six Congressmen elected were Democrats. Governor White surprised many political observers by piling up a plurality of over 200,000 votes over his Republican opponent, David Ingalls, a youthful and wealthy Clevelander, who had served the Hoover administration as Assistant Secretary of the Navy for Aeronautics.

The Ninetieth General Assembly of Ohio, which convened in January, 1933, was the first legislature of the state since 1917 whose lower house was controlled by the Democratic Party. The membership of the Senate was equally divided. Because of the continued persistence of the economic depression in the state and nation, a task of extreme difficulty awaited the attention of the members. The basic problem, which involved state appropriations for education and for poor relief, was that of raising necessary revenues from sources that tended to resist any additional burdens upon their resources, whose strength had been impaired by three years of economic stress. On the success of securing further levies, however, rested the continued operation of hundreds of elementary and secondary schools dependent upon state aid, and the supplying of the imperative necessities of life to thousands of families, who were unable to secure employment of any kind. Governor White at first proposed a program of "nuisance" taxes (on malt, tobacco, and so forth) and a diversion of funds from the gasoline tax. Early in May, however, he recommended the passage of a sales tax (a method that had previously been discussed in the legislature) and a graduated levy upon incomes. The sales tax proposal was strongly opposed by business interests represented in the Ohio Chamber of Commerce and by others who felt that it would be a severe blow at increased buying power, a factor recognized as essential to economic recovery. In the legislature the Governor's program was treated with scant courtesy, and following prolonged discussion, that body adjourned in July, after passing the general appropriation bill and sanctioning such "stop-gap taxes" as had survived the opposition of the powerful lobbies. To aid the impoverished public school districts, the cigarette tax was reënacted for two additional years, and a sales tax of one cent per gallon was levied upon all liquid fuels.[7] It was believed that assistance to school districts would be facilitated also by a new act that revised the existing intangible tax law and established a permanent system of allocation for revenue from intangibles. To provide for poor relief,

---

[7] By a companion measure, in order to compensate for the additional tax on gasoline, the state excise tax on that commodity was reduced from four to three cents a gallon.

a ten-per-cent tax was levied upon amusement admissions costing over forty cents, upon the retail price of cosmetics, and upon greens fees at golf clubs, with a five-per-cent tax upon golf club memberships. For the same purpose taxes upon beer (both in barrels and in bottles) were levied.

The revenues expected from these sources were clearly inadequate for the needs that they were intended to meet. Hence, two months later (in August) the legislature was convened in special session by the Governor, who submitted to the legislators five alternative plans for raising money. Dissension again arose, but further taxes placed upon the sale of malt and bottled beverages costing over five cents per unit were voted for poor relief. At the same time the cosmetic tax was extended until the middle of 1936 and the exemption from the admissions tax was reduced from forty cents to ten cents. Additional aid to poor school districts was complicated by a plea from Roman Catholic authorities, who asked approximately $2,500,000 aid annually for their parochial schools for a period of two years. Cries of unconstitutionality were heard, and Lutheran and other Protestant voices were raised against such an innovation. At length, after angry discussion, the adjournment of the legislature was secured without the granting of further assistance to either public or private schools.

While the legislature was thus fumbling its way toward some solution of the problems of taxation in the state, the new Roosevelt administration was commanding attention by its efforts to find a way of salvaging the economic structure of American life. At the time of the inauguration of the President, Ohio banks had already limited withdrawals from accounts in their institutions,[8] in part because

---

[8] A law permitting such restriction was pushed through the Ohio Legislature late in February.

of the heavy drain of money from Ohio financial organizations by Michigan depositors, whose own banking facilities had been curtailed two weeks before. Roosevelt soon proclaimed a national banking "holiday" of four days' duration, and Congress, summoned in special session, granted him dictatorial powers in dealing with the emergency. The Ohio Legislature gave similar authority to state officials in supervising the activities of banks, insurance companies, and building and loan organizations. Authority that approximated "war powers" over the closing, reorganizing, and liquidation of financial concerns was thus assumed by national and state officers. Gradually the banks of the state were reopened in practically all of the communities of Ohio, though for a time some continued to limit withdrawals. Loan associations which had earlier restricted or prohibited withdrawals continued that policy.

The advocates of social welfare, stimulated by the spirit of a "New Deal" in public affairs, introduced into the Ohio Legislature bills providing for unemployment insurance, old age pensions, and the minimum wage. The depression was effectively used as a reason or an excuse for opposing such enactments; but in June, following appeals from President Roosevelt and Secretary of Labor Frances Perkins, Governor White interceded for the passage of the O'Neil-Pringle Minimum Wage Bill. This act provides that the state director of industrial relations may appoint in certain industries boards of arbitration with power to establish minimum wages for women and children therein. By employing the initiative process, friends of old age pensions secured a popular vote in November, 1933, in Ohio, upon a pension proposal. This proposal received a favorable majority and paved the way for the establishment of a system of aid to impoverished persons who had attained the age of sixty-five, who had resided in Ohio for fifteen years, and who had no relatives legally responsible for their care.

The legislature also attempted to ease the plight of property owners who were victims of the depression by providing methods of paying off delinquent taxes without the customary penalties and by granting judges, for two years, discretion as to ordering the sale of mortgaged property in certain cases. In the same spirit a proposed amendment to the state constitution reducing the ordinary tax limitation upon real estate from fifteen mills to ten mills on each dollar of valuation was submitted to a popular referendum (in November, 1933). The proposal was carried by a very substantial majority, and there was presented the problem of finding new revenues to make up for the expected loss of about forty-five million dollars in real estate taxes.[9]

In the summer of 1933, the national government inaugurated its National Recovery Administration in a definite attempt to stimulate economic rehabilitation. The Ohio Legislature, in coöperation with this program, passed the Waldvogel-Smith Act to remove certain legal limitations upon cities and other political subdivisions that wished to secure Federal aid for public works. There was also enacted the Carney Law, setting aside the state's anti-trust legislation, permitting price-fixing within industries, and empowering the governor to accept, demand, and enforce codes of fair practice within industrial groups. Private citizens and corporations joined in supporting the plans of the aggressive President; and in Ohio, as elsewhere, there continued the hope, sometimes feeble, sometimes more

---

[9] At the same election a "County Home Rule Amendment" was also passed. It empowered counties to adopt alternative forms of county government.

vigorously expressed, that by some means—old or new— better times might come again.

Selected Bibliography

Ohio Legislative History (James K. Mercer, ed.) covers the period till 1926. Volumes III, IV, V, and VI deal with the last administration of James M. Cox, the term of Harry L. Davis, and the first two administrations of Vic Donahey. Much material for the present chapter was necessarily obtained from newspapers. The standard yearbooks and the magazines of contemporary opinion, like the *Literary Digest* and the *New Republic* (mentioned in the preceding chapter) are also of assistance for these years. Trends and facts on municipal affairs are readily obtainable in the *National Municipal Review* (1912–   ) and the *American City Magazine* (1909–   ).

The annals of the Ohio administrations in Galbreath, *History of Ohio*, Vol. II, continue to the fall of 1925. Special chapters in Galbreath are devoted to the temperance crusade and to the woman suffrage movement in Ohio, the latter contribution being by Mrs. Harriet T. Upton, for eighteen years president of the Ohio Suffrage Association. There are sections devoted to Ohio in *Standard Encyclopedia of the Alcohol Problem* (Ernest H. Cherrington, ed., 6 vols., Westerville, Ohio, 1925–1930) and in *History of Woman Suffrage* (Mrs. Elizabeth Cady Stanton *et al.*, eds., 6 vols., Rochester, N. Y., 1881–1922). An article by a noted political scientist who is sharply critical of the value of the administrative changes of the Davis administration is F. W. Coker, "Dogmas of Administrative Reform, as Exemplified in the Recent Reorganization in Ohio," *American Political Science Review*, Vol. XVI, pp. 399–411.

GOVERNORS OF OHIO

Name	Party	County of Residence	Period in Office
Edward Tiffin (resigned)	Republican[1]	Ross	1803–1807
*Thomas Kirker	Republican	Adams	1807–1808
Samuel Huntington	Republican	Geauga { In the part of Ohio now called Lake County	1808–1810
Return J. Meigs, Jr. (resigned)	Republican	Washington	1810–1814
*Othniel Looker	Republican	Hamilton	1814–
Thomas Worthington	Republican	Ross	1814–1818
Ethan Allen Brown	Republican	Hamilton	1818–1822
*Allen Trimble	Republican	Highland	1822–
Jeremiah Morrow	Republican	Warren	1822–1826
Allen Trimble	Republican	Highland	1826–1830
Duncan McArthur	National Republican	Ross	1830–1832
Robert Lucas	Democrat	Pike	1832–1836
Joseph Vance	Whig	Champaign	1836–1838
Wilson Shannon	Democrat	Belmont	1838–1840
Thomas Corwin	Whig	Warren	1840–1842
Wilson Shannon (resigned)	Democrat	Belmont	1842–1844
*Thomas Bartley	Democrat	Richland	1844–
Mordecai Bartley	Whig	Richland	1844–1846

---

[1] The early Republicans, who endorsed the political principles of Thomas Jefferson, should not be confused with members of the present Republican Party, an organization that arose during the decade prior to the Civil War.

* Governors so indicated were not elected but filled a vacancy due to a death or a resignation.

GOVERNORS OF OHIO (*Cont.*)

Name	Party	County of Residence	Period in Office
William Bebb	Whig	Butler	1846–1849
Seabury Ford	Whig	Geauga	1849–1850
Reuben Wood (resigned)	Democrat	Cuyahoga	1850–1853
*William Medill	Democrat	Fairfield	1853–1854
William Medill	Democrat	Fairfield	1854–1856
Salmon P. Chase	Republican	Hamilton	1856–1860
William Dennison	Republican	Franklin	1860–1862
David Tod	Unionist	Mahoning	1862–1864
John Brough (died in office)	Unionist	Cuyahoga	1864–1865
*Charles Anderson	Unionist	Montgomery	1865–1866
Jacob D. Cox	Unionist	Trumbull	1866–1868
Rutherford B. Hayes	Republican	Hamilton	1868–1872
Edward F. Noyes	Republican	Hamilton	1872–1874
William Allen	Democrat	Ross	1874–1876
Rutherford B. Hayes (resigned)	Republican	Sandusky	1876–1877
*Thomas L. Young	Republican	Hamilton	1877–1878
Richard M. Bishop	Democrat	Hamilton	1878–1880
Charles Foster	Republican	Seneca	1880–1884
George Hoadly	Democrat	Hamilton	1884–1886
Joseph B. Foraker	Republican	Hamilton	1886–1890
James E. Campbell	Democrat	Butler	1890–1892
William McKinley	Republican	Stark	1892–1896
Asa Bushnell	Republican	Clark	1896–1900
George K. Nash	Republican	Franklin	1900–1904
Myron T. Herrick	Republican	Cuyahoga	1904–1906
John M. Pattison (died in office)	Democrat	Clermont	1906–
*Andrew L. Harris	Republican	Preble	1906–1909
Judson Harmon	Democrat	Hamilton	1909–1913

* Governors so indicated were not elected but filled a vacancy due to a death or a resignation.

Governors of Ohio (*Cont.*)

Name	Party	County of Residence	Period in Office
James M. Cox	Democrat	Montgomery	1913–1915
Frank B. Willis	Republican	Delaware	1915–1917
James M. Cox	Democrat	Montgomery	1917–1921
Harry L. Davis	Republican	Cuyahoga	1921–1923
Vic Donahey	Democrat	Tuscarawas	1923–1929
Myers Y. Cooper	Republican	Hamilton	1929–1931
George White	Democrat	Washington	1931–

*Governors so indicated were not elected but filled a vacancy due to a death or a resignation.

INDEX

Bushnell, Simeon, case of, 256–257, 257 n.
Butler, Benjamin F., 164
Buttles, Joel, 148
Byrd, Charles W., 109

C

Caldwell, Captain William, 62
Calhoun, John C., 144, 212
Campbell, James E., 362–363, 364, 365, 367, 370
Campbell, John, 147
Campbell, Lewis D., 244, 335
Campbell, Reverend Alexander, 188, 193
Campbell, Senator Alexander, 123, 125 n.
Camp Charlotte, 49
Camp Chase, 270
Camp Dennison, 270
Camp meetings, pioneer, 184
Camp Sheridan, 481, 482
Camp Sherman, 481
Canal commissions, 138, 139, 140, 326
Canals (*See* Internal improvements.)
Canton, 173, 373
Capitals, territorial and state, 89, 119
Carleton, Sir Guy, 63
Carney Act, 522
Cary, Alice and Phœbe, 188, 388–389, 391
Cary, Samuel F., 339, 346
Cass, Lewis, 126, 219, 223–224
Catherwood, Mary H., 393
Catholicism:
    and schools, 421, 520
    and the "Geghan Bill," 340
    in Cincinnati, 188, 193, 194
    in Ohio, 194
Cat Nation (*See* Eries.)
Celoron de Blainville, 31–32, 34–35
Centennial celebrations, 360–361
Centinel of the Northwestern Territory, 200
Central Plains, 4, 6
Chamber of Commerce, Ohio, 519
Champaign County rescue cases, 254–255
Chapman, Horace L., 374
Chase, Philander, 199–200
Chase, Salmon P.:
    anti-slavery leader, 219
    aspirant for Presidency (1856), 249
    becomes Democrat (1851), 238
    Brown's Raid, 260
    calls Free Soil Convention, 223–224
    comments on early legislatures, 115
    death, 335
    elected United States Senator, 234–235
    fugitive slave cases, 254–257
    influence on Hoadly, 351 n.

Chase, Salmon P. (*cont.*):
    nominated and elected Governor, 245–248
    Presidential ambitions, 260, 288, 300
    reëlected Governor, 250–251
    resigns from Cabinet, 290
Chicago, University of, 430
Child Labor laws, 463–464, 500–503, 503 n.
Chillicothe:
    Camp Sherman at, 481, 484
    early lectures at, 188
    founded, 92
    group urges plan of territorial division, 104
    importance in 1830, 174
    newspapers, 200
    relation to slavery controversy, 210
Chisholm Bill, 450
Christian Church, 188, 193
Churches (*See also under various denominations.*), 184–185, 187, 188, 189–195, 291
Cigarette tax, 515, 519
Cincinnati:
    anti-slavery attitude, 212–213, 216
    art center, 403, 405
    churches, 192, 193, 194, 195
    Confederates threaten, 278
    constitutional conventions at, 230, 335
    early social life, 186–187
    educational interest, 197, 200
    events of 1884, 352
    growth, 1850–1880, 315–316
    home rule difficulties, 363
    importance in 1830, 176–177, 181
    in the World War, 474–475, 482
    labor center, 329
    liquor traffic, 474
    named, 89
    newspapers, 200, 201, 203
    race problem, 211–212
    schools, 196, 199, 420
    Southern relations, 266–267
    supports Lincoln, 263
    temperance movement in, 338
    under "Boss" Cox, 358
    vote in 1855, 247
Cincinnati *Commercial*, 323, 421, 433, 434, 437
Cincinnati *Enquirer*, 201, 437, 447, 460
Cincinnati *Gazette*, 201, 402
Civil service, state, 456, 461–462
Civil War:
    attitude toward secession, 266–268
    Brough's administration, 285–289
    crisis of 1863, 279–285
    first year, 268–274
    Ohio's contribution, 289–291
    reaction of 1862, 274–279
Clark, George Rogers, 55, 57, 58, 69, 70

Harding, Warren G. (*cont.*):
 Lieutenant-governor, 448–449
 nominates Taft (1912), 457
 President, 504
Hardin, John, 96
Harmar, Josiah, 79, 80, 95–96
Harmon, Judson, 451, 458, 460
Harper, John L., 133–134
Harper, William Rainey, 430
Harris, Andrew L., 451
Harris Line, 162
Harrison, Benjamin, 367, 368
Harrison, William Henry:
 abolitionist attitude toward, 218
 Cabinet, 218
 death, 218
 Delegate to Congress, 102
 elected President, 208–209
 elected United States Senator, 146 n.
 home at North Bend, 90
 Minister to Colombia, 148
 opponent of St. Clair, 106
 Presidential candidate in 1836, 168
 Secretary of Northwest Territory, 102
 Territorial division plans, 104
 war activities, 127
Harvey, Thomas W., 431
Hawke vs. *Smith*, 494
Hayes Memorial Library, 399
Hayes, Rutherford B.:
 attitude on inflation, 339
 elected Governor (1867), 296–297
 elected Governor (1875), 340
 elected President, 340–341
 estimate of, 341
 opinions, 345, 347
 quoted as to election of 1854, 244
 reëlected Governor (1869), 300
 Southern policy, 343
Hearst, W. R., 452–453
Heckewelder, John, 59–60
Henri, Robert, 404
Hentz, Mrs. Caroline, 186
Herrick, Myron T., 448–450, 477
Hillsboro, 338
Historical and Philosophical Society of Ohio, 399
Histories and historical writings, 396–399
Hitchcock, Peter, 229
Hoadly, George, 335, 351, 351 n., 354
Hocking Valley:
 coal strike (1884), 352–353
 industrial development, 318–319
 mine troubles, 365
Holmes County, draft resistance in, 280
Home Guards, in World War, 482
Homesteads, free, 227, 329
Hopewell culture, 12
Horner, John S., 165
Housing corporations, 517

Howard, Benjamin C., 163
Howe, Frederic C., 440
Howe, Henry, 398
Howells, William Dean, 385, 387, 388, 389, 393, 394, 437
Hubbard, Frank M., 436
Hudson, 200
Hull, General William, 126
Huntington, Samuel, 118
Hussey, Obed, 416
Hutchins, Thomas, 78

I

Impeachment of Judges George Tod and Calvin Pease, 118
Indiana Territory, 104
Indians, Ohio:
 campaigns of the 1790's, 95–99
 Dunmore's War, 45–51
 involved in French and English rivalries, 31–37
 land cessions, 43, 49, 69, 99, 178
 locations and characteristics of tribes, 16–20
 participation in American Revolution, 51–64
 Pontiac's Conspiracy, 39–42
 post-Revolution problems, 67–71
 relations with traders, 26–30
 War of 1812, 124–125, 127, 128, 129
Industrial Revolution (*See also* Corporations.):
 coal mining, 318–319
 effect on culture, 385–386
 growth of cities, 315–318
 iron industry, 315, 316, 318, 319
 manufacturing, 314–315
 political effects, 261–263, 319–320, 356–358, 440–443
Ingalls, David, 518
Inheritance taxes, 378–379, 379 n.
Initiative and referendum:
 adopted for state, 455–456, 463
 avoided by Governor Davis, 505
 in municipalities, 453, 463
 occasions used:
  old age pensions, 521–522
  prohibition, 493–495, 496
  state veterans' bonus, 506–507
  "uniform rule," 514–515
  woman suffrage, 499
Insane, provision for care of, 130
Internal improvements (*See also* Railroads.):
 and state debt, 228, 230
 canal system:
  canal lands commission, 326, 360
  construction, 138–141, 149, 151–152
  decline, 325–327
 Deposit Act, 160–161
 early problems, 135–138